G000144750

THE GLOBAL POSITIONING SYSTEM

ASSESSING NATIONAL POLICIES

SCOTT PACE • GERALD FROST • IRVING LACHOW

DAVID FRELINGER • DONNA FOSSUM

DONALD K. WASSEM • MONICA PINTO

Prepared for the
Executive Office of the President
Office of Science and Technology Policy

CRITICAL TECHNOLOGIES INSTITUTE

RAND

CIVIL AVIATION AUTHORITY
LIBRARY
CLASS No.....................
COPY No.....................

The Global Positioning System (GPS) is a constellation of orbiting satellites operated by the U.S. Department of Defense to provide navigation, position-location, and precision timing services to users worldwide. GPS applications have grown beyond their defense and transportation origins and are becoming crucial to a broad range of information industries. The evolution of GPS from a primarily military to a commercial and international resource has raised important policy questions about its regulation, control, protection, and funding.

This report describes the findings of a one-year GPS policy study conducted by the RAND Critical Technologies Institute for the White House Office of Science and Technology Policy (OSTP) and the National Science and Technology Council (NSTC). The goal of this research has been to assist OSTP and NSTC in assessing alternative national objectives, opportunities, and vulnerabilities in the exploitation of GPS as a national resource. The authors have taken a broad, top-level view toward GPS policy issues that should make this report of interest to a wide audience, including the increasingly large numbers of people who will be affected by GPS technologies in coming years. Policymakers concerned with balancing national security, foreign policy, and economic interests in emerging technologies may find GPS a particularly relevant example of the issues raised by dual-use (i.e., civil and military) technologies.

CTI was created in 1991 by an act of Congress. It is a federally funded research and development center (FFRDC) within RAND. CTI's mission is to

- provide analytical support to the Executive Office of the President of the United States,

- help decisionmakers understand the likely consequences of their decisions and choose among alternative policies, and

- improve understanding in both the public and private sectors of the ways in which technological efforts can better serve national objectives.

Inquiries regarding CTI or this report may be directed to:

Bruce Don
Director, Critical Technologies Institute
RAND
2100 M Street, N.W.
Washington, D.C. 20037-1270

CONTENTS

FIGURES

TABLES

The Global Positioning System (GPS) is a U.S. military space system operated by the U.S. Air Force. The space segment of GPS consists of a constellation of 24 satellites that broadcast precise time signals. When the satellites are in view of a suitable GPS receiver, these signals aid position-location, navigation, and precision timing. GPS was developed by the U.S. Department of Defense and deployed over two decades at a cost of over $10 billion. The U.S. armed forces are increasingly reliant on its signals for a variety of purposes from navigation to munitions guidance. However, over the past 10 years, GPS has evolved far beyond its military origins. It is now a worldwide information resource supporting a wide range of civil, scientific, and commercial functions, from air traffic control to the Internet. GPS has also spawned a substantial commercial industry in the United States and abroad with rapidly growing markets for related products and services.

THE POLICY PROBLEM

GPS policy issues cut across traditional boundaries, and national policy toward GPS has not kept pace with the system's rapidly expanding commercial and civilian roles. GPS is both a military and a civilian system, as well as a domestic and an international resource. Its multifaceted nature requires a complex balancing of different—and potentially competing—national interests relating to defense, commercial, and foreign policy objectives. This situation raises complex questions for U.S. policymakers, including:

- How should the United States integrate its economic and national security objectives into GPS policy decisions?

- How should the Department of Defense respond to the existence of widely available, highly accurate time and spatial data?

- What approach should the United States take toward international cooperation and competition in global satellite navigation systems?

- How should GPS and associated augmentations be governed in the future?

Clearly, policies intended to address this diverse set of questions will require trade-offs. Fashioning these trade-offs will require a clear policy direction. Given its ownership of GPS and prior experience with dual-use technologies such as computers, telecommunications, and the Internet, the United States is uniquely positioned to shape the international policy environment surrounding this increasingly important system. However, this window of opportunity is closing, as other nations become cabable of fielding rival satellite navigation and position-location systems.

PURPOSE

The purpose of this study is to assist the White House Office of Science and Technology Policy and the members of the National Science and Technology Council in addressing the key questions confronting GPS policymakers. The study identifies the major GPS policy issues, highlights opportunities and vulnerabilities in the defense, commercial, and foreign-policy arenas, discusses their implications for alternative governance and funding arrangements, and makes recommendations for U.S. policy. Assessing the effects of a dual-use technology like GPS may, in turn, provide a useful model for addressing future public policy issues in other technologies that cross traditional boundaries.

HOW GPS WORKS: A BRIEF OVERVIEW[1]

The Global Positioning System consists of three segments: a space segment of 24 orbiting satellites, a control segment that includes a control center and access to overseas command stations, and a user segment, consisting of GPS receivers and associated equipment.

GPS satellites transmit two different signals: the Precision or P-code and the Coarse Acquisition or C/A-code. The P-code is designed for authorized military users and provides what is called the Precise Positioning Service (PPS). To ensure that unauthorized users do not acquire the P-code, the United States can implement an encryption segment on the P-code called anti-spoofing (AS). The C/A-code is designed for use by nonmilitary users and provides what is called the Standard Positioning Service (SPS). The C/A-code is less accurate and easier to jam than the P-code. It is also easier to acquire, so military receivers first track the C/A-code and then transfer to the P-code. The U.S. military can degrade the accuracy of the C/A-code by implementing a technique called selec-

---

[1]For a detailed description of GPS operation, see Appendix A.

tive availability (SA). SA thus controls the level of accuracy available to all users of the Standard Positioning Service.

NATIONAL SECURITY ISSUES

The key national security issue for the United States is maximizing the military benefits of GPS while minimizing its risks. Secondary issues include the emergence of ground-based DGPS stations outside U.S. control and the status of SA.

Military Risks and Benefits

The benefits of GPS are substantial. It has become an integral component of U.S. military systems, and U.S. forces rely heavily on uninterrupted access to GPS signals. GPS provides accurate positioning and navigation for all types of military equipment, including land vehicles, ships, aircraft, and precision-guided weapons. The U.S. military is moving toward high reliance on GPS, and force structure decisions are being made that assume GPS availability. These developments carry obvious benefits, but there are risks as well. In particular, the more dependent U.S. forces become on GPS, the more vulnerable they are to disruptions in access to its signals.

The wide-scale availability of highly accurate (e.g., below 15 meters) positioning has many national security implications. First, the availability of accurate positioning is not a significant factor in major nuclear threats to the United States or its allies. Nuclear adversaries in the past, such as the Soviet Union, did not need GPS. Potential nuclear adversaries are not likely to be capable of a strategic nuclear counterforce strike and do not need GPS-level accuracies to cause great damage by the use of a few nuclear weapons.[2] GPS-aided cruise missiles, however, appear to be good platforms for delivering chemical and biological weapons of mass destruction.

Second, GPS-aided conventional weapons represent an air defense challenge to the United States and its allies. In particular, conventionally armed GPS-aided cruise missiles may pose a significant threat to large fixed targets, but they do not threaten most mobile targets. GPS-aiding means that weapons that are able to evade U.S. defense will have a greater potential for causing significant damage. (The spread of low-observable technologies can further increase the number of hostile aerial weapons leaking through U.S. defenses. However, the hos-

---

[2]Counterforce strikes have traditionally been thought of in terms of fixed installations such as airfield and ICBM silos. As sea-launched cruise missiles (SLBMs) make up a greater share of the U.S. nuclear arsenal, U.S. vulnerability to a counterforce attack will diminish.

tile use of low-observable technologies is an independent and distinct concern from the hostile exploitation of GPS.)

Third, selective availability has little effect on the accuracy of short- and medium-range GPS-guided ballistic missiles. GPS-aiding of Third World missiles such as the Scud and No Dong 1 can improve overall accuracy by 20–25 percent, but to no appreciable effect. Most of the advantages of GPS are achieved with the SPS-levels of accuracy, however, and SA is not a significant factor. Further improvements in missile accuracy involve much greater technical challenges than being able to access GPS signals. Missile proliferation—especially the spread of ballistic missiles—is (and has been) a serious problem independent of GPS. There is no question that use of GPS may allow Third World nations to develop accurate cruise missiles, but it is equally important to note that GPS is a facilitator, not a driver, of missile proliferation. Any potential solution to the problem of missile proliferation will require military, political, and economic components and cannot be effectively addressed by GPS policy decisions alone.

Fourth, while being able to deny access to GPS signals and GPS-related augmentations is important, this should not be done to the neglect of other countermeasures such as passive defenses, mobility, and avoidance of single-point failure modes, which can greatly reduce attack effectiveness. In particular, electronic combat against GPS must be integrated into U.S. planning and routine operations.

The magnitude of the current threat associated with hostile use of GPS is minor at present; however, future threats may be greater.[3] To cope with the wide range of possible future threats that may appear, the Department of Defense (DoD) should work on the development of selective GPS denial techniques for future theaters of operations. In the near term, this includes the development of tactical jammers to deny positioning and navigation information from GPS, DGPS (differential GPS-based systems), GLONASS (a Russian space-based system similar to GPS), and commercial position-location services. In addition, the United States needs to explore both active and passive defense programs against theater-area cruise missiles and ballistic missiles that may carry either conventional warheads or weapons of mass destruction.

---

[3]GPS-guided cruise missiles are likely to be the most significant future threat from the hostile exploitation of GPS. It is the marriage of GPS with other technologies such as low-observable materials, efficient turbofan engines, accurate inertial navigation systems, and weapons of mass destruction that poses the greatest threat to U.S. and allied forces.

Emergence of Differential GPS Networks

Another potential threat is emerging with the spread of DGPS networks, some with quite broad coverage areas. In the presence of such networks, potentially hostile weapons systems using GPS could emerge relatively rapidly (e.g., in 12–18 months). Thus, the United States and its allies need to plan for the possible emergence of DGPS weapons, even if widely acknowledged evidence of such systems is lacking. The threat posed by accurate GPS-aided weapons, aerial weapons in particular, is most acute for situations where the defender lacks air superiority. U.S. air power, when generated in theater, is quite formidable against any foreseeable threats.[4] U.S. allies can be at greater risk than the United States itself, say, in the opening period of conflict before U.S. air power can be brought to bear. Thus, U.S. regional allies should have greater incentives to deter or prevent the hostile exploitation of DGPS networks.

While creating appropriate responses to threats from long-range weapon delivery systems such as cruise missiles, the United States needs to think about how it can and should shape the international environment for space-based navigation services. For example, a stable and predictable GPS policy in the United States can help promote GPS as a global standard. In the case of DGPS services that cross international boundaries, it is in the security interests of the United States to have such systems under the direct control of allies, as opposed to potential adversaries or international civil organizations. Direct control can encompass a spectrum of techniques from using encryption of the DGPS communications link to ensure access only by authorized receivers to diplomatic agreements to limit areas and times of operation when international conditions warrant.

Selective Availability

Finally, the issue of selective availability is a controversial topic for some civil and commercial GPS users who would like to see it turned off in peacetime. However, the net effect of any SA decision on commercial growth and new applications is unclear. Technical alternatives in the form of DGPS and real-time-kinematic (RTK) techniques are increasingly available to users who need accuracies better than GPS alone can provide even with SA off. Although virtually all users would like better accuracy if it was costless, the commercial GPS market is driven much more strongly by declining prices than by the demand for accuracy only.

---

[4]Christopher Bowie, K. Braich, L. A. Arghavan, M. Agmon, and M. E. Morris, *Trends in the Global Balance of Airpower*, RAND, MR-478/1-AF, 1995.

The ability of SA to degrade the quality of civil GPS signals can be useful in wartime, assuming U.S. forces are not reliant on civilian GPS receivers. However, the military utility of leaving SA on in peacetime is unclear. The central arguments for leaving SA on in peacetime are that doing so discourages foreign military exploitation of GPS by making the signal less accurate and reliable than military users would want, and that turning SA on would be politically difficult, even in war or crises, because civil and commercial users would have depended on it while it was off. These arguments are being overtaken by events through the spread of DGPS techniques that can circumvent SA, initially by the use of ground-based reference beacons and potentially over wide areas by the use of reference beacons on geosynchronous satellites.

These arguments also highlight the importance of regional and international agreements on how GPS and its augmentations should be managed in times of war or crises. The most difficult questions about whether or when to turn SA on do not concern attacks on the United States, but attacks on allies or third-party conflicts where U.S. interests are unclear. One can imagine regional crises in which the United States would want a range of options, from working with allies to limit the performance of GPS augmentations, to turning SA on, actively jamming GPS signals, or attacking local DGPS ground stations. These actions would be facilitated by agreements that address regional security concerns with GPS and are likely to be more important than the single decision of leaving SA on or off in peacetime.

The risk of encouraging the proliferation of GPS-aided weapons must be balanced against the benefits of GPS as a global standard for satellite-based navigation. In this balancing, a decision on SA policy must consider U.S. interests in working with others to shape the international environment for GPS—not just individual military risks and uncertain economic benefits.

COMMERCIAL ISSUES

The key commercial issue is minimizing the political risks perceived by private industry. Currently, commercial GPS firms view political risk—that is, uncertainty surrounding future policy directions—as the greatest potential threat to U.S. world leadership in GPS products and services. Government policy decisions can create risks to commercial GPS in many ways. New taxes and fees can be imposed, spectrum licenses may be difficult or impossible to get, international trade disputes can hamper access to foreign markets, and governments may impose standards that fragment global markets into less attractive sizes. The problem of standards is particularly pervasive, as it cuts across civil, commercial, and military concerns in areas such as encryption, safety certification standards, and international spectrum allocations. Rapid changes in commercial GPS since the Persian Gulf War have created a strong industry interest in a national GPS policy that will provide a predictable environment for future business decisions.

The "No-Fee" Approach

The current U.S. policy of providing SPS free of direct user charges has stimulated the growth of commercial GPS applications and has been beneficial to the United States as well as the global community of users. In part, the "no-fee" approach is a technical necessity arising from the nature of GPS signals, and enforcing payments now would be difficult or impossible. This policy has minimized incentives for the entry of competitors, since it is difficult to compete against a free service.

Competition with GPS is a possibility that is sometimes raised. This seems to be unlikely provided the United States continues current GPS operating practices. Strong incentives for an alternative to GPS could be created if the United States were to fail to sustain the GPS constellation (e.g., as a result of funding instability), fail to operate GPS in a competent, reliable way (which would also put U.S. forces at risk), or attempt to charge users for access to signals, thus creating an economic niche for a competing system. GLONASS may be used as a supplement to GPS by some users, like other GPS augmentations, but it is unlikely to become a true alternative to GPS unless U.S. support of GPS falters.

Wide-Area Augmentations

The U.S. government plans to provide wide-area augmentations of GPS accuracy for aviation and maritime navigation. This has created concerns among DGPS service providers that government services will compete with them. While the economic harm from competition may be small relative to the benefits of wide-area GPS augmentations, U.S. government policy needs to find a balance between the requirements of public safety and avoiding competition with industry.

In deciding whether civil GPS accuracy augmentations should be selectively deniable, the primary concern should be to balance national security and public safety, including international acceptance. Commercial concerns are important, but of lesser national priority. International discussions are necessary to determine what types of selective denial would be both effective and broadly acceptable. Encryption is only one means of selective denial and need not be implemented if other means are available for national security purposes.

FOREIGN POLICY ISSUES

The key foreign policy issue is reassuring foreign users—especially governments—of a stable GPS policy and funding environment and continued access to GPS signals.

Reassuring Foreign Governments

Foreign governments have legitimate concerns about relying on a system controlled by the U.S. military as well as facing potential hostile uses of GPS. The greatest concerns are uses of GPS that involve public safety, such as air and sea transportation.

The GPS international environment can evolve in various ways. If the United States promotes GPS as a global standard, it must address the technology's dual-use nature through international agreements. If the United States does not actively support GPS, or becomes an unreliable steward, GPS augmentations will move forward independent of U.S. interests. The entry of foreign alternatives to GPS (e.g., GLONASS, or an INMARSAT service) will become a possibility. The United States might retain GPS for its own national security purposes, but it would risk losing the economic and diplomatic benefits accruing from past investments in GPS.

International Safeguards

The most important international safeguards for GPS involve preventing or deterring the hostile misuse of high-accuracy GPS augmentations. With the proliferation of long-range precision strike weapons, more of our allies are facing the kind of homeland strategic threat that the United States has faced for decades. The U.S. response in the case of air navigation aids was to create the SCATANA system, which provided for military control of air traffic control radars and other air navigation aids in times of war.[5] Beginning with traditional channels, NATO and the U.S.-Japan Treaty of Mutual Cooperation and Security could be used to create international "SCATANA" procedures with respect to wide-area GPS augmentations. In the event of war or a regional crisis, the operation of GPS-based navigation aids could be modified or suspended in an orderly way.

---

[5] Plan for the security control of air traffic and air navigation aids (Short title: SCATANA), 32 C.F.R § 245, 12 pp.

International Agreements

The principal problem in dealing with international GPS issues is the fact that no single organization or forum exists for addressing the full range of concerns regarding GPS or for making agreements. Foreign discussions of GPS tend to be segregated because separate communities depend on particular applications. This segregation results partly from the origins of GPS as a U.S. military system, but is also the result of domestic political constraints. For example, the Japan Defense Agency is highly constrained in its interactions with civilian ministries and it is difficult to forge a common Japanese government approach on the regional security and economic concerns arising from the spread of DGPS networks, including DGPS services provided by Japanese civil government agencies. The European Community is interested in GPS for transportation infrastructure applications, but does not have any jurisdiction over military matters. Similarly, NATO and the Western European Union are interested in the military benefits of GPS, but have difficulty addressing civil and commercial applications in a common forum.

The United States can have a unique role in creating and shaping an international dialog on GPS issues. Statements of U.S. intentions regarding GPS, as in the Federal Radionavigation Plan or by the FAA to the International Civil Aviation Organization (ICAO), are unlikely to be sufficient to reassure foreign governments; more formal mechanisms for making commitments are needed. Such commitments are not vital to private-sector acceptance, as demonstrated by current GPS export sales, but can help accelerate civil and commercial usage. International agreements other than treaties are feasible and perhaps the most effective means of overcoming foreign government objections to the official use of GPS and related augmentations.

A U.S. commitment to provide a specific level of GPS service can be verified by international integrity monitoring. Such monitoring may limit liability for accidents involving GPS, as timely warnings can be considered a form of "real-time" notice (especially relevant to international civil aviation). International integrity monitoring would not appear to compromise U.S. security interests, and the United States could agree to refrain from actively interfering with such monitoring.

To reach a sufficiently attractive international agreement, the United States could also consider turning SA off in peacetime. By sufficiently attractive, we mean an agreement that in toto provided significant national security or economic benefits to the United States. This prospect is likely to be easier in the course of bilateral discussions with traditional friends and allies such as Japan and Europe than in a multilateral negotiation affecting only one category of GPS users, such as civil aviation. On the other hand, U.S. allies may wish to see

SA kept on, so that they are able to control access to higher accuracy signals via their own GPS augmentations.

GOVERNANCE OF GPS AND AUGMENTATIONS

Given the worldwide popularity of GPS applications, the future governance of GPS is of interest to users in the United States and overseas. Aspects of governance include ownership, control, funding, and management decisionmaking. The pursuit of U.S. national security and economic interests in the use of GPS does not necessarily require U.S. control over all aspects of GPS and its technologies, even if that were possible. Pursuit of such interests does, however, require the United States to decide how it will deal with GPS international cooperation and competition.

To protect its national security interests, the United States should ensure that GPS itself remains subject to its control. By GPS itself, we mean the space and the control segments, consisting of the satellites and the master control stations, and access to overseas monitoring stations. The user segment making up the burgeoning market for GPS-related equipment, applications, and services is effectively in the hands of the private sector.

Next in importance is the nature of the international regime for GPS augmentations such as the Wide-Area Augmentation System (WAAS) and local-area DGPS networks. Local-area networks are already under the control of the private sector and national governments. Such networks are not good candidates for international management because of their limited range, the strong national interests in retaining local control, and the lack of a means for enforcing international control even assuming this were desirable. Wide-area augmentations, particularly those using space-based reference stations, are another matter.

Wide-area augmentations to GPS can provide at least three major enhancements to GPS: improved integrity, improved availability, and improved accuracy. The public safety and commercial benefits of improved GPS integrity and availability would be of global benefit, and international, regional, or national governance would not harm U.S. security interests but would enhance the international acceptance of GPS. It is likely that international organizations such as ICAO and the International Maritime Organization (IMO), as well as individual nations, would want independent oversight of augmentations to GPS integrity and availability; this could be provided in international agreements on GPS.

Accuracy augmentations are a more difficult issue, and accuracy governance should remain under the direct control of the nation providing the service. At present, the United States, Japan, Europe, and potentially Russia have the capability to provide wide-area accuracy augmentations. High levels of accuracy can pose risks to U.S. and regional security and require the development of military countermeasures. Wide-area accuracy augmentations should first be subject to bilateral agreements among the providers to address security and economic interests before considering multilateral agreements. Table S.1 summarizes the various preferred forms of GPS governance.

POLICY RECOMMENDATIONS

GPS enables unique military, civil, and commercial capabilities. The United States has an important opportunity to shape the direction of GPS applications and mitigate the risks of this new technology. Based on the questions posed in our definition of the GPS policy problem, the recommendations can be divided into four categories: the integration of U.S. economic and national security interests, the governance of GPS and its augmentations, national security, and foreign policy. Because of the dual-use nature of GPS, however, any policy decision in one of these realms has repercussions for the others.

Integrating Economic and National Security Objectives

- The United States should issue a statement of national policy (e.g., a Presidential Decision Directive) on the Global Positioning System to provide a more stable framework for public and private sector decisionmaking. This statement should identify U.S. interests and objectives with respect to GPS, address GPS management and acquisition issues, and provide guidance for the development of GPS augmentations and future international agreements.

Table S.1

Preferred Forms of GPS Governance

Regime	International	Regional	National, Bilateral	Local, Private
GPS segments				
Space/control			X	
User equipment				X
Wide-area GPS augmentations				
Integrity	X	X	X	
Availability	X	X	X	
Accuracy			X	
Local-area GPS augmentations			X	X

- The United States should initiate discussions with Japan and Europe on regional security and economic issues associated with GPS, potentially leading to international agreements. These agreements should be mutually beneficial to all parties but not involve the exchange of funds. The United States should be prepared to commit itself to providing the levels of GPS service defined in the Federal Radionavigation Plan.

Governance of GPS and GPS Augmentations

- The United States government should ensure that GPS is funded and maintained in a stable manner, free of direct user charges, to promote the adoption of GPS as a global standard for position location, navigation, and timing. The GPS space and control segments should remain under U.S. jurisdiction for the foreseeable future.

- In the case of DGPS services that cross international boundaries, it is in the security interests of the United States to have such systems under the direct national control of allies, as opposed to potential adversaries or international civil organizations.

National Security

- The DoD should reduce its reliance on civilian GPS receivers and the C/A-code for military purposes. The DoD should develop and introduce into operation GPS equipment capable of rapid, direct P-code acquisition as rapidly as practicable.

- The DoD should ensure that it can acquire GPS signals even in a challenged environment and should develop and field anti-jam receivers and antenna enhancements. The DoD should also ensure it has adequate electronic countermeasures to selectively deny GPS, GPS augmentations, and GLONASS signals to an adversary.

- Selective availability should be retained as a military option for the United States and not be turned off immediately. A decision on whether to turn SA off in the future should be made by the National Command Authority after international consultations and the demonstration of appropriate GPS and GPS augmentation countermeasures.

- The United States should not preclude or deter private DGPS services except for reasons of national security or public safety. In deciding whether civil GPS accuracy augmentations should be selectively deniable, the primary concern should be to balance national security and public safety, while taking international acceptance into account. Commercial concerns are important, but of lesser national priority.

Foreign Policy

- The United States should work to minimize international barriers to commercial GPS-related goods and services such as proprietary standards and inadequate spectrum allocations.

- However, the United States should refrain, and encourage others to refrain, from providing wide-area augmentations of GPS accuracy until appropriate mechanisms (e.g., military countermeasures, diplomatic agreements) are identified to deal with the potential misuse or denial of high accuracies. Subject to international agreements, the United States should encourage international integrity monitoring of GPS for public safety.

The international environment for GPS can evolve in various directions depending on the nature of U.S. policy. If the United States makes active efforts to promote GPS as a global standard, then it will necessarily need to address the dual-use nature of the technology through international agreements. On the other hand, if the United States does not actively support GPS, or becomes an unreliable steward, GPS augmentations will move forward independent of U.S. interests, and this will encourage the entry of foreign alternatives to GPS (e.g., GLONASS, or an INMARSAT service). The United States could still have GPS for its own national security purposes, but it would risk losing the economic and diplomatic benefits from its past investments in GPS.

The authors would like to thank Richard DalBello, Jeff Hofgard, Steven Moran, and William Clements of the Office of Science and Technology Policy for their assistance in and support for this research. For professional assistance, we are deeply indebted to Jules McNeff of the Office of the Under Secretary of Defense (Acquisition and Technology), Major Lee Carrick and Major Matt Brennan of the Air Staff, and Colonel Michael Wiedemer of the GPS Joint Program Office. We appreciate their gracious tolerance of our many questions.

We would also like to thank the U.S. GPS Industry Council, the Council's vice president for policy, Ann Ciganer, and executive secretary, Michael Swiek, for their insights into the commercial potential and challenges of GPS technology and the importance of U.S. policy decisions. We benefited from the kind assistance of Mr. H. Nishiguchi and Dr. M. Mizumachi of the Japan GPS Council and Mr. A. Fujita of the Embassy of Japan in Washington in gaining a better understanding of Japanese interests in GPS.

GPS is a technology that cuts across traditional lines, and we would like to express our appreciation to the many individuals who took the time to meet with us, provide us with references, and improve our understanding of how GPS technology is affecting many disparate interests. We would like to especially mention Charles Trimble of Trimble Navigation, Olaf Lundberg and Jim Nagel of INMARSAT, George Wiggers of the Office of the Secretary of Transportation, Dr. George Donohue and Norm Solat of the Federal Aviation Administration, Captain Chris Shank of the 50th Space Wing, U.S. Air Force Space Command, Captain Kenneth Smith of the U.S. Air Force Space and Missiles Systems Center, and Rob Conley and Ed Stephenson of Overlook Technologies.

While this study was being conducted, there were related GPS efforts under way at the National Academy of Public Administration (NAPA), the National Research Council (NRC), and the Defense Science Board (DSB). We benefited from invitations to attend working panels of these studies and, in the case of NAPA, coordination of international interviews in Japan and Europe. We would like to express our appreciation to Dr. William Delaney of the DSB, Alison Sandlin of the NRC, and Arnold Donohue, Roger Sperry, and Dr. Carole Nevas of NAPA, for their professional courtesy and insightful discussions, which we trust were of mutual benefit.

We are indebted to our RAND colleagues, Jeanne Jarvaise, Roy Gates, Greg Daniels, Joe Aein, Joel Kvitky, and David Vaughan, who provided important advice and counsel during the course of the study. In addition, Anna Slomovic and James Bonomo provided extensive and thorough reviews of the early draft that contained many constructive changes and corrections.

The RAND support staff is what keeps the work moving; we would like to especially thank Birthe Wenzel and Kathy Mills for their many contributions. We, of course, remain responsible for the observations and judgments contained in this report.

AJ	Anti-jamming
ADS	Automatic Dependent Surveillance
AGPS	Augmented Global Positioning Systems
C/A code	Coarse Acquisition code
CAT	Category
CDMA	Code Division Multiplex Access
CEP	Circular error probable
CGSIC	Civil GPS Service Interface Committee
CRPA	Controlled radiation pattern antenna
CW	Carrier wave
dB	Decibel ($X = 10 \, Log_{10} \times dB$)
dBW	Decibel Watts
DGPS	Differential GPS
DMA	Defense Mapping Agency
DME	Distance Measuring Equipment
DoD	Department of Defense
DOP	Dilution of precision
DoT	Department of Transportation
drms	Distance root mean squared
EIRP	Effective isotropic radiated power
ERP	Effective radiated power
FAA	Federal Aviation Administration
FRP	Federal Radionavigation Plan
GCM	GPS-aided cruise missile
GLCM	Ground-launched cruise missile
GDOP	Geometric dilution of precision
GLONASS	Global Navigation Satellite System (Russia)
GMT	Greenwich Mean Time
GNSS	Global Navigation Satellite System (ICAO)
GPS	Global Positioning System
GPSIC	GPS Information Center (U.S. Coast Guard)
HDOP	Horizontal dilution of precision

HE	High explosive
HOW	Hand Over Word
ICAO	International Civil Aviation Organization
ILS	Instrument Landing System
IMO	International Maritime Organization
IMU	Inertial measurement unit
Inmarsat	International Maritime Satellite organization
INS	Inertial navigation system
IOC	Initial operating capability
ION	Institute of Navigation
IVHS	Intelligent Vehicle Highway Systems
J/S	Jamming-to-signal ratio
JPO	Joint Program Office
L1	GPS primary frequency, 1575.42 MHz
L2	GPS secondary frequency, 1227.6 MHz
LADGPS	Local area differential GPS
LDC	Less developed country
MCS	GPS Master Control Station
MHz	Megahertz (10^6 Hz)
MLS	Microwave Landing System
MOA	Memorandum of Agreement
MOU	Memorandum of Understanding
MRC	Medium Regional Contingency/Conflict
MSL	Mean Sea Level
NAS	National Airspace System
NAV-msg	Navigation Message
NDB	Nondirectional beacon
NSA	National Security Agency
OEM	Original equipment manufacturer
P-code	Precision code
PDOP	Precision dilution of precision
Pos/Nav	Positioning and navigation
PPS	Precise Positioning Service
PRN	Pseudo random noise
RAIM	Receiver autonomous integrity monitoring
RDSS	Radio Determination Satellite Service
RF	Radio frequency
rms	Root mean squared
RTK	Real-time kinematic
SA	Selective availability
SAM	Surface-to-air missile
SEP	Spherical error probable

SPS	Standard Positioning Service
SSPK	Single-Shot Probability of Kill
SV	Satellite Vehicle
TACAN	Tactical Air Navigation
TEL	Transporter-Erector-Launcher
TLAM	Tomahawk Land Attack Missile
TTFF	Time to First Fix
UE	User Equipment
UHF	Ultra high frequency
USC	United States Code
USCG	United States Coast Guard
USNO	U.S. Naval Observatory
UT	Universal Time
UTC	Universal Time Coordinated
VOR	Very high frequency omnidirectional range
WAAS	Wide-Area Augmentation System
WDGPS	Wide-area differential GPS
WGS-84	World Geodetic System 1984
WMD	Weapon of Mass Destruction

DEFINITIONS[1]

Accuracy. The degree of conformance between the estimated or measured position and/or velocity of a platform at a given time and its true position or velocity. Radionavigation system accuracy is usually presented as a statistical measure of system error and is specified as:

- Predictable. The accuracy of a radionavigation system's position solution with respect to the charted solution. Both the position solution and the chart must be based upon the same geodetic datum.

- Repeatable. The accuracy with which a user can return to a position whose coordinates have been measured at a previous time with the same navigation system.

- Relative. The accuracy with which a user can measure position relative to that of another user of the same navigation system at the same time.

Availability. The availability of a navigation system is the percentage of time that the services are usable. Availability is an indication of the ability of the sys-

---

[1] Joint DoD/DoT Task Force, *The Global Positioning System: Management and Operation of a Dual-Use System*, Report to the Secretaries of Defense and Transportation, December 1993, Appendix B.

tem to provide usable service within the specified coverage area. Signal availability is the percentage of time that navigational signals transmitted from external sources are available for use. Availability is a function of both the physical characteristics of the environment and the technical capabilities of the transmitter facilities.

Coverage. The coverage provided by a radionavigation system is that surface area or space volume in which the signals are adequate to permit the user to determine position to a specified level of accuracy. Coverage is influenced by system geometry, signal power levels, receiver sensitivity, atmospheric noise conditions, and other factors that affect signal availability.

Differential. A technique used to improve radionavigation system accuracy by determining positioning error at a known location and subsequently transmitting the determined error, or corrective factors, to users of the same radionavigation system operating in the same area.

Distance Root Mean Square (drms). The root-mean-square value of the distances from the true location point of the position fixes in a collection of measurements. As used in this report, 2 drms is the radius of a circle that contains at least 95 percent of all possible fixes that can be obtained with a system at any one place. The percentage of fixes contained within 2 drms varies between approximately 95.5 percent and 98.2 percent, depending on the degree of ellipticity of the error distribution.

Full Operational Capability (FOC). For GPS, this is defined as the capability that occurs when 24 GPS (Block II/IIA) satellites operating in their assigned orbits have been tested for military functionality and certified as meeting military requirements.

Initial Operating Capability (IOC). For GPS, this is defined as the capability that occurs when 24 GPS satellites (Block I/II/IIA) operating in their assigned orbits are available for navigation uses.

Integrity. Integrity is the ability of a system to provide timely warnings to users as to when the system should not be used for navigation.

National Airspace System (NAS). The NAS includes U.S. airspace; air navigation facilities, equipment, and services; airports or landing areas; aeronautical charts, information, and service; rules, regulations and procedures; technical information; and labor and material used to control and manage flight activities in airspace under the jurisdiction of the United States. System components shared jointly with the military are included.

Nonprecision Approach. A standard instrument approach procedure in which no electronic glide slope is provided (e.g., VOR, TACAN, Loran-C, or NDB).

Precision Approach. A standard instrument approach procedure in which an electronic glide scope is provided (the Instrument Landing System (ILS)).

1. ILS Category I (CAT I). An ILS approach procedure that provides for approach to a height above touchdown of not less than 200 feet and with runway visual range of not less than 1800 feet.

2. ILS Category II (CAT II). An ILS approach procedure that provides for approach to a height above touchdown of not less than 100 feet and with runway visual range of not less than 1200 feet.

3. ILS Category III (CAT III).

    a. IIIA. An ILS approach procedure that provides for approach without a decision height minimum and with runway visual range of not less than 700 feet.

    b. IIIB. An ILS approach procedure that provides for approach without a decision height minimum and with runway visual range of not less that 1500 feet.

    c. IIIC. An ILS approach procedure that provides for approach without a decision height minimum and without runway visual range minimum.

Chapter One

INTRODUCTION

The Global Positioning System (GPS) is a U.S. military space system operated by the U.S. Air Force. It consists of three segments: The space segment of GPS is a constellation of 24 satellites that broadcast precise time signals. When the satellites are in view of a suitable GPS receiver, these signals can be used to aid position-location, navigation, and precision timing. The control segment consists of a control center and access to overseas command stations, and the user segment includes GPS receivers and associated equipment. The GPS space and ground segments were developed over two decades at the cost of more than $10 billion.[1] The purpose of this massive effort was to provide a highly accurate, secure, reliable way for U.S. forces to navigate anywhere in the world, without having to reveal themselves through radio transmissions.

GPS satellites transmit two different signals: the Precision or P-code and the Coarse Acquisition or C/A-code. The P-code is designed for authorized military users and provides what is called the Precise Positioning Service (PPS). To ensure that unauthorized users do not acquire the P-code, the United States can implement an encryption segment on the P-code called anti-spoofing (AS). The C/A-code is designed for use by nonmilitary users and provides what is called the Standard Positioning Service (SPS). The C/A-code is less accurate and easier to jam than the P-code. It is also easier to acquire, so military receivers first track the C/A-code and then transfer to the P-code. The U.S. military can degrade the accuracy of the C/A-code by implementing a technique called selective availability (SA). SA thus controls the level of accuracy available to all users of the Standard Positioning Service.

GPS had its wartime debut during the Persian Gulf War and was one of the most prominent military technologies of the war. Although the entire constellation of satellites was not yet complete, GPS signals were available for many hours a

---

[1] Senator James Exon, "GPS's Limitless Potential," April 30, 1993 speech on the floor of the U.S. Senate, reprinted in *Space News*, May 31–June 6, 1993, p. 15. The ground segment consists of the master control station and worldwide monitoring stations.

day over the Middle East. Soldiers, sailors, airmen, and Marines used GPS receivers to guide all manner of vehicles and themselves in a region with few landmarks. The news media reported that GPS receivers were so highly prized that troops were buying commercial GPS receivers with their own money or receiving them as gifts from family members in the United States. In the aftermath of the war, military analysts noted the importance of GPS to effective allied operations and cited the contribution of GPS satellites as an example of "space warfare."[2]

While the successful performance of GPS in war was a revelation to many, the rapid growth of commercial GPS applications after a 1983 decision by President Reagan to allow civilian access to GPS signals is perhaps just as striking. A robust commercial GPS industry had gone relatively unnoticed, but emerged into wider public view as GPS formally reached fully operational status.[3] The industry not only supplied the U.S. military in peacetime, but during war diverted its commercial production lines to meet military demands. GPS satellites, ground-control equipment, and military receivers continue to be built under government contracts, while GPS receivers have entered the consumer market to be used by hikers, truck drivers, and recreational boaters.

The commercial use of GPS receivers is growing rapidly in many diverse sectors. One of the first commercial applications was in surveying, where GPS is used in place of the visual sighting techniques that have prevailed for hundreds of years. Precise GPS timing signals are used to synchronize the operation of global telecommunications networks in a manner invisible to the consumer. GPS receivers are being embedded in products such as laptop computers and new generations of "smart" munitions. The intense cost and quality competition in commercial information and electronic markets is in turn making new capabilities available for military applications. This close interrelation of commercial and military applications is a common occurrence in "dual-use" technologies and systems, such as computers and communication networks. GPS itself can be thought of as a dual-use system, as can the technologies found in GPS user equipment.

THIS STUDY'S PURPOSE

GPS was designed and developed as a military system to serve the needs of the U.S. Department of Defense and U.S. allies for en route navigation. In the course of its development, GPS has expanded from primarily a U.S. military

---

[2]"Lessons of the First Space War," *Space Markets*, April 1991, p. 12.

[3]"AF Says GPS Fully Operational," *GPS World Newsletter*, May 22, 1995, p. 1. The story refers to an April 27, 1995 declaration by General Joseph Ashy of the U.S. Air Force Space Command.

resource into a commercial and even international resource. This evolution has created two broad sets of interests—military and economic—which overlap. These interests have come to the attention of the Executive Branch of the U.S. government, and the Office of Science and Technology Policy in particular, as the Departments of Defense, Transportation, Commerce, Interior, State, and others have found GPS to be an important factor in carrying out their missions, whether in support of national security, foreign policy, public safety, scientific research, or economic growth. The concerns of multiple agencies about the future of GPS and its impacts have raised policy questions about the management, funding, control, and regulation of GPS and its associated technologies. Among the questions national decisionmakers face are the following:

- How should the United States integrate its economic and national security objectives into GPS policy decisions?

- How should the Department of Defense respond to the existence of widely available, highly accurate time and spatial data?

- What approach should the United States take toward international cooperation and competition in global satellite navigation systems?

- How should GPS and associated augmentations be governed?

The purpose of this study is to assist the White House Office of Science and Technology Policy and the members of the National Science and Technology Council in assessing alternative national policy objectives, opportunities, and vulnerabilities related to GPS. This study provides an integrated assessment of how GPS policy decisions can and might affect diverse military and commercial interests and suggests how those interests might be balanced most effectively. The assessment of the impacts of a dual-use technology like GPS may, in turn, provide a useful model for addressing public policy issues in other technologies that cross traditional boundaries.

OTHER U.S. GOVERNMENT-SPONSORED STUDIES

Other recent government-sponsored GPS studies provide context and background for this report. The increasing military and commercial visibility of GPS has prompted a literature primarily concerned with the exploitation of GPS in specific applications, such as air traffic management or overcoming electronic countermeasures. A smaller number of studies, including this one, have focused on balancing military and commercial interests.

In 1993, the Departments of Defense and Transportation formed a joint DoD/DoT task force to examine the management and operation of GPS as a dual-use system. GPS was recognized as having benefits for both civil and military users and both departments agreed to encourage "maximum civil use of the system consistent with national security needs."[4] The report was notable for the range of interagency issues it covered and the degree of common ground the task force found in areas such as GPS management, funding, and the use of differential GPS technologies.

The joint task force recommended establishment of a joint executive board to resolve policy and management issues by consensus. In addition, it was recognized that many GPS-related applications need accuracies greater than what can be supplied by the GPS signals available to civil or even military users. Thus "augmentations" to GPS, e.g., differential GPS (DGPS) services, would be necessary even if civil users had access to the most accurate military-grade signals.[5] The task force recommended that the private-sector provision of DGPS services, which are not used for navigation purposes, should not be regulated. "Navigation" in this context essentially means applications where "safety of life" would be involved, as air traffic and ship navigation.

The joint task force also recommended a study of all differential GPS services then under development to meet the needs of maritime, railroad, and aircraft users. The study would assess the performance, economic benefits, and security implications of various services and how they might be optimally integrated. Both the Federal Aviation Administration (FAA) and the U.S. Coast Guard (USCG) have since been criticized by the General Accounting Office for potentially wasteful duplications of effort.[6]

The Department of Transportation then commissioned a study by the Institute of Telecommunication Sciences (ITS), within the U.S. Department of Commerce's National Telecommunications and Information Agency, to evaluate alternative GPS augmentations such as those made by the FAA and the Coast Guard.[7] After culling out almost two dozen alternatives, the study group looked at six composite architectures and evaluated them on detailed factors of performance, cost, and security. The study focused on expanded versions of the Coast Guard's local-area differential GPS system to provide nationwide coverage for marine and land users, supplemented by an FAA system for aviation. Notably, the analysts stopped short of recommending a particular architecture as the obvious choice. Instead, they acknowledged the need for a

---

[4]Joint DoD/DoT Task Force, *The Global Positioning System: Management and Operation of a Dual-Use System*, Washington, D.C., December 1993.

[5]See Appendix A for a discussion of how DGPS works.

[6]General Accounting Office, *Global Positioning Technology—Opportunities for Greater Federal Agency Joint Development and Use*, RCED-94-280, Washington, D.C., September 1994.

[7]U.S. Department of Commerce, Institute for Telecommunications Sciences, *A National Approach to Augmented GPS Services*, NTIA Special Publication 94-30, December 1994.

policy judgment on how national security and economic interests are to be balanced, in particular in the deployment of GPS augmentation systems.

The ITS study was criticized by some suppliers of differential GPS services as promoting U.S. government competition against private providers. One firm in particular, Differential Corrections, Inc., argued that it could provide services superior to the systems proposed by the FAA and the Coast Guard and at less cost to the U.S. taxpayer.[8] The Department of Defense was also critical of the report and argued that security concerns with wide-area broadcasts of differential GPS signals were not fully addressed.

The most recent, broad, nongovernment assessments of military uses of GPS and GPS augmentations have been by the Defense Science Board (DSB) and Overlook Systems Technologies, the latter under contract to the U.S. Department of Defense through the National Air Intelligence Center (NAIC). The Defense Science Board task force on GPS was cosponsored by the Director, Tactical Warfare Programs, and the Deputy Under Secretary of Defense for Advanced Technology.[9] The task force was asked to review and recommend options available to improve GPS jam resistance with particular emphasis on GPS tactical weapon applications. The main focus was on investigating techniques for improving the resistance of GPS-embedded receivers in tactical missiles and precision munitions and their delivery platforms. Recommended techniques were assessed in terms of ease of accomplishment, cost, risk, and anti-jam margin provided.

The study by Overlook Technologies concentrated on the technical feasibility and effectiveness of hostile exploitation of a Global Navigation Satellite System (GNSS).[10] The study looked at a wide range of threats, such as ballistic missiles, cruise missiles, precision-guided munitions and bomb-carrying aircraft, that could use GNSS signals. In contrast, the DSB study focused on improving the ability of GPS-aided U.S. systems to overcome electronic countermeasures— preventing denial of GPS to the United States. The Overlook study examined the potential misuse of GPS by hostile forces and did not judge whether such exploitation was politically or economically feasible.

---

[8]Ron Haley, *Response to NTIA Special Publication 94-30*, Differential Corrections, Inc., Cupertino, CA, January 1995.

[9]Memorandum for the Chairman, Defense Science Board, "Terms of Reference—Defense Science Board Task Force on Global Positioning System," from The Under Secretary of Defense for Acquisition and Technology, U.S. Department of Defense, June 2, 1994.

[10]Overlook Systems Technologies, *The Feasibility of a GNSS Exploitation Threat*, National Air Intelligence Center, Foreign Space Systems Analysis, TAG 07-02, April 25, 1995.

The largest outside studies of GPS have been mandated by Congress.[11] The Senate Armed Services Committee report on the National Defense Authorization Act for FY 1994 requested a study of future management and funding options for GPS. The motivations cited for the study were "pressures on the defense budget, the necessity for increased civil-military cooperation, the importance of dual-use technology for economic competitiveness and conversion, and the President's interest in effective infrastructure investments."[12] The study was conducted by the National Academy of Sciences (NAS) and the National Academy of Public Administration (NAPA), with the former taking the lead on technical issues and the latter taking the lead on management issues.

NAPA organized a study panel chaired by former Secretary of Defense James Schlesinger. After discussions with DoD and congressional staff, NAPA decided to address the following issues:[13]

- How should the GPS be structured and managed to maximize its dual utility for civilian and military purposes?

- How should the GPS program/infrastructure be funded to ensure consistent, sustainable, and reliable services to civilian and military users around the world? Are there equitable cost recovery mechanisms that may be implemented to make the GPS program partially or fully self-supporting without compromising U.S. security or international competitive interests?

- Is commercialization or privatization of all or parts of the GPS consistent with U.S. security, safety, and economic interests?

- Is international participation in the management, operation and financing of GPS consistent with U.S. security and economic interests?

The National Academy of Sciences placed its research arm, the National Research Council (NRC), under subcontract to NAPA to address such issues as future GPS technical improvements and augmentations to enhance military, civilian, and commercial use of the system "in the context of national security considerations." The NRC organized its own study panel, chaired by former Martin Marietta executive Laurence Adams. Issues addressed included:[14]

---

[11]U.S. Congress, Conference Report to Accompany H.R. 2401, The National Defense Authorization Act for FY 1994, Report 103-357, November 10, 1993.

[12]U.S. Senate, Committee on Armed Services, Report on the National Defense Authorization Act for FY 1994, July 28, 1993.

[13]National Academy of Public Administration, Committee on the Future of the Global Positioning System, Statement of Task, 1994.

[14]National Research Council, Commission on Engineering and Technical Systems, Committee on the Future of the Global Positioning System, Statement of Task, 1994.

- How can communication, navigation, and computing technology be integrated to support and enhance the utility of GPS in all transportation sectors, in scientific and engineering applications beyond transportation, and in other civilian applications identified by the study?

- What augmentations and technical improvements to GPS itself are feasible and could enhance military, civilian, and commercial use of the system?

- Given GPS-related threats, what are the implications of security-related safeguards and countermeasures for the various classes of civilian GPS users and for future management of GPS? In addition, are the selective availability and anti-spoofing capabilities of GPS meeting their intended purpose?

Both NAPA and the NRC found that most aspects of GPS technology, governance and management, and funding were sound.[15] They recommended retention of operational control and funding of the GPS satellites by the DoD, and the aggressive application of GPS technology to public safety and public service needs by civil government agencies. They also recommended that selective availability (SA), the capability by which the DoD can degrade the accuracy of GPS signals available to general users, be turned off. They saw SA as undercutting international confidence in GPS and imposing opportunity costs on commercial industry. On institutional matters, NAPA recommended that a Presidential Executive Order be given to create a GPS executive board. This board would resolve conflicts among and represent the interests of not only the U.S. Departments of Defense and Transportation, but other departments such as State, Interior, and Commerce as well. Finally, both studies saw the continued international acceptance of GPS as important to U.S. interests—a point that became an important theme in this study as well.

THE RAND/CTI GPS STUDY

The RAND/Critical Technologies Institute study was initiated by the Office of Science and Technology Policy (OSTP) in 1994 in response to the increasing interactions between commercial and national security interests as GPS applications grew. While addressing many of the same substantive topics as the other studies, this study has focused on alternatives for national policy as opposed to agency-specific management issues, system requirements and design, or GPS-related technologies per se.

---

[15]National Academy of Public Administration, National Research Council, *The Global Positioning System—Charting the Future, Summary Report*, Washington, D.C., May 1995.

Research Approach

Study efforts began with a comprehensive literature review and attendance at panel meetings of the Defense Science Board, National Academy of Public Administration, and National Research Council, where industry and government briefings were presented. We interviewed a wide range of U.S. government and industry officials, primarily in Washington, D.C., California, and Colorado (the location of the GPS Master Control Station). Individual U.S. GPS industry interviews were conducted in late September 1994, with follow-up discussion throughout the study. Interviews with Japanese government agencies and the Japan GPS Industry Council were conducted in Tokyo in October 1994. Interviews with European government and international agencies were conducted in Paris, London, and Brussels during late January 1995.

As part of our assessment of potential military threats and countermeasures to the use or denial of GPS, we calculated the effectiveness of ballistic missiles and cruise missiles aided by GPS and GPS augmentations (see Chapter Three). Although many factors contribute to the effectiveness of a weapons system, we focused on the effects of varying levels of GPS accuracy, because this was a common concern that came up in interviews. We did not attempt to predict the impact of GPS on combat outcomes, since realistic simulations are subject to so many variables and assumptions that a reliable, conclusive statement would not be possible.

Another concern that arose from our interviews was that space-based GPS augmentations posed a qualitatively different military risk from ground-based augmentations because of the wider area of coverage. To better understand how some civil GPS augmentations, such as differential GPS ground stations, might be exploited by hostile military forces, we analyzed signal propagation for specific areas of conflict such as Northeast Asia and the Persian Gulf (see Chapter Three). While the missile analysis addressed the performance of individual weapons, the signal propagation analysis addressed the range over which such weapons might exploit GPS augmentations. The exploitable ranges of GPS augmentations for civil and military uses are not the same, leading to differing perceptions of the risk.

We next assessed the commercial impacts of GPS technology. To do this, we combined our interview results with market studies by GPS industry associations in the United States and Japan. These market studies focused on GPS equipment sales, however, and not the underlying technologies. To understand the international environment for GPS-related technology, a subcontract was let to Mogee Associates, an experienced patent analysis firm, to assess international trends in patents of GPS technology. This provided a view of the competitive position of U.S. GPS technology and firms, a matter of interest to policy-makers.

U.S. and international legal literature was searched to understand the international legal environment for using GPS. Many of our international interviews tended not to emphasize GPS technology or operations, but rather its institutional structure and the ability of foreign countries to use GPS for civil public safety functions. This review of international and domestic law relevant to civil uses of GPS led to an analysis of the "nature" of GPS—for example, whether it is a natural monopoly, public good, or utility. Debates over what GPS is or should be is an important concern of policymakers as they balance competing interests.

We integrated national security, commercial, and institutional and legal findings in reaching our conclusions. We then made recommendations based on those conclusions, recommendations that would address what we felt were the most important or difficult questions in GPS policy. This has necessarily required some judgments about the relative importance of national interests such as security, public safety, and economic growth. While we hope that the study recommendations will lead to a broad national consensus on GPS policy, those recommendations do not represent the views of any particular person, agency, firm, or the study sponsor.

Organization of the Report

This report consists of six chapters, including the Introduction. Chapter Two provides an overview of GPS policy issues and who the major stakeholders are in the development and implementation of GPS policy.

Chapter Three is a national security assessment of GPS that treats both the need for access to GPS by the United States and the need to deter and respond to the misuse of GPS signals by others.

Chapter Four assesses the growing commercial uses for GPS, the status of commercial GPS technologies, and policy issues that affect the international market for GPS technologies, products, and services.

Chapter Five addresses international legal and institutional issues in the characterization and management of GPS. Choosing appropriate funding and management structures is an important focus of this chapter, because those structures are of central interest to both policymakers and the GPS community.

Chapter Six summarizes our conclusions and recommendations on how GPS policy can best integrate the diverse interests of the United States in GPS technology and applications.

Appendix A provides a more detailed description of the GPS system and potential alternatives such as the Russian GLONASS and inertial navigation technologies. Appendix B describes the history and budget of the GPS program, including a chronology of major program events. Appendices C and D contain copies of significant GPS policy documents and legal citations. A bibliography and list of interviews are also included.

Chapter Two

NATIONAL INTERESTS AND STAKEHOLDERS IN GPS POLICY

GPS satellites may be thought of as accurate, stable "clocks in space" that bathe the earth with a weak, consistent time signal. These radio waves allow receivers to passively calculate where they are and what time it is by comparing the signals of multiple satellites in the same constellation. GPS is a sophisticated space system developed and operated by hundreds of highly trained people; it is also a technical innovation that is transforming many diverse areas of human activity. In one sense, GPS is a model dual-use technology in which a military development leads to civil and commercial benefits beyond what was originally intended for the program. In another sense, GPS is a commercially driven information technology, like high-speed data networks and mobile communications, which is affecting the nature of national and international security.

This chapter provides an overview of the many interests affected by the Global Positioning System and those who may be considered stakeholders in GPS policy—that is, groups whose interests are so affected by GPS and GPS technologies that they will seek to shape GPS policy. The chapter is divided into three major sections. The first describes various national interests that are affected by GPS. The second section describes the range of views about GPS to be found in U.S. and foreign organizations, both public and private. In some cases, a single national interest is represented by one organization, such as national security in the case of the U.S. Department of Defense. In other cases, an agency may have multiple interests—the U.S. Department of Commerce is concerned with a mixture of GPS security, scientific, and commercial issues. The third section reviews current U.S. policy commitments with respect to GPS and key future policy decisions that will need to balance the stakeholder interests described in the chapter.

The views of U.S. government agencies and industries, foreign governments and industries, and international organizations should be considered in the U.S. formulation of GPS policy. In part, this is because there is no single source of expertise on GPS matters, and a variety of views are needed for a complete picture of potential problems. Perhaps more pragmatically, the effective implementation of policy requires an understanding of which interest groups will support or oppose specific policy decisions. Our study looks at only the most crucial decisions affecting GPS policy for national decisionmakers. We do not attempt to be exhaustive in addressing lower-level organizations and technical questions that properly belong in government channels or the private sector.

GPS policy issues arise not only from questions about the operation of GPS itself, but from the applications enabled by GPS and the potential of this technology to create both benefits and risks for the United States and the world. Public policy decisions affect the operation of the GPS space and control segments, as well as the purchase of GPS receivers for such government purposes as national defense. Public policy decisions affect the growth and competitiveness of commercial GPS-related product and service providers, the denial or misuse of GPS signals, and the character and shape of the international environment for GPS and its alternatives.

GPS POLICY AFFECTS DIVERSE NATIONAL INTERESTS

National Security and Public Safety

GPS was developed by the Department of Defense to improve en route navigation. An accurate space-based system of satellites was intended to be more cost-effective and survivable than a multiplicity of ground-based radio navigation aids. National security has historically been the first concern in GPS policy. Since the dramatic demonstrations of GPS in Operation Desert Storm and the increasing integration of GPS receivers into U.S. military forces, the state of GPS has become of increasing interest to military commanders at all levels. At one time, the most important military space function was the detection of intercontinental missile launches. Today, judging by the calls that come in to U.S. Space Command from deployed U.S. forces, it is the performance and stability of the GPS signal.

Virtually every mobile platform in the U.S. military forces has or is intended to have access to GPS signals. Original applications include navigation for aircraft, tanks, ships, and other vehicles. As the cost of GPS receivers declines, the equipment is being purchased in large numbers for infantry, artillery, and support (medical and logistics) functions. The U.S. Army has been the largest military purchaser of GPS receivers (Figure 2.1). Specially designed, rugged, and compact GPS receivers are used by Special Forces, and the GPS signal is necessary for some intelligence functions. In less than a decade, U.S. military forces have moved into a position of great reliance on GPS for routine operations. Over the next 10 years, U.S. military forces may move from reliance to dependence on GPS.

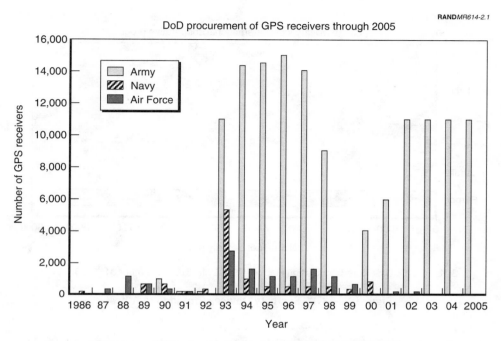

Figure 2.1—The Army Dominates DoD Receiver Purchases

With its global presence, the United States has long led the development of international standards and procedures for long-range military and civilian navigation. In addition, how the United States chooses to equip its forces has a major influence on the force structures of its allies. With some significant time lags, GPS receivers are being added to allied military forces in parallel with the growth of GPS use in the DoD. It is difficult to precisely estimate the numbers of GPS receivers in use in U.S. or allied forces because commercial GPS receivers are often bought by individual military personnel outside of official procurement channels.[1] In contrast, cryptographic security devices for GPS receivers are strictly controlled by the United States through export regulations, approved foreign military sales, and international cooperative programs. Security devices may be seen as a proxy for allied military use of GPS, and it is not surprising to see that Europe has the greatest number of such devices. (See Figure 2.2.) Like the United States, allied military organizations such as NATO are becoming dependent on access to GPS signals.

---

[1]DoD statistics on the procurement of military GPS receivers do not reflect the purchase of several thousand commercial "small lightweight GPS receivers" (SLGRs) during the Persian Gulf War in 1991. Because of a U.S. inability to waive the lowest-cost certification, many of the devices had to be purchased by Japan and then provided to the allies. U.S. Department of Defense, *Conduct of the Persian Gulf War: Final Report to Congress*, Appendixes A–S, April 1992.

RAND*MR614-2.2*

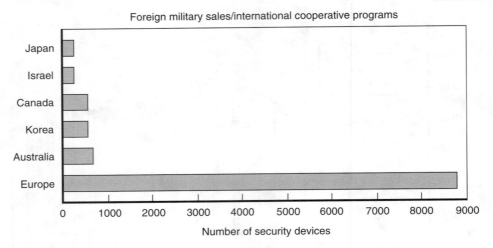

Figure 2.2—GPS Security Devices Provided to Allies

SOURCE: DoD Selected Acquisition Report, DD-COMP 823, December 31, 1993.

In contrast to the growing reliance of conventional military forces on GPS, U.S. nuclear forces have not been and are not dependent on GPS,[2] partly because of the recent arrival of GPS as a fully operational system as opposed to an experimental development. There has also been a long-held reluctance to depend on space systems that may not survive a nuclear exchange, for a secure retaliatory response. The U.S. ICBM force moved to self-contained inertial navigation systems (INS) and away from radio-based guidance (such as used by Atlas ICBMs) in the 1960s.[3] In the post–Cold War era, some previously strategic platforms, such as the B-52, B-1, and B-2 bombers, are emphasizing conventional missions and are adopting GPS receivers for nonnuclear operations.

While the threat of a massive nuclear exchange between the United States and the Soviet Union is gone, the threat from the proliferation of weapons of mass destruction persists. In addition, there are increasing threats from the spread of ballistic missiles and cruise missiles that can carry out rapid, long-range, precision strikes.[4] The improved navigation and guidance capabilities offered by

---

[2]Each GPS satellite carries nuclear detonation detectors that are used for monitoring nuclear test ban agreements as well as the hostile use of nuclear weapons. The network of space-based detectors, a by-product of the GPS constellation, is a unique national capability.

[3]Steven J. Isakowitz, *International Reference Guide to Space Launch Systems*, American Institute of Aeronautics and Astronautics, 1991, p. 185.

[4]William C. Potter and Harlan W. Jencks (eds.), *The International Missile Bazaar: The New Suppliers' Network*, Westview Press, Boulder, CO, 1994. See also K. Scott McMahon and Dennis M.

GPS could thus be used by hostile forces in conflict with the United States and its allies. The extent that GPS contributes to the threat from ballistic missiles and cruise missiles is thus a topic of concern for policymakers and this study. GPS is not the only satellite-based navigation system available or potentially available, which can lead to tensions between the impulse to limit GPS access to specifically authorized users and the creation of incentives for competing systems that would be subject to less U.S. influence than holds today.

The increasing use of GPS by military forces has been paralleled by the civilian use and dependency on GPS public safety applications. GPS is of great interest to civil air and maritime transportation operators and government agencies that provide navigation and geographic reference services. The Federal Aviation Administration is developing new air traffic management systems based on the use of GPS signals and the U.S. Coast Guard uses GPS in its maritime beacon system to serve both marine and nearby land users. At the same time, other U.S. navigation aids such as Omega, Transit, and Loran are being shut down or transferred to foreign operators.[5] The National Oceanic and Atmospheric Administration (NOAA) maintains a National Geodetic Reference System (NGRS) that was originally intended to maintain uniformity in land surveys. With the dramatic improvement in accuracies resulting from GPS, spatial data information is in increasing demand by federal, state, and local governments, utility companies, emergency service providers, and commercial firms. GPS is thus enabling the creation of an accurate, single geographic reference system for the United States and potentially for other countries as well.[6]

A more subtle issue for public safety is the increasing use of GPS time signals for the synchronization of fixed and mobile communication systems, including computer networks. Accurate timing is needed for the smooth routing of information packets, a function that becomes more challenging as data rates increase. GPS is a cost-effective means for distributing precision time "stamps" uniformly over national and international distances. Precision time from standard sources (such as the U.S. Naval Observatory) may be delivered via fiber optic lines or atomic clocks, but there is no obvious substitute for GPS time, given the increasingly large installed base of modern telecommunication networks. Public safety depends on modern communications, which in turn is dependent on the reliable distribution of accurate time via GPS.

Gormley, *Controlling the Spread of Land-Attack Cruise Missiles*, American Institute for Strategic Cooperation, AISC Papers, No. 7, Marina del Rey, CA, January 1995.

[5]U.S. Department of Transportation and the U.S. Department of Defense, *1992 Federal Radionavigation Plan*, U.S. Government Printing Office, Washington, D.C., January 1993.

[6]National Research Council, Committee on Geodesy, *Forum on NOAA's National Spatial Reference System*, National Academy Press, Washington, D.C., 1994.

Economic Growth

The United States has a rapidly growing GPS industry whose global sales are expected to exceed $8 billion by 2000, up from 1995 sales of $1.2 billion.[7] This rate of growth is plausible when considering that the similar sales figure for 1990 was only $80 million.[8] These sales are for GPS equipment used in consumer applications, car navigation, tracking, survey and mapping, geographic information systems, civil aviation and marine applications, and military sales. Exports are a major proportion of GPS sales, estimated to be 52 percent in 1995.[9]

The commercial sales figures do not include the manufacture, launch, and operation of GPS satellites or the costs of maintaining the ground-control segment. The follow-on to the current GPS program, known as Block IIF, was expected to cost $6 billion, with the space-based portion accounting for a third of that.[10] Originally, 51 satellites were planned to be procured to sustain the GPS signal past the year 2000, with the first Block IIF GPS satellite available in 2004.[11] In 1995, the planned procurement was reduced from 51 to 33 satellites, to be purchased in three lots for a total of $3 billion. The initial contract would be for six satellites in 1996, followed by a 1998 contract for 15 satellites, and a final contract in 2002 for 12 satellites.[12]

GPS technology and the use of the GPS signal affect many industries at varying points in economic "food chains." Unlike the situation with many other defense procurements, the commercial stakeholders in GPS extend beyond just those seeking to compete for DoD contracts. They include firms supplying GPS products to the private sector directly (e.g., original equipment or original equipment manufacturers [OEM]), firms that use GPS products to enhance the competitiveness of their products (e.g., luxury car builders), firms that use GPS products to meet the needs of their customers (e.g., surveyors), service providers (e.g., ambulance operators), and firms that benefit from the improvements to the public sector brought about by GPS (e.g., commercial airlines and long-distance communications firms).

The growth of commercial GPS firms has in turn provided benefits back to the U.S. government. In the Persian Gulf War, commercial suppliers were able to

---

[7]"GPS in Year 2000: $8 Billion," *GPS World Newsletter,* April 11, 1995, p. 1

[8]U.S. Department of Commerce, *Space Business Indicators,* U.S. Government Printing Office, Washington, D.C., 1992, p. 4.

[9]Personal communication with Michael Swiek, U.S. GPS Industry Council, May 5, 1995.

[10]"GPS 2F Hinges on Procurement Strategy," *Space News,* May 1–7, 1995, p. 3.

[11]Ibid.

[12]"Air Force Chops GPS Contract Plan," *Space News,* July 24–30, 1995, p. 1.

meet the higher-than-expected demand for GPS receivers, even if suppliers or GPS receivers could not meet all military specifications. The revenues from commercial sales of GPS receivers have supported private R&D investments, which have led to technical innovations that did not require taxpayer funds. These innovations have led to international patents by U.S. firms, declining prices, and increasing export sales. The lower costs, lighter equipment, and improved performance of commercial GPS receivers have provided stringent competitive benchmarks for military receiver manufacturers. The existence of a strong commercial GPS industry means that a significant part of the U.S. defense industrial base can be maintained without government funding.

The productivity benefits of GPS are contributing to economic growth in industrial sectors in the United States and overseas. U.S. industry leaders do not see major risks to further international growth as coming from technical or financial factors, but from market risk resulting from government policies.[13] Further growth depends on the continued supply of a stable, high-quality GPS signal, international acceptance of commercial GPS products and services, and the absence of competing systems or technologies providing similar benefits. Because U.S. industry is not in a position to control these factors, they constitute significant business risks. As will be argued later, the U.S. government can control or at least mitigate these risks.

Foreign Policy

GPS is a strong symbol of U.S. international economic and technical influence as well as military capability. The economic power of U.S. firms supplying or using GPS technology is creating opportunities for cooperation and competition with foreign firms in the international market. Foreign firms may seek to use government supports or market barriers to narrow the U.S. lead in GPS technology, leading to trade tensions. Alternatively, foreign governments' decisions to open their markets to GPS technology can create new export opportunities for the United States as well as benefit foreign productivity through their use of GPS. These decisions are all essentially political judgments involving sovereign powers who may be influenced by U.S. foreign policy.

The Soviet Union was the only country to build a space-based navigation system—GLONASS—that could duplicate the global coverage and accuracy of GPS. Other countries, such as France, considered and rejected the construction of a fully independent space constellation as too expensive. Instead, foreign governments have constructed GPS augmentations, such as local-area differential GPS (DGPS) reference stations, and are developing space-based versions

---

[13]Swiek, op. cit.

of these reference stations to provide wide-area services (see Appendix A). Like GPS itself, these augmentations have dual-use applications and these governments will have to balance the risks and benefits of providing highly accurate navigation information over their territory. They may be expected to look for any U.S. policy precedents on combining commercial, civil, and military interests.

INMARSAT, the international maritime satellite organization, provides mobile aeronautical and maritime communications services and is seeking to enter the market for land mobile communications. INMARSAT has a broad international membership that includes the United States, and it has expressed interest in providing space-based services to monitor the quality of GPS signals and augment them with space-based reference signals to provide accuracies comparable to differential GPS on a global basis.[14] As a civil international organization, INMARSAT does not directly address the security concerns of its members, although it does provide services to military users. It may thus be difficult for the United States to directly address its security concerns with wide-area DGPS services within INMARSAT alone.

Agreements involving international navigation and commerce are among the oldest and most common international accords to which the United States is a party. As a new form of navigation aid, GPS raises both familiar and new issues for U.S. foreign policy. Aside from specific regional security, trade, regulatory, and safety questions, there are overarching questions on whether GPS will be a global standard for navigation, position location, and timing (which are distinct functions made possible by the same set of signals) and what the international regime will be for that standard. For example, other nations may choose to rely only on GPS or seek to ensure there is more than one GPS-like system (e.g., by using GLONASS).

With respect to GPS augmentations, the leading Western space powers (i.e., the United States, Japan, and Europe) may cooperate to create an interoperable system based on satellite systems under their national control.[15] Alternatively, INMARSAT or some other single international organization could provide global coverage from a common set of geostationary satellites. An important decision for U.S. policymakers is whether it is desirable to have a set of bilateral agreements with traditional allies on GPS augmentations or a single international organization providing GPS augmentations.

---

[14]Olaf Lundberg, "Waypoints for Radionavigation in the 21st Century," keynote speech delivered at the Institute of Navigation Conference, ION GPS-94, Salt Lake City, UT, September 20, 1994.

[15]For example, the United States, Japan, and Europe could each provide standardized GPS augmentation signals from their own geostationary satellites. The satellites would be chosen to provide seamless, global coverage except for the poles.

Scientific Research

The military decision to develop GPS and the growth of commercial markets have enabled a host of scientific applications. GPS signals can be used to measure relative positions at or above the earth's surface to better than 1 centimeter. The declining cost of GPS equipment means that multiple ground stations can acquire information over large areas, thus permitting precise geographic control networks. The original impetus for much of this line of research came from NASA's Crustal Dynamics Project, which has sought to apply the techniques of very-long-baseline interferometry (VLBI) and satellite laser ranging (SLR) to the measurement of tectonic plates on a global scale.

GPS permits a better understanding of the atmosphere through which the signals travel. As signals from GPS satellites pass through the atmosphere, they are distorted by the ionosphere and other effects (such as water vapor). As the operation of the GPS constellation has matured, extensive research has gone into compensating for these distortions and eliminating other effects. GPS time signals are so precise, for example, that GPS is the only operational military or civil system that routinely compensates for general relativistic effects as the satellites orbit in earth's gravitational field. It has been speculated that GPS signals may be useful in distinguishing between earthquakes and underground explosions caused by nuclear devices.[16] An explosion produces a limited acoustic wave pulse that travels up through the atmosphere, producing subtle distortions in the transit of dual-frequency GPS signals, whereas an earthquake does not. Events detected by seismographs could be correlated with the behavior of GPS signals to indicate if they could have been caused by explosions.

The use of GPS has sparked interdisciplinary research in diverse fields, including geology, atmospheric science, volcanism, oceanography, polar studies, and geospace physics. In addition to basic research, GPS is being used in applied research on earthquakes, landslides, climate change, environmental assessments, toxic waste dispersal, coastal erosion, and the integrity of public works such as dams, bridges, and highways. There is a rich interaction between various scientific fields and between private industry and universities using GPS technologies.[17] GPS is thus an international scientific resource as well as a military space system.

---

[16]Jean-Bernard Minster, "Some Applications of GPS in the Earth Sciences," Scripps Institute of Oceanography, Institute of Geophysics and Planetary Physics, presentation to the Committee on the Future of the Global Positioning System, National Research Council, July 29, 1994.

[17]For a more detailed description of scientific research projects using GPS, see the UNAVCO Science Plan, University Navigation Consortium, University of Colorado, Boulder, CO, September 1993. This document can be found on the World Wide Web at http://www.unavco.ucar.edu/

VIEWPOINTS WITHIN THE U.S. GOVERNMENT

As might be expected, the diverse range of interests affected by GPS is reflected in the differing viewpoints of U.S. government agencies. The national interests described above do not map neatly onto the agencies, although some interests predominate over the others. It is helpful to understand the mixture of agency concerns and motivations in assessing how differing policy proposals might be received.

We interviewed a number of government officials during the course of this study and have attempted to reflect an accurate understanding of their views in this study. Nonetheless, the authors alone are responsible for the interpretations presented here, which do not represent official agency positions.

Department of Defense

After satellite communications, GPS is the most widely used military space system, which generates strong feelings about its future. Within the DoD, viewpoints on GPS tend to cluster around those who are concerned with the system itself, those who seek to apply GPS to specific problems, and those who are concerned with the global spread of GPS technology. The GPS Joint Program Office (JPO), based in El Segundo, California, is concerned with sustaining the GPS constellation and with the procurement of the next set of GPS satellites, known as Block IIF. Like other major and minor programs, the GPS program has had to work to justify its claim to a share of the declining defense budget. The Air Force Space Command, 50th Space Wing, operates the GPS master control station in Colorado Springs, Colorado. As might be expected, their primary concern is the management of a large constellation of spacecraft that serve military units around the world. As GPS has become integrated into the U.S. force structure, deviations in the performance of GPS tend to be quickly noticed and commented on by field commanders, creating feedback pressure on the system operators.

The military usage of GPS has spread beyond originally intended applications, such as en route navigation, and into more demanding areas such as munitions guidance. The potential usage of GPS by weapons has brought debate over performance specifications for the next generation of GPS satellites. The current system is performing better than original specifications in terms of accuracy, reliability, lifetime-on-orbit, etc., so that most users say that they just want guarantees that this level of performance will continue with future satellites. The JPO and industry contractors respond that although they may be able to do this, to guarantee current performance levels will require extra resources. Neither the GPS program office nor the DoD users wishing to exploit better-than-expected GPS performance have budgets for these additional resources.

To those involved in the procurement and operation of GPS, the system is first and foremost a military system, but the increasing civil and commercial users of the system are impossible to ignore. Like military users, civil and commercial users are interested in the current and future performance of GPS and seek to impress their views on the JPO and the 50th Space Wing by formal and informal means. This interest is seen as a mixed blessing. On one hand, the GPS system has benefited from civil and commercial expressions of support in earlier budget reviews. On the other hand, the GPS user community is so large and diverse that it is difficult, if not impossible, to channel nonmilitary interests into the military decision process in any uniform way. The DoD tends to welcome the idea of the Department of Transportation becoming responsible for coordinating civil and commercial inputs, but has been frustrated by the slow progress in implementing such coordination.

For most of the armed services and the Joint Staff, the central problem with GPS is getting military-qualified receivers and equipment integrated into the force structure rapidly enough. Since Operation Desert Storm in 1991, GPS technology has been embraced at all levels, especially at the lower ranks, with the availability of low-cost commercial receivers. Some senior commanders are more wary of GPS and concerned about depending on an electronic system that may be jammed or spoofed. Senior DoD civilian leaders recognize the immense value of GPS, but have also been concerned about paying for integration costs. While it may be possible to give a soldier a $500 commercial GPS receiver that benefits him and his unit, integrating a GPS-based navigation system into a modern fighter plane starts with costs of $100,000. Nonetheless, Congress has imposed a mandate that GPS installations be completed by Fiscal Year 2000 or funding for the platforms without GPS may be terminated.[18]

DoD users appreciate the military advantage created by GPS but are concerned that this advantage may be eroded by international developments and new technologies. The United States has concentrated its counterproliferation efforts on weapons of mass destruction, but there are concerns that the spread of other technologies such as submarines, unmanned air vehicles, and advanced civilian command, control, communication, and intelligence (C3I) capabilities—including GPS—could pose significant new threats to U.S. forces.[19] Aside from the concern that civilian levels of GPS accuracy could be militarily useful, there is even deeper concern over plans to provide highly accurate (< 5 meter)

---

[18]The National Defense Authorization Act for FY 1994 (P.L. 103-160), Division A, Subtitle D, Sec. 152(b), states that after September 30, 2000, funds may not be obligated to modify or procure any DoD aircraft, ship, armored vehicle, or indirect-fire weapon that is not equipped with a GPS receiver.

[19]Henry D. Sokolski, "Nonapocalyptic Proliferation: A New Strategic Threat?" *The Washington Quarterly*, Vol. 17, No. 2, Spring 1994, pp. 115–127.

differential GPS signal corrections over global distances for civil airlines. DGPS accuracy is superior to the military signals available from GPS alone; because civil airliners depend on that signal, the DoD is concerned about denying that access in wartime.

The DoD seems to be more concerned with wide-area civil DGPS than local-area DGPS or the Russian GLONASS system for at least three reasons. The first is that global usage of DGPS by airliners will mean higher commercial production rates for suitable receivers. No such large commercial market exists for GLONASS receivers, and thus the potential for enemy exploitation, while significant, is much less. Second, there is a perception that local-area DGPS systems are easier to shut down, jam, or destroy if necessary, as opposed to space-based systems whose signals cover major portions of the globe. Third, the global availability of DGPS signals might encourage foreign military forces to exploit GPS capabilities more than they otherwise would if GPS remained a U.S. monopoly. That is, foreign militaries might calculate that the United States would be unable to deny access to wide-area DGPS signals, and thus they themselves could depend on such signals for military operations. Clearly, if such operations were conducted against the United States or its allies, this could pose a military risk. As a result, many in the DoD would prefer that space-based distribution of DGPS signals over wide areas not occur at all, or—if they do occur—that such signals be encrypted for positive control and offset from GPS frequencies to facilitate jamming. However, the magnitude of the military risk is likely to be more dependent on exogenous factors such as enemy sophistication and force levels.[20]

With growing awareness in DoD of the potential for denial or misuse of GPS signals has come an increasing interest in offensive and defensive electronic warfare (EW) techniques for GPS. Offensive EW includes jamming or spoofing an enemy's attempt to use GPS signals. Defensive EW means acquiring GPS signals, especially the Precise Positioning Service, in the face of enemy jamming, spoofing, or other actions. Defensive EW capabilities are part of what distinguishes a military receiver from a commercial one. Null-steering antennas, for example, seek to find the weakest areas of jamming when using a GPS signal in a challenged environment. Cryptographic capabilities on a GPS receiver help verify that it is getting a true GPS signal and is not being spoofed. Intentional jamming and spoofing are not a current concern in commercial applications, but this could change in the future.[21]

---

[20]Allan R. Millett, Williamson Murray, and Kenneth H. Watman, "The Effectiveness of Military Organizations," *International Security*, Vol. 11, No. 1, Summer 1986, pp. 37–71.

[21]GPS signals to commercial aircraft might be jammed as an act of terrorism, or GPS time stamps on financial transactions spoofed as part of a criminal act.

Perhaps the most contentious area of GPS operations is the practice of "selective availability" in peacetime. Selective availability (SA) intentionally degrades the accuracy of the coarse acquisition (C/A) signal used to provide the Standard Positioning Service (SPS). Without SA, SPS accuracy could be increased from 40 meters to as much as 5–10 meters CEP.[22] SA was turned off during the Persian Gulf War so that U.S. forces could use commercial GPS receivers (the enemy was not similarly equipped). When U.S. forces entered Haiti in 1994, SA was again turned off to permit use of commercial GPS receivers. As might be expected, these actions fed calls from some commercial users to turn SA off in peacetime. The DoD has resisted turning SA off, fearing that it may be unable to activate SA in wartime because important nonmilitary users may have become dependent on the more accurate signal. DoD also fears that turning SA off would encourage a faster spread of GPS technologies to foreign military forces and a narrowing of the U.S. military advantage provided by GPS.

GPS-aided navigation and position location is seen as particularly effective in improving the effectiveness of air-to-ground attacks. If a military force has air superiority, however, it should be able to defeat many hostile uses of GPS. U.S. air power is seen as the most capable and effective in the world today and likely to maintain that position.[23] Unfortunately, air superiority is not something that can be maintained at all times and in all places and allied air forces may not be able to guarantee air superiority. Particularly in the opening phase of hostilities, there is concern that U.S. allies could find themselves under attack from GPS-aided weapons. Thus, many in the DoD would like to slow the spread of GPS technologies, discourage their use for military purposes, and maintain as many advantages in the operation and control of GPS as possible. Such objectives may not be realistically achievable for more than a few years, sparking a consequent interest in other approaches to preserving U.S. military advantages.

Department of Transportation

Like the Department of Defense, the Department of Transportation expects GPS to play an increasingly important role in accomplishing its missions. Also like the DoD, the DoT is expecting to make major investments in ground and space systems that depend on GPS. Unlike the DoD, the DoT interest in GPS was initially championed through one application—civil air navigation and

---

[22]CEP (circular error probable) refers to a 50 percent level of confidence. SPS accuracy is more commonly referred to in terms of a 95 percent level of confidence. SA reduces the accuracy available from the C/A signal from 20–30 meters to 100 meters (95 percent). The latter figure is specified as the required accuracy for SPS service in the Federal Radionavigation Plan.

[23]Chris Bowie et al., *Trends in the Global Balance of Airpower*, MR-478/1-AF, RAND, 1995.

management by the Federal Aviation Administration. The U.S. Coast Guard has become interested in GPS for enhanced maritime navigation using both GPS and DGPS techniques to update its existing beacon system. DoT discussions of an "intelligent vehicle highway system" has meant that GPS is a "multi-modal" issue, an important characteristic in balancing the diverse transportation interests within the DoT.

The productivity benefits of GPS are a primary motivation for the DoT, which is challenged with providing high-reliability navigation information for increasingly crowded and complex national air and water transportation networks that must also be integrated into global transportation networks. The SPS-level of GPS accuracy is satisfactory for some applications such as en route navigation, but not for others such as final approach and landings, especially in inclement weather or when maneuvering a ship in port. As a result, the FAA and the U.S. Coast Guard have developed DGPS system concepts that they believe will be more cost-effective than current radio-based navigation aids such as Loran-C. Accuracy alone is not the only concern for these systems; they must also be available when needed, 24 hours per day, and they must have a high degree of integrity—that is, the user must be able to tell when bad information is being received. When landing an aircraft in bad weather, the integrity requirements may be severe and require warning within seconds.

One of the key attractions of GPS is that is has already been built and the marginal cost of serving additional users is zero. Thus GPS is especially attractive to the DoT, which is facing severe budget pressures and demands for new investments to improve an aging air traffic control system.[24] Even if the DoT decided not to augment GPS, it would recognize a public safety need to monitor the availability of GPS signals and their performance. In the case of the FAA, the incremental cost of providing differential correction signals is seen as low, and thus there is a compelling case to do so. This has led to conflicts with the DoD, which sees potential security threats from the provision of highly accurate correction signals, especially over the wide areas necessarily served in air traffic control.

The policy conflict between DoD and DoT over how to balance the risks and benefits of wide-area GPS augmentations has raised international issues as well. International airlines prefer to work in a "seamless" navigation network that minimizes the need for different types of equipment and crew training. International certification authorities want to have a clear understanding of the potential risks in using a particular navigation system. The Federal Aviation

---

[24]"GPS: What Can't It Do?" Hearings before the Committee on Science, Space, and Technology, Subcommittee on Technology, Environment, and Aviation, U.S. House of Representatives, March 24, 1994.

Administration plays a major role in developing aviation standards within the International Civil Aviation Organization (ICAO), and is thus sensitive to foreign government concerns with U.S. policies and operations when GPS is proposed as the basis for global air traffic management. Understandably, foreign governments are reluctant to certify the use of a satellite-based navigation system they may not understand and certainly do not control. Thus, DoT views on GPS are affected by perceptions of its political acceptability as well as by its technical effectiveness.

When debates between the DoD and DoT over conditions for moving forward with FAA plans for a wide-area augmentation system (WAAS) became public in early 1995, there were concerns that the United States was about to become more restrictive in allowing access to GPS. To help allay these concerns, President Clinton sent a letter to ICAO restating that no change had occurred in U.S. policy with regard to providing GPS signals to the international aviation community.[25] In the past, the DoT thought that it might acquire an operational role in GPS, with civil DoT personnel stationed at the master control station in Colorado Springs and at the GPS Joint Program Office in Los Angeles. Currently, the department sees the need for a strong liaison function, but not for DoT personnel actually operating the satellites. It has focused instead on being an advocate for civil requirements, especially those involving public safety, and having an impact at the national policy level through interagency fora. This is seen as helping promote international acceptance for countries that feel more comfortable dealing with a civil agency than with the DoD.

Whereas the first concerns with satellite-based navigation for civil transportation have been with technical feasibility and signal access, there are more subtle, less articulated concerns with the security of GPS augmentations used for civil transportation networks. The basic GPS system is seen as secure—the satellite constellation is designed to operate for up to 180 days in the event of the loss of ground control. The satellites themselves are in high earth orbit and military receivers have access to encrypted signals that are jam-resistant and difficult to spoof. Civil GPS signals are relatively easy to jam, as are the associated differential GPS correction signals proposed for air traffic control uses. This has raised questions about what backup systems (preferably ground-based) would be in place in the event of the loss or failure of the GPS augmentation system and the operational security of satellite-based navigation in the event of a terrorist threat. The DoT, through the FAA, has paid some attention

---

[25] "WAAS Frequency Offset," briefing by Joe Dorfler, FAA SatNav Program Manager, February 15, 1995; and letter from President Clinton to the International Civil Aviation Organization at its Montreal Conference, March 16, 1995.

to backups but relatively little to terrorist threats, which are perceived as unlikely.

DoT perceptions of low operational security risks in using GPS are not shared by DoD, which has objected to the provision of wide-area differential correction signals because of concerns that national and international dependence on such signals will make their denial in crises or wartime difficult if not impossible. Even in peacetime, the wide availability of such signals is thought to be an incentive to develop high-accuracy weapons and military platforms that could be used against the United States and its allies. The GPS Joint Program Office has proposed various countermeasures to the potential misuse of differential correction signals, such as encrypting correction signals exclusively for authorized users and widely separating their operating frequencies from GPS frequencies to allow them to be jammed more easily.[26] The DoT has objected to such ideas for a variety of reasons that come down to the issue of international acceptability. Those steps which enhance military security are seen as undercutting the political and technical acceptability to foreign civil government authorities.[27]

As the DoT has pressed forward with plans for civil aviation and maritime GPS augmentations, it has encountered resistance from suppliers of private DGPS services. These suppliers, some based in the United States but operating worldwide, provide encrypted DGPS correction signals through FM subcarriers, and authorized customers can get various levels of accuracy by paying fees for decryption keys. The service areas are typically larger than those of a DGPS-equipped survey team with one or more base stations, but smaller than the beacons proposed by the U.S. Coast Guard or the satellite-based FAA WAAS concept. These firms feel that the U.S. government would unfairly compete with them and have argued that the government should purchase DGPS services from them instead.[28] The DoT does not feel that any of the service providers can meet the technical and reliability requirements imposed by safety-of-life applications. While it is possible to promulgate regulations that would allow uses of commercial services for safety-of-life purposes, there are uncertainties with the allocation of liability to private firms. Given the budget

---

[26]"Augmented Global Positioning System," briefing by Colonel Michael Wiedemer, System Program Director, GPS Joint Program Office, June 1994.

[27]The larger commercial communities using GPS have been largely uninterested in this debate. The question of international acceptance depends on decisions by governments on whether to use GPS for civil purposes, not on acceptance by private markets. The DoD already has processes for use of GPS by friendly foreign military forces.

[28]*Response to NTIA Special Publication 94-30, "A National Approach to Augmented GPS Services,"* Differential Corrections Inc., Cupertino, CA, January 24, 1995.

pressures on DoT that have made GPS attractive in the first place, it is likely that the cost-effectiveness of private DGPS services will come in for close scrutiny.

The FAA has been the primary advocate within DoT for adoption of GPS as the basis for a new, more efficient global air navigation system. The U.S. Coast Guard has played an important role in working with civil GPS users through its public information center and meetings of the Civil GPS Service Interface Committee (CGSIC).[29] Despite the individual expertise (or perhaps because of it) within DoT agencies, the formation of a common policy framework for DoT interests has been difficult and slow. To a greater degree than other civil agencies, such as the National Aeronautics and Space Administration (NASA) or the Department of the Interior, the DoT sees GPS both as an important technology to accomplish its missions and representative of significant policy issues (e.g., the relative balance of civil and military interests in the exploitation of GPS as a global resource). Within the Office of the Secretary of Transportation, there is an awareness that if the DoT is to have a substantive role in GPS policy, it will have to speak with one voice in both interagency and international fora.

Department of Commerce

The Department of Commerce (DoC) has a variety of interests in GPS. The National Oceanic and Atmospheric Administration (NOAA) within DoC uses GPS in routine activities such as environmental monitoring, fisheries management, and coastal mapping. The Bureau of Export Administration (BXA) regulates the export of military GPS receivers. The International Trade Administration (ITA) is interested in encouraging the growth of a competitive domestic industry. Thus DoC interests in GPS cover a spectrum of direct agency applications, regulations, and trade policy. GPS is an interesting success story in dual-use technology in which government investments led to unexpected commercial benefits, and the DoC wants to have a role in shaping GPS policies that influence commercial interests.

The Department of Commerce has been involved in a number of decisions affecting the commercial development of GPS. NOAA has historically chaired the Federal Geodetic Control Committee, which sets standards for mapping and geodesy. In 1984, the first draft standards allowing use of GPS were published

---

[29]The CGSIC is sponsored by the U.S. Department of Transportation Assistant Secretary for Transportation Policy and the U.S. Coast Guard Navigation Center. The U.S. Coast Guard provides information on the status of various navigation aids through its Navigation Center in Alexandria, VA.

in the *Federal Register*. In 1995, virtually all geodetic standards are GPS-based.[30] This acceptance of GPS data by a civil government agency helped spur the growth of commercial survey and mapping applications that could take advantage of the superior productivity of GPS over traditional survey techniques. In 1991, the Bureau of Export Administration published revised export regulations that more clearly defined military versus civilian GPS receivers.[31] The former would continue to be treated as "munitions" and face strong export restrictions, whereas the latter would be available for general export without restrictions. This has helped accelerate U.S. industry penetration of overseas markets. In the future, the DoC's National Telecommunications and Information Administration (NTIA) will likely see industry requests to use the U.S. government spectrum for new applications of differential GPS and communications.

The DoC has pointed to the technical and sales leadership exhibited by U.S. GPS companies to highlight areas of U.S. industrial strength. As hardware costs continue to drop, a greater proportion of the value-added in typical GPS products has been in software, a traditional U.S. strength. GPS devices have become smaller and more deeply embedded in other systems, such as laptop computers and automobiles. This has played to another U.S. strength—systems integration. As a result, fears that GPS receivers would become another consumer electronics industry lost to Asian competitors have not been realized and U.S.-Japanese relations in particular have exhibited a mixture of cooperation and competition.[32]

The U.S. commercial advantage in GPS has a number of sources, such as being first to market and having considerable investment in commercial R&D.[33] In addition, there has been close cooperation between economic agencies, such as DoC and the U.S. Trade Representative (USTR), and the Department of Defense on policy matters affecting the GPS industry. Changes in export regulations are one example, as well as the extensive use of civilian GPS receivers during the Persian Gulf War. The USTR has worked with DoC and DoD to discourage for-

---

[30]Interview with Captain Lewis A. Lapine, Chief of the National Geodetic Survey, NOAA, June 6, 1995. The Federal Geodetic Control Committee is now a subcommittee of the Federal Geographic Data Committee chaired by the Department of the Interior.

[31]*Federal Register*, "7A05A Global Positioning Satellite (GPS) receiving equipment with a null-steerable antenna, and specially designed components therefor," Vol. 56, No. 168, August 29, 1991, p. 42890.

[32]U.S. Department of Commerce Press Release, "Remarks by U.S. Secretary of Commerce Ronald H. Brown before the Magellan Systems Corporation GPS Consortium Announcement, San Dimas, CA," Office of the Secretary, Washington, D.C., August 26, 1993.

[33]In 1989, Trimble Navigation spent 27 percent of its revenue on R&D. In the first quarter of 1995, this has lessened to 15.7 percent of sales, still a considerable level of commitment. See Trimble Navigation, "First Quarter Financial Report," Sunnyvale, CA, 1995.

eign governments from establishing proprietary standards for local differential GPS services, thus ensuring that U.S. firms can compete.

As GPS applications have spread to more and more industries, the DoC has begun talking about GPS as an element of national and global information infrastructures, which in turn contribute to the competitiveness of other industries. In a speech before a space conference in 1995, Secretary of Commerce Ronald Brown said that "The commercial application of GPS receivers is a prime example of how many defense-related technologies, developed for military purposes, can be used to improve our economic competitiveness in the post–Cold War world."[34]

Department of State

The economic and security aspects of GPS technology affect multiple U.S. foreign policy interests in regional security, alliance relations, nonproliferation, economic development, and international cooperation. Reflecting this range, many offices within the State Department have an interest in GPS policy. The Bureau of Politico-Military Affairs might look at the effect of GPS on military alliances, regional security, and nonproliferation. The Bureau of Economic and Business Affairs might look at how GPS could aid economic development and create opportunities for U.S. industry. The Bureau of Oceans and International Environmental and Scientific Affairs tends to follow applications of advanced technology, such as satellite systems, and would be interested in how GPS could be used for international scientific cooperation. Of course, each country and regional desk would be concerned with how GPS policy might affect the countries they cover.

At perhaps the most basic level, GPS enhances the effectiveness of U.S. military forces and thus their diplomatic value. GPS is also useful in operations other than war, such as humanitarian relief, which may be important in achieving U.S. foreign policy objectives. GPS guidance can be used, for example, in dropping relief supplies to isolated villages in rough terrain. Other applications of GPS, however, may help undermine U.S. foreign policies. One common concern is that the availability of GPS signals for accurate guidance will stimulate the proliferation of ballistic missiles and cruise missiles, contributing to regional instabilities.

The economic benefits from GPS technology to local transportation and construction infrastructures have come with no requirement for payment or other

---

[34] U.S. Department of Commerce press release, "Remarks by U.S. Secretary of Commerce Ronald H. Brown before the Global Air & Space Conference, Arlington, VA," Office of the Secretary, Washington, D.C., May 2, 1995.

compensation to the United States. The United States has arguably provided an important gift to other countries for its own reasons. On the other hand, the United States is under no obligation to provide this gift, and as GPS applications become more pervasive, foreign governments may worry about becoming dependent on a system in which they have little voice. For commercial users, U.S. or international, this does not seem to be a significant concern or impediment to the adoption of GPS technology. For governmental users, the question of whether to adopt GPS is more acute.

There are established procedures for foreign military use of GPS that involve direct negotiations with the Department of Defense. There are no similar procedures for foreign civil government use of GPS in safety-of-life applications such as air traffic management. This has led to numerous discussions with international organizations, such as ICAO, about how and under what conditions civil authorities should support the use of GPS. The economic attractions are profound, yet uncertainty over U.S. GPS and international use of GPS in particular has slowed adoption of GPS in some public-sector applications.

The dual-use nature of GPS makes for complex foreign policy questions—the military and commercial aspects of GPS are not separable into distinct channels. Adoption of GPS for air traffic control raises nonproliferation questions. Conversely, the military management of GPS raises concerns for foreign civil governments depending on the system. Foreign governments understandably have to be careful in making decisions on the use of GPS for public purposes, especially those involving military forces or public safety. The foreign government concerns constitute the major international policy questions raised by GPS. The strong commercial export sales exhibited by GPS indicate that foreign nationals have decided on their own that GPS is worth adopting.

As the United States addresses GPS international issues, commercial and military questions arise in a broader context of alliance relations and existing international organizations. For example, if the United States were to discuss GPS policy with Europe, would it address NATO, the European Community, the Western European Union, or go directly to states such as France and the United Kingdom? Or should it seek to deal with GPS in specialized international organizations such as ICAO or INMARSAT? There is no obvious single place to treat the full range of international GPS issues simultaneously, and that is a problem for U.S. foreign policy. An underlying challenge for the Department of State in addressing GPS, as well as other technologies, is a shortage of staff with strong technical backgrounds. This can lead diplomats and negotiators to depend on information from other agencies and private industry, which may or may not support U.S. foreign policy objectives.

The Executive Office of the President

The twin streams of GPS national security and economic issues cut across multiple government agencies and come to the White House for integration. Staffs of the National Science and Technology Council, the National Security Council, and the National Economic Council have all found themselves dealing with GPS-related issues in the past year. GPS has figured as an example in policy issues and initiatives that the Administration has wanted to highlight, such as the importance of dual-use technologies, the National Information Infrastructure, and the modernization of international air traffic management. The President himself signed a letter to ICAO reassuring it that GPS would remain available for use by civil aviation.[35]

A comprehensive White House review of GPS policy is under way as of this writing.[36] The review is co-chaired by representatives of the Office of Science and Technology Policy and the National Security Council, with participation from across the government. The last presidential policy on GPS was by President Reagan, so it is expected that this review will update the earlier policy to take account of the events of the last decade and provide a framework for the future management, operation, and exploitation of GPS. A policy review could also address the relative balance of civil, commercial, and national security interests in GPS and provide guidance on how GPS can advance U.S. foreign policy interests as well.

Congress

Congress is interested in GPS policy for the same diverse reasons found among GPS users and managers as a whole. In addition, Congress is concerned with the funding needs of GPS and how those needs stack up against other priorities. Since GPS is a DoD program, the responsibility for funding GPS satellites and ground operations falls under the Senate Armed Services Committee and the House National Security Committee and their counterparts in the Appropriations Committees. Congress has recognized the importance of GPS to the U.S. military and has been impatient with the slow pace at which GPS receivers have been integrated into military platforms such as aircraft, tanks, and ships.[37] GPS funding must compete against other military space programs and

---

[35]Letter from President Clinton to the International Civil Aviation Organization at its Montreal Conference, March 16, 1995.

[36]Letter from Vice President Gore to Mr. Charles Trimble, CEO of Trimble Navigation, April 21, 1995.

[37]The National Defense Authorization Act for FY 1994 (P.L. 103-160), Division A, Subtitle D, Sec. 152(b).

against other DoD programs. The next major budget commitment will be the follow-on series of GPS satellites, Block IIF, to maintain GPS service well into the next century.[38]

Consistent with pervasive concerns over the federal budget, a common question is how GPS is funded and whether other agencies and civil users should contribute directly to its maintenance. Both in the military and civil committees, the "free rider" question comes up—since we (the United States or the DoD) are paying for the system, why are others using it for free? This study addresses this question later in examining institutional alternatives for GPS (see Chapter 5).

In recent years, the Senate Armed Services Committee has taken the lead in raising GPS issues—see, for example, speeches and articles by the former Chairman, Senator J. James Exon (D-NE).[39] Nonmilitary congressional committees have also "discovered" GPS, particularly drawn by its potential to affect the future shape of the nation's air traffic control system.[40] To date, there seems to have been only informal communications between the civil- and military-oriented congressional committees, reflecting the tendency to segregate civil and military GPS interests.

Dual-use technologies and programs pose a challenge for Congress and its elaborate committee structure. The structure created for traditional issues tends to be unwieldy and difficult to adapt for newer, interdisciplinary issues like GPS. It can be expected that Congress would welcome a statement of Administration policy on GPS as a convenient place to begin debates, rather than attempt to create a complete policy framework of its own.

VIEWPOINTS IN U.S. INDUSTRY

As with Congress, it is difficult to uniformly characterize the wide range of viewpoints to be found within GPS-related U.S. industries. One can place firms along an economic "food chain" from satellite builders to users of GPS-derived information. At one end, there are the firms that build satellites under government contracts. At the other end are users who care only about how GPS improves their productivity or allows them to meet some market need. In the

---

[38]"GPS 2F Effort Hinges on Procurement Strategy," *Space News*, May 1–7, 1995; "Navstar Global Positioning System Block IIF Acquisition—Intent to Release Draft Request for Proposal," *Commerce Business Daily*, May 18, 1995.

[39]"The Future of the Global Positioning System," Senator J. James Exon, *Congressional Record*, April 30, 1993, pp. S5274–S5276; "GPS on Capitol Hill: Policy and Progress," *Professional Surveyor*, July/August 1994, p. 18.

[40]"Civil Aircraft Usage of GPS," Hearings before the Committee on Transportation and Infrastructure, Subcommittee on Aviation, U.S. House of Representatives, June 8, 1995.

middle of the chain, there are the original equipment manufacturers who translate GPS receiver technology into commercially competitive solutions.

The original equipment manufacturers (OEMs) are the most interesting firms in terms of policy development because they are aware of the needs of every possible GPS user—commercial, academic, military, or civil government. They form strategic partnerships with larger firms to exploit emerging markets, compete in the development of GPS technologies, and seek to leverage advantages in one market when entering others. They also cooperate when common interests are at stake, as was the case when export controls on civilian GPS receivers were defined in 1991. In the United States, OEMs are represented by the U.S. GPS Industry Council and in Japan by the Japan GPS Council. There is no comparable industry organization in Europe.

The OEMs support DoD management and operation of the GPS constellation as both competent and fair. There would seem to be little incentive to be misleading on this point because military sales are an increasingly small proportion of revenues. As businesses, the firms routinely manage technical, market, and financial risks, so their primary concern with political risk is that GPS policy remain stable and predictable. This translates into specific concerns such as maintaining the quality of the GPS signal and continuing support for replacement satellites, as well as not charging direct user fees for access to the GPS signal.

While taking a conservative approach toward the government's role in GPS, the U.S. GPS Industry Council recognizes the need to address the rapidly changing nature of commercial GPS uses. The current rapid growth of GPS has led to fears that one or another user segment—whether aircraft, automobiles, or even the military—will attempt to shape GPS for its own needs and neglect other segments. The divided nature of congressional committees makes this a plausible concern; hence a presidential statement of policy would provide a balanced framework for future developments.

A balanced policy framework would have commercial value. As U.S. OEM firms and GPS-dependent products and services expand into international markets, there are a variety of ways in which foreign governments can seek to block entry. Nontariff measures such as local content requirements, specialized standards, special licenses, and inadequate spectrum (e.g., for DGPS communication links) can be used to provide unfair barriers to market competition. These barriers may affect a wide variety of goods and services that may have no immediate military significance. It is therefore important for the U.S. GPS industry that there be a good understanding of GPS across the U.S. government (e.g., USTR, Commerce, Transportation, and State), not just within the DoD, to counter such barriers. In turn, it is important to U.S. industry that DoD understand the nature of commercial pressures as they affect the cost and quality of GPS technology available to U.S. and allied forces.[41]

There are several U.S.-based firms that provide differential GPS signals using FM and other radio waves. These signals can provide varying levels of position accuracy to subscribers. Subscribers may have many reasons for wanting more accuracy than is available from civil GPS signals alone, but do not want to support their own dedicated differential GPS system. These service providers are concerned by the plans of the U.S. Coast Guard and the FAA to provide differential GPS services to civil aviation and maritime users over wide areas. They feel that their customers, even if they are not aboard planes or ships, may opt to use the free signals from those systems, which overlap with their current service areas. These firms are asking that the civil government signals be encrypted and that fees be charged to limit competition with their services.

On one hand, it is easy to understand the interest in ensuring that the government does not compete with private firms. On the other hand, the government also has an interest in seeing that high-quality navigational aids exist for the public safety. Imposing direct charges for navigation signals may result in some users forgoing them to avoid the fee or the effort of subscribing to a service, thus placing themselves and others at risk.[42] Imposing indirect charges does not have a similar safety risk, but such charges do not solve the problem of government competition with the private sector. For example, the FAA funds its radionavigation aids from indirect user charges deposited in the Airport and Airways Trust Fund. As a result, users perceive a zero marginal cost of using these FAA services, but would experience additional costs to acquire the same service from a private provider.

The challenge for policymakers is to minimize competition with the private sector in a manner consistent with public safety (as well as national security) needs. This debate is ongoing as of this writing, but DGPS service plans by both the U.S. Coast Guard and FAA are proceeding. The U.S. GPS Industry Council supports the government efforts, recommending only that a decision on user fees—direct, indirect, or none—be made soon to provide a more stable environment for business planning. In addition, the council has recommended that

---

[41]The slow nature of the foreign military sales (FMS) process is a source of frustration to military GPS receiver manufacturers working with increasingly short product life-cycles. FMS products lag behind the best commercial technologies. Direct commercial sales of military receivers may be no faster, however, if a Memorandum of Understanding (MOU) for the transfer of encryption devices is needed. Government-to-government negotiations of MOUs and equipment transfers seem to consume the most time in both processes.

[42]Such behavior is particularly likely among general aviation pilots and recreational boaters, where mandatory use of navigation equipment is difficult to enforce.

private DGPS service providers be subject to appropriate regulation if their services are to be used in public safety navigation applications.[43]

INTERNATIONAL VIEWPOINTS

Because GPS is a global service, all nations can be expected to take an interest in GPS policy. From the standpoint of U.S. policy, however, the most important stakeholders are traditional U.S. allies in Europe and Asia, particularly Japan. These areas are where the most significant commercial markets are, as well as the security risks from the potential misuse of GPS. Europe and Japan are the source of competing GPS technologies and, after the United States, they will likely be models for the integration of civil and military GPS policies, and thus key to the future international environment for GPS.

Other regions of the world are less significant at the present time. The Middle East and Southwest Asia may see regional security problems in the wide use of GPS, but the commercial markets are relatively small. Although Russia has a competing satellite navigation system, GLONASS, there is not a large market in commercial GLONASS receivers. China, however, is a major potential source of military and commercial GPS competition. Chinese firms with both civil and military backgrounds are actively exploring the use of GPS. One fear is that past Chinese exports of advanced military equipment could be repeated with integrated GPS capabilities.

Japan

After the United States, Japan is the leading producer of GPS equipment and technology. While all types of GPS applications are found in Japan, the use of GPS in car navigation is the major force in the domestic market. GPS is treated as a form of consumer electronics, with an emphasis on driving hardware costs down to expand demand. Japanese industry has taken the lead in promoting GPS application while Japanese government ministries and agencies attempt to sort out their respective roles in the diverse aspects of GPS.

The Japan GPS Council (JGPSC) is an industry organization and does not represent official views, but it is "sponsored" by the Ministry of Posts and Telecommunications and the National Police Agency. The JGPSC, a vocal and influential group promoting the use of GPS in Japan, exchanges information with the U.S. GPS Industry Council on government policies that may affect commercial markets. Not surprisingly, the two organizations have much in

---

[43]U.S. GPS Industry Council, "Augmented Services Offered by the U.S. Government vs. Private Augmentation Services," unpublished issue paper, September 1, 1995.

common with respect to GPS policy. When the RAND study team visited Japan, even discussions with small GPS equipment suppliers outside of Tokyo echoed the theme of "policy stability and no user fees." The main point made by Japanese GPS firms was that GPS should be viewed as a global resource and that the current civil signal (i.e., the C/A code) should not be changed. In return, the firms saw a responsibility to help develop new markets and international standards for GPS with a thin line between cooperation and competition. As a way of recognizing the benefits provided to Japan by the U.S. provision of GPS, it has been informally suggested that fees for U.S. ship dockings and aircraft landings could be lowered for those using GPS. This type of fee reduction, although mostly symbolic, could be a positive political statement between the United States and Japan.

The Ministry of Transport is the most active part of the Japanese government promoting GPS applications, particularly for ports and harbors, maritime, and civil aviation users. Under the Bureau of Ports and Harbors, real-time GPS kinematic surveys are used for dredging, placement of structures, and measuring tide levels. Plans are under way for the placement of a DGPS station at Kita-Kyushu for safe maritime passage in a narrow strait. For civil aviation needs, a multifunctional transport satellite (MTSAT) is planned for the acquisition and dissemination of weather data and to provide GPS integrity signals to civil aviation users. The Loral Corporation was recently selected to build the combined weather and air traffic control satellite for about $100 million.[44]

The Ministry of International Trade and Industry (MITI) has a small program related to GPS. There is no central office for GPS technologies, and applications are addressed separately depending on the underlying industry—automobiles, ships, computers, etc. The largest single project, arising from MITI's responsibility for Japan's energy policy, is a feasibility study for the installation of a DGPS station at the Malacea Strait to ensure safe passage of oil shipments from the Middle East. The Ministry of Construction is similarly focused on immediate applications such as using GPS for basic mapmaking and to monitor earth movement for earthquake prediction. The ministry has installed about 200 GPS receivers at reference stations throughout Japan and is trying to integrate the massive network flows of data from these stations.

The Ministry of Posts and Telecommunications (MPT) is primarily involved with GPS through its Communication Research Laboratory, which maintains the time standard for Japan. MPT also has the sole responsibility for managing the radio frequency spectrum and providing frequency allocation licenses to users, which includes other ministries. This gives it a powerful position in the

---

[44]"Loral Awarded Contract for Japanese Satellite," *Space News*, March 6–12, 1995.

future development of GPS applications that require wireless communications, as in the case of mobile computing and mobile network services. While other ministries are concerned with GPS applications for their own missions, the MPT may be in the best position to integrate the diverse range of interests in GPS because of its influence in the International Telecommunications Union and meetings of the World Administrative Radio Conferences.

The Japanese Defense Agency (JDA) has had an agreement with the DoD for many years for access to military-level GPS signal accuracy. Military GPS receivers and encryption devices are being integrated into the Japan Self-Defense Forces, mostly with the Maritime Defense Forces. Parts of the JDA are aware of the potential benefits and risks of having widespread, overlapping differential GPS services given the local geography around Japan. This has not led, however, to open discussions with Ministry of Transport or the Ministry of Foreign Affairs about how to balance commercial and Japanese security interests. The type of civil-military dialog that has been going on for years between the DoT and DoD in the United States has yet to occur in Japan. As a result, the United States will likely have to play a leading role in starting that dialog to protect its own interests in regional stability and commercial markets in Asia affected by GPS.

Europe

Europe is behind the United States and Japan in the general level of awareness of GPS technology and applications. There is no comparable GPS industry association as there is in the United States and Japan, but there is a growing network of GPS product and service suppliers. Firms supporting North Sea oil exploration and recovery make extensive use of differential GPS. Firms in the United Kingdom and Norway in particular have developed DGPS equipment for reliable operation in hostile weather. German automobile firms such as BMW and Mercedes-Benz are developing car navigation products to meet U.S. and Japanese competition. On the whole, however, European interest in GPS is focused on government-driven public transportation planning for aircraft, trains, and future "intelligent vehicle highway systems."

Internal European discussions of satellite navigation and GPS seem to be driven by questions of government management, government contracts, and European community politics rather than military or commercial concerns. Within the European Commission, DG VII (Transports) has paid the most attention to GPS in the hopes of improving the dense European transportation networks, followed by DG XIII (Telecommunications), and DG XII (R&D). A tripartite group consisting of the European Commission (EC), the European Space Agency (ESA), and Eurocontrol (the European air traffic control organization) was formed to update the European air traffic system with satellite navigation. Eurocontrol is developing a European version of the U.S. Federal Radionavigation Plan, which is due in 1997. Dominant national voices seem to be France, the United Kingdom, Germany, and Sweden (a recent member of the European Union).

Despite misgivings about the United States, Europeans have largely decided that GPS is the world standard for satellite navigation. In a series of separate decisions, France decided not to build a French GPS, ESA decided not to build an ESA GPS, and the French space agency (CNES) decided not to build its own GPS augmentation system and instead to concentrate on integrity monitoring. Ten years ago, CNES was thinking about a European complement to GPS. That thinking formed the technical basis of the European Geosynchronous Overlay System (EGNOS), which consists of a geostationary satellite, a ground control station, and lots of small stations for wide-area integrity monitoring. Like the FAA's Wide Area Augmentation System, this approach could be extended to provide wide-area differential GPS signal corrections as well. Aside from the value to aviation, European interests in GNSS are primarily to use it to gain useful experience for future commercial ventures and to participate in GPS operations via integrity monitoring. Europe seems to be accepting dependence on GPS, but it is not ready to accept U.S. dominance in augmentation systems and would like to have its own regional system.

Europeans are reluctant to base their infrastructure on a U.S. space system, especially a military one, and thus they entertain ideas such as using GLONASS or launching "complementary" European satellites. In contrast, the Japanese do not seem to care who owns the GPS satellites because they are interested in capturing ground-equipment markets. While selective availability does not create significant technical problems, it does create political and emotional problems. To a significant degree, this political concern with the United States and the attendant attention on the space segment are in tension with the real commercial receiver market.

A systemic problem in implementing aviation uses of GPS in Europe is the difficulty of interstate coordination of standards. Only the United States seems to coordinate its position with all internal agencies (or so it appears to the Europeans) through instruments such as the Intergovernmental Aviation Agreements (IGA). Other countries do not coordinate to such an extent and persons at meetings sometimes represent only their agencies or themselves, not their governments. As a result, the Europeans find themselves struggling for focus in their planning processes.

European airspace cannot be characterized as seamless, and national sovereignty issues continue to arise.[45] Eurocontrol focuses on technical architecture matters, the EC focuses on institutional arrangements (e.g., who pays whom), and the ESA seeks to design future satellites and space-rated GPS equipment. A second systemic problem is the allocation of money and payments, with each country wanting to see returns to its own industries commensurate with funds contributed for common projects. A third major problem is European labor unions that resist consolidations and labor reductions. In a discussion of the benefits of GPS to air traffic control, the union representative objected to the phrase "enhanced productivity" and preferred "reduced controller workload."[46]

The most difficult problems for European aviation usage of GPS are not technical but bureaucratic and legal. Many European states have laws requiring navigation aids for safety-of-life application be under state control—clearly not the case with GPS. In addition, the Civil International Aviation Authority of the United Kingdom has a rather rigorous process for certification of aviation systems that it needs to adapt for satellites. One of the key difficulties in such adaptation is the need for knowledge of potential GPS vulnerabilities, which the United States is unlikely to share with a foreign government, even a military ally, for nonmilitary purposes. At base is the question of who would be liable in the event an accident occurs in which GPS may be a factor. At a minimum, international civil aviation authorities want to be able to monitor the integrity of GPS and have rapid notification if the system is not operating correctly. These difficulties have led some organizations, such as the Royal Institute of Navigation, to conclude that GPS will not be acceptable for European aviation use until it is under international control.

A major alternative for Europe would be to use the International Maritime Satellite (INMARSAT) organization as a means of international management of GPS augmentations. INMARSAT seems to have the capability and the will to move ahead on a Global Navigation Satellite System (GNSS) that would rely on GPS, and possibly GLONASS, and use INMARSAT satellites to broadcast integrity monitoring and differential correction signals on a global basis. This system could obviate the need for regional augmentation systems such as WAAS, MTSAT, and EGNOS. On the other hand, this concept could be blocked if the members decide to develop separate systems or support the U.S. WAAS concept on a global basis.

---

[45]Interview with Norman Solat, International Programs Manager, FAA, in Brussels, Belgium, January 30, 1995.

[46]Ibid.

INMARSAT is moving aggressively to position itself as the obvious choice for international management of satellite navigation aids and it offers a comfortable venue for Europe, with states' voting shares based on their contributions. Future GPS augmentations could be on the model of INMARSAT-P, where participants buy shares that may be more or less than their percentage of INMARSAT itself. INMARSAT would likely compete with or co-opt a European system and thus limit competition to its position. A significant concern for the United States would be the civil nature of INMARSAT. While attractive for civil and commercial users of GPS, an international civil satellite navigation system could pose regional security problems for the United States and its allies if INMARSAT wide-area differential GPS services were used by hostile forces. INMARSAT would not want to take sides in any conflict and the United States could be faced with the need to take military countermeasures against a civil satellite system.

As in Japan, there is a wide chasm between the civil and military GPS communities in Europe and an almost willful inattention to international security issues in European civil organizations. There does not seem to be any competent organization, except perhaps NATO, to address the military issues raised by wider civil use of GPS technology. The Western European Union (WEU) is often cited as the eventual forum for common European military issues, but it is still in an early stage of development. In our interviews, it was striking how European militaries were not part of civil aviation coordination processes. The only exception for military issues is the NATO Coordination of European Airspace Control (CEAC), which handles NATO air defense with the 16 members and the new "Partners for Peace" of the former Warsaw Pact. At present, civil/military airspace coordination in CEAC is the only place where civil/military GPS policy issues are discussed in a common European forum.

The key problem for NATO in adopting GPS is a lack of will to abandon old systems because of fears of political dependency. Thus the productivity of GPS does not contribute as much as it might to cost savings, a source of some frustration to NATO officers. Regional European security concerns that do arise center mostly on the misuse of differential GPS and concerns with potential attacks from North Africa. Some NATO people are uncomfortable with GPS because it can be easily jammed, and they are more concerned with assured access than with misuse of the signal. A NATO group called the CNAD (Conference of National Armament Directors) has a triservice group for military equipment. Within that, there is a subgroup on navigation equipment, including GPS. This subgroup meets with the GPS Joint Program Office to discuss satellite procurements and military GPS-related issues.

The lack of dialog between European civil and military GPS communities makes it hard for the United States to develop a GPS policy that takes into account

European concerns. In the United States, awareness of GPS has started with its identity as a military system that has become available to civil and commercial users. In Europe, awareness of GPS has occurred as a U.S. satellite system that can benefit civil aviation and potentially other transportation functions. The military identity of GPS then arises as a seemingly unfortunate aspect of its parentage that should ideally be "fixed." Not surprisingly, the United States has not been supportive of the idea that the U.S. control of GPS is a problem. Yet if the United States is to actively support the international acceptance of GPS as a global standard for safety-of-life applications such as aviation, it will need to address legitimate European concerns with integrity monitoring, liability, standards, and dependence on a system over which Europeans have no direct legal authority. There appear to be no realistic alternatives to GPS, including GLONASS, but addressing European concerns is likely to be an important part of the post–Cold War agenda of the Atlantic alliance.[47]

KEY GPS DECISIONS FOR THE FUTURE

Stakeholders in GPS policy are those concerned with the GPS system itself (access to it and preventing misuse) and the interests affected by applications of GPS (users, providers, and supporters). This chapter has shown how interdependent GPS policy issues are, as summarized in Figure 2.3.

The central issue is the management of GPS—who controls, funds, and defines the standards for the core space and ground segments. Augmentations such as local-area and wide-area differential correction signals depend on the existence of GPS. Potential competitors to GPS, such as GLONASS or an independent civil system, face a global market defined by GPS standards and expectations (e.g., no user fees, global availability). The spread of GPS augmentations creates national security concerns by undercutting the effectiveness of selective availability and creating opportunities for the misuse of GPS. At the same time, the wide use of GPS creates opportunities for international civil and military cooperation that can bring other nations closer to the United States. The rapid growth of commercial GPS applications creates further opportunities for cooperation and conflict by adding economic interests to the assessments of national security and foreign policy interests. GPS technology is being driven by many of the same forces driving other information and electronic technologies. Interests in GPS are thus affected by trends in miniaturization, software, and

---

[47]The EC sent a demarche to the State Department in March 1995 requesting clarification of U.S. GPS policy before proceeding with internal EC debates on using GPS in transportation systems.

RAND*MR614-2.3*

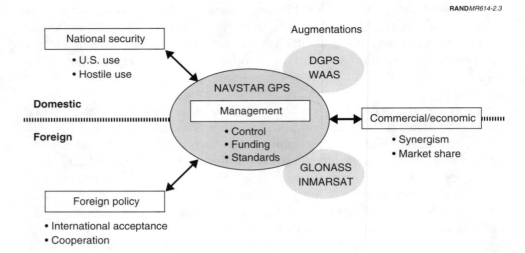

Figure 2.3—GPS Policy Issues Are Interdependent

complementary technologies such as inertial navigation and geographic information systems.[48]

Current Commitments

Current GPS policy commitments by the United States are fairly straightforward. In the aftermath of the Soviet downing of Korean Air flight 007 in the Far East, President Reagan declared that GPS facilities would be available to civilian aircraft to help prevent future accidents from navigation errors. The GPS program was still in an early experimental phase and not yet ready for adoption as a global navigation standard, but the U.S. announcement was interpreted as allowing access to the C/A (coarse acquisition) signal and what became known as the Standard Positioning Service for international civil aviation. The offer was unilateral by the United States and nothing was said about non-aviation uses.

FAA administrators have traditionally reinforced the Reagan announcement and pushed for greater specificity in order to gain international acceptance of GPS. In a 1994 letter to ICAO, the FAA administrator reiterated the U.S. intention (notably not a commitment) to make GPS-SPS available on a continuous, worldwide basis, free of direct user fees for the indefinite future. This service level was defined as providing horizontal accuracies of 100 meters with a 95

---

[48]GPS can be used to create accurate digital maps based on high-resolution remote sensing images. These maps, like the underlying technologies, can themselves have dual military and civilian uses.

percent probability. The United States would expect to provide at least six years notice prior to termination of GPS operation or elimination of the GPS-SPS and would attempt to provide at least 48 hours advance notice before any intentional disruption of SPS.

As distinct from U.S. statements, there is no overarching international agreement or treaty on GPS. The DoD has executed numerous agreements with allied militaries (and even civil government agencies) to provide access to the encrypted P-code, or Precise Positioning Service (PPS). There are some 15 international agreements to which the United States is a party that mention GPS, but usually in terms of providing assistance in using GPS-derived data for mapping and geodesy or providing mutual assistance for "safety-of-life at sea." The international agreement that created INMARSAT mentions navigation, but some modifications would be needed for INMARSAT to offer navigation services in the same manner in which it offers mobile communications. In short, the United States has not entered into any commitment to provide GPS services to particular parties or to agreed-upon specifications.

National and International Interests in GPS

The fundamental challenge for policymakers in balancing the interests of the various stakeholders in GPS is how to blend economic and national security interests. This is a particular challenge for implementation in foreign policy, given the potential for both conflict and cooperation in the exploitation of GPS. The time when GPS could be thought of as a purely military system is past. At the same time, GPS has such implications for international security and public safety that it cannot be treated as a purely private good. While it may be tempting to treat the various aspects of GPS policy in separate channels, the close interaction of decisions made in one venue with other interests argues for an integrated policy approach.

The need for an integrated GPS policy may also be debated, but the views of the various stakeholders, both U.S. and international, argue that current policy is ill-defined for current realities and that it is desirable to have a stated policy in order to make plans for the future—military, civil, or commercial. A diversity of approaches may be desirable in technology, but not in public policy. The first task in defining a national GPS policy is the definition of national interests and how they might be effectively balanced and advanced. The next task is to define the scope of policy, such as whether it should address GPS augmentations or just the GPS system itself, and to what extent it should treat potential competitors and alternatives to GPS.

The key policy decisions regarding GPS can be organized into three categories: U.S. government decisions, foreign government decisions, and international decisions. U.S. policy decisions include decisions on the funding and management of GPS, when to use selective availability, what level of commitment to make in the Federal Radionavigation Plan, and what services to offer concerning U.S. augmentations such as WAAS and the U.S. Coast Guard beacon system. The most important foreign government decisions are whether to officially accept GPS for certain uses, such as for navigation aids and military forces. Foreign consumers are already making their own decisions on the use of GPS for private purposes.

Finally, there are policy decisions that are not the province of any one government. International discussions are needed for issues such as liability, standards, and preventing the misuse of GPS and its augmentations. In particular, regional and international cooperation is likely to be needed to minimize the risks of GPS systems deployed for civil and commercial benefits. The United States has been concerned for decades about precision strikes on its homeland. GPS is creating the potential for similar risks (with or without weapons of mass destruction) for many other countries. As the United States works to enhance regional stability, it will need to coordinate with other countries in creating mechanisms to mitigate the potential risks of GPS.

Decisionmakers are being challenged not only by the dual-use nature of GPS, but by the fact that whenever a useful technology comes on the market, people find multiple unexpected applications for it. It is impossible to know in advance what these applications will be or how they will affect the technology's original intended use. In the case of GPS, the DoD was the prime mover behind the system and continues to give first priority to national security considerations, but commercial and civil applications appear to be growing so fast they eclipse military applications in importance. The unexpected spread of GPS creates tension among U.S. government agencies, industry, and foreign governments.

The following chapters discuss national security, commercial, and institutional issues created by GPS in greater detail. Neither the spread of technology nor the creation of new applications is over yet. Now that GPS has created (or uncovered) a need for precise time and position information, users may be expected to find other systems or other technologies to provide them with this information if the current GPS becomes unreliable or unavailable.

Chapter Three

NATIONAL SECURITY ASSESSMENT

Although GPS can support U.S. and allied military activities, it can at the same time create a dependency. Furthermore, enemy uses of GPS can threaten U.S. forces and broader security interests. This dual aspect of GPS—its utility in American and allied hands, along with the risks of dependency and enemy use—highlights a fundamental dilemma for decisionmakers seeking to maximize the benefits of GPS technology while minimizing its risks. To help policymakers deal with this dilemma, this chapter sets forth the benefits and risks associated with military uses of GPS.

The first section considers U.S. military use of GPS. Because U.S. forces rely on GPS, we pay particular attention to potential vulnerabilities and threats that could prevent U.S. forces from taking full advantage of the system. The second section evaluates the threats arising from hostile use of GPS against U.S. assets or those of its allies. Rather than placing equal emphasis on all potential uses of GPS by hostile forces, this study considers those situations that appear to be the most threatening to U.S. forces. For example, the use of GPS by enemy navies appears much less serious than the enemy use of GPS on cruise missiles. It is our assertion that by examining the threats that appear the most significant, we can make a reasonable assessment of the overall risks associated with hostile use of GPS.

The third section of this chapter analyzes how GPS augmentation systems could be exploited by hostile forces. Third-party local- and wide-area differential GPS (DGPS)[1] systems can be used by one nation to attack another. The fourth section examines the effectiveness of two signal modifications implemented by the U.S. government: selective availability (SA) and anti-spoofing (AS). The

---

[1] DGPS enhances the accuracy of the basic GPS signal through the use of differential corrections to the basic GPS timing signals. DGPS is based on comparing positioning measurements with known locations at one or more ground reference stations. These differential corrections are then transmitted to the users so that they can make corrections to their GPS receivers. Differential corrections can improve the 100-meter SPS accuracy to about 5–10 meters, or even less, for many GPS applications.

former is designed to decrease the accuracy of signals available to civilian users. The latter was implemented to prevent civilian access to the authorized users' signals. The final section of this chapter summarizes our findings and discusses how they fit into the overall scope of this report.

U.S. MILITARY USE OF GPS

GPS is becoming an integral component of U.S. military forces. It can provide navigation for all types of land vehicles, ships, missiles, munitions, aircraft, and troops. It can be used to supply accurate targeting information and as a common position grid for joint operations. GPS can also improve battle management and command-control-communication-computer-intelligence (C4I) operations. GPS receivers are passive; they provide information to U.S. forces without revealing the location of those forces. GPS can also be easily integrated with other technologies such as inertial navigation systems and telecommunications.

Given the above, it comes as no surprise that GPS equipment is found in almost every type of vehicle fielded by the DoD. In fact, Congress has declared that after the year 2000, any aircraft, ship, armored vehicle or indirect-fire weapon that is not equipped with a GPS receiver will not be funded.[2] The Joint Chiefs of Staff have identified more than 80 missions that can be improved through use of GPS.[3] These missions encompass air, land, sea, and space environments.

It is evident that the U.S. military is moving towards high reliance on GPS, and force structure decisions are being made assuming GPS availability. These developments carry obvious benefits, but there are costs as well. In particular, the more dependent U.S. forces are on GPS, the more vulnerable they are to disruptions of access to GPS. Threats to U.S. military use of GPS can be divided into two classes: internal threats and external threats. The former are generally within the control of the U.S. government while the latter are essentially exogenous.

Internal Threats

There are three basic internal threats to successful U.S. and allied military use of GPS: mismanagement of the system, inadequate funding for operation and maintenance, and excessive reliance upon civilian GPS equipment. Although

---

[2]U.S. Congress, *National Defense Authorization Act for Fiscal Year 1994*, P.L. 103-160, Division A, Subtitle D, Section 152(b). See also Senate Armed Services Committee Report 103-112.

[3]*CJCS Master Navigation Plan*, CJCSI 6130.01, May 20, 1994. GPS is also useful for peacekeeping and peacemaking operations. For example, GPS was used to accurately air-drop food and supplies to safe havens in Bosnia.

all three problems are potentially troublesome, they can be avoided through foresight and careful planning.

Stewardship of GPS through routine maintenance, technical upgrades, and the training and retention of skilled personnel is the most immediate requirement for continued use of GPS. For example, the GPS master control station at Falcon Air Force Base is using extremely old equipment and outdated software whose maintenance is increasingly difficult. Depending on the length and severity of the problem, a systems failure at this site could seriously affect the quality of GPS information.

Inadequate funding of the GPS space and control segment and inadequate acquisition of military receivers are other obvious threats. For example, budget reductions and competition with other programs could limit the number of replacement satellites that the Air Force will be able to purchase in the next two decades and force longer reliance on aging systems. Reliance upon civilian GPS receivers is another concern. While it is difficult to get an exact estimate on the number of civilian receivers (often termed "standard lightweight GPS receivers" or SLGRs) in use by U.S. forces, there are indications that the figure is in the tens of thousands.[4] There are two drawbacks associated with U.S. military use of civilian GPS receivers. First, the accuracy of the position and velocity information provided by SLGRs will be degraded by SA. This leaves the U.S. government with two choices: it can leave SA on and allow some of its forces to operate with degraded information, or it can turn SA off and allow opposing forces to have the same accuracies as U.S. forces.[5] More important, U.S. forces relying on the C/A-code will be much more vulnerable to jamming than those using the P-code.

External Threats

External threats to GPS originate outside the direct control of the U.S. government. These threats may be directed at either the system segments or the GPS signal itself. There are unintentional and intentional threats. The former include phenomena such as natural disasters and malfunctions. The latter include military attacks and terrorist actions. The GPS master control station at Falcon Air Force Base is well protected, and the high altitude of GPS satellites makes them hard to attack with anti-satellite weapons.[6] Consequently, unin-

---

[4]Interview with Colonel Michael Wiedemer, GPS Joint Program Office, August 25, 1994, and Charles Trimble, Trimble Navigation, February 15, 1995.

[5]SA was turned off in 1990–1991 during Operations Desert Shield and Desert Storm and in 1994 during Operation Uphold Democracy in Haiti.

[6]For a discussion of Third World threats to U.S. satellites, see Allen Thomson, "Satellite Vulnerability: A Post-Cold War Issue?" *Space Policy*, Vol. 11, No. 1, pp. 19–30.

tentional threats are probably a larger concern for the GPS control and space segments.

If an accident did occur, what might its effect be on the overall GPS performance? The most serious disruptions would occur if the control segment became inoperable. The timing accuracy of the GPS satellites would begin to drift and the positioning accuracy would degrade with time. Current specifications call for the GPS Block IIA satellites to maintain an accuracy of 16 meters spherical error probability (SEP) for 14 days after the last update. The Block IIR satellites will improve on this as a result of autonomous navigation capabilities from multiple satellite cross-ranging. These satellites should provide accuracies of 16 meters (SEP) for 180 days after the last update.

The cessation of service from specific satellite vehicles (SVs) can affect both the area covered by GPS and the accuracy available to users. Although other satellites would continue to broadcast, they might not be positioned well for a particular GPS user, who would experience a geometric dilution of precision (GDOP) (see Appendix A for further discussion). However, because the system was designed to operate with only 21 satellites in orbit (there are currently 24 functioning satellites), up to three satellites could malfunction before serious degradations took place.

The most significant threat to U.S. military GPS use is signal denial. GPS transmissions can be easily jammed by both intentional and unintentional sources. The power of GPS signals when they reach the earth is approximately 10^{-16} Watts. Because the GPS signal strength is so low, small jammers can cause a GPS receiver to lose lock at long ranges. For example, tests indicate that a one-Watt jammer can incapacitate a commercial GPS receiver (causing it to lose both code and carrier tracking) at a distance of 22 km.[7]

There are two approaches an adversary can take in an effort to jam U.S. forces using GPS—smart jamming and noise jamming. Smart jamming is often called spoofing. Signals are transmitted that attempt to duplicate the characteristics of the GPS signals being received by users. The goal is for a receiver to track the false GPS signals rather than the real ones. The weapon or user can then be led off-course or crashed into the ground. Spoofing can be accomplished by low-power devices, and may be somewhat effective in preventing C/A-code acquisition, but it will not work well once the GPS codes are being tracked. The P(Y)-code, in particular, will be nearly impossible to spoof because of its one-week code length and encryption.

---

[7] "Jamming Danger Raises Doubts About GPS," *Aviation Week & Space Technology*, October 19, 1992, p. 61.

Noise jammers are a more pervasive threat to GPS signals than spoofing. This approach attempts to overwhelm a GPS receiver (by brute force) with radio noise. Adversaries are likely to pursue one of two options—narrowband or wideband jamming. Narrowband methods include carrier wave (CW) jamming (also known as "tone" jamming), swept CW jamming, and pulsed jamming. These methods have the advantage of concentrating a great deal of power into a narrow spectrum. Narrowband jamming is not, however, an effective strategy for jamming military GPS receivers because they can filter such signals without much degradation in performance.

A better method for jamming U.S. forces is to spread the jammer noise across the entire bandwidth of the P-code (which is 20 MHz, versus 2 MHz for the C/A-code). This strategy is difficult to counter because the jammer signal cannot be filtered before processing. The only effective techniques for countering wide-band jammers are those that minimize the amount of jammer energy that enters the antenna. Two such techniques are narrow beam steering and adaptive nulling (which is usually accomplished with a controlled radiation pattern antenna or CRPA). Both of these anti-jam techniques are difficult to implement and expensive, and the latter method only works against a limited number of jammers.[8]

Jammer power can easily range anywhere from 1 to 10,000 Watts. A small jammer could be battery powered and weigh in the neighborhood of 1–2 lb. A medium-sized jammer in the 100–1000 Watt range could be man-portable. However, large jammers transmitting 1,000 to 10,000 Watts would have to be transported by truck or helicopter. While large jammers appear to provide the largest threats to U.S. forces, they are also the easiest to detect and destroy. On the other hand, large numbers of low-power jammers would be difficult both to locate and counter. For this reason, the proliferation of small wideband jammers is the greatest concern of the U.S. military.

Finally, it is important to note that jammers can be deployed on airborne platforms. Airborne jammers are more effective than ground-based jammers for two reasons. First, their altitude allows them to jam a much larger area than ground-based jammers, especially against low-altitude targets. Second, an airborne jammer's signal will approach a receiver from the same direction as some GPS satellites; thus, it will be much harder to block out such signals using physical obstacles. However, placing an airborne jammer at the right time and location to jam U.S. forces is not easy to do. In addition, such airborne targets

---

[8]A good description of these techniques is provided in N. B. Hemesath, "Performance Enhancements of GPS User Equipment," *Global Positioning System*, Vol. I. Institute of Navigation, Washington, D.C., 1980, pp. 106–107.

would be extremely vulnerable to both electromagnetic countermeasures and direct attack from U.S. forces.

Options for Improving Signal Access

Options for improving GPS signal access include modifications to both the space and user segments. Space segment improvements include increases in the transmission power and/or signal spread spectrum bandwidth. Both of these improvements are technically feasible, but they would be costly and would need to be incorporated in future satellite designs. Thus, they could not be implemented for several years. In addition, the latter option would require modifications in current GPS receivers. The highest-payoff area for improved signal access is likely to be in the user segment—in the GPS receivers themselves and antenna designs.

GPS receivers use spread-spectrum processing to detect, track, and demodulate extremely weak signals transmitted from the satellites. Proper operation requires a minimum threshold ratio between the GPS signals and the combined sum of receiver thermal and jamming noise. Typical values for current GPS receivers are shown in Table 3.1 as a function of tracking state. The jamming-to-signal (J/S) limits are shown for a moving GPS user with an inertial navigation system (INS) or for an unaided stationary receiver. The incremental J/S contribution from INS-aiding is about 10–15 dB. The J/S ratios shown assume an antenna gain of 1 (0 dB). As shown, loss of both carrier and code tracking, defined as State 3, occurs for current receivers at a J/S ratio of about 54 dB. GPS anti-jam enhancements possible for advanced military receivers are shown Table 3.2.

In Table 3.2 note that a GPS receiver is most vulnerable to jamming when it is trying to acquire the C/A-code. A potential solution to this problem is for U.S. forces to be equipped with receivers that can acquire the P-code directly.

Table 3.1

Current GPS Receiver Performance

Tracking State	Description	J/S Threshold (dB)	
		SPS	PPS
1	Normal start, C/A-code acquisition	25	25
2	Hot start, direct P-code acquisition	—	34
5	Maintain code and carrier track	33	43
3	Maintain code track	44	54

NOTE: Assumes IMU aiding (ΔJ/S = 10–15 dB).

Table 3.2

Advanced GPS Receiver Anti-Jam Enhancements

GPS Receiver Anti-Jam Enhancements	J/S (dB)
Advanced receiver designs: multiple correlators, increased dwell time	9
Data stripping (aiding or wiping)	6
Practical limit of advanced receiver	54+15 = 69

Unfortunately, direct P-code acquisition is difficult because of the length of the code (6×10^{12} bits versus 1023 bits for the C/A-code). This is an important and challenging technical problem and work is in progress to address this source of U.S. vulnerability.

Other goals of advanced GPS receivers are to decrease their size, weight, and power, to provide higher anti-jam margins against jammers, and to minimize the time-to-first-fix. With INS aiding, the J/S performance for advanced military receivers operating in State 3 (maintain code tracking) has been increased from about 54 to about 64 dB against wideband noise jammers by using multiple correlators and increasing the signal dwell time. The multiple correlators are used so that the signal does not drift outside the observation window. The longer dwell time allows for narrowing the loop bandwidths, which results in a J/S improvement of about 6 dB. An additional 3 dB of processing gain is obtained for wideband jamming as compared with narrowband jamming.[9] The typical GPS receiver performance of 54 dB J/S is normally referenced to a narrowband jamming signal.[10]

An additional anti-jam margin of about 6 dB J/S can be obtained by data stripping, also referred to as data aiding or data wiping. Data stripping requires knowledge of the current navigation message so that the message can be removed from the GPS signal. This results in narrowing the tracking bandwidth, which in turn provides higher J/S margins. Prior to the mission, the navigation message would need to be loaded into the receiver. Collecting the navigation message data and accounting for unexpected changes in the data for many weapons is not expected to be operationally simple.

Additional anti-jam enhancements can be obtained by changing the differential gain pattern of the GPS antenna (spatial filtering). The use of a narrow beam antenna that focuses on the GPS satellites would provide 10 to 20 dB of addi-

---

[9]Based on conversation with Jack Murphy, Rockwell International, Collins Avionics and Communications Division, Cedar Rapids, IA, November 8, 1994.

[10]Interview with Tyler Trickey, Rockwell International, Collins Avionics and Communications Division, Cedar Rapids, IA, November 9, 1994.

tional jamming resistance. Adaptive null steering places a null in the direction of a jammer. These antennas are extremely effective—they can provide 30 to 40 dB of jamming resistance—but they only work against a limited number of jammers. The current CRPAs under development by the DoD can null either six or three jammers, depending on the model.

The jamming ranges for various GPS receiver states with INS-aiding are shown in Figure 3.1. Without additional anti-jam enhancements, a 1-Watt jammer can cause loss of code track for a P-code receiver at about 4.3 km. The jammer can also prevent direct P-code acquisition out to a range of 45 km. An advanced GPS receiver with –10 to –20 dB antenna gain can maintain code track to about 4 km from a 1-kW jammer source.

It is clear that the use of GPS for military applications is extremely vulnerable to jamming without a design that includes additional anti-jam enhancements and an adequate INS to ensure graceful degradation after loss of GPS. Anti-jam GPS enhancements would include an advanced receiver and an antenna with a shaped pattern.

As stated earlier, military GPS receivers expected to operate in a "challenged" environment need to provide enough anti-jam enhancements such that the adversary is forced to employ a jammer that can be effectively attacked if necessary.

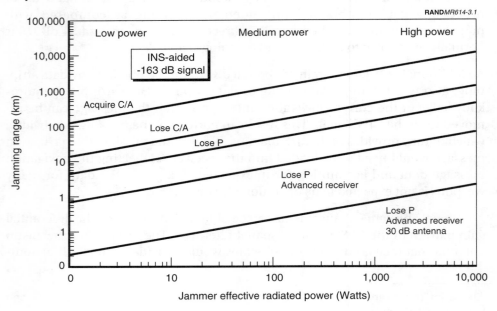

Figure 3.1—Jamming Range Versus Jamming Power

The growth of the vehicle navigation error after loss of the GPS signal is shown in Figure 3.2 for various levels of INS quality.[11] The quality of the inertial navigation system is expressed in terms of an equivalent gyro drift rate that results in position errors arising from uncertainties in the gyroscopes, accelerometers, and platform/sensor misalignments.

After loss of the GPS signal, the short-term navigation error growth during the first 1 to 2 minutes results primarily from random gyro drift terms, assuming a conventional transfer alignment of the INS. The parameter used to specify INS quality is equivalent gyro drift rate, which accounts for gyro, accelerometer, and alignment errors. The navigation CEP from both targeting and guidance errors is arbitrarily assumed to be 10 meters prior to loss of GPS carrier and code tracking. The quality and representative costs of these hypothetical inertial platforms, assuming large-quantity purchases in the year 2000, are shown in Table 3.3.[12] For comparison purposes, a 0.01 degree/hr quality INS in a high-performance aircraft costs in the range of $100,000 to $200,000.

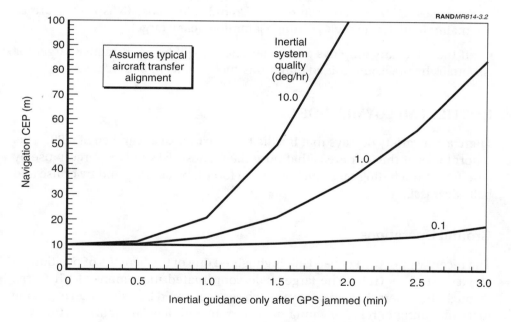

Figure 3.2—CEP Degradation After GPS Loss-of-Lock

---

[11]This curve is based on work by Sean Gilmore and William Delaney of Lincoln Laboratory, Lexington, Massachusetts.

[12]Ibid.

Table 3.3

Missile INS Quality

Equivalent gyro drift rate (deg/hr)	Type of INS	Estimated cost ($K)
0.1	Interferometic fiber optic gyro	20–50
1	Advanced micromechanical	2–5
10	Near-term micromechanical	1

The findings of this analysis can be summarized as follows:

- A major jammer threat arises from the proliferation of low-power, wide-band jammers. It is therefore important for U.S. forces to acquire P-code before entering a jamming environment. In addition, an aided military receiver can be designed to achieve a jamming resistance of about 70 dB. Antennas can provide an additional anti-jam margin of from 10 to 30 dB. In all cases, GPS-guided weapons will require low-cost INSs if they are to maintain high accuracies through jamming near a target.

- If the adversary employs a large jammer, it will be an attractive target for attack by precision-guided munitions such as anti-radiation missiles.

HOSTILE EMPLOYMENT OF GPS

There are a variety of ways that hostile forces can take advantage of GPS. This report looks at the four areas that pose the highest risks to U.S. forces: use by land forces (including targeting), by naval forces, by aircraft, and by cruise and ballistic missiles.

Ground Operations

The recent war in the Persian Gulf highlighted one of the benefits of positioning services such as GPS. The large-scale coordinated movement of VII Corps through the desert showed one way such services could be used by an attacking force operating in relatively unfamiliar terrain with few landmarks. However, that movement, while facilitated by GPS receivers, would not have been possible had U.S. forces not been well trained for complex maneuver warfare, with apparatus available to support forces movement. Warfare, especially ground warfare, is facilitated by technology such as GPS, but is dependent on the underlying people and equipment. In assessing GPS in the hands of an adversary, it is important to determine if they have all that is necessary to allow them to capitalize on the system.[13]

There are a few areas where GPS/DGPS might be helpful, at least on a small-unit level:

- Improved capability to conduct shoot-and-scoot operations when operating away from presurveyed regions if the units are trained and equipped for that class of operation.

- Improved helicopter operations, provided accurate digital charts and flight software are available.

- Improved technical intelligence by exploiting timing signals and avoiding the need for more expensive distributed timing devices.

- Improved capability to establish mine fields, or safe corridors through mine fields.

In sum, GPS provides three major benefits for land-based military operations—self-location accuracy, navigation, and target location.[14] Self-location accuracy is crucial because simple projectile-type weapons must be programmed to fly a given distance. The accurate positioning information provided by GPS can increase the lethality of artillery, rocket-launchers, and mobile missiles by reducing their location uncertainties at launch.

In addition to its high accuracy, GPS allows users to determine their location passively; that is, users can find out where they are without transmitting signals that could be detected and targeted by enemy forces. Improved self-location information can also reduce fratricide (i.e., unintentional attacks on one's own forces) if the information is processed effectively, which depends on the command, control, communications and intelligence (C3I) capabilities of a given military.

Accurate navigation information provided by GPS can be crucial in environments where other navigation methods falter. For example, GPS was an invaluable asset to U.S. forces during the Gulf War in part because they were operating in a featureless terrain. Good-quality navigation information can also increase the movement rate of ground troops and improve movement coordination and attacks. However, many developing nations may not have the

---

[13]Allan R. Millett, Williamson Murray, and Kenneth H. Watman, "The Effectiveness of Military Organizations," *International Security*, Vol. 11, No. 1, Summer 1986, pp. 37–71.

[14]This section is partly based on material found in Irving Lachow, "The GPS Dilemma: Balancing Military Risks and Economic Benefits," *International Security*, Vol. 20, No. 1, Summer 1995, pp. 126–148.

necessary prerequisites—including equipment and training—to take full advantage of the information provided by GPS.[15]

The third benefit that land forces can gain through the use of GPS is accurate target location. The drawback of this application is that a GPS receiver must be located at or near a target to determine its coordinates.[16] Forward observers could use GPS to more accurately locate U.S. units on the move. Furthermore, GPS position information could be combined with high-resolution remote sensing data to accurately locate fixed targets. In addition, fixed facilities such as docks, airfields, and warehouses could be pretargeted with GPS receivers before a conflict began.

Naval Operations

For naval forces, the story is a little different. Naval forces are usually moving to patrol an area or seek/avoid an enemy force. However, GPS/DGPS can help specific classes of operations:

- Mine warfare, since GPS/DGPS provides a fixed reference point for mines being laid, mine sweeping, and corridors through mine fields.

- Locating ships by providing better location information from surveillance platforms and assisting in signal intelligence that can locate emitters at sea.

- Providing location information for anti-ship missiles in flight to decrease guidance drift after launch.

As with the earlier discussion of ground forces, one of the prerequisites for an improved capability is having a force capable of exploiting it. The effective use of GPS usually assumes other related capabilities and the ability to bear additional costs. For example, anti-ship missiles might employ GPS-aided guidance schemes to decrease the cost of the onboard IMU, and the initial fix may be better, but this could increase the cost of onboard radar or other sensors employed to search the area where the target ship might be located.

Operating navies is an expensive and difficult proposition, and few nations operate significant blue-water (deep ocean) forces. However, the major concern then is that GPS/DGPS might be useful to forces operating near their homeland, and could enhance the threat from green water (coastal) forces. Position information can certainly help such forces, but it would not appear to alter the

---

[15]Brigadier General Robert H. Scales, Jr., Director, Desert Storm Study Project, *Certain Victory: United States Army in The Gulf War,* United States Army, Washington, D.C.: 1993, pp. 117–118.

[16]A technique called relative targeting allows one to determine the position of a target relative to a landmark with a known location.

primary threats to the U.S. Navy, which will likely remain anti-ship missiles, submarines armed with torpedoes, and naval mines.

The problem for the United States is not just GPS/DGPS, but the proliferation of advanced conventional weapons.[17] The contribution of GPS/DGPS to potential threats is to somewhat decrease the entry cost for parties wishing to begin a process of denying easy access to nearby waters. The additional cost for a GPS/DGPS-aided capability might be a few tens of thousands of dollars, which—unless the price of the total system is driven down dramatically—will make only a small difference in terms of the quantitative and qualitative threat faced.[18]

Air Operations

Foreign air forces can benefit from the use of GPS in three areas: aircraft navigation, air-to-air missions, and air-to-surface missions. One of the fundamental factors hindering the capability of many foreign air forces is the limited skills of their air crews. Reliable and inexpensive navigation systems like GPS can assist air crews in navigating to and from target areas. The ability to find their airbases at night or in bad weather will greatly increase the range of conditions under which these air forces might operate.

In air-to-air operations, the ability to accurately locate friendly, enemy, and unknown aircraft is extremely important. A radar site might be able to detect and track aircraft, but there are significant errors associated with such measurements. By using GPS in conjunction with data links and radar data, ground controllers can more effectively control an air battle. Furthermore, when air-to-air operations occur within close proximity of friendly surface-to-air (SAM) missiles, a nation's aircraft must avoid flying into keep-out areas. The precision-location information provided by GPS allows aircraft to operate with smaller safety margins, thus potentially increasing the number of SAM engagements against opposing aircraft. On the whole, however, the contribution of GPS will likely be minor except for the most-capable air forces. The training and command-control-communications capabilities needed for effective counter-air operations, with or without GPS, are considerable.

In air-to-ground operations, GPS can help aircraft navigate to and from a target, coordinate air operations, and increase the accuracy of air-delivered ordnance. Of these applications, the most important is probably the latter. By minimizing

---

[17]For a description of the anti-ship missile threat, see Steven Zaloga, "Harpoonski," *Naval Institute Proceedings*, February 1994, pp. 37–40.

[18]A more serious threat is probably the proliferation of stealth technology that can decrease the utility of anti-ship defense systems.

their self-location errors, aircraft can determine their bomb drop points more accurately, which increases the likelihood that their bombs will hit designated targets.[19] If GPS information is combined with sophisticated radars and targeting algorithms on a weapon that can compensate for ballistic errors and wind effects, bomb accuracy can begin to approach that of precision-guided weapons (10 meters or less). While such technologies are currently out of reach for most Third World nations, their basic building blocks will be in the hands of several countries fairly soon. It is also possible that such systems will become available on the international arms market along with other advanced conventional weapons.

GPS-Guided Ballistic Missiles

The proliferation of Third World ballistic missiles is a major U.S. concern.[20] These missiles can carry weapons of mass destruction, reach targets quickly, and are difficult to intercept. The ballistic missile activity of selected developing nations is shown in Table 3.4.

Most of the guided ballistic missiles possessed by developing nations today are based on the Scud B, a missile developed by the former Soviet Union more than 40 years ago and, in turn, based on the German V-2 rocket design of World War II. This missile has a nominal range of about 300 km and can deliver a 1000-kg payload with an accuracy of approximately 500 to 1000 meters. The Scud B has a single-stage, liquid-fueled rocket and a single warhead that does not separate from the booster. The Scud B is a low-tech, inaccurate missile with limited military utility. However, it has been suggested that the accuracy of Scud missiles could be improved by an order of magnitude through the use of GPS guidance.[21]

We examined two of the most common guided ballistic missiles in the world— the Scud B and the No Dong 1. The No Dong 1 is a medium-range North Korean missile. It is based on a Scud design, but the No Dong 1 has four strap-on engines and the warhead separates from the booster after thrust cutoff. This design change allows the missile to have a longer range than the Scud B

---

[19]Miniature GPS receivers can also be placed aboard bombs to create "smart munitions" that can guide themselves to a target. This is a technically demanding task that is unlikely to be successfully accomplished by developing nations. See Gerald Frost and Bernard Schweitzer, "Operational Issues for GPS-Aided Precision Missiles," paper presented at the 1993 National Technical Meeting of the Institute of Navigation, Washington, D.C., January 1993.

[20]This section is based on Gerald Frost and Irving Lachow, "GPS-Aided Guidance for Ballistic Missile Applications: An Assessment," paper presented at the 51st Annual Meeting of the Institute of Navigation, Colorado Springs, CO, June 5–7, 1995.

[21]Raffi Gregorian, "Global Positioning Systems: A Military Revolution for the Third World?" *SAIS Review, A Journal of International Affairs,* Vol. 13, No. 1, Winter–Spring 1993, pp. 133–148.

Table 3.4
Ballistic Missile Capability of Selected Developing Countries

Nation	Range Category (km)			Supplier
	300–500	500–1000	1000+	
China	M-11	M-9	CSS-2	Indigenous
Egypt	Scud B			USSR
	Scud B	Scud C		North Korea franchise
		Vector		Indigenous (Condor)
India			Agni	Indigenous
Iran	Scud B			USSR
	Scud B	Scud C		North Korea franchise
Iraq	Scud B			USSR
	Scud B	Scud C		North Korea franchise
		Al Hussein		Indigenous (Scud)
			Al Aabed	Indigenous (Condor)
Israel	Jericho 1		Jericho 2	Indigenous
Libya	Scud B			USSR
		Scud C		North Korea
		M-9		China
			Al Fatah	Indigenous
North Korea	Scud B	Scud C	No Dong 1	Indigenous
Pakistan	M-11			China
	Hatf 2			Indigenous
Saudi Arabia			CSS-2	China

without sacrificing payload. However, the No Dong 1 has poor accuracy at the longer range.   The estimated characteristics of the two missiles are given in Table 3.5.

The boost guidance concept assumed for Scud-type short-range ballistic missiles (SRBMs) is a simplified velocity-to-be-gained guidance law. Prior to launch, a ground-based computer calculates the sensed burnout velocity state that must be attained for a missile to hit a given target. An accelerometer mounted in the direction of the missile's longitudinal axis measures the vehicle's sensed velocity. When the difference between the calculated velocity and the actual velocity approaches zero, booster thrust is terminated. For liquid propellant engines, thrust is terminated by closing the valves to the fuel and oxidizer tanks. An open-loop, body-mounted inertial system as described above is assumed to be representative of that used by Scud-type missiles. A more complex boost guidance system can improve accuracy. Such a system

Table 3.5

Characteristics of the Scud B and No Dong 1

Parameter	Scud B	No Dong 1
Length (m)	11.3	15.5
Diameter (m)	0.9	1.3
Range (km)	300	1000
Payload (kg)	1000	1000
System CEP (m)	500–1000	1500–3000
Total mass (kg)	5400	19000
Propellant mass (kg)	4000	16000
Burn time (sec)	70	70
Thrust (kN)	130	540
Reentry ballistic coefficient (N/m^2)	190,000	36,000–48,000

NOTE: Data taken from David Wright and Timur Kadshev, "An Analysis of the North Korean No Dong Missile," *Science & Global Security*, 1994, Volume 4, pp. 1–32, and U.S. Congress, Office of Technology Assessment, *Technologies Underlying Weapons of Mass Destruction*, OTA-BP-ISC-115, (Washington, DC: U.S. GPO, December 1993), pp. 208–209.

could include a full axis gimbaled or strapdown inertial reference system, digital computer, and a separating warhead with a vernier control system for providing fine velocity adjustments during payload deployment. An advanced missile would also be designed to minimize the other major factors contributing to the weapon system CEP, such as reentry errors.

Tables 3.6 and Table 3.7 show the estimated accuracy for the Scud and No Dong 1 based on use of a velocity-to-be-gained guidance law.[22] As one can see, in both cases velocity cutoff errors make significant contributions to missile CEP. These errors arise from two primary sources—the longitudinal accelerometer and the thrust termination control system. The former depends on the quality of a missile's accelerometers. The latter results primarily from errors in the booster cutoff control system, which include contributions from thrust impulse after cutoff and timing errors in the cutoff signal to the engine valves. Thrust impulse variations differ for each specific booster and with environmental conditions such as pressure and temperature.

Ballistic missiles use inertial sensors to navigate to the desired burnout state. When a missile reaches the desired position and velocity state, thrust is terminated and the weapon hits the designated target. GPS receivers can provide accurate position and velocity measurements, which may improve the CEP of

---

[22]The calculated accuracies for both the Scud and the No Dong 1 fall within the range of published values.

Table 3.6

Baseline Scud Accuracy

Error Sources	1-σ Downrange (m)	1-σ Crossrange (m)
Initial conditions		
Position, alignment	100	300
Boost phase		
Accelerometers	100	200
Gyros	100	200
Alignment	100	200
Cutoff control	400	100
Reentry		
Winds, density, aerodynamics	440	360
Target location	100	100
Root-sum-square	640	600
Weapon system CEP	730	

NOTE: Error estimates are for a Scud B missile fired to a range of 300 km. Error components for the baseline Scud are based on reasonable technical assumptions for a system that has an overall weapon system CEP of about 0.5 to 1.0 km.

Table 3.7

Baseline No Dong 1 Accuracy

Error Sources	1-σ Downrange (m)	1-σ Crossrange (m)
Initial conditions		
Position, alignment	100	900
Boost phase		
Accelerometers	300	300
Gyros	200	700
Alignment	200	700
Cutoff control	800	200
Reentry		
Winds, density, aerodynamics	900	1100
Target location	100	100
Root-sum-square	1300	1800
Weapon system CEP	1850	

NOTE: Error estimates are for a No Dong 1 missile fired to a range of 1000 km. The assumptions used for the Scud calculations also apply to the No Dong 1 case.

ballistic missiles. In addition, the use of GPS can allow for simplified initialization and alignment methods. Table 3.8 describes the position and velocity accuracies for GPS in various operating modes.

Table 3.9 describes the three scenarios examined in this chapter. We note that the improvements described in Cases B and C are technically challenging and may be beyond the reach of many developing nations for some time.

Table 3.8

GPS Position and Velocity Accuracy

GPS Signal	Position (m)		Velocity (m/s)
	2 drms	1 σ	1 σ
SPS	100	36	0.3
C/A without SA	20–30	7–11	0.1
PPS	21	8	0.1
DGPS	5	2	0.01

NOTE: Velocity estimates are approximate. The quality of a user's velocity measurements will depend on a variety of factors such as the type of receiver, the kinematics of the user vehicle, the geometry and distance between the user and a differential station, and so forth.

Table 3.9

GPS-Aided Ballistic Missile Cases

Case	Description
A	Baseline missile with a simplified guidance and control system, and GPS aiding.
B	The same as Case A except vernier controls are added in the boost thrust direction.
C	The same as Case B except that reentry and targeting errors are reduced by 50 percent.

NOTE: All cases assume that GPS is used to correct all of the errors that accumulate during the boost phase. This is a generous assumption, but it allows us to consider worst-case scenarios.

Figure 3.3 shows the overall weapon system accuracy for a Scud-type missile as a function of GPS velocity measurement errors for the cases described in Table 3.9.

Case A: GPS velocity measurements improve the overall CEP of a Scud by about 20 percent through reductions in the initial-condition and boost-phase errors. However, a missile using DGPS shows little improvement over one using the Standard Positioning Service (SPS) because contributions from other error sources such as cutoff control and reentry effects dominate the weapon system CEP.

Case B: As expected, the CEP in Case B is smaller than that in Case A because of a reduction in the cutoff control errors by the vernier engines. The overall weapon system accuracy is still relatively insensitive to changes in the quality of the GPS velocity measurement errors because the largest remaining errors arise from reentry dispersions.

Case C: The Scud's overall CEP for this case is about 40 percent less than Case A. Again, however, one can see that the missile's accuracy is fairly insensitive to

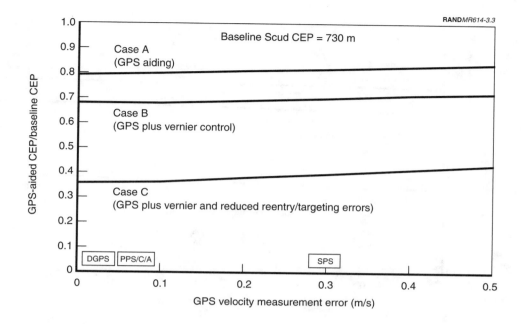

Figure 3.3—Scud Accuracy Versus GPS Velocity Measurement Error

GPS velocity measurement errors. For example, the difference in CEP between missiles using SPS and DGPS is almost insignificant—because reentry errors remain sufficiently large to dominate the weapon system CEP.

In sum, GPS-aiding can improve the accuracy of Scud-type missiles by about 20 percent. Greater gains in accuracy can then be achieved by reducing thrust termination errors and reentry dispersions. Scuds gain little benefit by using DGPS instead of the SPS because GPS velocity measurement errors are insignificant compared with other error sources.

Figure 3.4 illustrates the effect of GPS-aiding for the No Dong 1 missile. The findings here are similar to those for the Scud case. Use of GPS velocity aiding improves the accuracy of a No Dong missile by about 25 percent. However, there is little difference in CEP between No Dongs using the SPS and those using DGPS. This result holds for all three cases. Thus, the velocity degradations resulting from selective availability have almost no effect on the accuracy of GPS-guided short- and medium-range ballistic missiles.

This study has examined the application of GPS for short- and medium-range ballistic missiles, finding that these missiles experience modest gains in accuracy from GPS-aiding. It appears, however, that long-range ballistic missiles can experience significant accuracy improvements with GPS-aided inertial

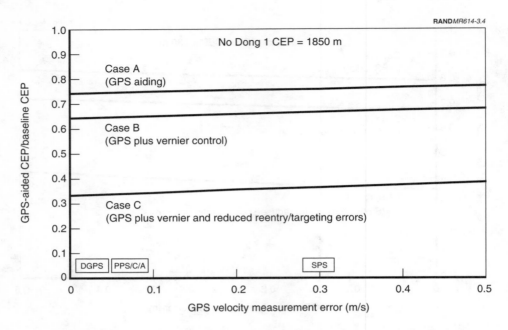

RAND*MR614-3.4*

Figure 3.4.—No Dong 1 Accuracy Versus GPS Velocity Measurement Error

guidance. This is true because velocity errors in the range-sensitive direction at burnout can lead to large downrange impact errors for missiles traveling long distances. For example, a missile with a 10,000-km range using accelerometers meeting the Missile Technology Control Regime (MTCR) control guidelines (130 ppm scale factor), will have a velocity measurement error of about 1 m/s at burnout. This will result in a downrange error of about 1900 meters. A missile using the SPS will have a downrange error due to velocity measurement uncertainties that is a factor of three smaller than the one calculated above, but still not one that could be described as precise.

The other major error that can be significantly reduced through the use of GPS is initial azimuth alignment uncertainty at the launch site. Accurate ICBMs require azimuth alignments to a few arc-seconds because the crossrange error sensitivity for a 10,000-km-range missile is about 30 m/arc-sec. The use of GPS-aiding in the boost phase would allow for low-cost gyrocompassing and rough azimuth alignment because these errors would be reduced to the position and velocity uncertainties associated with GPS. The remaining errors would result from reentry vehicle dispersions that are not corrected by GPS (unless the reentry vehicle can be maneuvered) and target location uncertainties.[23]

Advanced Short-Range Ballistic Missiles

Might the effects of GPS-aiding be significantly greater for a more advanced short-range ballistic missile? Selective availability may have only a minor benefit for the most common ballistic missiles, but would there be significant benefits for more-advanced missiles and thus a proliferation incentive for advanced missiles if SA were turned off or DGPS were widely available? To examine this possibility, the effects of differing levels of GPS service were examined for the case of a notional single-stage ballistic vehicle that can be quickly launched from a mobile transporter-erector-launcher (TEL).

The major performance improvements of this advanced short-range missile compared with Scud- and No Dong-type missiles are the ability to accurately deploy the payload and an attitude control system that aligns a separating payload vehicle to achieve zero angle of attack at reentry. These improvements reduce major contributions to the weapon system's CEP. A missile of this type could deliver a 500-kg payload to a range of 600 km with a CEP of approximately 600 m (0.1 percent of range). This section investigates the possible further reduction in weapon system CEP through application of GPS-aiding of the missile's inertial navigation system.

Accurate thrust termination control will reduce some of the major impact errors that were significant for Scud- and No Dong-type missiles. The transformation of burnout velocity uncertainties into impact miss errors for short-range ballistic missiles is approximated by

$$\Delta R_0 / \Delta V_0 = 2 V_0 / g \sin 2\gamma_0$$

where

$$V_0 = \text{missile burnout velocity (m/s)}$$

$$\gamma_0 = \text{burnout flight path angle (deg)}$$

$$g = \text{acceleration due to gravity (m/s/s).}$$

---

[23]A standard civilian GPS receiver could determine a target's location to about 10 meters by time-averaging the SPS signals. The limiting factor is the ability of a single frequency receiver to model the ionospheric delays experienced by L-band radio waves.

For a minimum energy trajectory (neglecting aerodynamic drag and assuming instantaneous boost velocity), the miss sensitivity is about

$$\Delta R_O / \Delta V_O = 500 \text{ m/m/s}$$

assuming

$$R_O = 600 \text{ km}, V_O = 2400 \text{ m/s, and } \gamma_O = 45 \text{ deg.}$$

The actual miss sensitivity will be less than this partial at the point of payload separation. The downrange impact miss due to an inertial accelerometer with a measurement uncertainty of 130 ppm (which falls within the MTCR export control limits) would then be about 150 meters. This particular error source, plus other position and velocity errors at burnout, could be greatly reduced by GPS-aiding of the missile's inertial navigation system. The GPS receiver provides accurate corrections for missile position and velocity errors that accumulate up to the point of payload deployment. These errors result from uncertainties in missile initialization and booster navigation and control. The magnitude of CEP reduction will depend on the quality of the position and velocity measurements and type of GPS receiver.

The advanced-missile CEP is also improved compared with the Scud and No Dong missiles because of reductions in reentry errors associated with the ballistic coefficient, atmospheric density and winds, and vehicle angle-of-attack effects. Targeting and payload separation uncertainties also contribute to weapon system CEP.

The quality of the velocity measurements obtained by a GPS receiver depends on the type of receiver and the GPS operating mode.

SPS Mode. GPS provides civilian users a 100-m horizontal accuracy (2 drms) with SPS. This level is set by policy and achieved by intentional degradation of the basic signal by selective availability (SA). There is no equivalent standard for velocity accuracy; however, observations show that the rms velocity accuracy of the SPS signal is about 0.3 m/s.[24]

PPS Mode. The rms velocity accuracy for a P-code receiver is specified to be 0.1 m/s for any axis; however, typical receiver performance is better than specifica-

---

[24]J. Clynch, G. Thurmond, L. Rosenfeld, and R. Schramm, "Error Characteristics of GPS Differential Positions and Velocities," *Proceedings of the ION-GPS-92*, Albuquerque, New Mexico, September 16–18, 1992; R. Galigan and J. Gilkey, "Providing Highly Accurate Velocity Data for an Airborne Platform Using Differential GPS Velocity Corrections from a Non-Surveyed Reference Receiver," *Proceedings of ION National Technical Meeting*, San Francisco, CA, January 20–22, 1993.

tions.[25] We assumed a horizontal rms velocity accuracy range of 0.05 to 0.1 m/s per axis, where the vertical component is larger than the horizontal component by a factor of about 2. Similar performance is also expected for a C/A-code receiver operating without SA. The accuracy of GPS velocity measurements also depends on the severity of the vehicle kinematics. Receiver kinematics introduces noise into the phase tracking loop and can cause the oscillator frequency to drift. Therefore, it is best to perform GPS-aiding during free flight after booster burnout. A small velocity-correction package on the payload would be needed.

DGPS. A DGPS operation assumes that a GPS reference station is located near (100–200 km) the missile at payload deployment. The objective of DGPS is to improve missile position and velocity in the presence or absence of SA. Errors in the known location and velocity of a GPS reference station are measured and pseudo-range and pseudo-range rate corrections are sent to the missile, using conventional broadcast standards such as RTCM SC-104.[26]

The major factors that influence the velocity accuracy of DGPS corrections are the quality of the base station and missile receivers, separation distance, effects of geometry (which is given by the Position Dilution of Precision [PDOP] factor), and user kinematics. For the case of a stationary remote GPS user, where the DGPS ground station receiver takes several seconds to form a correction and transmits every few seconds, the rms horizontal velocity error for a PDOP of 1.5 to 2.0 is found from test results to be about 2.5 cm/sec.[27] The velocity estimates are determined by measuring the Doppler shift in the carrier frequency. This quality-of-accuracy measurement results from the short wavelength (19 cm) of the carrier frequency. Estimated carrier phase measurement errors of a few percent taken every second with a PDOP of 2 results in a vehicle velocity accuracy estimate of 1–2 cm/sec, which compares favorably with test results.

However, experiments have shown that the accuracy of the velocity corrections will degrade depending on the level of receiver kinematics. For example, the uncertainty in the missile's velocity could be greater than 0.1 m/s during boost. Therefore, it is important to perform the GPS measurements after completion of the boost phase. For this analysis, DGPS is assumed to provide an rms velocity accuracy in the range of 0.02 to 0.05 m/s if the corrections are made during the free flight phase after booster burnout.

GPS-aiding for an advanced short-range ballistic missile provides significant improvement in weapon system CEP. With SPS, the CEP is reduced from an as-

[25]ARINC Research Corporation, *GPS User's Overview,* YEE-82-009D, March 1991.

[26]Radio Technical Commission for Maritime Services, Special Committee 104, Washington, D.C.

[27]J. Clynch et al., op. cit.

sumed baseline of 600 m to about 215 m. For this case, the uncorrected errors arising from payload separation, reentry vehicle dynamics, and targeting are assumed to be 150 meters (see Figure 3.5).

For C/A-code without SA, the comparable accuracy is about 160 meters. As shown, SA has more of an effect for this system than for a Scud missile; however, SA has only a moderate effect on system performance. Weapon system CEP improvements for GPS velocity measurement accuracy below 0.1 m/s is minor; therefore, the addition of a ground-based DGPS system with associated uplink to the missile is not warranted. Besides the obvious improvements in weapon system CEP, GPS-aiding relaxes the initial positioning and alignment requirements. This allows the use of low-cost inertial instruments for initial azimuth alignment, which provides for a fast missile launch.

The findings of this section can be summarized as follows:

*   GPS-aiding of Third World missiles such as the Scud and No Dong 1 can improve overall missile accuracy by 20–25 percent. Further improvement in missile accuracy cannot be achieved simply by reducing the burnout velocity measurement errors. Vernier engines are needed to minimize cutoff control uncertainties. More important, thrust termination control and reentry dispersion errors need to be minimized. The latter can be

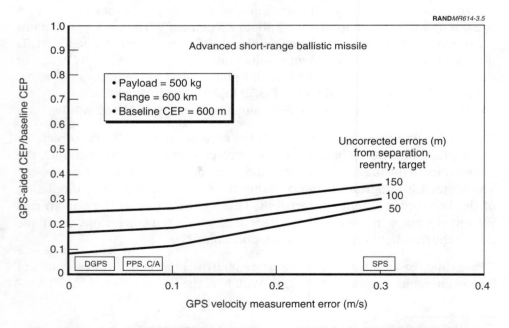

Figure 3.5—Advanced Missile Accuracy Versus GPS Velocity Measurement Error

accomplished by spin-stabilizing the reentry vehicle or designing it to have a high ballistic coefficient. This is a significant technical challenge.

- Selective availability has little effect on the accuracy of short- and medium-range GPS-guided ballistic missiles.

- GPS-aiding of ICBMs can significantly improve their CEP. It allows the use of low-cost inertial instruments for initial azimuth alignment and can minimize the effects of boost-phase inertial instrument errors. These benefits may be achieved with the SPS; DGPS is probably not required.[28] These missile systems require sophisticated post-boost vehicles (PBVs) if they are to accurately deliver their warheads.

GPS-Guided Cruise Missiles

In the last few years, interest in the problem of cruise missile proliferation has grown substantially.[29] One of the main reasons for this interest in cruise missiles, especially land-attack cruise missiles, is the fact that less-developed nations can use GPS to obtain high navigation accuracies. Whereas there is general agreement among analysts that GPS-guided cruise missiles (GCMs) pose a potential threat to U.S. security, there is wide disagreement on the magnitude of that threat. This section summarizes the results of research to assess the risk posed to U.S. forces by GCMs using GPS.

The analyses focus on attacks against U.S. forces in a theater of operations; attacks against the Continental United States (CONUS) are not considered for two reasons. First, the likelihood that the United States will become involved in a military conflict with an adversary both capable of and willing to conduct military attacks against CONUS is small. Second, terrorist attacks against CONUS are an ever-present danger. GCMs may provide terrorists with another weapon, but their overall contribution to the risks already facing U.S. citizens from terrorism is marginal.

To understand how GPS can significantly affect cruise missile guidance, one must understand the inherent limits of inertial navigation systems.[30] Although INS packages are commercially available and are jam-proof, they have one major drawback—the physical forces that affect the gyroscopes and accelerometers used in inertial navigation systems create errors that accumulate over

---

[28]GPS can be of particular benefit to sea-launched ballistic missiles (SLBMs) and mobile ICBMs because it reduces their position uncertainty at launch.

[29]In this report, a cruise missile is defined as an unmanned, self-propelled vehicle that sustains flight through the use of aerodynamic lift over most of its flight path.

[30]An inertial navigation system consists of gyroscopes, accelerometers, and some type of processor.

time. The navigation errors resulting from inertial drift are large enough to undermine the military utility of INSs for all but short-range missions. To illustrate this point, Figure 3.6 shows CEP as a function of inertial drift for three inertial navigation systems and compares these accuracies with the accuracy provided by GPS.[31]

The drift error of the 10 deg/hr INS surpasses the position error of GPS almost
immediately. The drift error for the 1 deg/hr INS surpasses the GPS error in approximately two minutes. For a 0.1 deg/hr INS, the two errors are equal after 10
minutes. In assessing the availability of these systems, note that the 10 deg/hr
INS is an extremely low-quality system; a less-developed country (LDC) will al-

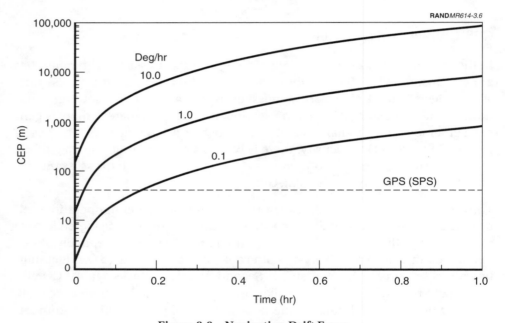

Figure 3.6—Navigation Drift Error

---

[31]Figure 3.6 shows the accuracy available to civilian users when SA is turned on. The graph is based
on an inertial navigation model found in Edward R. Harshberger, *Long-Range Conventional
Missiles: Issues for Near-Term Development*, RAND, N-3328-RGSD, 1991, p. 121. Although the model
expresses its navigation errors in deg/hr rather than nmi/hr, the model does include the errors from
both gyroscopes and accelerometers. An excellent discussion of all the errors that have to be
included in such a model is given in Morris M. Kuritsky and Murray S. Goldstein (eds.), "Inertial
Navigation," *Proceedings of the IEEE*, Vol. 71, No. 10, October 1983, pp. 1156–1176.

most certainly be able to do better. The 1 deg/hr INS is very close to the limit of what an LDC could purchase legally. The 0.1 deg/hr INS is a high-quality system that falls under export restrictions.[32]

Before discussing the lethality of GCMs, we review cruise missile survivability. This is a vital topic for one simple reason—if a cruise missile cannot reach a target, its lethality is irrelevant. A missile attempting to attack U.S. forces will probably have to penetrate several layers of air defenses. An analysis of a missile's ability to do this must consider the physical characteristics of the missiles, the number of missiles employed in an attack, and the deployment strategy.

The survivability of individual cruise missiles depends on two factors: how easy they are to detect and how easy they are to intercept once they are detected. The ability of U.S. forces to detect GCMs depends on the radar cross section, altitude of flight, and velocity of the missiles, as well as the capabilities of U.S. radars. These characteristics are as important in assessing the threat of GCMs as the guidance accuracy and payload. Many GCMs are likely to have small radar cross sections and fly at low altitudes, making them hard to detect because their radar returns will be buried in ground clutter. In addition, slow-flying low-technology cruise missiles could be hard for airborne radars to detect.

If they are detected, individual GCMs will probably be easy to shoot down because they do not react to fighters or SAMs employed against them.[33] However, large numbers of missiles employed in a coordinated attack can stress both defensive fighters and terminal surface-to-air defenses.[34] For example, while penetrating an area defended by fighters, a spreadout group of GCMs could force fighters to expend their fuel pursuing individual missiles, thus decreasing the total number of possible engagements or exhausting the available missile loadout of the fighter force. Similarly, GCMs might overwhelm terminal defenses by saturating a single SAM site—by exploiting the limited line-of-sight that ground-based radars have against low-flying missiles and by attacking in large numbers.

---

[32]High-accuracy gyroscopes, accelerometers, and INSs are export-controlled. For example, U.S. law prohibits the sale without licenses of gyroscopes with drift rates of 0.1 deg/hr (at linear accelerations of less than 10 g) and INSs with navigation errors of 0.8 nmi/hr (CEP). See *Code of Federal Regulations* (C.F.R) Vol. 15, Chapter VII, Part 799, Section 799.1, Item 7A03A, Office of the Federal Register, National Archives and Records Administration, Washington, D.C.,1993.

[33]Some GCMs may pose a challenge for air defenses. For example, slow-flying missiles may be hard for aircraft to intercept, particularly if they are flying at low altitudes. High-flying, supersonic cruise missiles could also be difficult to intercept because they compress time lines to the point where few shot opportunities are available for the defense.

[34]GPS timing and navigation information could be useful in coordinating such attacks. It could also provide increased flexibility for mission planning.

Once cruise missiles penetrate enemy defenses, the central issue becomes how much damage the missile can inflict on a target. To understand this problem, we will examine two cases: cruise missiles carrying high explosives, and cruise missiles carrying weapons of mass destruction (WMD). Through this analysis we will assess the effect that GPS can have on the lethality of cruise missiles. This will give us a better understanding of the implications of enemy use of GPS for cruise missile guidance.

The lethality of conventionally armed GCMs depends on several variables— their horizontal and vertical navigation accuracy, the angle of their terminal dives, their range and payload characteristics, their targeting accuracy, and the size and hardness of a given target.[35] The following graphs show the single-shot probability of kill (SSPK) for GCMs carrying high explosives (HE) as a function of GPS accuracy for several scenarios.[36]   Figure 3.7 illustrates the effects of conventionally armed GCMs against soft point targets such as a wooden building. Figure 3.8 illustrates the effects against a hard target such as a sturdy industrial installation.

It is evident that the lethality of GCMs attacking point targets is highly dependent on the magnitude of targeting errors. Neither soft nor hard point targets face high risks from GCMs with large targeting uncertainties. If targeting errors are small, then the lethality of GCMs depends on their navigation accuracy. Cruise missiles attacking soft point targets will have low SSPKs if they use SPS, and high SSPKs if SA is off and/or if they use DGPS. GCMs attacking hard point targets will require the accuracies associated with DGPS to achieve high SSPKs.

Figures 3.9 and 3.10 show that the lethality of GCMs is higher against area targets than against point targets. The larger the target, the higher the lethality. It is also apparent that the utility of SA diminishes as a target's area increases.

In summary, the lethality of conventionally armed GCMs depends on several factors. A key variable is targeting accuracy. If targeting errors are large, the ability of GCMs to successfully attack point targets drops significantly. In addition, many important point targets are mobile. Third World nations will have an extremely hard time trying to locate such targets. Thus, it is highly

---

[35]Irving Lachow, *The Global Positioning System and Cruise Missile Proliferation: Assessing the Threat*, CSIA Discussion Paper 94-04, Kennedy School of Government, Harvard University, June 1994.

[36]These curves assume the attacking cruise missile performs near-vertical terminal dives. Thus, they represent a worst case from the point of view of U.S. military planners.

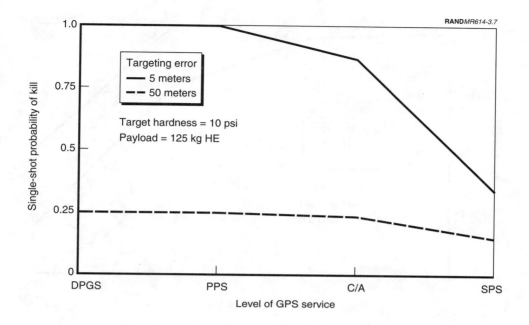

Figure 3.7—GCM Attacks Against Soft Point Targets

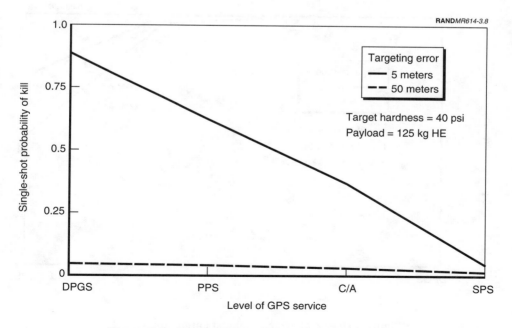

Figure 3.8—GCM Attacks Against Hard Point Targets

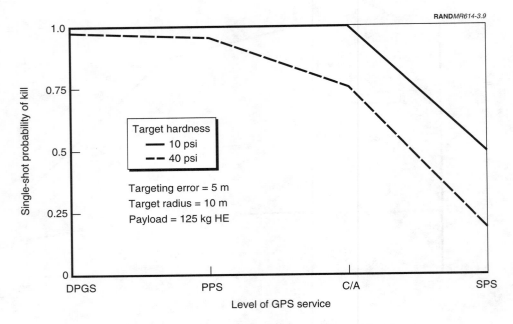

Figure 3.9—GCM Attacks Against Small Area Targets

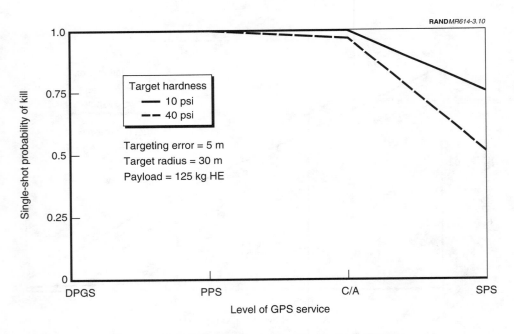

Figure 3.10—GCM Attacks Against Large Area Targets

unlikely that GCMs will pose a significant threat to point targets in the near future.

On the other hand, fixed area targets such as ports, warehouses, and airfields are much more vulnerable to cruise missile attacks. Locating such targets should be relatively easy and many of them could be pretargeted before a conflict began. In addition, GCMs do not require DGPS accuracies to achieve high SSPKs against these structures; SPS is sufficient.

The story is somewhat different for cruise missiles employing weapons of mass destruction than for GCMs carrying ordinary conventional warheads. In the former case, the attacker's problem is to ensure that small numbers of valuable warheads arrive on target. Similarly, a defender facing missiles carrying WMD must ensure that no weapons leak through the defenses.

Many of the cruise missiles that Third World nations are likely to acquire for land-attack missions will either have long ranges and small payloads (e.g., unmanned aerial vehicles) or short ranges and large payloads (e.g., converted anti-ship cruise missiles). This may limit their ability to effectively deliver chemical and nuclear weapons.[37] On the other hand, biological weapons are so lethal that even small payloads can completely cover a city, though the effects are far less predictable than for nuclear weapons.

In contrast to conventionally armed cruise missiles, GCMs carrying nuclear weapons could land within hundreds of meters of most targets and still accomplish their mission. The same is generally true of missiles carrying chemical and biological weapons. In most cases, SPS provides more than enough accuracy for cruise missiles carrying weapons of mass destruction. Thus, SA does little to limit the threat posed by such missiles—other defenses will have to be used against them.

In sum, the threat posed by GPS-guided cruise missiles is highly dependent on the physical characteristics of the missiles, the type of payload they are carrying, the intelligence and reconnaissance capabilities of the adversary, and the performance of air defenses. Specific conclusions are scenario dependent, but the analyses conducted herein point to some general observations.

---

[37]For an analysis of the coverage areas of GCMs carrying chemical and biological weapons, see Irving Lachow, "GPS-Guided Cruise Missiles and Weapons of Mass Destruction," in Kathleen C. Bailey (ed.), *The Director's Series on Proliferation #8*, Lawrence Livermore National Laboratory, Livermore, CA, June 1, 1995, pp. 1–22. Note that nuclear weapons produced in the Third World will probably weigh at least 500 kg, which is more than many cruise missiles can carry. However, warheads obtained from other sources may be more compatible with cruise missile delivery. See Eric H. Arnett, "The Most Serious Challenge in the 1990s? Cruise Missiles in the Developing World," in Eric H. Arnett and Thomas W. Wander (eds.), *The Proliferation of Advanced Weaponry: Technology, Motivations, and Responses*, American Academy for the Advancement of Science, Washington, D.C., 1992, p. 111.

- Conventionally armed GCMs may pose a significant threat to large fixed targets but do not threaten most mobile targets.

- GPS-guided cruise missiles appear to be good platforms for delivering chemical and biological weapons (CBW), especially the latter. However, the efficacy of CBW attacks may be greatly reduced if slow-flying cruise missiles are detected early enough to warn U.S. forces and be destroyed.

- At present, it is highly unlikely that nuclear weapons will be delivered by GPS-guided cruise missiles. That situation may change if advanced cruise missiles or small nuclear warheads become available to less-developed countries.

- SA can be quite effective when hard point targets are attacked. If soft or large targets are attacked, SA has minimal effect on the lethality of GCMs. In any case, GCMs using DGPS can achieve high SSPKs.

There is no question that GPS provides LDCs with access to signals that can be used to guide cruise missiles. However, it is the availability of the basic GPS signal itself that provides the greatest benefit to Third World nations. Selective availability may reduce the lethality of GCMs in some situations, but it does not eliminate the threat to U.S. forces. In addition, the proliferation of both local- and wide-area DGPS services will give Third World nations access to high accuracies in the near future. In sum, GPS-guided cruise missiles are a new feature on the landscape. The threat posed by cruise missiles using satellite navigation will exist whether SA is on or off, and may exist even if GPS should be turned off in the future.

PROVISION OF DGPS SERVICES

The Wide-Area Augmentation System (WAAS) is a space-borne system for providing differential GPS corrections over large areas of North American airspace. It may also serve as the prototype of a worldwide system of space-borne DGPS systems. However, the basic attributes of the system as currently articulated— to provide high accuracy to all users over wide areas—pose some concerns for national security planners. Since the DGPS accuracy provided will be better than the PPS available to the U.S. military and allied forces, hostile forces and groups might make use of the system.[38] There is also concern that in conflicts between third parties, DGPS signals might be used to support military operations, and hence make the United States politically, if not legally, culpable.

---

[38]In discussions with foreign officials, security matters concerning GPS were conspicuously treated as an American matter, provided these matters did not interfere with other aspects of the system such as maintaining system availability at its current levels or altering the cost structure to end-users.

Differential correction signals can be distributed through several possible technologies. Figure 3.11 lists several approaches. The corrections themselves are obtained by combining information from a known reference location, or set of locations, and comparing that to the location obtained by observing a set of satellites. A receiver is placed at a surveyed location (i.e., a location whose position is known precisely). The GPS signals that arrive at that location contain errors that offset the position of the surveyed point by some amount. The errors in the GPS signal are determined by comparing the site's known position with its position according to GPS. Correction terms for each satellite can then be calculated and transmitted to users. Those correction terms allow a user's receiver to eliminate many of the errors in the GPS signal.[39]

The DGPS correction signals can be transmitted many different ways, ranging from maritime telephones to satellite transmissions. The extent of the coverage is determined by the distribution of reference stations and the physical range of the transmitters. Long-range transmission of signals is practical if a sufficient number of reference stations are available to ensure that the appropriate correction can be applied in a region of interest and if the stations can be networked with the transmitters.

The operation of space-based DGPS transmitters with no intrinsic selective denial capability creates a dilemma for U.S. security officials, because interfering with the transmissions or the satellite might adversely affect other nations in the satellite's antenna footprint. Figure 3.12 illustrates the coverage available from three notional satellites located at geosynchronous orbits. The contours denote elevation angles (0, 15, 30, and 45 degrees) at the ground terminal.

RANDMR614-3.11

Space-based	Terrestrial
WAAS (L1 band)	FM-subcarrier
Low earth orbit communication satellite (LEO COMSAT)	Medium-frequency radio beacons
MTSAT	Maritime phones
INMARSAT	L1 band transmitters
	Cellular networks

Figure 3.11—Selected DGPS Distribution Methods

---

[39]All bias errors are eliminated. The remaining errors vary randomly and therefore cannot be corrected in this manner. However, the random errors contribute little to a user's position uncertainty.

RAND *MR614-3.12*

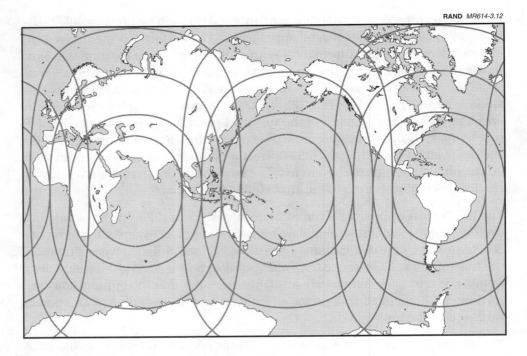

Figure 3.12—Representative Space-Based DGPS Coverage

While options—such as encryption and steerable antennas—can improve a system's ability to deny use of its signal to hostile groups, these options add cost and operational complexity to the use of the satellite. Thus, they run counter to the civil/commercial aspects of the system that call for its widespread availability at low cost. Also, the idea that a civil navigation system might be so configured has concerned allied governments, receiver manufacturers facing adverse impacts on sales, and those not wishing to foster support for alternatives to GPS.

In addition, uplinks (transmissions to the satellite) and downlinks (transmissions from the satellite to users) may be vulnerable to spoofing (where another transmitter inserts false information into the data-steam to mislead the receiver). National security planners are concerned about any system being constructed without prudent security precautions. However, any options to address system security would add at least marginally to the cost of the system, and are somewhat at odds with the motivation of a civil/commercial enterprise.[40]

An alternative to basing a DGPS system in space is to place an array of differential transmitters on the earth's surface. Such transmitters might use FM-subcarriers, cellular phone networks, or maritime radios (all of which cover relatively short ranges), or might use medium-frequency (MF) transmitters such as the U.S. Coast Guard and Army Corps of Engineers' system being established in the United States. Ground-based systems have some vulnerabilities from the national security perspective in that many transmission sites in a conflict would be located in a belligerent nation and would be subject to either physical destruction or electronic warfare.

There is, however, a wrinkle to this matter, at least if MF systems are used. Because of the propagation characteristics of the MF signal, it is possible to use the signal at significantly long ranges from a transmitter site—particularly at night. Also, if networked into arrays of ground stations that provide the correction signals, modest numbers of transmitters can cover extended areas. One could intentionally place DGPS sites to support one's own military activity or a neighboring nation's activity as part of an overtly civilian system that is available to all end-users. Furthermore, DGPS sites are readily immunized by placement on or near sensitive installations such as hospitals, and by their overt use in the civilian sector. Even military transmitters could be survivable given their relatively low power requirements of 1–120 Watts and their small size. Hunting down and destroying a proliferated network would be difficult, although electronic warfare against the sites appears relatively simple.

An MF DGPS signal may propagate in several ways (see Figure 3.13). The signal may propagate via a direct wave when the receiver has an unobstructed line-of-sight to the transmitter. The signal can propagate via a ground wave (the primary mode for a DGPS system) that is diffracted (and to some extent refracted by the atmosphere) around the earth's surface, and is attenuated by varying amounts depending on the conductivity and dielectric constant of the earth's surface along the signal's path. At night, when the absorptive D-layer of the lower ionosphere is depleted, the MF signal may traverse it and be reflected off the higher E-layer, and thereby be received at longer ranges than a ground wave.

---

[40]Interestingly enough, if the system were purely commercial, many of the security precautions suggested by the national security community might be needed to avoid liability for the space-based DGPS system (protecting the signal uplinks and downlinks), and to allow for revenue production (controlling end-user access). However, there is no guarantee that a commercial company would in fact be U.S. or that it could be forced to follow the direction of the United States government.

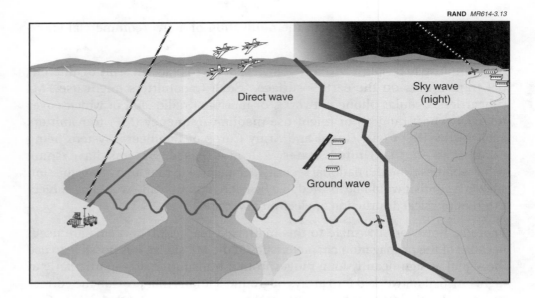

Figure 3.13—Medium-Frequency Propagation Modes for DGPS Signals

A system designer might design the system to exploit only the ground wave, since it is the most robust of the modes (allowing 24-hour propagation) and would constitute conservative design practice. A military planner might attempt to exploit the signal at longer ranges by opting for nighttime operations when the sky wave is strong, although utility at longer ranges is lessened because of the difficulty in maintaining view of the same satellites and the lesser accuracy available at significant distances from a reference location. There is also the possibility of networking remote reference stations together (possibly even covert reference stations passing information over other communications media), and propagating the signal via MF transmitter.

The difference between the extent of coverage that the system designer might anticipate and the range a military planner might achieve is exploitable under well-understood circumstances. (See Figure 3.14.) As one can see, concerns over DGPS signals being available to belligerent nations is not removed by promoting terrestrial DGPS systems over space-based systems. Consider the problems arising in the example shown if the sites illustrated were located in neutral territory. Extending the conflict to neutralize these sites could be of uncertain value while escalating the conflict dramatically.

To quantify the problem, signal transmission and reception were analyzed using a simulation that evaluates signal propagation over paths radiating away

RAND *MR614-3.14*

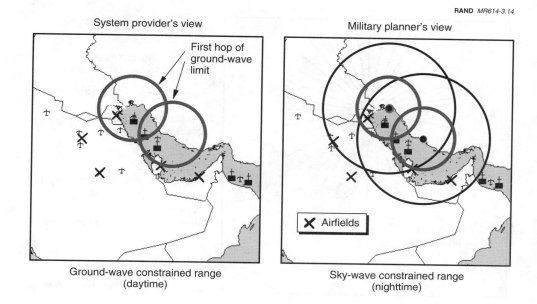

Figure 3.14—Designers' and Military Planners' Views of Medium-Frequency DGPS Signals Differ Significantly

from the broadcast stations. Figure 3.15 shows the basic approach toward assessing the impact of multiple transmitters on coverage throughout a region. Each transmitter had a set of spokes assigned to it, along which pseudo-receivers were located. The strength of the received signal was calculated for each pseudo-receiver along the spokes and repeated for all transmitter sites considered. Calculations were made for Southwest Asia and the Far East to demonstrate the effects of differing terrain on ground conductivity with line-of-sight calculations. Simulation runs examined the impact of seasonal variations (winter/summer), and time of day (noon, dawn, dusk, and midnight). Receiver altitude was also examined to better understand the effect of equipping missiles and aircraft with DGPS receivers and the expected strength of the signal at the time of reception. The added signal strength at altitude could be important in properly assessing the possibility of jamming the DGPS signal.

Figure 3.16 shows the output for a single spoke with signal strength plotted against range from the transmitter. Signal components from the direct wave, ground wave, sky wave, and the resultant total signal wave are plotted, along with representative thresholds for the receiver. A sky-wave/ground-wave interference calculation was explicitly modeled for the region where sky wave and ground wave interact. The case shown is for a single spoke radiating away from a transmitter site located on the Korean peninsula.

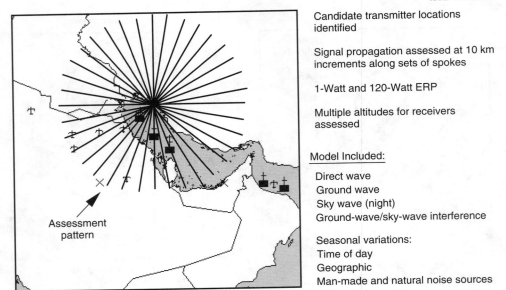

Figure 3.15—Medium-Frequency DGPS Signal Propagation Assessment Methodology

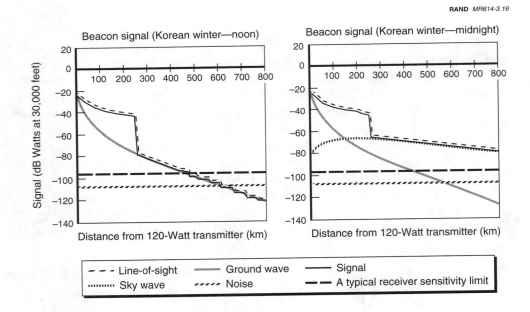

**Figure 3.16—Nations Can Take Advantage of Enhanced Ranges
by Exploiting the Sky Wave**

There is an appreciable difference between the strength and range of the signal during daylight hours and at night. In both cases, night and day, the dominant portion of the signal is the direct wave until line-of-sight is broken, when it falls to the signal from the ground wave. For the noon case (Figure 3.16, left), the signal decreases with range, following the ground-wave's attenuation contour. For the midnight case (Figure 3.16, right), the signal follows the ground-wave portion of the curve until it intercepts the sky wave, and then falls off with range as does the sky wave. The region where the sky wave and ground wave have approximately the same strength can involve either positive or destructive interference. However, an airborne vehicle would probably traverse that region in a short time.

If the system accuracy is acceptable at longer ranges, and the technical limitations associated with maintaining view of the same satellites and remote reference stations are overcome, the longer range should be exploitable by friendly and hostile forces. In the case of a signal provided by a neutral party, a logical option would be to reduce its transmitter power. In civil and commercial applications, transmitted power is reduced to avoid interference with remote AM radio stations operating at frequencies close to DGPS stations.

Figure 3.17 shows the propagation of DGPS signals in Northeast Asia from sites at which 120-Watt ERP DGPS transmitters could be located. The four cases shown are for winter, with variations in the necessary signal-to-noise threshold for the GPS receiver(10 dB/0 dB) and for the time of day (noon/midnight). The 10-dB receiver thresholds are based on the performance of commonly available equipment, whereas the 0-dB values represent a more sophisticated receiver. Noon was chosen as the representative time that system designers might use, and midnight was chosen to highlight the maximum range to which the signal might propagate.

In the cases shown, receiver stations falling within ±3 dB of the target sensitivity are highlighted. Rings with large open regions indicate that receivers were still outside the receiver threshold when calculations were terminated. The striking aspect of this is that a relatively small number of transmitter stations, as distinct from monitoring stations, can cover large areas.

The other point to keep in mind is that all regions of the world are not of equal interest to the United States either in geopolitical or economic terms. When one examines the regions where the United States has significant interests (such as Northeast Asia, Southwest Asia, and Europe), two facts become apparent: (1) terrestrial DGPS services will quite possibly be used within those regions, and (2) DGPS distribution services that cross borders might pose a problem. Wide-scale deployment of DGPS services could likewise cover many regions of interest.

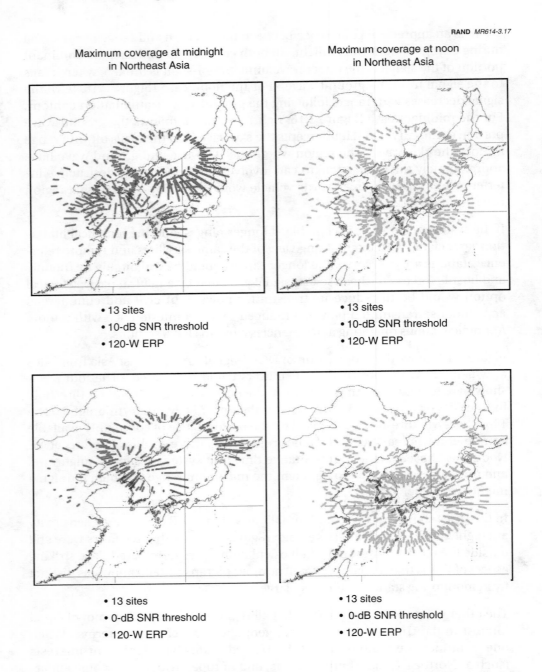

RAND *MR614-3.17*

Maximum coverage at midnight
in Northeast Asia

Maximum coverage at noon
in Northeast Asia

- 13 sites
- 10-dB SNR threshold
- 120-W ERP

- 13 sites
- 10-dB SNR threshold
- 120-W ERP

- 13 sites
- 0-dB SNR threshold
- 120-W ERP

- 13 sites
- 0-dB SNR threshold
- 120-W ERP

Figure 3.17—DGPS Reference Station Propagation in Northeast Asia

The key attributes of DGPS services are shown in Figure 3.18. In all likelihood, it will be difficult to interfere with DGPS stations in near-war situations. The inability to interfere with this class of target arises from the nonmilitary use of the system, including possible safety-of-life functions within the target country. Even if those attributes could be set aside, DGPS signals will not necessarily respect borders, and it is possible that critical regions like the Middle East will have neutral-nation systems overlapping regions of interest. This is especially true for many space-based systems with intrinsically wide-area coverage, some of which may not be under the control of the United States.

Assuming that DGPS services are a possible problem—whether or not space-based distribution of corrections occur, how can the United States mitigate the fact that hostile groups have access to GPS/DGPS signals? It would be helpful to have a range of options, such as agreements with countries hosting DGPS networks to limit their operations upon request, as well as to ensure the ability to jam or attack such networks if necessary. To the maximum extent possible, it is in the security interest of the United States to have DGPS systems that cross international boundaries under the direct control of allied nations, as opposed to potential adversaries or international civil organizations. Direct control may or may not include encrypting the DGPS communications link or limiting transmissions to ground-based sites. The important point is that such systems be subject to control for international security purposes.

A higher-order question is whether DGPS and other improvements over the SPS signal would substantively alter any current U.S. defense plans, or substantively alter the ability of U.S. forces to operate around the world. The ability to deter or negate the hostile use of DGPS signals may be part of layered missile and air defense strategies, but it is not likely to be the most important factor. Other capabilities, such as target detection and interdiction as well as the direct suppression of attacks will justifiably consume more resources and attention.

RAND*MR614-3.18*

- Most applications of DGPS are nonmilitary in nature.

- DGPS is likely to be in critical safety applications.

- Space-based and some terrestrial systems do not respect borders.

- DGPS cannot be easily interfered with during near-war situations.

- The United States is only one of several possible actors.

Figure 3.18—Key Attributes of DGPS Systems

SELECTIVE AVAILABILITY

Selective availability is a technique that intentionally degrades the accuracy of GPS signals available to civilian users. A random process dithers the satellite clocks and falsifies the satellite ephemerides so as to produce position and time errors for SPS users of the service. When SA is active ("on"), the horizontal position accuracy of the civilian signals drops from 20–30 meters to 100 meters (95 percent probability) and the timing accuracy is reduced from 200 nanoseconds to 340 nanoseconds (95 percent probability) relative to Coordinated Universal Time (UTC).[41] This accuracy is available worldwide and without restriction to any user. The actual accuracy of SPS with SA off can approach about 5 meters, which is much better than the system specification.

The main justification for SA is that it prevents the use of high-accuracy signals by adversaries. However, it is not evident that SA is successfully accomplishing this mission; high-accuracy signals can be obtained through the use of differential GPS methods. In fact, it is possible that the SA control policy has actually encouraged some users to turn to differential services because the SPS accuracies were not adequate for their needs. Whether or not this is true, both local and wide-area DGPS services are spreading rapidly around the world. It has also been stated that the current SA policy benefits U.S. companies that currently have an edge over foreign competitors. This benefit, however, is limited to a few firms and may only be a short-term artifact that could quickly change.

Another problem with the argument that SA alone prevents the hostile use of GPS is that many factors affect the lethality of a weapons system. For example, the lethality of a GPS-guided cruise missile depends on its navigation accuracy, its targeting accuracy, the angle of its terminal dive, its payload, and the size and hardness of a given target. Although GPS provides positioning information that can be extremely useful to military forces, that information can only be exploited to the extent that the forces are properly equipped and trained to use it. It has also been stated that SA is important because it degrades the velocity information inherent in GPS signals. Such information could be used to update the inertial systems on board hostile ballistic missiles. This concern was addressed in previous sections that showed that much of the benefit of GPS is already realized with access to SPS accuracy levels.

On the other side of the debate, it has been argued that turning SA off in peacetime would help to promote international acceptance and reliance on the U.S. GPS system. A comparison of the advantages and disadvantages of selective

---

[41]The spatial and temporal accuracies for GPS with SA on are defined in the U.S. Federal Radionavigation Plan and also in the GPS SPS signal specification document. These accuracies are given and have not been estimated or calculated by the authors.

availability is shown in Table 3.10. The SA issue is more fully discussed in Chapters Four and Six.

ANTI-SPOOFING

GPS anti-spoofing (AS) encrypts the P-code so that only authorized users can have access to it. The resulting signal is known as the Precise Positioning Service (PPS). Access to PPS can be obtained only with receivers equipped with a cryptographic key. PPS provides users with a horizontal accuracy of 22 meters (95 percent probability) and 200 nanoseconds (95 percent probability). In addition to protecting access to the P-code, AS makes the PPS signal extremely difficult to spoof (hence its name). Despite its benefits, the AS policy does have some drawbacks such as expensive receiver equipment and the need for a cryptographic key management infrastructure.

Table 3.10

Pros and Cons of Selective Availability

SA	Pro	Con
On in Peacetime	Denies high accuracy (10–15 CEP) to adversaries, required for some military missions	SPS satisfies many military needs and DGPS methods circumvent SA
	Shows political resolve, which may discourage foreign military dependence on GPS	Encourages reliance on DGPS, wide-area DGPS or other satnav systems (e.g., GLONASS)
	Would be difficult to reactivate SA if turned off	Clear policy stating conditions for reactivation of SA reduces concern
	Prevents accurate GPS velocity updates for ballistic missile applications	Significant CEP errors such as reentry dispersions not corrected by GPS; also DGPS can provide velocity updates
	Benefits DGPS companies; maintains edge over foreign competitors	Benefits limited to certain companies—a short-term view that could quickly change
Off in peacetime	Promotes international acceptance of, and reliance on, GPS-based technologies.	Foreign users primarily concerned with DoD control of GPS rather than status of SA
	Provides improved accuracy to all GPS users, less reliance on DGPS	Less revenue for companies that provide DGPS services
	Reduces DGPS correction update rate, conserving spectrum bandwidth	Amount of conservation not significant

OVERALL THREAT ASSESSMENT

There are many possible uses of GPS and augmented GPS in the military arena. GPS information can influence many aspects of warfare, including the operation of space, air, ground, naval, and special forces. In most cases, the benefits provided by GPS are not revolutionary; rather, they increase the efficiency of forces in the field. The military benefits of GPS to U.S. forces in large part draw from the way the United States has chosen to organize, train, and equip those forces. As with other information technologies, the effective use of GPS requires an extensive infrastructure, training, and—perhaps most important—a doctrine that combines GPS information with other systems for operational employment. Indeed, a relatively small number of nations are capable of truly exploiting the full potential of GPS technology over the near to mid term, and virtually all of them are U.S. allies.

Aside from the performance of individual weapons, the number and type of weapons threatening the United States need to considered. Typically, potential adversaries have access to tens to low hundreds of the kind of precision weapons that we have discussed. By comparison, the United States employed 288 TLAMs (Tomahawk Land Attack Missiles) during Operation Desert Storm against Iraq,[42] and these were only a small portion of the total number of precision weapons used during the conflict. Given a nominal assignment of two to six missiles per militarily significant aim point, the coverage expected from a small cruise-missile-equipped force would not be very extensive.

Precision weapons could be used against small numbers of politically sensitive targets. In this role, the actual damage is not as important as the effort itself. In the Persian Gulf War, attacks by Iraq against Saudi Arabia and Israel were political attacks, and they served that role well. Presumably, a more accurate system with a better chance of striking a particular target, such as a parliament building, would have greater effect. However, GPS-aided weapons are not the only means of delivering such attacks (enemy special operations forces might be effective here). Whereas improved accuracy helps in the attack of politically sensitive targets, the nature of the targets themselves and their disposition within a country usually lend themselves to other lines of attack as well.

The examination of GPS-aided ballistic and cruise missiles shows that improvements in performance are possible; however, those improvements need to be seen within a broader set of considerations such as the nature of the threat (e.g., numbers and types of warheads on the weapons), planned U.S. re-

---

[42]U.S. Department of Defense, *Conduct of the Persian Gulf War; Final Report to Congress Pursuant to Title V of the Persian Gulf Supplemental Authorization and Personnel Benefits Act of 1991*, Public Law 102-25, Washington, D.C., April 1992, p. T-201.

sponses to the threat already being deployed (e.g., upgrades to the Patriot air defense system), as well as additional countermeasures necessitated by the availability of GPS (e.g., better jammers and receivers able to acquire P-code directly), and the costs associated with both sets of responses.

National security threats to the United States will continue to exist independent of the possible exploitation of GPS/DGPS, but we must understand whether the potential for hostile GPS exploitation and denial will drive current U.S. force structure and R&D investment plans in different directions, or change how the United States conducts military operations or its strategy for particular regions. For example, will the existence of GPS-aided cruise missiles change plans to conduct defensive operations against modest-sized forces exploiting weapons of mass destruction? For the most part, the answer appears to be no. U.S. planning will still need to avoid single-point failure modes vulnerable to small numbers of weapons. In addition, air defenses will have to be sized to handle raids consistent with a larger-scale conventional attack or a WMD attack masked by decoys and conventional weapons.

Placing the Threat in Context

Hostile forces using GPS for guidance can pose some risk to U.S. forces, but that risk must be placed in context. Figure 3.19 summarizes the magnitude of the GPS-based threat to U.S. national security.

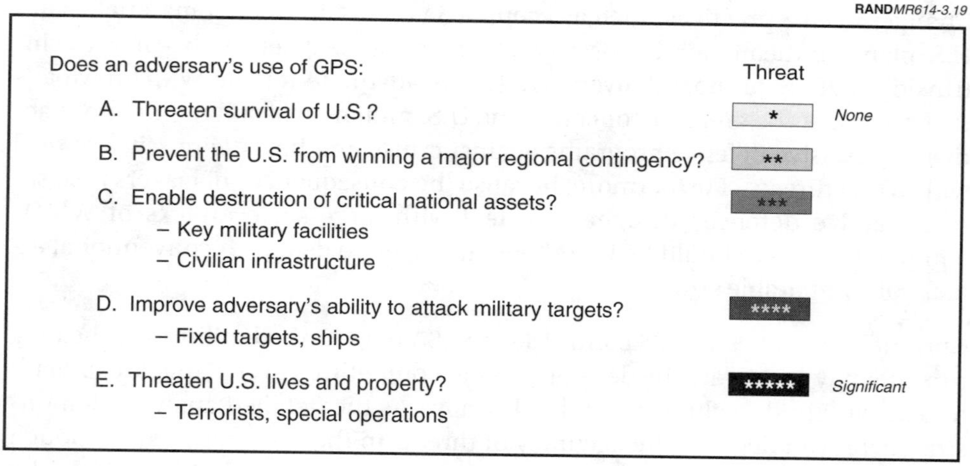

Figure 3.19—Assessing the Threat of Hostile Forces Using GPS

Thus, enemy forces using GPS can threaten U.S. lives and property and can probably improve an adversary's ability to attack U.S. military targets. However, these forces' ability to destroy critical national assets is marginal, and the likelihood that they will either prevent the United States from winning a medium regional contingency (MRC) or threaten the survival of the United States itself is quite low.

National Security Findings

During the course of the analysis, a number of national security findings were reached. While the detailed analyses highlighted the impact of GPS on specific types of operations as well as methods of exploiting augmented signals, these findings must be placed in the context of high-level decisions. GPS/DGPS services can improve the ability of properly trained and equipped forces to operate against the United States. However, the overall magnitude of that threat appears manageable provided the United States proceeds prudently in preparing an array of defensive measures designed to operate in a world where precision time and location services are available. These measures might include fielding theater air defenses designed to operate against raids that might intermix conventional weapons and weapons of mass destruction, electronic warfare assets to degrade the guidance of conventionally armed weapons, passive defenses to protect personnel and installations, and mobility to avoid creating an attractive target for the enemy.

Changes in GPS practices, such as keeping SA on or off, will not materially alter U.S. plans for theater air defenses and theater missile defenses, because the intrinsic accuracy of most delivery systems is adequate for the WMD payloads that represent the greatest concern. The U.S. military will still require both active and passive defense programs against cruise and ballistic missiles to deal with WMD threats. Furthermore, because the consequences of leakers is so serious, active defenses designed to deal with large-scale attacks of WMD-equipped missiles should be more then adequate to deal with conventional attacks of comparable size.

Current approaches to GPS control such as SA have limited utility over the long run and may accelerate the development of competitors to GPS that are difficult to deal with both technically and politically. As the detailed analyses demonstrated, SA can degrade the accuracy of threats in the short term, even though access to the C/A-code already provides most of the added utility. Also, the costs of approaches like SA create conditions conducive to the creation of competing systems that might undermine the benefits of maintaining ultimate control of the GPS constellation.

The United States needs to think about how it can and should shape the international environment for space-based navigation services at the same time it considers appropriate responses to changing threats from long-range weapons delivery systems such as cruise missiles. For example, a stable and predictable GPS policy in the United States can help promote GPS as a global standard. In the case of DGPS services that cross international boundaries, it is in the security interests of the United States to have such systems under the direct control of allies, as opposed to potential adversaries or international civil organizations. Direct control can encompass a spectrum of techniques, from using encryption of the DGPS communications link to ensure access only by authorized receivers through diplomatic agreements to limit areas and times of operation when international conditions warrant.

Examination of the technology underlying GPS indicates that the United States cannot count on maintaining a monopoly on precision time and location services forever. Indeed, because of the relative simplicity of GPS-like technologies, it is vital that the United States begin preparing to operate in a world where access to GPS-type and augmented GPS services are the norm. The economic and technical barriers to entry for a competing satellite navigation system are shrinking with the creation of LEO communication satellite networks (which may lower the costs of building and launching satellites). Thus it will become increasingly risky to assume that no other party will be able to introduce a competing system should GPS become unavailable or unreliable.

Chapter Four

COMMERCIAL ASSESSMENT

The commercial uses of GPS are diverse and many, with applications across industry. Some applications are simple, such as determining a position, whereas others are complex blends of GPS with communications and other technologies. The rapid growth of commercial applications in recent years has come as a surprise to many industry observers and firms building GPS satellites and equipment for the U.S. Department of Defense. As a result, there has been a lag in understanding the commercial implications of government policy decisions and how commercial developments can create both opportunities and challenges for policymakers.

This chapter discusses the commercial growth of GPS applications and technologies, with special attention to potential implications for national policy. The first section reviews the various kinds of civil and commercial applications of GPS and how they are categorized. Attention is paid to the demand for "high end" applications, such as submeter positioning and precision timing, which represent areas of particular commercial importance. The second section reviews U.S. and Japanese projections for the growth of commercial GPS markets, with particular attention to the use of GPS in car navigation, which is expected to represent a large segment of the consumer market. The third section rates the competitive position of firms and countries in GPS technology through analysis of patent trends. Although government funding was vital to the initial development of GPS technology, a competitive commercial market now provides the major incentive for further advances.

Moving from the technical and economic realities of commercial GPS to the policy environment, the fourth section looks at potential changes to the civilian GPS signal now being provided. Commonly discussed changes include the elimination of selective availability and greater nonmilitary access to the Precise Positioning Service. We discuss the potential commercial implications of these changes. Looking beyond the GPS system itself, the U.S. government intends to provide civil augmentations to GPS to improve public safety and navigation services to aviation, maritime, and other users. The fifth section briefly reviews the proposed GPS augmentations and areas where public and private interests conflict. The final section reviews potential threats to the future growth of commercial GPS markets. All of the significant threats arise from potential U.S. and international government policies, hence attention to policy issues should be a priority with GPS industry.

COMMERCIAL AND CIVIL USES OF GPS

The differing needs of commercial and civil GPS users and the availability of alternative solutions for meeting them have led to a highly diverse and competitive market for GPS technologies, equipment, and services. The market for commercial uses of GPS can be segmented by the differing needs of customers for time and spatial information. Not all users need or desire the same level of accuracy; for example, a surveyor will want more accuracy than a ship captain, and a truck fleet manager will need real-time data in a way that a scientist studying crustal motion does not.

There are varying levels of spatial accuracy available to civil and commercial customers. The basic GPS signal—the Standard Positioning Service (SPS)—provides 100-meter horizontal accuracy (and in practice may be as good as 70–80 meters). If greater accuracy is needed, as is often the case, differential GPS (DGPS) techniques can employ one or more reference stations in addition to the SPS, providing accuracies to less than 10 meters and to submeter (e.g., centimeter) levels with data post-processing. An important distinction in DGPS operations is that some systems provide accurate data only to receivers in fixed positions, others function well even while the receivers are moving (also known as real-time-kinematic [RTK] performance), and some can provide the most accurate data possible, but only after extensive post-processing. These differences in performance have cost implications as well for both the equipment itself and how it is used by the customer in specific operations. A fleet manager who needs to know where a shipment is at any moment is not interested in hours of processing time to gain a few meters of accuracy.

Accuracy is addictive and, if cost were no object, virtually all customers would ask for the greatest accuracy possible subject only to how many decimal places they cared about.[1] Accuracy is not the only (or even primary) concern for some users of GPS. Persons operating ships and aircraft far from land, for example, will be concerned with how available the GPS signal is("Will it be there when I need it?") and with its integrity ("Can I trust the information I'm getting?").

---

[1]One of the authors recalls that during a boating trip, his GPS receiver adequately told him where he was relative to the shore; however, it also said the boat was 10 meters under water. In situations where reality is not so obvious, there is concern that users will trust GPS positions provided on electronic displays to the exclusion of other observations.

Surveyors can schedule when to take their measurements (these commercial uses of GPS were possible before the full constellation was completed). Transportation system operators are driven by customer schedules and may not be able to adjust rapidly if GPS signals are interrupted. Similarly, some periods of GPS use can be especially critical, such as aircraft landings and harbor movements. During such times, GPS users want rapid notification of any problems with GPS signal integrity—sometimes in seconds. Figure 4.1 shows how sample GPS users segment themselves with differing needs for accuracy, integrity, and availability.

The needs and interests of GPS users are a significant input to the formulation of GPS policy because they drive the technology and markets for GPS and, to put it bluntly, each U.S. user of GPS is a potential voter.[2] As discussed in Chapter Two, there is a diverse array of viewpoints on the commercial and civil uses of GPS within U.S. and foreign government agencies. The users them-

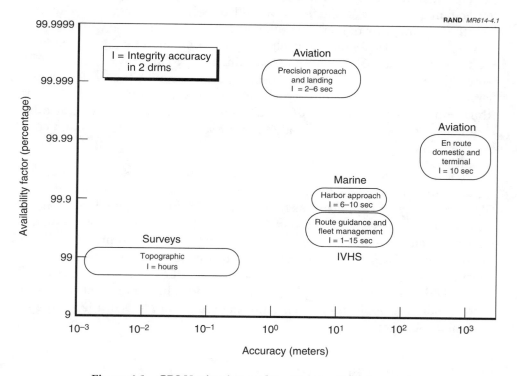

Figure 4.1—GPS Navigation and Positioning Requirements

---

[2]Voters have often made their views known in areas of mass technology, such as cable television and telephone service.

selves have similarly diverse opinions on the management and operation of GPS. In the course of our interviews and other research, however, some common themes repeatedly emerged.

Above all, civil and commercial users want the GPS signal to be a reliable, stable standard that they can plan around, much like electrical power from a wall socket. Closely related to signal stability is the political stability of GPS operations and management. This is important to international civil authorities who contemplate using GPS for safety-of-life applications such as air and ship navigation. Price is a major concern of commercial users, particularly as GPS is integrated into other consumer electronic products in computers and automobiles. As prices for GPS equipment drop, more commercial users adopt GPS or explore its use—even with no change in the GPS policy environment.

According to a leading GPS manufacturer, civil and commercial buyers are price elastic, and thus price is a greater influence per se on overall demand levels than accuracy.[3] While users would like perfect accuracy if it were costless, the vast majority of markets not using DGPS seem satisfied with the accuracy of SPS. The DGPS market itself has been stimulated by the gap between the accuracy available from SPS and that which DGPS can provide. This market would still exist, however, even if all users had access to the Precise Positioning Service signal (used by the military), or selective availability were turned to zero (thus improving the accuracy of the Standard Positioning Service), or other technical improvements were made to improve GPS service to civil and commercial users.

In broad terms, all users want the continued existence of a stable, predictable signal. For commercial GPS users, the primary concern is the price of using GPS technology and applications that meet their needs. For international and civil government users interested in GPS for safety-of-life applications such as navigation aids, the primary concern is political stability and predictability in the provision of GPS, usually expressed in technical terms such as system integrity, reliability, and availability. For some scientific users, the primary concern is with absolute accuracy (with and without differential techniques) in such demanding applications as monitoring crustal motions or measuring atmospheric occultation.

Categories of GPS Applications

One of the original purposes of GPS was to improve en route navigation for military ships and aircraft. Today there are dozens of uses of GPS, with new

---

[3]Interview with Charles Trimble in Salt Lake City, UT, September 20, 1994.

applications being reported each month in academic, business, and public media. One list compiled by the U.S. Department of Transportation provides multiple examples of GPS usage in

- aviation

- maritime and waterways

- highway and construction

- public transportation

- railroads

- communications

- emergency response (e.g., ambulance and fire)

- surveying

- weather, scientific, and space

- environmental protection

- recreation (e.g., sports events)

- law enforcement and legal services

- agriculture and forestry.[4]

Such lists are useful for demonstrating the diversity of GPS users, but often do not show important underlying trends in GPS applications and technology. Rather than providing another review of GPS applications, we found it more useful to think of GPS applications evolving in response to three types of questions. GPS began by answering the question "Where am I?" and with the addition of communications could answer "Where are you?" questions. More recently, GPS can answer "Where is it?" in tracking assets and packets of information.

"Where am I?" applications involve the most visible kinds of GPS equipment such as hand-held receivers used by hikers, drivers, and pilots and surveyors. Information such as latitude, longitude, altitude, and time are provided from a GPS receiver for further action by the user. The information may be translated into more easily understood forms, such as position relative to an existing terrain or street map, or used to provide relative information such as distances to user-defined "waypoints" or positions specifically identified by the user. Applications by surveyors and hikers are mirrors of each other. A hiker wishes

---

[4]U.S. Department of Transportation, Office of the Secretary, "Civil Uses of GPS," September 1994.

to know his position relative to the terrain. A surveyor taking control points over an unknown area wishes to precisely describe where he has been. Both applications directly use GPS-generated information.

"Where are you?" applications occur when GPS information for multiple users is communicated to another party. For example, the manager of a trucking fleet can use GPS and mobile phone communications to stay in touch with the drivers. At a very sophisticated level, GPS and mobile communications can help manage international air traffic where hundreds of aircraft are moving constantly in complex patterns. As noted above, the GPS user may convert basic time and space information into another form before it is communicated. For instance, insurance adjusters evaluating fire or earthquake damage in a residential neighborhood have GPS receivers combined with laptop computers, digital cameras, and cellular phones. A standard form is filled in on the computer, a digital picture is attached to the file, and GPS determines the damage location address. All of this information can then be communicated rapidly to a central location, allowing more-efficient claims processing. In some cases, a GPS application need not require deliberate action by the user. GPS receivers have been integrated into some experimental automobile airbag and cellular phone systems. In the event the airbag detonates, the phone automatically contacts emergency services and reports the location of the detonation relative to local highway maps.

"Where is it?" applications are ones in which GPS tracks assets such as cargo shipments or manages packets in dense information networks. These applications may be thought of as variations on the previous two categories. GPS receivers may be used to ask "Where are you?" when the object is a scientific instrument or cargo out of direct human contact that cannot communicate its position by itself. GPS can provide input to remote machinery that has some autonomy, as for example when GPS-based navigation systems provide position updates to a satellite. Self-correcting actions by remote machines can in turn lower the workload of central monitoring facilities such as ground-control networks.[5]

Real-Time Kinematic Techniques

Differential GPS techniques began by providing correction signals from a base station to a stationary receiver. Many commercial (and military) applications would like to have submeter or even centimeter accuracy while moving in real time. Real-time differential techniques require more-sophisticated software

---

[5]Some brief examples of space-based GPS applications can be found in "Dividends in Space," *GPS World*, June 1995, p. 16.

and communication systems to make corrections "on-the-fly" without having to wait for post-processing analysis. Examples of commercial applications that use real-time kinematic (RTK) GPS techniques include surveying, construction, mining, transportation, and utilities management, often in combination with Geographic Information Systems (GISs) that incorporate position data as they are taken.

Real-time kinematic operations use measurements of GPS carrier and code information from both the frequencies (but not encrypted military data). In an initialization process, the GPS receiver calculates the integer number of carrier-phase wavelengths between it and the GPS satellites in view. Once the integer number of wavelengths is known, the data are combined with phase measurements of the carrier waves to allow a precise calculation of the "pseudo-range" between the GPS satellite and receiver at a particular instant. Pseudo-range measurements from multiple GPS satellites are then combined, after being suitably corrected by a communications link with a fixed station, to calculate a precise real-time position.

While using principles similar to those employed in wide-area differential GPS systems (such as proposed by the FAA and the U.S. Coast Guard), the signal structure of RTK GPS is quite different. The data volume is much higher than for code-based DGPS techniques (see Appendix A) and the range over which RTK provides superior accuracy is much shorter than for common code-based DGPS—typically 10–20 km compared with 500 km.[6] An alternative to RTK is commercial DGPS services broadcasting on FM subcarrier bands. These services work well in areas covered by FM stations, but the best accuracies typically require being within 10–20 kilometers of the transmitter as well. Many RTK users operate in remote areas (e.g., mining areas) that are not served by FM stations, thus requiring local reference stations.

GPS and Precision Timing

Timing is one of the less-obvious uses of GPS, yet it affects a wide variety of information-driven activities. GPS provides an inexpensive and standard mechanism for the distribution of precise timing signals over a large area. It can facilitate the synchronization of signaling on digital networks both on landlines and over the airwaves, allow for more effective exploitation of limited bandwidths for communications, provide a means of reliably time-stamping activities for

---

[6]"Need for Nationwide Frequencies for RTK GPS Applications," Memorandum from Mark Nichols to Ann Ciganer, Trimble Navigation, May 12, 1995.

authentication and security activities, and support widely distributed scientific and military activities that might benefit from time-correlation of events.[7]

Perhaps the most pervasive use of GPS is in supporting wide-area communication networks. Precise GPS-based time signals are used in Internet protocols to manage the flow of information packets. The "Slow Start" protocol helps reduce congestion by monitoring a network; when congestion appears imminent, it delays the transmission of packets anywhere from milliseconds to a second. The actual delay is calculated on the basis of factors such as the current available capacity of the network, as well as round-trip transmission times (i.e., distance) between the packet sender and the chosen destination. The protocol was introduced in 1987 and has helped the Internet function while it has grown more than a thousandfold.[8] In a similar manner, precise time-stamps can be applied to audio packets, and controlled delays enable voice conferences over the Internet with suitably equipped computers. The next section discusses GPS-based time applications.

One of the difficulties with addressing timing is that it is largely unseen by the end-user. Applications of GPS in the timing world are becoming notable. Currently, AT&T is using GPS-originating time signals to synchronize the timing signal produced at 16 primary nodes, which in turn govern digital communications across the 300,000 kilometers of its transmission facility network. The actual timing precision reported on the AT&T network is on the order of several parts in 10^{-12} seconds, far better than the 1 part in 10^{-11} seconds required by ANSI and CCIT standards. Indeed, the ability to use GPS for a timing signal has allowed AT&T to significantly better its performance over current international standards. Precise timing information can facilitate communication services such as Asynchronous Transfer Mode (ATM) over fiber-optic communications at speeds up to 1–2 Gbits/s. The data-communication rates expected in the near term are much greater than anything seen in wide-scale deployment only a few years ago.

Precise timing can be significant in exploiting wireless communications. Here the focus is not so much on synchronization for high speed, though that can apply on some types of network links. Rather, timing comes to the fore in exploiting the scarce electromagnetic spectrum allocated for wireless communications. The Time Division Multiple Access (TDMA) communications process allows many users on a single network. Under TDMA, users are allocated cer-

---

[7]Eric A. Bobinsky, "GPS and Global Telecommunications," briefing for the National Research Council Committee on the Future of the Global Positioning System, Washington, D.C., July 29, 1994.

[8]Jeffery Kahn, *Building the Information Highway*, Summer 1993. This document can be found on the World Wide Web at http://www.lbl.gov/Science-Articles/Archive/information-superhighway.html

tain times on a network; during that slice of time they can communicate. The time divisions envisioned are short and are largely imperceivable to the end-users, provided they are communicating in a relatively slow manner such as voice. How many people can practically use the system without excessive delay is in part dependent on how finely the network services can be divided. Very precise timing allows smaller amounts of overhead to be assigned per user, and thus more time is available for end-users.

Another use of GPS-provided time, either directly or indirectly, is for security and authentication of electronic transactions. Time stamps and their verification can be very important in some schemes for rotating passwords that allow access to secure systems, as well as for some types of electronic commerce in which timing is a reference marker for sensitive financial information. For such applications, the timing accuracy of GPS per se may not necessarily be an issue, but rather it is the ubiquitous nature of the signal that can be significant. For international transactions, the ability to access a single dependable time server at low cost can help foster the use of time stamps for transactions. GPS's time stamp can be used both in the United States and abroad as a global standard.

The GPS timing signal can also support precise measurements. In this role, GPS timing signals are used to synchronize clocks at distant points so events can be compared. Applications include interferometry studies of distant stars and galaxies, precise measurements from remote seismographs, measurements of minute amounts of time associated with transactions occurring at 1–2 Gbit/s network interfaces, and provision of Time Distance of Arrival (TDOA) for military signals intelligence functions. In all of these applications, a common time base is needed for the operation of distributed receiving sites and to lower the cost of each site.

As the amount of wireless communications increase, GPS will be needed to tell data packets "where and when" when they are merging onto the global information superhighway. A user's location must be known to select a communications path (e.g. cellular phone or satellite link), and, as mentioned above, knowing a user's precise time smooths network management. Trimble Navigation and Socket Communications have placed integrated GPS engines on PCMCIA Type II cards which, combined with an external antenna, can fit into laptop computers.[9] In 1995, an industry observer estimated that there are 13.6 million laptop computers in use, up from 5.9 million the year before. By 1997, it is expected that there will be 40.1 million laptops in use.[10] While not every

---

[9]Trimble Navigation, *1993 Annual Report,* p. 14. PCMCIA stands for Personal Computer Memory Card International Association.

[10]Interview with David Atkinson, April 25, 1995. Mr. Atkinson was formerly an AT&T vice president for consumer products and is now with the investment banking firm of Hunterberg Harris.

laptop will have a GPS engine, this is a large potential market if prices continue to drop.

COMMERCIAL GPS MARKETS

The diversity of GPS applications makes it difficult to characterize the industry as a whole. A broad view of the GPS industry would include original equipment manufacturers (OEMs) of GPS receiver "engines," suppliers of GPS-related peripheral equipment such as displays and antennas, and GPS-related service providers. Some firms compete in the consumer electronics market, whereas others use GPS to provide professional services such as surveying and mapping. Some GPS products are tied to the fortunes of their platforms, such as the automobile and aircraft markets, while other GPS products aid commercial activities such as managing transportation and communication networks. One can imagine an economic "food chain" beginning with government contracts to build the GPS satellites, to commercial firms building GPS receivers, to firms using those receivers to provide services, and value-added firms that use GPS to enhance other commercial products.

From a narrow military beginning, GPS technology is spreading to more and more industries and sectors of the economy. As GPS applications become more sophisticated, they are also becoming more deeply embedded in economic activities. New commercial exploitations of GPS are increasingly dependent on other technologies, such as wireless communications and software that are closely tailored to specific customer needs. At one end of the applications spectrum, there is an individual user holding a GPS receiver to determine his position; at the other end, there is a distributed group of persons sharing a GIS database over the Internet without a direct awareness of GPS at all.

Categorizing GPS is of conceptual interest as well as a concern of government statisticians and industry analysts. The Standard Industrial Classification System (SIC) of the U.S. Department of Commerce is a detailed, numerical structure that tracks U.S. economic activity. Government reports, academic studies, and private industry studies typically use SIC codes to assess corporate product lines, relative industry productivities, potential investments, and the effects of taxes and tariffs.[11] GPS, a relatively new technology, is currently placed in a subcategory of Satellite Communications Systems (SIC 36631.38).[12] Some commercial GPS firms advocate a separate categorical identity for GPS

---

[11]SIC codes are used despite criticism that they are weighted toward traditional manufacturing activities and do not consistently represent emerging technologies and services.

[12]U.S. Department of Commerce/International Trade Administration, *U.S. Industrial Outlook 1994*, U.S. Government Printing Office, Washington, D.C., January 1994, p. 30-21.

that would acknowledge that GPS is an industry and not just a product on a list.[13]

A potential benefit of a new SIC code for GPS is that a standard classification would make it easier to conduct and evaluate market studies. Openly available market studies typically lack hard data on production levels, sales, and market shares that would come from the OEMs. Lacking such data, most studies tend to focus on estimates of prospective markets and qualitative arguments about adoption rates and critical price points (below which demand increases significantly). The problem of varying definitions is likely to become more acute as GPS continues to become an embedded technology in other products and services rather than a stand-alone product.

Like other information-based technologies, the generic applicability of GPS makes it an enabler of productivity improvements through reducing costs, enabling new functions, or enhancing revenues. The economic benefits of civil and commercial applications of GPS are thus broader than might be measured by sales of GPS equipment and service-related sales alone. At the same time, projecting future benefits is uncertain at best—it is difficult to predict where GPS-dependent productivity benefits might be found in the economy. Lowering the cost of using GPS is seen by industry as a crucial aspect for the growth of GPS, not only in terms of increasing demand from people who know what they want to use GPS for, but also in terms of encouraging experimentation with GPS by persons who are not sure if it will be useful.[14]

Industry Survey by the U.S. GPS Industry Council

The U.S. GPS Industry Council (USGIC) is an industry association of U.S. GPS satellite and equipment manufacturers: Ashtech, Interstate Electronics, Magellan Systems, Martin Marietta Astro Space (now Lockheed Martin), Motorola, Rockwell, and Trimble Navigation. The USGIC, formed in 1991, does not include foreign firms or service providers, preferring to focus on the common interests of U.S. GPS manufacturing firms.

In 1995, the USGIC surveyed its membership and developed a common set of market projections on global GPS equipment sales through the year 2000. The model was based on company proprietary studies of expected average sale

---

[13]"SIC Effort Could Make GPS an Official Industry," *GPS World Newsletter*, October 13, 1994, p. 1.

[14]Aside from the potential for hostile military use, there can be negative commercial "misuse" as well. Criminal uses of GPS might include more-efficient smuggling networks using small, unmanned, GPS-guided aircraft. Criminal organizations have been early adopters of other new technologies such as pagers and cellular phones and may be expected to experiment with GPS as equipment prices drop.

prices and unit sale projections and represents a consensus of the member firms.[15] Worldwide sales revenue projections are made in nine product categories; the totals do not include value-added services (e.g., GPS-enhanced mapping) or differential GPS services.[16]

The USGIC projections, in current dollars, are shown in Table 4.1. Worldwide sales in 1993 were $510 million and sales in 2000 are expected to total $8.47 billion, for an average annual growth rate of 50 percent per year. The two largest components of this market are expected to be car navigation and consumer/cellular applications, such as GPS-equipped mobile phones and personal computers. Car navigation not only tells a driver where he is, but can include roadside assistance, summoning emergency services, and stolen vehicle recovery. Military sales are relatively minor and are expected to account for an increasingly smaller share of U.S. GPS ground-equipment sales (i.e., excluding satellites). Similarly, aviation sales are expected to be significant, but are unlikely to drive commercial investments.

Figure 4.2 is a graphical representation of the data in Table 4.1, with the market segments regrouped into (civil) land, marine, and air applications as well as military sales. The large size of the car navigation and consumer/cellular markets, combined with the traditionally strong survey market, makes land-based GPS applications the largest expected portion of future equipment sales.

Table 4.1

Global GPS Market Projections
(Sales in millions of dollars)

Component	1993	1994	1995	1996	1997	1998	1999	2000
Car navigation	100	180	310	600	1100	2000	2500	3000
Consumer/cellular	45	100	180	324	580	1000	1500	2250
Tracking	30	75	112	170	250	375	560	850
OEM	60	110	140	180	220	275	340	425
Survey/mapping	100	145	201	280	364	455	546	630
GIS	25	35	50	90	160	270	410	650
Aviation	40	62	93	130	180	240	300	375
Marine	80	100	110	120	130	140	150	160
Military	30	60	70	80	90	100	110	130
Total	510	867	1266	1974	3074	4855	6416	8470

SOURCE: U.S. GPS Industry Council, 1995.

---

[15]"GPS in Year 2000: $8 Billion," *GPS World Newsletter*, April 11, 1995, p. 1.

[16]There are several U.S. firms, including Differential Correction (DCI), AccQPoint, and John E. Chance & Associates, that provide differential GPS services via FM broadcasts. None are members of the USGIC.

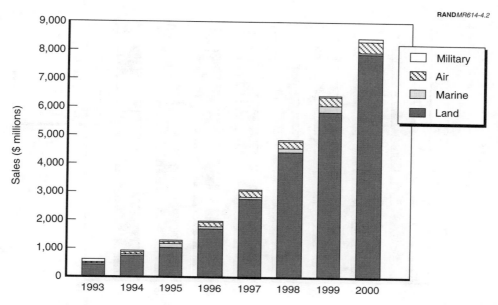

SOURCE: U.S. GPS Industry Council, March 1995.

Figure 4.2—Global GPS Market Projections

The market shares held by military, aviation, and marine applications are expected to continue to shrink, as shown in Figure 4.3. These market segments were the first users of GPS and the rationale for constructing the system. They will likely continue to contribute to GPS policy as a result of public safety and national security interests. Thus, the value of military, marine, and aviation GPS applications will depend more on how they serve public interests than the size of their sales alone.

Hardware costs in vehicle navigation applications have declined an average of 30 percent per year in line with the competitive pressures seen in other areas of consumer electronics.[17] GPS unit prices of $700 may be tempting to private pilots and boaters, but they have not been attractive to U.S. car buyers. Lincoln-Continental cars for 1996 will offer GPS navigation systems as an option for $350–$500. This represents entry into the upper end of the U.S. car market, and a mass-market price point may be 18–24 months away.[18] While prices of consumer GPS products are falling, professional and commercial GPS

---

[17]"Trimble Discusses GPS Markets, Applications at the FCC," *Global Positioning and Navigation News,* May 30, 1995, via NewsPage on the World Wide Web at http://www.newspage.com/ NEWSPAGE/newspagehome.html

[18]Interview with David Atkinson, April 25, 1995.

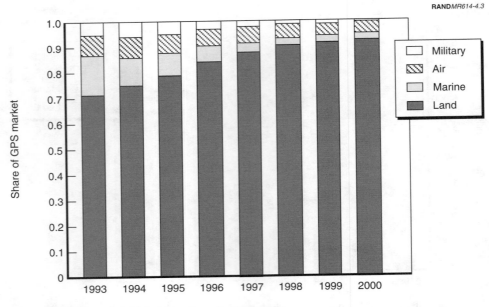

RAND*MR614-4.3*

SOURCE: U.S. GPS Industry Council, March 1995.

Figure 4.3—Global GPS Market Share Projections by Operating Regime

equipment at the upper end of the market have maintained higher price levels with increasing contributions from embedded software. That is, as the profit margins for hardware decline, some GPS firms are relying on software to provide added value to their products.[19] In established markets such as surveying, systems may cost $30,000 rather than the $300 that can now be paid for GPS consumer units.[20]

Figure 4.4 is a graphical plot of the USGIC sales projections for each of the market segments making up the category of land applications. Notably, sales in the most price sensitive categories—car navigation and consumer/cellular—are expected to grow most rapidly after 1997. There are significant product sales in these categories now, but it is expected that continuing declines in hardware

---

[19]A primary example is new software that enables real-time kinematic survey, that is, the ability to take survey points on the move and thus cover a site more rapidly.

[20]"Survey Continues to Be a Strong GPS Market," *Global Positioning and Navigation News*, May 2, 1995, via NewsPage on the World Wide Web at http://www.newspage.com/NEWSPAGE/ newspagehome.html

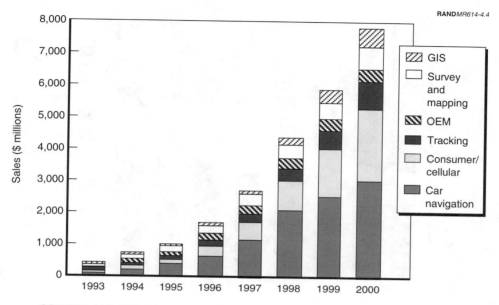

SOURCE: U.S. GPS Industry Council, March 1995.

Figure 4.4—Global GPS Land Use Sales Projections

costs will require another two years to reach price points for the start of mass-market sales. Figure 4.5 shows the same sales data for land applications in terms of market share. GIS and tracking applications are expected to retain a roughly constant share of a growing market. Survey and mapping uses, as well as OEM sales, are expected to account for about 10 percent of the land market in the year 2000, although they make up almost 50 percent now. Assuming expected price points are met, the USGIC is projecting that the strongest market share growth will occur in car navigation and consumer/cellular applications. The car navigation market share is shown as peaking in 1998—presumably a year after prices decline enough to spark mass-market sales—then declining slightly in the face of continued consumer/cellular growth.

GPS has a tendency to grow in waves as different markets adopt the technology. In the United States, GPS equipment sales were at first predominately military, moving into the surveying market as the GPS constellation grew. With the completion of the GPS constellation and continuing decline in hardware costs, the most rapidly growing segments of GPS are expected to be mass consumer markets in which GPS adds functionality to cars, computers, and mobile communi-

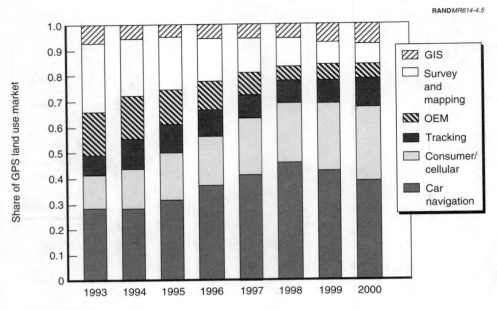

RAND*MR614-4.5*

SOURCE: U.S. GPS Industry Council, March 1995.

Figure 4.5—Global GPS Land Use Market Share Projections

cations. At the same time, competitive pressure on hardware prices will create incentives for GPS firms to add value through software and service niches in their existing markets (e.g., survey, mapping, and geographic information systems). In some respects, GPS is likely to become an "add-on" capability like modems or sound cards for personal computers. Consumers may be able to do without GPS in their personal applications, but they will buy GPS equipment if the price is right and the technology does not require much training to use. In other respects, GPS will become increasingly embedded in the functioning of international telecommunications and transportation networks, as well as in the U.S. armed forces, so that losing access to GPS will be considered intolerable.

Japanese Industry Survey

The Japan GPS Council (JGC) is the Japanese counterpart to the U.S. GPS Industry Council. It was established in 1992 by eight GPS receiver manufacturers, application suppliers, and users: ASCII, Central Japan Railway, Nippon Motorola, Mitsui & Co., Pioneer Electronic, Sharp, Sony, and Toyota Motor. By the end of the year, the council had 72 corporate members and 15 supporting parties, such as nonprofit corporations and other technical associations. In addition to private firms, the JGC is sponsored by the Ministry of Posts and Telecommunications (MPT) and the Japan Police Agency.[21]

In 1994, the JGC cooperated with the Electronics Industry Association of Japan in conducting a survey of 23 GPS-related manufacturers, including OEMs (as in the case of the USGIC survey) and firms that include GPS in products such as automobiles.[22] The survey covered the amounts and values of GPS shipments in several market segments. In 1993, Japanese sales were estimated to be ¥24 billion (about $240 million), about half the size of comparable U.S. sales. The survey also projected a ¥160 billion receiver market in 1995, growing to ¥360 billion (about $3.6 billion) in the year 2000. In comparison to overall Japanese electronic equipment sales of ¥21 trillion in 1993, GPS is a tiny market, but one that is growing much more rapidly than the electronics market as a whole.[23]

Figure 4.6 is a summary graph of the Japanese survey projection of sales by Japan-based GPS firms. The Japanese survey defines GPS product lines in a slightly different manner than the USGIC survey. Military and OEM segments are not separately identified. The relatively small amount of GIS applications are included in the geodetic/surveying market, and vehicle lines are divided into business and leisure applications (e.g., commercial fishing and recreational boating) rather than marine and aviation markets. Car navigation is the largest market, accounting for some 70 percent of the total GPS market, and thus is shown separately. The "other" category consists of sales to academic institutions and aeronautical navigation (the latter is a separate category in the U.S. survey). These differences appear to arise from differences in the historical development of the different markets and assumptions about the nature of GPS technology.

In the United States, military equipment sales were an important source of initial GPS ground equipment revenues, followed by the adoption of GPS in the survey and mapping market and the idea that GPS technology not only sold hardware, but improved productivity as well. In Japan, GPS has been traditionally thought of as another form of consumer electronics in which low-cost,

---

[21]"Launching of the JGPSC," *News Release of the Japan GPS Council*, 3-24-11 Yushima, Bunkyo-ku, Tokyo, 113 Japan, May 5, 1993.

[22]The firms were Icom, Alpine, Kenwood, Sanyo Electric, Car Electronics, Sony, Taiyo Musen, Trimble Japan, NEC, Nihon Denso, Nihon Musen, Pioneer, Fujitsu Ten, Furuno Denki, Matsushita, Mitsubishi Electric, Yokokawa Navitec, Clarion, Topcon, Miigata Tsushinki, NEC Home Electronics, Leica Japan, and Maspro Denko. *Report on the Japan GPS Market* (in Japanese), Electronics Industry Association of Japan, June 3, 1994, p. 17.

[23]"Japanese GPS Receiver Market: $240 Million and Climbing Fast," *GPS World Newsletter*, December 29, 1994, p. 1.

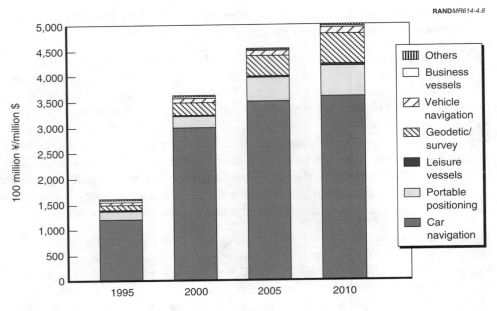

SOURCE: Japan GPS Council Survey, 1994.

Figure 4.6—Projected GPS Sales in Japan

high-quality mass manufacturing is the key to winning market share and commercial leadership. Thus, although Japanese firms are aware of the benefits of GPS to transportation networks and surveying, they have tended to concentrate on promising mass markets such as automobiles and portable GPS receivers for hikers and fishermen. The Japanese construction industry is only starting to shift from older triangular net survey systems to GPS-based survey systems, a process the United States started over ten years ago.[24] In the last year, some Japanese government and industry leaders have become increasingly interested in the information highway and in using GPS to build competitive fixed and mobile telecommunication networks."[25]

The U.S. and Japanese industry surveys were similar in that both concentrated on manufacturers' perceptions of achievable price points over time and likely unit volume sales. They differed on the expected areas of growth, with Japan focusing on car navigation and the United States looking at both car navigation

---

[24]Interview with Kazuo Inaba, Head of Survey Guidance Division, Planning Department, Geographical Survey Institute, Ministry of Construction in Tokyo, Japan, October 21, 1994.

[25]Interview with Akio Motai, Director-General of the Radio Department, Telecommunications Bureau, Ministry of Posts and Telecommunications, Tokyo, Japan, October 24, 1994.

and embedded uses of GPS in information applications such as mobile communications and computing. They also differed in their expectation of achievable prices, with the U.S. firms projecting more-rapid price declines. Table 4.2 compares expected prices in the year 2000 derived from the U.S. and Japanese surveys. The U.S. firms expect to reach price levels two to five times below those of their Japanese counterparts. In the surveying market, where the United States has long experience and a competitive advantage in high-end, software-intensive systems, expected sales prices differ by (are lower than) as much as a factor of 12 from those in Japan.

It may be tempting for U.S. firms and policymakers to interpret the Japanese prices as a reason either to be complacent or to fear a new round of disputes in high-technology trade. In past U.S.-Japanese trade disputes, high domestic prices have been used to allegedly support lower overseas prices (i.e., "dumping"). However, direct comparisons of average sale prices can be misleading for a variety of reasons, such as differing definitions of market segments, the degree of competition expected in the market addressed, and exchange rate fluctuations. The U.S. numbers, for example, are expected average sale prices in the global market and presumably include Japanese competition. The Japanese numbers represent sale prices in Japan that may not include an expectation of U.S. competition in the home market. Domestic Japanese GPS prices can also be higher for fundamental economic and technical reasons, as in the surveying and tracking markets where the United States maintains

Table 4.2

Estimated Average Sale Price of U.S. and Japanese GPS Products in the Year 2000 (dollars)

Product	U.S.	Japan	Ratio
Car navigation	600	1500	3
Consumer cellular	250	400	2
Tracking	500	2385	5
OEM	50	na	
Survey/map	5000	60,000	12
GIS	1500	na	
Aviation	5000	na	
Marine	800	2500	3
Military	1200	na	

SOURCES: U.S. GPS Industry Council and Japan GPS Industry Council.
NOTE: na = not available.

technical and pricing leadership. In the case of car navigation and consumer products, the differences in projected average sale prices are lower, possibly reflecting independent agreement on the pace of manufacturing technology and consumer price points.

Based on our interviews with U.S. and Japanese industry and government officials, we believe trade tensions are low to non-existent, in spite of aggressive commercial competition in GPS equipment. There have even been several examples of cooperation between U.S. and Japanese firms in terms of partnerships and joint ventures.[26] Domestic Japanese trade barriers are a common concern for many firms exporting to Japan, but such barriers do not seem to be a major issue for U.S. GPS firms.

Although the wide differences in average sale price projections may be an artifact of the studies, they highlight the question of whether U.S. firms can be competitive in high-volume electronics manufacturing. If U.S. firms are not able to meet or beat foreign manufacturers (particularly the Japanese), then they will need to shift manufacturing overseas while attempting to retain control of the underlying technology (e.g., software and chip integration) and value-added services. U.S. firms have largely lost the ability to compete in high-volume, low-cost consumer electronics, and a recent assessment of U.S. electronics manufacturing suggests that this may be a competitive handicap for the United States in emerging markets.[27] A panel of industry experts working for The Japanese Technology Evaluation Center concluded that Japan leads in electronic equipment production and controls technology, materials technology (e.g. ceramics and epoxies), process technology, component technologies (e.g., packaging, batteries, and displays), and consumer markets, while the United States leads in industrial markets (e.g., communication networks), software, and microprocessors.[28] The significance of this for competition in GPS markets is that emerging GPS applications exemplify fusion of integrated circuits, electronic packages, and advanced displays as GPS combines with high-volume consumer products—all areas where the United States is weak. While U.S. competitiveness in electronics is beyond the scope of this study, policymakers must understand that the competitiveness of GPS is tied to the competitiveness of U.S. firms in other industries as well. The next section briefly addresses factors affecting car navigation markets, which are expected to see fierce competition in the near future.

---

[26]One U.S. firm licensed GPS technology for the Japanese domestic car market in return for Japanese assistance in improving the quality of its manufacturing production line. Another firm is exporting large numbers of GPS receivers to a group of Japanese car manufacturers.

[27]"Study Faults U.S. Daring in High-Volume Products," *New Technology Week*, May 30, 1995, p. 1.

[28]*Electronic Manufacturing and Packaging in Japan*, Japanese Technology Evaluation Center, ISBN 1-883712-37-8, National Technical Information Service, Washington, D.C., 1995.

Car Navigation Competition

Car navigation units typically consist of a GPS receiver and antenna in combination with a CD-ROM player and a display screen. The CD-ROM accesses digital maps and databases and displays map scenes to the driver. The GPS receiver then calculates the position of the car and places a highlighted point on the map display. The driver can locate potential destinations from an onboard database while seeing his own position. According to the Japanese industry survey, unit sales of GPS receivers for automobiles tripled in one year from 53,000 (1992) to 159,000 (1993), and 1994 sales were expected to reach 300,000 units.[29] More-recent estimates are that 35,000 GPS units per month are being installed in Japanese cars.[30] These sales are predominately aftermarket, when car owners add accessories from various suppliers.

Given the strong U.S. and Japanese projections for the car navigation market, Japanese domestic market experience would seem to make the Japanese formidable competitors and raises the question of why they are not more visible in the U.S. market today. Our interviews indicate that the lack of Japanese penetration of the U.S. automobile navigation market arises from the different market conditions in the two countries. Except for the largest boulevards, roads in Japan rarely have names—even in Tokyo, and postal numbers are not sequential. Even for taxi drivers and professional truck drivers, finding an unknown address is a complex affair with the added challenge of congested urban traffic. Car owners in Japan tend to add expensive accessories such as high-quality stereos and TV sets to their cars and are less price sensitive than their U.S. counterparts. Thus, when GPS car navigation equipment first became available, it was adopted quickly by many car owners and sales have strengthened with declining prices. The early adoption process has been stimulated by the existence of digital maps at a scale of 1:50,000 for all roads and at a scale of 1:25,000 for 50 percent of all roads (usually near major cities).[31]

The U.S. automobile market and driving environment are very different from those of Japan, and Japanese car navigation units are fewer. The United States is a larger country, and computerized map databases, including local streets, are not available except for a few cities and the State of California.[32] Road layouts and postal numbering are more logical and addresses are relatively easy to find with current paper maps. U.S. professional and nonprofessional drivers

---

[29]*GPS World Newsletter*, op. cit.

[30]"Trimble Discusses GPS Markets, Applications at the FCC," *Global Positioning and Navigation News*, May 30, 1995, via NewsPage on the World Wide Web at http://www.newspage.com/NEWSPAGE/newspagehome.html

[31]Interview with Kazuo Inaba, October 21, 1994.

[32]"Car Navigation Expected to Spark GPS Growth," *Space News*, March 13–19, 1995.

have not been receptive to navigating based on the "pattern recognition" typical of Japanese systems but prefer getting specific routing information to a desired destination.[33] Car navigation units now being tested in the United States provide only specific directions, such as "turn left" or "destination ahead." Most important, U.S. car buyers are more price sensitive, and the cost of car navigation units has only recently fallen to a point where luxury car owners are taking an interest in GPS.

With approximately 100 million private vehicles in the United States alone, there is potential for substantial sales of GPS receivers even if the market for new vehicles were to be saturated.[34] Penetration of the U.S. market will depend on competitively priced, high-quality, mass-market hardware; easy-to-use software; and widely available digital maps. The hardware challenge is not just for GPS, but for other technologies, such as low-cost inertial guidance, dead-reckoning instrumentation, and radio communications that may be combined in a single car-navigation system. As noted above, the United States is generally weak in high-volume electronics manufacturing and must be technically innovative and must price aggressively to meet foreign competition.

GPS TECHNOLOGY PATENTS AND INTERNATIONAL COMPETITION

The GPS technology of most interest to commercial markets is ground equipment, the most competitive area. Like other electronic products, GPS ground equipment has been steadily declining in size and price. Personal GPS receivers used in the Persian Gulf War were the size of a medium-sized hardcover book. Four years later, personal GPS receivers are the size of pocket calculators and have greater capabilities—they can track more satellites, store more waypoints, acquire GPS satellites faster, etc. As more functions are compressed onto single integrated circuit boards, the largest and heaviest items for a GPS receiver are turning out to be the antenna, power supply, and input/output devices like keyboards and displays, as is the case for most other modern electronic products.

The pace of innovation in GPS receiver technology continues to be rapid. Product life-cycles of 12–18 months are considered typical, compared with the years or even decades associated with military and space equipment. The rate of GPS technical innovation is widely believed by industry to be most rapid in the United States, followed by Japan with Europe a distant third. This seems to

---

[33]Interview with Robert Denaro, Director, Position and Navigation Systems, Motorola, Northbrook, IL, September 29, 1994.

[34]U.S. Department of Commerce/International Trade Administration, *U.S. Industrial Outlook 1994*, U.S. Government Printing Office, Washington, D.C., January 1994, p. 35-2.

have less to do with knowledge of GPS per se and more to do with the relative strengths of domestic electronics and software industries as well as knowledge of GPS markets. To gain a more analytical understanding of the state of GPS technology competition than could be provided by interviews alone, Mogee Research and Analysis Associates, under a subcontract to RAND,[35] provided an international patent analysis of GPS technology.

Patent analysis is not a perfect measure of technical competitiveness; for example, it does not capture innovations that are kept as trade secrets, and differing international standards for filing patents make direct comparisons tricky for the nonspecialist. Nevertheless, patent analysis is increasingly used as an objective measure and a means of testing anecdotal perceptions of technical competition. According to legal counsel for U.S. GPS manufacturers, this is the first time a comprehensive international patent analyses has been done for GPS. This section is largely drawn from that report.

An electronic search of the Derwent World Patents Index resulted in 763 GPS-related patent families for analysis. (A "family" is a collection of related patents and published patent applications.) Of these, 336 (44 percent) were international families. GPS technology has experienced a rapid growth in international patent families since 1988, as shown in Figure 4.7. Japan is showing the highest level of technical activity, followed by the United States. Germany, Great Britain, and France have much lower levels of activity, and other countries (e.g., Australia, Israel) have few families. The five leading countries patent heavily in each others' markets. More than three-quarters (78 percent) of U.S.-origin international patent families have patent documents in Germany and Great Britain. The United States found France to be the next most attractive market (70 percent), followed by Italy (53 percent), Sweden (45 percent), Canada (43 percent), the Netherlands (42 percent), Australia (41 percent), and Japan (33 percent).

The United States began filing patents earlier than Japan, but the Japanese overtook the United States in cumulative families by 1993. The Japanese lead should be treated carefully, however, because its domestic patent systems and commercial culture give rise to unusually high levels of domestic patenting, even for "inventions" that would be considered trivial or obvious elsewhere. Nonetheless, although the Japanese have increased their level of international patenting quickly and have more international patent families than the United States, U.S. firms continue to hold more foreign patents than the Japanese. The

---

[35] *Global Positioning Systems Technology: An International Patent Trend Analysis,* Mogee Research & Analysis Associates, Great Falls, VA, April 6, 1995.

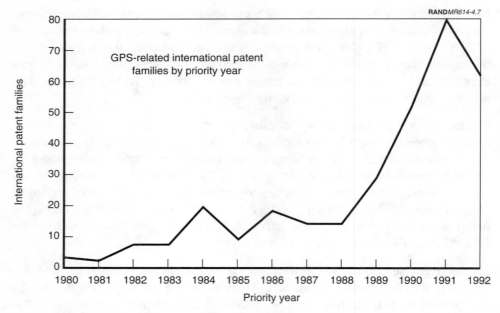

SOURCE: Mogee Associates, Derwent World Patents Index.

Figure 4.7—Recent Growth in International GPS Patent Families

GPS patent "trade" between the United States and Japan flows heavily toward the United States. Although the United States files only 33 percent of its international families in Japan, Japan files 65 percent of its international families in the United States. Even at this level, the United States has been more successful than other major countries in protecting its GPS inventions in the Japanese market.

The United States continues to maintain a substantial lead in its share of foreign patents. The share of foreign patents is significant for what it indicates not only about the level of technical activity, but also about the breadth with which patent applications have been filed around the world, thus indicating competitive technical position as well. The U.S. position shows a broader breadth of protection for its GPS inventions worldwide, which should be a competitive advantage in international markets.

The WPI records include International Patent Classifications (IPCs), a technology classification assigned by national patent examiners. More than one IPC may appear on a record. An examination of the IPCs on GPS patents can provide a broad picture of the particular aspects of GPS technology that are of international interest. The most frequently occurring IPCs are in radionavigation, radio transmission systems (including satellite communication systems), navigational instruments, digital data processing equipment, and aerials (as in antennas).

It should be noted that the rise in U.S. patents began about the same time as government R&D spending for GPS user equipment began a long-term decline (see Appendix B). We cannot say whether the decline in government R&D spending "caused" the rise in commercial patents or was the result of a strong commercial industry available to conduct R&D that the government could no longer afford. Nonetheless, the U.S. commercial technology position as measured by patents does not appear to depend on continued government investment in user equipment R&D.

Table 4.3 ranks companies by the number of international GPS patent families they hold. Inventions covered by these patents presumably have more commercial value than single-country patent families and are intended for international exploitation. Of the top 11 companies—those with 2 percent or more of all international families—four are Japanese, six are in the United States, and one is French. While Japan has conducted R&D and has exploited GPS technology internationally, it has not protected its GPS inventions as broadly as has the United States. In addition, the relative breadth with which U.S. GPS inventions are protected around the world should provide a competitive advantage to U.S. companies.

Number counts could not indicate the value of any particular patent or patent family, how fundamental the patents are, or how difficult they might be to

Table 4.3

Top Assignees of International GPS Patent Families

Company	International Families	Percent
Pioneer Electronic Corp.	53	15.8
Motorola Inc.	19	5.7
Mitsubishi Denki KK	12	3.6
Caterpillar Inc.	10	3.0
Trimble Navigation Ltd.	10	3.0
Hughes Aircraft Co.	8	2.4
ITT Corp.	7	2.1
Magnavox Co.[a]	7	2.1
Nissan Motor KK	7	2.1
Sony Corp.	7	2.1
Thomson CSF	7	2.1

SOURCE: Mogee Research & Analysis Associates.

[a]GPS business acquired by the Swiss firm of Leica in February 1994.

design around. They did illustrate the intense international competition in GPS technology and which firms and countries are the major players. Industry interviews gave the impression that the nature of GPS is changing, from very basic, broad patents to narrow applications such as vehicle tracking and aircraft collision avoidance. One firm told us that they knew of about 200 patents on file involving GPS and cellular communication and that some of the most "interesting" competition was coming from non-GPS companies that were finding innovative GPS uses.[36] The significance of changes in who develops new GPS technology is hard to assess at present, but it is clear that innovations are coming from private firms, not governments. In addition, innovations are coming from firms that are close to the end-users (e.g., Caterpillar). GPS manufacturing firms are likely to seek strategic partnerships with firms that are leaders in particular markets they wish to enter (e.g., telecommunication, automobiles) to gain technical advantages as well as distribution channels and market intelligence.

POTENTIAL CHANGES TO CIVIL GPS SERVICES

Civil and commercial communities are interested in potential changes in the GPS signal they receive as well as better ways of manipulating and using that signal. The widespread use of GPS has stimulated an increasingly competitive environment for receiver technology over the past decade. As the GPS constellation has matured, there has been interest in making changes to the GPS satellites themselves and how they are controlled in order to benefit various user communities. At the same time, there has been resistance to change in view of the increasingly large installed base of GPS receivers. This section discusses sources of GPS signal errors and two commonly discussed changes—turning selective availability (SA) to zero and providing greater nonmilitary access to the Precise Positioning Service.

The National Research Council has extensively reviewed potential technical improvements and enhancements for GPS.[37] From various published sources, they summarized the types and magnitudes of positioning errors that have been observed by GPS receivers in calculating a four-satellite position solution (i.e., four GPS satellites acquired by the receiver). These errors for the Standard Positioning Service (SPS), with and without SA, and the Precise Positioning Service (PPS) are shown in Table 4.4. The total user equivalent range error (UERE) is calculated as the square root of the sum of the squares of all the range

---

[36] Interview with James Janky, Trimble Navigation, January 27, 1995.

[37] National Research Council, Committee on the Future of the Global Positioning System, *The Global Positioning System: A Shared National Asset*, National Academy Press, Washington, D.C., 1995.

Table 4.4

Observed GPS Positioning Errors with Typical Receivers

Error Source	Range Error Magnitude (meters, 1 σ)		
	SPS (SA on)	SPS (SA off)	PPS
Selective availability	24.0	0.0	0.0
Atmospheric error			
Ionospheric	7.0	7.0	0.01
Tropospheric	0.7	0.7	0.7
Clock and ephemeris error	3.6	3.6	3.6
Receiver noise	1.5	1.5	0.6
Multipath	1.2	1.2	1.8
Total user equivalent range error	25.3	8.1	4.1
Typical horizontal dilution of precision	2.0	2.0	2.0
Total horizontal accuracy (2 σ)	101.2	32.5	16.4

SOURCE: National Research Council, pp. 68, 80.

errors. The 2 drms (distance root mean squared) horizontal positioning error is equal to two times the UERE times the horizontal dilution of precision (HDOP).

Positioning results depend on the geometric arrangement of the satellites, atmospheric conditions, specific receiver characteristics, and other factors. Atmospheric error caused by delays in the GPS satellite signal as it passes through the atmosphere can be largely removed by comparing the time of arrival of parallel signals arriving on different frequencies and by software modeling.[38] Clock errors occur in the atomic clocks on each GPS satellite and ephemeris errors result from errors in the orbital positions reported for the satellites. Multipath errors occur when satellite signals reflect off buildings and bodies of water and interfere at the receiver antenna, a particular problem for GPS reception in urban areas. The total observed error, however, can be different from performance specifications and is often better. For example, the specified horizontal accuracy for the PPS at 2 drms is 21 meters; the National Research Council study shows observed values of about 16 meters.[39] Under favorable conditions, the level of SPS without SA has been observed to approach the PPS-design level.[40]

Suggestions on improving the signal available to civil and commercial users typically start with a listing of the various sources of GPS errors and ideas for how to reduce them. For example, most civil receivers access only one GPS fre-

---

[38]A second L-band frequency to actively correct for atmospheric propagation errors enhances the accuracy of PPS.

[39]ARINC Research Corporation, *GPS Navstar User's Overview,* Fifth Edition, March 1991, p. 59.

[40]Overlook Technologies Inc., "Assessment of Recent SPS Performance Transients," briefing to the Office of the Assistant Secretary of Defense (C3I), October 15, 1994.

quency (the L1 signal), whereas military receivers are dual-frequency (using L1 and L2 signals) to help correct for atmospheric errors. Some civil receivers track the L2 carrier frequency to partially correct for atmospheric errors. A common suggestion is to add a second frequency, called an L4 signal, for civil users.[41] Clock and ephemeris errors can be reduced by improvements in the atomic clocks themselves as well as more frequent updating of satellite orbital positions from GPS ground-control stations. The received signal-to-noise ratio can be increased by improvements in receiver design and by boosting the transmitted power of GPS signals.

These kinds of technical fixes represent marginal improvements, however, and changes to the civil GPS signal almost inevitably return to changing the definition of what the civil signal should be. The most common proposal is to remove selective availability and the second is to allow for greater civilian PPS access. Since SA is a technical capability built into the GPS architecture, "removal" does not mean taking out hardware, but turning the bias it generates to zero. PPS access means using "P-code capable" GPS receivers and encryption keys. These proposals are discussed below.

Selective Availability and Commercial Markets

The removal of SA has been advocated by many civil and commercial interests and was recommended in a recent joint report on GPS by the National Academy of Public Administration and the National Research Council (NRC).[42] Turning SA off would benefit current GPS-SPS users who gain accuracy, improved availability for any given level of accuracy, and better integrity monitoring. DGPS users would see a reduction in the data rate requirements and bandwidth needs for differential corrections.[43] As stated earlier, GPS users would like greater accuracy if it were costless, and having SA turned to zero appears to be a costless option for civil and commercial users. There are GPS users who need accuracy better than SPS but do not wish to use DGPS techniques for a variety of reasons.[44] They may not want to pay the extra cost of DGPS equipment (typically several hundred dollars), may be unable to establish a fixed reference station, or may be out of range of commercial DGPS service providers. Finally, the removal of SA considerations can improve the operation

---

[41] The so-called L3 frequency is associated with GPS-based nuclear detonation detectors.

[42] Joint Report of the National Academy of Public Administration and the National Research Council, *The Global Positioning System: Charting the Future*, May 1995.

[43] National Research Council, op. cit., pp. 79–82.

[44] Examples include hikers, fishermen, and scientists conducting field work that requires them to roam over large areas.

of GPS augmentations, such as local-area and wide-area differential signals, for those users who need accuracy greater than SPS even with SA turned off.

A market analysis by Booz.Allen & Hamilton (BAH) for the NRC indicated that the North American market for GPS and DGPS equipment would expand dramatically if SA were removed.[45] This study estimated that the cumulative 1994–2004 market for GPS (including receivers, subsystems, DGPS network services, systems integration and software, and data communications) would increase from $42 billion to $64 billion if SA were turned off. In both situations, GPS hardware itself made up 47 percent of the cumulative market, for a total of $19.8 billion with SA on and $30.1 billion with SA off. In comparison, the cumulative 1994–2000 projection by the USGIC for total U.S. GPS product sales (including North America), which assumed no change in SA policy, was $27 billion. If one assumes an average annual growth rate of 25 percent for the years 2001–2003, half the rate of the preceding eight years, the cumulative total would be $67.3 billion.

The BAH and U.S. GPS Industry Council projections are difficult to compare because of

- different market focus (global versus regional)
- different definitions of the market segments
- different time periods
- different methodologies.

However, the BAH projection of approximately $1.5 billion in North American GPS product sales in the year 2000 could be consistent with the USGIC projection of $8.47 billion for global U.S. GPS sales that year depending on export sales assumptions. Similarly, the BAH projection of approximately $2 billion in GPS product sales if SA were turned to zero could also be consistent. Both projections agree that commercial GPS goods and services are experiencing rapid growth and will be multibillion dollar industries in the near future.

There is essentially no way to say one projection is right and the other wrong. The USGIC might be expected to have a bias toward inflating its projections of future growth, although that does not appear to be the case. The BAH projections predict a large increase in commercial GPS growth as a result of turning SA to zero. The GPS firms that might be expected to support turning SA to zero

---

[45]Michael Dyment, Booz.Allen & Hamilton, *North American GPS Markets: Analysis of SA and other Policy Alternatives*, Final Report to the National Academy of Sciences, Committee on the Future of the Global Positioning System, May 1, 1995.

have in fact taken a more ambivalent position, noting the national security interest in keeping SA and noting a slight advantage to commercial firms now providing DGPS services and equipment in doing so. With SA on, potential customers who need better than 100-m horizontal accuracy have an incentive to purchase DGPS equipment and services. The source of the different perceptions of the result of SA arise from differing economic assumptions about the future behavior of the GPS market, as shown in the simplified demand curves of Figure 4.8.

In Case 1, the current demand for GPS products is shown as the line labeled "Today." As the price for GPS products declines, the demand for them becomes greater. If SA is turned off, it is assumed that the demand curve will shift well to the right, as shown for the line labeled "SA off." Thus, with no change in the price level, there will be more demand for GPS products because of the greater accuracy available. In Case 2, the same demand curve for "Today" is shown. As the GPS market evolves, this case assumes that the market will become both more dependent on GPS and more price sensitive (i.e., increasing the price elasticity of demand), even with SA remaining on. As a result, the demand curve will shift to the right and become more shallow, representing a GPS market that is both more consumer-driven (e.g., GPS receivers in personal communication devices) and more infrastructure-driven (e.g., GPS receivers in telecommunication networks, highways, ports, and construction projects). Case 1 seems to be the view of the BAH assessment, whereas Case 2 seems to be the view of the USGIC members.

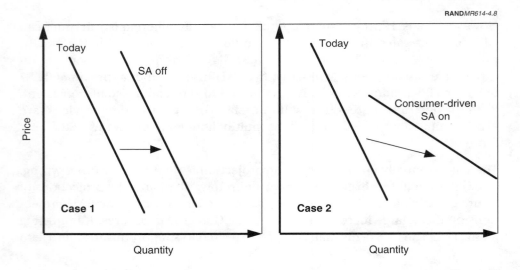

Figure 4.8 —Alternative GPS Demand Levels

The demand curves of Figure 4.8 could be estimated for each GPS market segment of interest and then aggregated. Different markets will naturally have different sensitivities to price and accuracy, as well as other factors. The USGIC firms seem to believe, as apparently do the members of the Japan GPS Council, that hitting various price points in individual markets is more important to their growth than SA. Again, if turning SA off were costless, they likely would not object, but other competitive factors appear dominant in their minds. The situation might be different if there was a competitive alternative to GPS that offered a free signal at better accuracy, but no such competitor has yet emerged. The Russian GLONASS has some acceptance as a supplement, but it is not seen as an alternative to GPS for civil and commercial users.

The key uncertainty in the economic value of turning SA to zero is whether the elasticity of demand for GPS is of greater or lesser significance than the position of the demand curve. To put it more bluntly, does the future of commercial GPS depend more on low prices or on greater accuracy? The BAH assessment seems to be driven by estimates of market penetration rates and market share rather than by pricing. Thus, it is understandable that a costless change would increase acceptance of GPS and lead to greater sales over time. The firms selling in the GPS market today seem to believe the answer is low prices, assuming all other factors remain equal (e.g., stable government policy, no real alternative to GPS itself). While there are often political arguments for using government decisions to economically benefit one group or another, in the case of SA it is not clear that there is a compelling national economic justification to do so. Leaving SA on will not create obvious economic harm and turning it to zero may not create dramatic economic benefits beyond the current path of GPS development.

Civil Access to the Precise Positioning Service

Another option for users wanting accuracy better than GPS-SPS is to gain access to the Precise Positioning Service through GPS receivers that can access the GPS signal's P-code in addition to the C/A code. The C/A (coarse/acquisition) code on the L1 frequency repeats every millisecond, allowing for rapid acquisition by the GPS receiver. In contrast, the P (precision) code on both the L1 and L2 frequencies repeats only every seven days, so that knowledge of the phase of the P-code is needed to acquire the signal. This information can be gotten from a hand-over-word (HOW) contained in the NAV (navigation) message. The NAV message contains the GPS system time of transmission, the HOW, ephemeris data, clock data for the particular satellite signal being acquired, almanac (health) data for the remaining satellites in the constellation, coefficients for calculating UTC (Universal Time Coordinated), and the ionospheric delay model for C/A-code users. This message is superimposed on both the C/A-code and P-code signals and can be captured within 30 seconds of signal acquisition.[46] P-code receivers use the HOW and the acquired C/A-code signal to minimize the search requirements for acquiring the P-code. If the C/A code is being jammed, a P-code receiver can attempt to bypass the C/A acquisition step and directly acquire the P-code, but this is difficult unless an external synchronized atomic clock is available to provide the exact GPS time.

Access to PPS is technically controlled in two ways. The first is through SA, which degrades the accuracy available to SPS users, and the second is through an anti-spoofing (AS) feature. AS can be invoked at random times to prevent hostile imitation (spoofing) of PPS signals. AS has the effect of encrypting the P-code, which is then called the Y-code, without affecting the C/A-code. Authorized users thus have an additional level of assurance that the signals they are receiving are genuine. Encryption keys provided to authorized users allow them to remove the effects of SA and AS. PPS receivers can use either the P(Y) code, the C/A code, or both. As a result of the technical differences between using the C/A- and P-code, military GPS receivers have three major differences over civil GPS receivers: (1) a faster corrector (10 MHz versus 1 MHz) to search for and acquire the P-code, (2) security-approved electronic chips and cables to handle Y-code information, and (3) cryptographic keys to access the Y-code. The addition of controlled cryptographic keys is what makes the military GPS receiver itself a controlled item and subject to special protection.

Access to PPS is administratively controlled by the U.S. Department of Defense; it is typically limited to such users as U.S. and allied military forces. PPS access requires the use of security devices that are specifically authorized and are predominately employed by allied military forces, as shown in Figure 4.9. Most of these devices have been sent to the allied NATO forces in Europe. An increasing number of civil government agencies, including the U.S. Coast Guard, the U.S. Forestry Service, NASA, and the National Science Foundation, have applied for and received PPS access in support of their missions. Figure 4.10 shows a current count and projection of GPS receivers bought by civil U.S. government agencies. Changes to SA are "top-down" in that they affect all GPS receivers without regard to user. In contrast, access to PPS is "bottom-up" in that access to better accuracies is limited to specific P-code-capable receivers that are specifically authorized and have associated agreements for their protection.

---

[46]Bill Clark, *Aviator's Guide to GPS*, TAB Books, New York, 1994, p. 20.

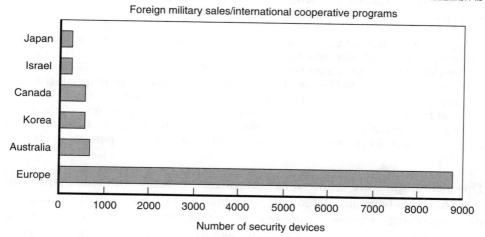

SOURCE: DoD Selected Acquisition Report, DD-COMP 823, December 31, 1993.

Figure 4.9—GPS Security Devices Provided to Allies

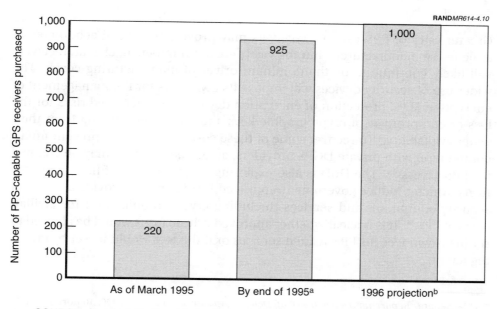

SOURCE: Overlook Systems Technologies, Inc. and the NAVSTAR GPS Joint Program Office.

[a]Figures are estimates.

[b]Current users of PPS GPS include the U.S. Departments of Agriculture, Commerce, Energy, and Interior; NASA; and NSF.

Figure 4.10—GPS-PPS Receivers Bought by U.S. Civil Government Agencies

U.S. policy, as expressed in congressional report language, says that PPS access is to be

> restricted to U.S. Armed Forces, U.S. Federal agencies, and selected allied armed forces and governments. While GPS/PPS has been designed primarily for military radionavigation needs, it will nevertheless be made available on a very selective basis to U.S. and foreign private sector (non-governmental) civic organizations. Access determinations will be made by the Government on a case-by-case evaluation that: (1) access is in the U.S. national interest; (2) there are no other means reasonably available to the civil user to obtain a capability equivalent to that provided by GPS/PPS; and (3) security requirements can be met.[47]

These conditions are followed in current DoD practice and statements, but there have not been any statements more binding by the President or Congress than this report language. In the same report, Congress went on to say that the Department of Defense should not compete with civil interests, such as differential GPS service providers, for accuracies greater than that provided by SPS. DoD was therefore directed to

> take whatever actions are appropriate to prevent the GPS from competing with existing civil systems that provide accuracies greater than the SPS accuracies . . .[48]

Greater sales of PPS-capable receivers may provide beneficial economies of scale to the manufacturers, but the vastly greater numbers of civilian receivers will likely continue to be the dominant driver of manufacturing costs. The wider use of security devices will impose its own costs for the management of encryption keys, protection of encryption devices, and increased risks for the loss or compromise of cryptographic keys and equipment arising from their wider availability. To recover some of these costs, as well as to prevent unfair competition with private DGPS providers, an annual user fee may be charged for PPS access.[49] The DoD is also exploring the possibility of having private firms, which produce government-approved PPS receivers, provide associated security equipment and services (including cryptographic keys) for civilian users of PPS.[50] It is unclear whether approved private firms would be allowed to set their own fees for PPS-related services or if the fees would be set by law or regulation.

---

[47]U.S. Senate, *Report for Department of Defense Appropriation Bill, 1990*, Report 101-132, September 14, 1989, Washington, D.C., p. 332.

[48]Ibid.

[49]Presentation by John Martel, Overlook Technologies, Inc., to the 25th Meeting of the Civil GPS Service Interface Committee (CGSIC), Tysons Corner, VA, March 2, 1995.

[50]Letter from Edgar L. Stephenson, Overlook Technologies, Inc., to F. Michael Swiek, U.S. GPS Industry Council, May 19, 1995.

The significance of current U.S. PPS policy to commercial markets is that while specific firms and organizations may be able to gain improved accuracies through PPS, this is not an applicable approach for mass markets. The central question is to define what is in the "national interest" as posed by Congress in its report language. Civil government agencies are virtually by definition performing public service work in the national interest, and the question of PPS access turns more to protecting the security devices and ensuring that commercial alternatives are not more cost-effective than PPS. The question of national interest is more difficult to answer for private firms such as airports, utilities, and telecommunications.[51] The definition of national interest could be construed so broadly as to become meaningless; that is, if the U.S. government approves PPS access for one firm, on what basis could it say no to another on national interest grounds?

The desire of civil and commercial markets for greater accuracies will likely result in continued political pressures to reduce SA to zero and open access to PPS. Barring changes in national policy, the market response will be a continuing development of technical solutions that provide greater accuracies (such as differential GPS) and other technologies. For example, miniature inertial navigation and communication systems can be combined with GPS receivers to provide better performance than GPS alone.[52] Such combinations can be applied to guide advanced munitions as well as automobiles. In the longer term, interest in SA and PPS may fade as new opportunities and dangers emerge from technical advances in competing and complementary GPS technologies.[53] Today, however, safety-of-life applications such as aircraft and ship navigation require better accuracies than SPS can deliver. The next section addresses U.S. government plans to provide differential GPS services for these and other purposes.

AUGMENTATIONS TO GPS

Various government augmentations to GPS are intended primarily to provide signals for specific applications, such as civil aviation and maritime navigation, but other users may have access to the signals. Such access may create competition for private providers of DGPS services as well as fan debates over the appropriate roles of the public and private sectors in providing precise positioning

---

[51]Al Fisch, "GPS Timing Signals Support Simulcast Synchronization," *Mobile Radio Technology*, May 1995.

[52]Joseph Aein, *Miniature Guidance Technology Based on the Global Positioning System*, RAND, R-4087-DARPA, 1992.

[53]Edward J. Krakiwsky and James F. McLellan, "Making GPS Even Better with Auxiliary Devices," *GPS World*, March 1995.

and timing information. Like GPS itself, unintended usage is expected to create challenges for government policymakers—as will be discussed later.

Augmentations to GPS provide levels of accuracy, availability, and integrity beyond what is normally possible with the SPS (or sometimes the PPS) level of GPS service. The most common augmentation is local-area differential GPS correction, in which one or more base stations provide a common reference point for submeter or even centimeter accuracies. If the user is traveling over long distances, local-area DGPS broadcasts may be impractical. Wide-area distribution of differential correction signals is possible through a network of DGPS systems, as shown in Figure 4.11. A number of reference sites over a given area are connected to a central facility that processes the corrections from each site and sends the information to satellites in orbit above the earth. These communication satellites can then transmit the differential corrections and other information (such as integrity data) for each GPS satellite to users over a large area. The ground network continually monitors the performance of the GPS constellation within view of the users roaming within the service area.

Federal Aviation Administration GPS Augmentation

A prime example of a wide-area differential GPS system is the Wide-Area Augmentation System (WAAS) being planned by the Federal Aviation

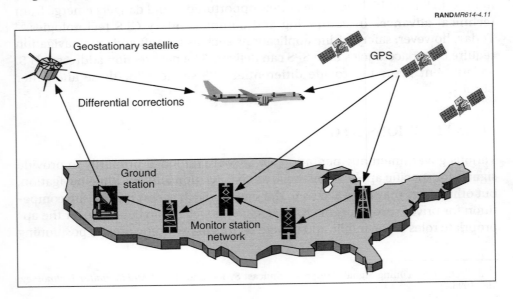

RAND*MR614-4.11*

Figure 4.11—Wide-Area Differential GPS

Administration to serve civil aviation. Whereas use of GPS promises to be much more reliable and less expensive than current air navigation aids, the GPS system as it currently exists cannot meet at least three critical requirements for safety of flight and must have some form of augmentation. These requirements are

- integrity—the ability of a system to provide timely warnings to users or to shut itself down when it should not be used for navigation

- accuracy—the difference between the measured position at any given time and the actual or true position

- availability/reliability—the ability of a system to be used for navigation whenever and wherever it is needed.[54]

The WAAS is intended to fill the "requirements gap" for aviation users who need something more than simple GPS but are not within range of local-area differential systems. The WAAS concept calls for a ground-based communications network of 24 reference stations, two master stations, and two satellite uplink sites as well as "L1-like" signals broadcast from at least three geostationary satellites.[55]

The current GPS system can be used for en route navigation when its integrity can be verified by another source, such as a qualified INS. In addition, GPS integrity can be monitored by modified airborne GPS receivers using Receiver Autonomous Integrity Monitoring (RAIM); this has been certified for en route flight over oceans. RAIM techniques generally rely on redundant measurements from six or more GPS satellites as a means of detecting unreliable satellites and inconsistent position solutions. Accuracy and time-to-alarm integrity requirements for en route oceanic navigation are less stressing than any other phase of flight. RAIM is acceptable in this application but has not been certified for other phases such as approach and landing.[56]

The most demanding phases of flight are approach and landing, particularly when visibility is impaired in Category II and III conditions (Category I denotes good visibility). In such conditions, the WAAS signals may not be adequate to

---

[54]Robert Loh, "Seamless Aviation: FAA's Wide-Area Augmentation System," *GPS World*, April 1995, p. 21.

[55]Federal Aviation Administration, System Operations and Engineering Branch, *Wide-Area Augmentation System Request for Proposal*, DTFA01-94-R-21474, Department of Transportation, Washington, D.C., June 8, 1994.

[56]National Research Council, op. cit., p. 29. Accuracy and time-to-alarm requirements for en route oceanic navigation are 23 km and 30 seconds, respectively. The same requirements for a Category III approach and landing are 0.6–1.2 m (vertical) and 2 seconds, respectively. RAIM alone cannot meet the latter requirements.

land safely, and if GPS were to be used it would be through a local-area augmentation systems (LAAS) based at or near individual airports. Local-area augmentations may be needed in any event to coordinate the movement of aircraft and vehicles on the ground at major airports as well as to prevent runway incursions. An overview of how various GPS augmentations, including WAAS, might support each phase of flight is shown in Figure 4.12.

Interest in and support for WAAS comes from both the FAA and the aviation industry, especially the major airlines.[57] The airlines expect that implemen-

RAND*MR614-4.12*

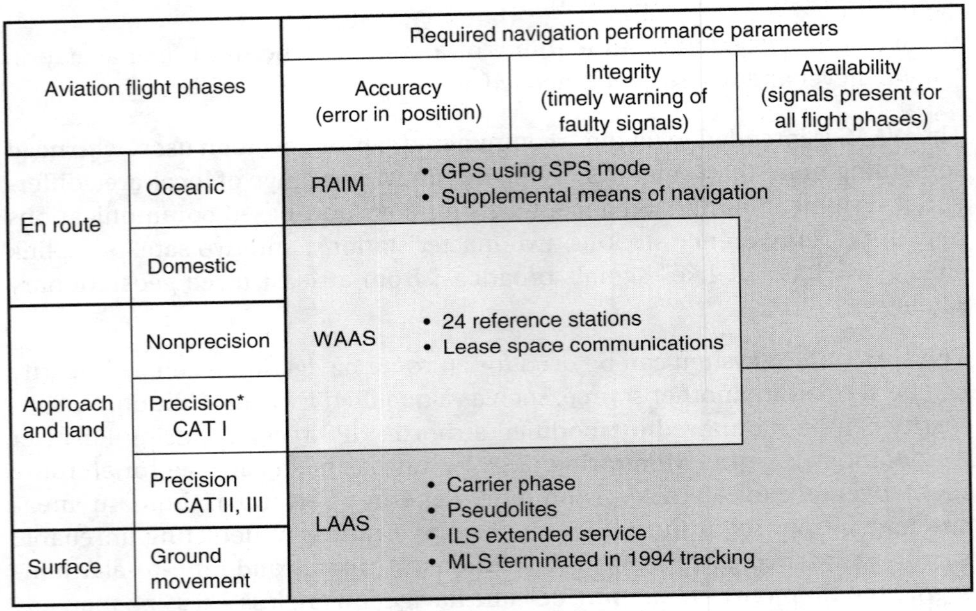

Aviation flight phases		Required navigation performance parameters		
		Accuracy (error in position)	Integrity (timely warning of faulty signals)	Availability (signals present for all flight phases)
En route	Oceanic	RAIM	• GPS using SPS mode • Supplemental means of navigation	
	Domestic			
Approach and land	Nonprecision	WAAS	• 24 reference stations • Lease space communications	
	Precision* CAT I			
	Precision CAT II, III	LAAS	• Carrier phase • Pseudolites • ILS extended service • MLS terminated in 1994 tracking	
Surface	Ground movement			

RAIM = Receiver Autonomous Integrity Monitoring provides GPS signal integrity.

WAAS = Wide Area Augmentation System provides differential corrections and integrity signals to users.

LAAS = Local Area Augmentation System provides high accuracy, integrity, and reliability.

ILS = Instrument Landing System.

*LAAS may be needed to support CAT I approach if WAAS signals are restricted by local terrain.

Figure 4.12—GPS Augmentations to Support Civil Aviation

[57]U.S. General Accounting Office, *National Airspace System: Assessment of FAA's Efforts to Augment the Global Positioning System*, Statement of Kenneth M. Mead before the Subcommittee on Aviation, Committee on Transportation and Infrastructure, U.S. House of Representatives, GAO/T-RCED-95-219, Washington, D.C., June 8, 1995, p. 4.

tation of a qualified satellite-based navigation system will allow more-efficient routing, shorter flight times, fuel savings, and safer all-weather operations. The airline industry continues to be under severe financial and competitive pressures, and infrastructure improvements that promise major cost savings are of great interest. Similarly, the FAA's own budget is under great pressure at a time when it seeks to upgrade and modernize an increasingly outmoded air traffic control system. Implementation of a satellite-based navigation system could allow removal of older navigation aids, and the expectation that WAAS will be available by 1997 has allowed the cancellation of a multibillion-dollar microwave landing system (MLS) program.[58] The United States is a major influence in international aviation, and the technical precedents established by WAAS will likely influence foreign developments. The operational and cost benefits of GPS-based navigation are greatly enhanced when implemented on a global basis. The FAA has been a strong advocate of GPS and its associated augmentation in international fora such as the International Civil Aviation Organization (ICAO). It helped coin the term Global Navigation Satellite System (GNSS) to refer to the idea of a "seamless" worldwide air navigation architecture based on augmentations of satellite signals provided by GPS—and possibly GLONASS as well.[59]

The U.S. Department of Defense and the U.S. Department of Transportation agreed in 1993 that a Wide-Area Augmentation System should be implemented to enhance GPS integrity and availability, but did not come to agreement on the wide-area augmentation of GPS accuracy.[60] The differential corrections provided by WAAS are expected to increase the accuracy available to civil and commercial users from 100 m horizontal (the SPS level) to about 15 m.[61] The DoD continues to be concerned that the unprotected broadcast of WAAS accuracy information at the L1 GPS frequency (1575.42 MHz) will have potential for hostile use of the WAAS accuracy information. As discussed in Chapter Three, highly accurate DGPS signals might be exploited by hostile military forces such as aircraft and cruise missiles. If the United States were to jam WAAS accuracy signals, it would also interfere with normal GPS operations. Since WAAS signals by definition cover wide areas, jamming or shutting off WAAS accuracy signals in one area of military conflict may disrupt distant civilian activities as well.

---

[58]Ibid.

[59]Loh, op. cit., p. 30.

[60]U.S. Department of Transportation and U.S. Department of Defense, *The Global Positioning System: Management and Operation of a Dual-Use System—Report to the Secretaries of Defense and Transportation*, Joint DoD/DoT Task Force, Washington, D.C., December 1993.

[61]"GAO Questions Schedule for GPS Augmentation," *Aviation Week and Space Technology*, June 19, 1995, p. 42.

The prospect of major civilian disruptions may then deter the United States from protecting its forces in the most effective way possible.

Several options have been discussed for balancing the civil/commercial interests in WAAS with national security concerns over the availability of wide-area DGPS information. One idea is to move or offset the WAAS operating frequency away from the L1 frequency. Figure 4.13 shows the relative frequency positions of GPS signals, the potential offset positions, and nearby operating positions for GLONASS and mobile satellite communications. Another idea is to encrypt the WAAS accuracy information so that it is available only to authorized users and presumably can be denied to non-authorized users. Finally, there is the prospect of deleting or deferring the broadcast of WAAS accuracy information entirely while moving ahead with the WAAS integrity and availability augmentations.

The DoD proposed an offset of 10.23 MHz between the L1 and WAAS positions, a sizable separation. The FAA opposed this idea as incompatible with its plans to broadcast the WAAS signal through an INMARSAT III satellite. INMARSAT could not technically accommodate such a large offset before 1999 and counterproposed a 1.023 MHz offset.[62] The DoD did not feel that the counterproposal allowed enough separation to deny the WAAS signal while allowing con-

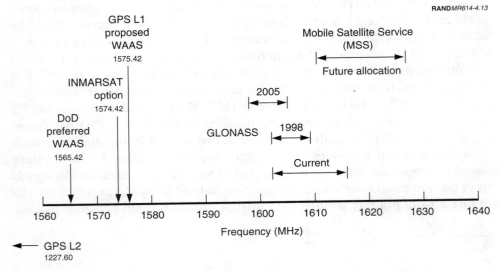

Figure 4.13—Frequency Locations for GPS Augmentations

---

[62]Joe Dorfler, SatNav Program Manager, "WAAS Frequency Offset," Briefing by the Federal Aviation Administration, February 15, 1995.

tinued operation of the L1.[63] The FAA did not embrace the smaller offset either, as it felt that a decision to operate WAAS at a position other than L1 would undercut its goal of a seamless global air navigation system and would not likely be internationally accepted—other countries would fear precisely the denial capability DoD requires.

The encryption option was also opposed by the FAA as costly and unlikely to be internationally accepted. The secure management of cryptographic systems for all international aircraft operating around the world was seen as a formidable challenge. As with hybrid avionics equipment for dissimilar air navigation regimes, the commercial airlines were expected to oppose actions that would increase their equipment costs and decrease hoped-for operational savings from the move to GPS. In addition, current ICAO practices discourage (but do not forbid) encryption of navigation signals as contrary to the goal of enhancing safety for all of civil aviation. Preventing hostile uses of GPS augmentations is not the only use of encryption, however, and this topic is discussed further in a following section.

If compromises on frequency offsets and encryption are not mutually accept-able to the U.S. civil and military communities, there is the final option of not providing WAAS accuracy signals at all. This would certainly be opposed by the FAA and international aviation users because it leaves a gap in the phases of flight that can be serviced by GPS alone or ground-based DGPS networks. The FAA also feels that the small marginal costs (to the FAA) for adding accuracy signals and the economic benefit from the signals make the case for accuracy augmentation compelling. Although the DoD is uncomfortable with wide-area accuracy broadcasts, they recognize that benefits from GPS augmentation would be available to U.S. and allied military forces. The question is how to avoid the exploitation of that capability by hostile forces.

Beyond technical concerns with unprotected WAAS broadcasts at the L1 fre-quency, a key strategic military issue appears to be the entire concept of space-based distribution of DGPS accuracy signals. For example, the DoD raised the idea of modifying the WAAS architecture so that accuracy signals are broadcast from space (in some secure manner) to local or regional ground-based net-works and then openly retransmitted to aircraft. This would allow denial of WAAS accuracy signals in the event of a conflict without requiring aircraft to carry hybrid avionics or decryption keys. The FAA feels that this idea is imprac-

---

[63]Recall that military GPS receivers currently require access to the C/A code at L1 to access the more accurate P-code. Direct P-code-accessible receivers have yet to be developed. Recent techni-cal analyses by the Defense Science Board suggest that it may be technically possible to deny a WAAS signal operating at L1 without interfering with the C/A code. Personal communication to S. Pace, March 29, 1995.

tical and that it would be too difficult and expensive to incorporate such a major change. The FAA also claims that the space-based distribution of WAAS signals to aircraft is cost-effective compared with distributing such signals from a ground networks. While acknowledging the disruption that the DoD idea would cause, we were unable to find a comprehensive cost-effectiveness analysis of space-based versus ground-based DGPS distribution concepts for WAAS.

The dependence of international air navigation on a few satellites is another issue. In some regions, there may be only one geosynchronous satellite providing WAAS signals. Reliability calculations can provide assurances against accidental failure, but they do not account for the risk of hostile action. If space-based WAAS links are lost and selective availability remains on, it is not clear that the nation's air navigation system could function effectively on just GPS and the planned remaining ground systems. On the other hand, if SA were turned to zero, a satisfactory international air navigation system might be built on GPS, a WAAS that provides only integrity and availability augmentations, and ground-based DGPS networks. In addition to the national security costs that WAAS accuracy signals may impose, the rapidly declining cost of GPS equipment (compared with the high cost of space systems) indicates a long-term trend favoring ground-based systems wherever possible. Is preserving SA more important to U.S. security than deterring the spread of space-based distribution of DGPS accuracy information? We will return to this question in Chapter Six.

A detailed systems analysis of alternative WAAS architectures was outside the scope of this study, but the debate over WAAS illustrates the competing civil, commercial, and national security tensions in the discussion over the future of GPS. The WAAS characteristics favored by airlines and the FAA—accurate, non-interruptable, nondiscriminatory, global coverage—are contrary to DoD desires for a service that can be selectively denied without undue political or technical costs. If WAAS accuracy information should be used by forces hostile to the United States or its allies, does the United States have any options short of the use of force to deny the information? As discussed in Chapter Three, if DGPS signals are coming from a neutral country or spacecraft, the United States may not be able to suppress those signals directly and will consequently need other defenses and electronic countermeasures. Resolving these conflicts requires both technical tradeoffs and efforts to shape a future international environment in which many nations have local DGPS networks and a few nations and organizations have their own satellites providing GPS augmentations from space.[64]

---

[64]Examples include the Japanese MTSAT project, the European Geostationary Navigation Overlay Satellite system, and INMARSAT's proposals to provide international navigation services.

WAAS began as a U.S. concept, and U.S. interests will be affected by whether the rest of the world decides to cooperate or compete with U.S. proposals.

Other U.S. Government Augmentations of GPS

The WAAS concept is the most sophisticated GPS augmentation, but it is not the only example of government agencies building GPS-based systems. The Department of Defense, NASA, and the National Science Foundation own and operate permanent DGPS reference stations. NASA cooperates with several other countries to maintain over 50 GPS tracking sites around the world that are used for geodetics and geoscience research.[65] The tracking sites produce highly accurate post-processed GPS orbital data that are available on the Internet within a few days. In addition to the Federal Aviation Administration, eight other federal agencies own and operate permanent DGPS reference stations or plan to do so by fiscal year 1996, including the Army Corps of Engineers, the Bureau of Land Management, the Environmental Protection Agency, the National Oceanic and Atmospheric Administration (NOAA), the St. Lawrence Seaway Development Corporation, the U.S. Forest Service, the U.S. Coast Guard, and the U.S. Geological Survey.[66] Even state and local governments have established or plan to establish DGPS reference sites for use in local geographic information systems or to improve emergency services, notably in California and Florida.

The U.S. Coast Guard is establishing an extensive network of 50 DGPS stations along the U.S. coastline, the Great Lakes, Puerto Rico, Alaska, and Hawaii. This network, expected to be complete in 1996, broadcasts differential corrections on Coast Guard marine radio frequencies. These corrections enable position accuracies of 1.5 m (2 drms) up to a distance of 250 nautical miles from an individual radio beacon.[67] The Coast Guard hopes to be able to meet the more demanding accuracy requirements of navigating on inland waterways by combining this network with another DGPS network operated by the U.S. Army Corps of Engineers along the Mississippi River and its tributaries.[68]

---

[65]J. Zumberge et al., "The International GPS Service for Geodynamics—Benefits to Users," *Proceedings of ION-GPS 94: 7th International Meeting of the Satellite Division of the Institute of Navigation,* Salt Lake City, UT, September 20–23, 1994.

[66]U.S. General Accounting Office, *Global Positioning Technology: Opportunities for Greater Federal Agency Joint Development and Use,* GAO/RCED-94-280, U.S. Government Printing Office, Washington, D.C., September 1994.

[67]U.S. Department of Transportation/U.S. Coast Guard, *U.S. Coast Guard GPS Implementation Plan,* Washington, D.C., June 1994.

[68]Ibid.

Since DGPS reference stations radiate inland as well as over the water, it was quickly noticed that about two-thirds of the United States was covered by the Coast Guard and Army Corps of Engineers. The addition of beacons in the North and Southwestern states (perhaps by the U.S. Geological Survey) could create a national geodetic network if common standards could be created. Toward that goal, NOAA's program of Continuously Operated Reference Stations (CORS) is attempting to ensure that GPS data provided from all federal DGPS reference stations are in a common, accessible format. Users could access the data electronically to provide post-processed accuracies of 5 to 10 cm.[69] In 1994, President Clinton issued an Executive Order establishing a "National Geospatial Data Clearinghouse" that called for the development of a National Spatial Data Infrastructure (NSDI) to support both public- and private-sector applications of geospatial data.[70]

Whereas the extensive federal activity in DGPS is technically interesting and attractive to the agencies involved, it has not been uniformly welcomed by the private sector. Unlike GPS itself, there are a number of competitive private suppliers of DGPS services. Differential corrections are broadcast directly to users from geostationary communication satellites or rebroadcast from local FM radio stations. Direct satellite reception in the C- and L-band frequencies is possible with relatively small antennas and receivers. Reception of DGPS signals and data on inaudible FM subcarriers requires a device the size of a standard pager. When linked to a normal commercial GPS receiver, accuracies below five meters are routinely available. Private firms such as Differential Corrections, Inc. provide various levels of accuracy to their subscribers using a set fee schedule and relatively simple encryption.

Private DGPS suppliers oppose FAA plans for both a WAAS and local-area DGPS systems as a form of unfair competition.[71] They feel that U.S. civil government needs for DGPS data should be met by commercial purchases and that they should have been allowed to compete for the FAA and Coast Guard programs. The DGPS suppliers claim that they offer superior services in some instances— that for example, FM subcarrier broadcasts are more reliable in bad weather than the marine radio frequencies used by the Coast Guard. Most important,

---

[69]U.S. Department of Commerce/National Telecommunications and Information Administration, *A National Approach to Augmented GPS Services*, Institute for Telecommunication Sciences, NTIA Special Publication 94-30, Washington, D.C., November 1994, p. G-9.

[70]Executive Order of the President, *Coordinating Geographic Data Acquisition and Access: the National Spatial Data Infrastructure*, The White House Office of the Press Secretary, Washington, D.C., April 11, 1994.

[71]Bruce A. Noel, Vice President, Differential Corrections, Inc., *Preventing Delays and Cost Overruns in the FAA's New Global Positioning (Satellite Navigation) System*, testimony before the Subcommittee on Aviation, Committee on Transportation and Infrastructure, U.S. House of Representatives, Washington, D.C., June 8, 1995.

they believe that while the FAA and Coast Guard systems are intended for specific users, the free, nondiscriminatory DGPS signals provided by civil agencies will be used by others and thus compete with established businesses.

A group of major private DGPS service providers has recommended that DGPS corrections broadcast by any government agency be encrypted and appropriate user fees charged, as is done for their services. In their view, safety-of-life applications, such as air and sea navigation, might be provided free since indirect fees and trust funds can be used for their support, but commercial users should not get a free government DGPS service. They usually go on to note that encryption would be favored by national security interests as well. The next section addresses the choices faced by advocates and opponents of encrypting wide- or local-area DGPS signals.

Encryption

For national security, foreign policy, and economic reasons, the ability to ensure that augmentation signals go only to desired parties is usually provided by encryption. A GPS-related cryptographic system can be used for two purposes: denial of the signal to unauthorized users, and protection of the message itself to prevent alterations or the creation of a substitute message (spoofing). The former makes a critical portion of the message unavailable to non-authorized users. In military schemes preservation of a unilateral advantage may be of interest; in a commercial setting the ability to exclude nonpaying users is necessary to collect revenue. Authenticating the message through use of an encrypted signature block that might both authenticate the sender of the message and verify the contents is consistent with application in the civil government sector, where ensuring integrity of the message is important.

In a DGPS context, encryption might be inserted at one of several points in the transmission of the signal to the user. As shown in Figure 4.14, encryption might protect the uplink in a satellite relay, the original messages to the satellite, and the command functions on the satellite. Or encryption might protect the signature region of a message that indicates its authenticity and the integrity of the main message payload. A third option might be to encrypt the entire message. Other variants include encrypting only selective portions of the message.

In testimony before the U.S. House of Representatives, Dr. Dorothy Denning succinctly listed the arguments for and against government DGPS encryption,

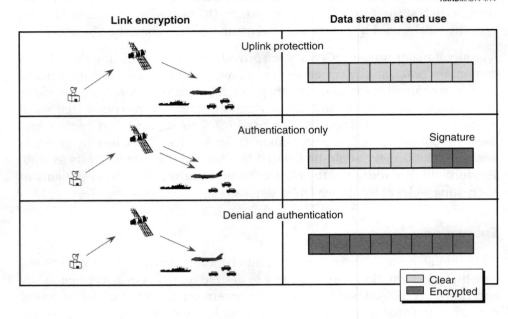

Figure 4.14—Some Encryption Modes for DGPS Signal

with emphasis on the WAAS case.[72] The arguments in favor of encryption were that it

- provides a method of denying access to adversaries

- enhances safety by protecting against spoofing

- provides a mechanism for recovering costs and enforcing fees

- protects private DGPS providers from government competition.

The motivations of recovering costs and preventing government competition are both variations on the first reason—denying access to undesired parties. The arguments against encryption are that to implement it (in the case of WAAS) would

- potentially undermine U.S. leadership in GPS by encouraging international augmentations that lacked encryption

---

[72]Dr. Dorothy Denning, Computer Science Department, Georgetown University, testimony before the Subcommittee on Aviation, Committee on Transportation and Infrastructure, U.S. House of Representatives, Washington, D.C., June 8, 1995.

- require a complex key management infrastructure

- require a major redesign and development effort, causing delays and increasing costs to the government

- create new safety risks if the key management system failed, particularly in an emergency.

The transaction costs imposed by encryption would have to be balanced against the benefits expected.

During the hearing, there was disagreement over how complex the key management infrastructure needed to be. The underlying policy question was how secure and reliable the encryption should be. As Dr. Denning put it, "in any encryption, something must remain secret." For some proprietary algorithms, no keys need to be distributed, and this is usually sufficient for commercial systems such as cable TV and the DGPS providers. If an open algorithm is used, keys and an associated key management system are needed to gain international acceptance. The desired future of electronic, over-the-air rekeying is not yet here. In the case of military systems, both keys and classified algorithms are used.

There are several technical approaches that might be taken to encrypting the signals for local- and wide-area DGPS applications using private-key and public-key encryption schemes. Some schemes involve over-the-air "rekeying" devices to enable/disable the ability of specific units to receive messages. Other schemes involve relatively simple authentication mechanisms that would not have to be tied to individual units and would depend on the ability to prevent alteration or forging of a message.[73] As one would suspect, trying to deny signals to end-users is an involved process from the standpoint of managing keys and of keeping track of which unit belongs to which person or group. Nevertheless, if the goal is to allow control of the use of a signal rather than, say, prevention of reception of the signal by cutting of transmissions in a given area (e.g., by turning off or jamming GPS signals), then one is forced to these more elaborate schemes.

The goal of encryption should be decided before selecting a particular approach (see Table 4.5). If the primary goal is authenticating the message and preventing false messages, there is no need to go to the expense and complexity of a system that denies the basic message by encrypting the entire message

---

[73]For a good overview of modern cryptographic techniques, see Bruce Schnier, *Applied Cryptography: Protocols, Algorithms, and Source Code in C,* John Wiley and Sons, New York, 1994. For a user-oriented focus emphasizing a popular public-key encryption system, see Simon Garfinkel, *PGP: Pretty Good Privacy,* O'Reilly and Associates, Inc., Sebastopol, CA, 1995.

Table 4.5

Functions of Encryption

Means	Goal	
	Authentication	Denial
Full-stream encryption	Yes	Yes
Signature/verification	Yes	No

stream. If encrypting the stream in the future is desired, it may be appropriate to use a more elaborate scheme as long as the possible future benefits are expected to offset associated costs and possible opposition. The complexity of denial-focused approaches plus the specter of selectively controlling the signal will create incentives for alternative standards and systems outside of U.S. control.

Public Versus Private Interests in GPS Augmentation

Both the public and private sectors have an interest in providing reliable, high-quality augmentations to GPS. Disagreements arise over how to deal with unintended uses and what the balance between competing national security, public safety, and economic interests should be. The central question is whether civil government GPS augmentation services should discriminate among potential uses. There is no argument that commercial DGPS providers should not be able to discriminate, typically by encryption, to enforce payments. There is similarly no argument that military DGPS systems should not be able to deny access to unauthorized users. Advocates of civil GPS augmentations, however, typically oppose discriminatory service, and encryption in particular, for public safety applications.

Debates over encrypting civil GPS augmentations tend to span three broad areas—who should provide the service, what the primary purpose of the service is, and who should pay. Those in favor of encryption make several arguments: (1) The government should not compete with the private sector, (2) the ability to selectively deny service is necessary to prevent hostile exploitation, and (3) those who use the service should be required to pay. Those opposed to encryption argue that: (1) The government has a unique responsibility to provide navigational aids, (2) public safety and international acceptance will be harmed by encryption, and (3) users will pay for the service through indirect fees.

Advocates of civil GPS augmentations acknowledge that the private sector is likely to be more innovative and respond faster to market opportunities than will the government. These advocates also argue that the government has a responsibility to ensure that services vital to public safety, such as navigational aids, are provided even if they are not financially viable for commercial firms. Commercial DGPS providers argue that they can provide navigation services if the government defines its requirements clearly and is willing to pay.

Whereas commercial DGPS providers would welcome being paid to provide government-mandated navigation services, they are more concerned with the prospect of government DGPS services becoming a source of competition for existing customers. There is broad agreement that the government should not provide services that are also available from the private sector, but disagreement over how far the government can or should go to prevent unintended (as distinct from unauthorized) users from accessing government-provided signals. Thus, some commercial DGPS firms argue that government services should be encrypted to ensure that only authorized users have access. This may limit unwanted government competition. However, such encryption could also hinder use of the navigation aids for the very purpose they were created—public safety.

Since the government itself uses GPS augmentation services, government agencies will argue that they should have flexibility in deciding whether to acquire services or provide them internally. Choosing a commercial service usually involves negotiations on the price, extent, and quality of service to meet government needs. The option of providing the service to itself, contracting for the service, or subscribing to a commercial service can create greater leverage for the government in obtaining the best deal for the taxpayer. Whether these services should be provided by government employees, by contractors, or by government purchases of services from private suppliers can be a difficult question to resolve. This study did not examine the system architecture tradeoffs that would be necessary to conclude that the FAA or U.S. Coast Guard augmentations are cost-effective compared with potential private providers.

The WAAS encryption debate between the DoD and FAA has raised questions that require balancing national security and civil interests. For example, if WAAS accuracy signals were encrypted, are commercial practices acceptable? Or would military security be required? Encryption is not just a domestic but an international issue if WAAS is to be a model for global air navigation systems. On one hand, international aviation authorities have historically opposed encryption of navigation aids for obvious safety reasons. On the other hand, the potential for hostile exploitation of DGPS may be more worrisome than earlier threats, and increased global dependency on GPS may raise interest in authenticating navigation information.

Another major question is whether wide-area GPS augmentations should be managed on a national, regional, or international basis. There are arguments that national authorities may welcome WAAS and local-area DGPS encryption to control at least some navigation signals in their airspace, if not the civil GPS signals themselves.[74]   Several countries have expressed interest in WAAS participation, including Canada, Australia, New Zealand, and Japan.   There is a long history of Canadian cooperation with the United States through the North American Air Defense Command in controlling air navigation aids in times of crises or war. A final decision on the encryption of GPS accuracy augmentations, and on what basis such augmentations should be managed, will need to consider national and international interests beyond those of the civil aviation authorities. Whether and what kind of encryption would find wide acceptance must be determined in international discussions, and it should not be assumed that compromise is impossible.

The debate between the DoT and private industry over government DGPS systems involves balancing commercial interests with those of public safety in providing geodetic data and navigation information. In particular, commercial DGPS firms argue that a fee should be charged for access to government GPS augmentations rather than making the signal available at no cost. The imposition of direct charges for navigation signals raises public safety issues, however. Users may forgo the service to avoid paying the fee (or avoid the paperwork and nuisance of subscribing to a service) and thus place themselves and others at risk. The DoT contends that such behavior is particularly likely by general aviation pilots and recreational boaters, where mandatory use of navigation equipment is difficult to enforce. Furthermore, the large number of persons engaged in these activities means that the number of accidents, injuries, and fatalities could be significant despite the low probability of any individual incident.

Imposing indirect charges does not create a similar safety risk, but it does not solve the problem of government competition, since indirect charges ensure only that the intended users pay. For example, the FAA funds WAAS and its other radionavigation aids from indirect user charges deposited in the Airport and Airways Trust Fund. Unintended non-aviation users, say hikers or sport fishermen, would perceive a zero marginal cost of using these FAA services and may forgo buying access to a commercial DGPS service in favor of the "free" government service.

From the broader perspective of the U.S. GPS industry as a whole, the economic impact of debates over civil GPS augmentations is likely to be minimal and most strongly affect the relatively small segment of commercial DGPS service providers, not sellers of GPS equipment and software. Not surprisingly, the

---

[74]M. Ananda, P. Munjai, R. Sung, and K. T. Woo, "A Simple Data Protection Scheme for Extended WAAS," unpublished paper, The Aerospace Corporation, Los Angeles, CA, June 1995.

USGIC has been notably silent on government plans for GPS augmentations, whether local or wide area. The following findings and observations summarize this section:

- The government is responsibile for ensuring that navigation aids are provided, either by the government directly or through the private sector. We did not reach any conclusion on whether the public or private provision of GPS augmentations would be more cost-effective in meeting government requirements.

- In deciding whether civil GPS accuracy augmentations should be selectively deniable, the primary concern should be to balance national security, public safety, and international acceptance. Commercial concerns are important, but of lesser national priority. International discussions must determine what types of selective denial would be both effective and broadly acceptable. Encryption is only one means of selective denial and need not be implemented if other means are available for national security purposes.

- The ability to impose direct user fees depends on being able to selectively deny service, usually with some form of encryption. Thus, a decision not to employ encryption for civil GPS augmentations will most likely preclude this option. Alternatively, one can have encryption for national security reasons but choose not to impose user fees for public safety reasons. Again, while commercial concerns are important, they are secondary to those of public safety. Government competition with commercial DGPS providers may be an unavoidable consequence in areas where both services overlap.

POTENTIAL THREATS TO COMMERCIAL GPS

The rapid growth and diversity of GPS applications are impressive. Further growth is expected from technical innovation, declining prices, and increasing international acceptance of GPS as an embedded standard for navigation, position location, and precision timing in many different markets. The most significant potential threats to commercial GPS benefits are likely to come from governments and government policy. Policy decisions by the United States to date have, intentionally or not, been supportive of commercial GPS applications. In this section we will briefly review major risks to commercial GPS that could arise from policy decisions and government action or inaction.

Barriers to the Entry of GPS Competitors

GPS is a unique system, more because of the many "barriers to entry" for potential competitors than any ability of the United States to enforce a global monopoly. Other nations are capable of building GPS-like space systems, just as they build GPS receivers. They have not done so for a variety of economic and political reasons that derive from their assessment of the U.S. position and their own needs.

National decisions to acquire space capabilities can be thought of as occurring on a spectrum from commercial-driven to autonomy-driven.[75] That is, the most immediately profitable space activities that a nation might pursue are in commercial niches, such as GPS applications, interpreting remote-sensing imagery, or selling satellite ground stations. As nations seek to become more autonomous in space and have their own satellite manufacturing and space launch capabilities, the commercial rationales become weaker and entering these markets requires other justifications such as national security, international prestige, or support for scientific research. In the case of GPS, there was no commercial rationale for expending over $10 billion to develop and implement the GPS constellation and control segment. The reason for doing so was to gain military advantages for the United States. After GPS existed, however, a commercial market appeared for GPS user equipment, and with commercial pressures and incentives this market has advanced more rapidly and made greater investments than the government could have justified for its purposes alone.

The only space-based system fully comparable to GPS is the Russian GLONASS. GLONASS is similar in many respects to GPS in that it was developed to aid military navigation with a constellation of 24 satellites (see the description in Appendix A). Although the GLONASS constellation should be complete in 1995, its future is uncertain because of economic strains on the Russian military and the relatively short lifetimes of its satellites.[76] The Russian government has tried to increase international interest in and support for GLONASS, even going so far as to develop a public Internet site.[77] The most important difference between GPS and GLONASS is not technical, however, but economic. There is a thriving global market in GPS receivers but not in GLONASS receivers, and such receivers might be best described as rare outside of Russia. Some U.S. and European firms have built receivers that can access both GPS and GLONASS signals, usually for scientific and aviation testing purposes, but sales of such

---

[75]The authors acknowledge Jeff Kingwell of the Australian CSIRO Office of Space Science and Applications for this insight from Australian space efforts.

[76]Nicholas L. Johnson, "GLONASS Spacecraft," *GPS World*, November 1994, p. 52. Periodic reports on GLONASS are also prepared by the U.S. Air Force's National Air Intelligence Center at Wright-Patterson AFB, OH.

[77]The Russian Space Defense Forces home page on GLONASS can be found at http://mx.iki.rssi.ru/SFCSIC/SFCSIC_main.html

equipment have been minor.[78] In Russia's case, they carried all the expenses of building an independent system but have not been able to reap commercial benefits from it.

Other nations have decided that they do not want to pay for developing, deploying, and operating their own global satellite navigation system. Instead, they have focused on GPS equipment, services, and applications markets. In part, this is because only Russia, Europe, and Japan have the necessary range of satellite manufacturing and space launch capabilities. Another reason is that the United States is already providing GPS signals, at least the civil ones, for free. Against a free good on the market, it is difficult to compete economically or to recover investment costs. A competing good would have to be different in some way and fill a different need than the free good to induce customers to pay for it. The difference could be technical—greater accuracy provided by DGPS services. Or the difference could be political—regional or international ownership and control to meet the needs of national pride or to ensure uninterrupted service. In both cases, the different signal could be encrypted to enforce payment.

The barriers to entry could decline if space system costs were dramatically reduced. In one study of the potential cost of a stand-alone civil navigation satellite system, the "replacement" cost of the GPS constellation ranged from $1.4 billion to $770 million.[79] The upper number was based on government procurement costs, whereas the lower number was for smaller "civilianized" GPS satellites that lacked military features such as nuclear detection systems, emergency maneuvering fuel, and 180-day data storage capabilities. Another approach would be to place navigation "hitchhiker" payloads on communication satellites, such as the low earth orbit (LEO) constellations being planned for mobile communications. Challenging technical problems include compensating for Doppler effects resulting from the faster transit times of LEO satellites compared with the higher GPS orbits, and continually calculating an accurate ephemeris so the payloads know where they are. If geosynchronous satellites were used, additional satellites would be needed in high inclination orbits to provide truly global coverage. Cost estimates for both the LEO and geosynchronous approaches range from $1 to $2 billion.[80]

---

[78]The GLONASS system uses Frequency Division Multiple Access (FDMA), in which each satellite transmits on a slightly different channel in the L-band. The time base used is slightly different than for GPS and it uses a Soviet coordinate system rather than the World Geodetic Systems (WGS 84). See also Yuri G. Gouzhva et al., "Getting in Sync: GLONASS Clock Synchronization," *GPS World*, April 1995.

[79]Keith McDonald, "Econosats: Toward an Affordable Global Navigation Satellite System?" *GPS World*, September 1993.

[80]Ibid.

A less expensive approach to greater autonomy from both GPS and GLONASS is to build a GPS "supplement" rather than a replacement system. A global, space-based wide-area augmentation system could take advantage of the existence of GPS and GLONASS signals while providing a hedge against unwelcome changes in both systems. For example, a recent estimate of the cost for 15 "lightsat" navigation satellites was $85 million.[81] The navigation satellites would be launched as "hitchhiker" payloads and operate in intermediate circular orbits to provide wide-area augmentation services. A commercial spin-off from INMARSAT, INMARSAT-P, is intended to provide worldwide mobile communications using 12 satellites in intermediate circular orbits, and it may provide GPS augmentation services as well.[82] The INMARSAT-P concept for GPS augmentation appears consistent with the $85 million cost estimate, but no public estimate of the cost or pricing of this capability was available as of this writing. Presumably, fees could be charged for the augmentation signals alone or as part of a bundle with other communication services such as paging.[83]

The ability to recover costs may not be a consideration for space systems built for national security, public safety, or scientific purposes. But cost recovery is a top consideration for systems built for commercial purposes. A $100 million investment will typically require creating about $200 million per year in revenue and about $100 million per year in profit.[84] Who could or would pay such sums? It is unlikely to be price-sensitive individuals or GPS equipment manufacturers. It is most likely to be foreign governments or commercial firms, such as telecommunications, with billions of dollars in revenues and a crucial dependence on GPS navigation and time signals. They would invest in an augmentation or even an alternative to GPS to serve internal rather than external customers.[85]

---

[81]J. R. Nagel et al., "Global Navigation Satellite System (GNSS) Alternatives for Future Civil Requirements," presented at the INMARSAT Plans '94 Technical Program, April 12, 1994.

[82]Hale Montgomery, "INMARSAT Goals," *GPS World*, September 1995, p. 16.

[83]The U.S. government might be able to use these commercial networks as well. Nuclear detonation detectors now on GPS satellites and small remote-sensing instruments could be flown as "hitchhikers" on commercial satellites. The U.S. Army has experimented with pagers to relay missile warnings to troops in the field.

[84]Notionally, assume $100 million is borrowed at 10 percent and invested over three years before first launch. About $15 million per year will be needed to service the debt, $20 million per year to pay down the investors, $30 million per year to achieve a standard 20 percent return on investment, and $35 million per year for taxes. Excluding any margin, this requires a profit of $100 million per year. This implies a revenue stream of $200–$250 million per year from individuals, corporations, or countries.

[85]Another option would be to invest in maintaining GLONASS. That, however, would require that GLONASS be seen as more technically and politically reliable than GPS, in addition to the cost of adapting the installed base of user equipment.

Although building an alternative to GPS is not economically attractive in the face of a stable, free, high-quality GPS signal, it could be seen as a necessary step in a larger venture under the right conditions. One mobile satellite communications venture was concerned about its reliance on GPS time for its network and examined the cost and feasibility of providing its own precision time source for communications. It concluded that it was possible to substitute for GPS, but that doing so would lengthen the payback time for its investment by about one year. The venture decided to rely on GPS but to maintain the independent approach as a fall-back option if access to GPS were to change.[86] In the case of this commercial venture, the primary barrier to entry was an economic calculation based on perceptions of U.S. policy, not technology or markets.

To summarize, an incentive for a competing GPS-like system would be U.S. policy instability. GPS accuracy, reliability, and availability are already quite good and augmentations are available to meet needs beyond the SPS or even PPS level of service. On the other hand, if the United States failed to maintain the GPS constellation, failed to provide a continuous, stable signal, unilaterally initiated changes to the civil signal (such as encryption or user fees), then other countries might decide that they could not depend on GPS or needed a complementary system. International interest in the FAA's wide-area augmentation system and a role for INMARSAT in distributing augmentation signals can be attributed to a desire to hedge against changes in U.S. policy while avoiding the costs of complete autonomy.

DoD Policies and Management

Since stable funding and competent operation of GPS are integral to the continued growth of commercial applications, DoD policies and management are paramount. Maintaining GPS and ensuring competent management may be national responsibilities, but funding for the GPS space and control segments comes from the DoD budget—the Air Force in particular. GPS must compete with other military programs for funding and attention in an environment of constrained defense spending. DoD funded the development of GPS and is the most likely source of continued government support: GPS is critical to national security missions, there is no other budgetary "home" for GPS (the U.S. Department of Transportation is already occupied with various GPS augmentations), and there is no obvious way to fund GPS except through the public treasury.

---

[86]Personal communication to S. Pace, January 3, 1995.

In a time of declining budgets, one can ask whether the Air Force is willing to continue maintaining GPS. The answer appears to be yes, provided the Air Force budget does not decline so far as to force triage decisions that could affect U.S. air superiority. One impression from discussions at the U.S. Space Command is that shifting post–Cold War priorities would seem to favor GPS over other U.S. military space forces. During the Cold War, early warning satellites, such as the Defense Support Program, seemed to receive the greatest amount of attention as a critical part of the U.S. nuclear deterrent. Today, with the prospect of massive nuclear confrontation lessened, GPS has moved to the center of attention as a service that is used every day by U.S. forces around the world. When the GPS signal moves outside of normal performance bounds, calls start coming into the Master Control Station at Falcon AFB from concerned military users—some at senior levels. Funding GPS is recognized as a significant commitment, but if the Air Force were to drop support for GPS it would likely raise questions about the willingness of the Air Force to use space systems in support of conventional forces.

While DoD support of GPS has been and continues to be crucial, certain military interests can conflict with commercial interests. Selectivity availability is one of the most commonly cited examples of conflicting interests, yet the evidence of economic harm from SA is questionable. A more subtle conflict stems from how DoD efforts to preserve its control and freedom of action have sometimes reinforced international fears that the DoD cannot be trusted to manage GPS fairly for civil users.[87] Perceptions of the DoD role among civil government users (both U.S. and foreign) tend to be complex and sometimes contradictory, whereas commercial users tend to be satisfied if the GPS signal is available and predictable. Some civil users are critical of DoD control yet also expect the DoD to go to extraordinary measures to ensure GPS remains operational in peace or war. Other civil users interested in GPS services for specific groups want to have a greater say in GPS management. At the same time, they acknowledge that the DoD has been successful in balancing the needs of diverse operating locations (land, sea, air, and space).

A more concrete concern of commercial users is how available GPS will be in time of war. To date, the United States has not only maintained GPS signals during conflicts but has turned SA to zero to allow U.S. forces to use commercial GPS receivers. As more military receivers enter into use, SA may be expected to stay on and civil GPS signals as well as GLONASS signals may be jammed in a combat theater (possibly by all sides). The DoD is seeking to im-

---

[87]John M. Beukers, "Civil Versus Military Use of Satellites for Positioning and Navigation," presented at the First International Radionavigation Conference, Radionavigation Intergovernmental Council of the Commonwealth of Independent States, Moscow, Russia, June 26–30, 1995, p. 2.

prove its ability to selectively deny GPS access in narrow geographic areas, including through improved jamming techniques.

Selective area denial of GPS may be a more or less serious problem for civil and commercial GPS users depending on how wide the conflict is and how integral GPS is to the local infrastructure. Civil aircraft using GPS would certainly be advised to stay out of the combat theater, but areas remote from combat may also be affected if a wide-area augmentation system is disrupted. Some users of GPS, such as information networks, will not be able to operate, and jamming can be expected to cause collateral damage to local communications and computer networks. The degree of resiliency such networks might exhibit against various levels of GPS jamming is poorly understood.

The National Research Council report on GPS provided a comprehensive listing of technical improvements that could benefit civil, commercial, and military users. As discussed earlier, DoD actions that could significantly improve the GPS signal available to civil and commercial users involve major policy decisions or levels of resources (e.g., adding additional satellites to the constellation). Some technical improvements could be incorporated in future GPS satellites, such as the NRC recommendation to authorize an L-band frequency to provide an unencrypted L4 signal. Access to a dual-frequency GPS signal would help correct ionospheric errors and reduce interference problems experienced by civil and commercial users.[88]

The impediments to making GPS improvements, assuming DoD is willing, are budgetary and process-driven. GPS is a military system and funding for specific improvements need to be based on military requirements. Discussions between DoD and DoT are under way on how to respond to civil and commercial needs, but at present there is no defined path for civil agency funding of GPS improvements, much less commercial or international funding. Policy decisions at a national level, rather than an agency level, are likely to be needed to create a process for incorporating non-military-driven GPS changes.

Other DoD policies and practices that can help (or hurt) the commercial GPS industry include procurement rules, foreign military sales, and export controls. The DoD benefits from a strong domestic GPS manufacturing and software industry, but government procurement rules sometimes limit those benefits. During the Persian Gulf War, several thousand commercial GPS receivers were purchased. Because the DoD was unable to quickly get a waiver for a lowest-

---

[88]National Research Council, op. cit., pp. 90–91.

cost certification, many of the receivers had to be purchased by the Japanese government and donated to the allies.[89]

Foreign military sales (FMS) of PPS-capable receivers represent another area of concern. DoD supports the integration of military GPS receivers into allied armed forces for which it has a Memorandum of Understanding (MOU) on security procedures. Obtaining approvals from the DoD, State Department, and the GPS Joint Program Office can result in a government process that takes from nine months to two years to complete a sale.[90] In comparison, commercial product cycles can be 12 to 18 months, resulting in the allied militaries lagging behind commercial capabilities. Although FMS sales are not a major part of overall GPS sales, a slow U.S. process encourages entry by foreign competitors who can gain a foothold in the GPS market through military sales.

In contrast, DoD support of reforms to U.S. export controls in 1991 is acknowledged by industry as helping to establish a dominant position for the United States in international sales.[91] Military GPS receivers are classified as "munitions" and subject to strong export controls. A military GPS receiver is defined as one that is capable of providing navigation information at speeds in excess of 1000 nautical miles per hour and at altitudes in excess of 60,000 feet (e.g., as with ballistic missiles), has a "null steering" antenna to overcome jamming, or which has an encryption device, such as the kind needed to access the GPS P-code.[92] Civilian receivers are classed as "general destination" items and face fewer restrictions. GPS manufacturers are able to routinely include modifications in their electronics so that civilian GPS receivers will not function above the speeds and altitudes defined in the regulation. In this case, military and commercial interests have been able to cooperate in a way that benefited both.

Taxes and User Fees

Both the GPS Standard Positioning Service and Precise Positioning Service are provided without user fees (although fees for PPS access have not been ruled out). U.S. government DGPS services, such as the FAA and U.S. Coast Guard systems, are intended to be free of direct fees—transportation trust funds from

[89]U.S. Congress, Office of Technology Assessment, *Assessing the Potential for Civil-Military Integration*, OTA-ISS-611, U.S. Government Printing Office, Washington, D.C, September 1994.

[90]Interview with Gary Sauser, Collins Avionics and Communications Division, Rockwell International, November 9, 1994.

[91]"Manufacturers Hail Revised Export Rules, GPS Industry Council," *GPS World*, July/August 1991, p. 22.

[92]U.S. Government, *Federal Register*, Rules and Regulations, Vol. 56, No. 168, August 29, 1991, p. 42890, sections 7A05A and 7A25B.

indirect fees (e.g., ticket taxes) are likely to be used instead. GPS equipment it-self is subject only to normal sales taxes and import tariffs.

The primary motivation for taxes and user fees is usually to recover costs, but there can be other motivations such as controlling access, discouraging use, or limiting competition to other goods and services. Access fees are used to con-trol access to cable TV, for example, and excise taxes are used to discourage consumption of goods while not banning them outright. In the case of GPS, user fees have been proposed for government DGPS systems so they will not compete with private service providers. For selected users, such as airline pi-lots, user fees may be waived as in the public interest to encourage use of GPS for safety-of-life applications.

Taxes and fees cannot be levied solely because the government wishes to do so; a good or service must first be subject to fee collection. General tax revenues are used to pay for traditional public goods, such as national defense, because it is too difficult (or impossible) to levy special charges. In the case of SPS, it was originally decided not to impose user charges in order to encourage use of GPS by government policy[93] and because the transaction costs associated with fee collection and enforcement were judged to be high relative to expected rev-enues. In addition, there was an awareness that charging fees for GPS would encourage use of foreign systems such as GLONASS or private sector proposals such as Geostar (a commercial radio determination satellite system).[94]

There are three general categories of taxes and fee collection mechanisms—those that apply to user equipment, those that apply to differential GPS signals, and those that apply to GPS signals themselves. Taxes and fees are most easily imposed on user equipment that is tangible and already subject to traditional taxes. A one-time tax on receivers would raise their prices, lower sales, and slow acceptance in new markets. The commercial GPS market is becoming increas-ingly price competitive, and a large fee (say, over $50 each) could seriously de-press sales of mass-market receivers whose prices are heading toward less than $200 each.[95] Assume the U.S. government did not want to discourage GPS re-ceiver sales and was able to collect an average of $50 for every U.S. receiver ex-pected to be sold in the year 2000. On sales of about 1.5 million units (including 25,000 to the military), that total revenue is only $75 million—less than the cost

---

[93]U.S. Department of Defense, *Global Positioning System User Charges,* Report to the Senate and House of Representatives Committees on Appropriations and Armed Services, Washington, D.C., May 1984.

[94]Op. cit., p. 14. See Appendix A for a description of Geostar.

[95]The price of GPS "engines" themselves are often in the range of $35 to $50 each, with other parts of GPS equipment and software making up the rest of the cost.

of two GPS satellites.[96] This is before subtracting collection costs or considering the depressive effect of the tax on U.S. sales. On one hand, $75 million is not insignificant compared with annual costs on the order of $400 million. On the other hand, there is no plausible way to pay for GPS on the basis of GPS equipment sales. The imposition of a tax would raise U.S. prices and improve the competitive position of foreign suppliers. One might impose additional tariffs on GPS equipment imports to protect domestic sales, but international sales would still be hurt by a U.S. receiver tax regardless of any foreign retaliation.[97]

Taxes and fees on GPS augmentations are more difficult to impose because there must be an enforcement mechanism to deny signal access. For private DGPS service providers, this is typically done by encrypting the signal and charging a fee for access to the decryption key. A similar process could be applied to government DGPS systems if the ability to encrypt were included in the system design. Whether to actually impose user fees would be both a policy-driven and a practical decision. In policy terms, the rationale for imposing a fee could be to recover costs, limit competition to private service providers, or to ensure that unintended users (e.g., non-aircraft users of the FAA's WAAS signal) paid their share when the intended users have already paid indirect fees via trust funds or other mechanisms. Reasons not to charge include promoting use of the government signal, an unwillingness to encrypt a navigation aid, and the expected costs of fee collection.

From a commercial perspective, taxes and fees for governmental GPS augmentations may be justified on the policy principle of preventing competition with private-sector providers. A decision to charge fees would have to be balanced against the cost of enforcing fee collection and the public interest to be served by the augmentations (e.g., safer air and marine navigation). One way of deciding this would be to allow private firms to compete for the supply of DGPS signals to meet public purposes such as navigation or surveys. The government could provide a DGPS service, wide area or local, in the event the private sector could not cost-effectively meet government requirements. The central question is where the burden of proof should lie—on the government or the private provider—to show who is best qualified.

---

[96]The 1.5 million unit sales projection is from the 1995 U.S. GPS Industry Council survey.

[97]Current European Community tariffs on GPS equipment are about 6–8 percent and Japanese tariffs are zero. GPS equipment is not treated as a separate item but categorized by end use, such as navigation, survey, or aviation. If all GPS equipment were categorized as telecommunications, the global tariff rate would drop to about 4 percent. Interview with Paul Sakai, Trimble Navigation, January 27, 1995.

These same considerations can be applied to regional and international GPS augmentations. One proposed model is that of COSPAS/SARSAT, the international search and rescue system.[98] Satellites and ground networks of a GPS augmentation system can be contributed on a voluntary basis by individual states cooperating in a regional or international structure. Costs may be recovered directly by charging end users or indirectly through trust funds or general tax revenues from cooperating nations. The states all would have to agree on how to charge end users, but they could take separate paths if indirect fees or general taxes were chosen. International cooperation by the United States is typically on a no-exchange-of-funds basis, and the operation of GPS itself would probably be considered a more than fair contribution. Some organizations, such as the European Space Agency, have elaborate procedures for ensuring each state gets a "just return" for its financial contribution. An international GPS augmentation system in Europe can be expected to have similar financial balancing requirements.

GPS signals are unlike satellite communications signals in that they flow one way from the satellite to the passive receiver.[99] In order to impose a user fee, there must be a way of denying the signal to enforce payment. The signal can be encrypted or periodically changed in a manner that requires purchase of a government-controlled key or software update. This approach was contemplated early in the GPS program for the SPS signal, but it was not implemented. Enforcing a fee collection for SPS today would be impossible without costly changes (both technical and political) to the GPS architecture. PPS access is controlled by government encryption, so fees could be imposed. To date, users have been predominately the U.S. military, allied forces, and civil government agencies, free of any fee. With wider civil access to PPS, it is possible that a user fee would be introduced. The purpose of the fee would likely be to recover the cost of administering PPS access for nongovernment users, as opposed to recovering costs of the GPS program as a whole, and possibly to stem complaints of government competition from DGPS service providers.

It might be argued that the United States is already getting a return on its investment in GPS through enhanced national security and taxes from the growing commercial uses of GPS. The problem with many simple fees and taxes, however, is that they are invariably designed for current uses of GPS, not future uses. As shown in this chapter, the uses of GPS technology continue to grow and change. Taxes and fees that slow market experimentation and growth thus carry hidden costs in terms of forgone or delayed growth that are impossible to

---

[98]Beukers, op. cit., p. 6.

[99]The private U.S. Geostar concept provided position location and navigation information through a two-way radio communication between the satellite and receiver. See Appendix A.

quantify. In more mature markets, say the sale of television sets, the effects of a tax increase can be calculated with some confidence. This is not the case in a changing, technology-driven market like GPS. As a theoretical idea, one might tax firms using GPS in proportion to the productivity benefits achieved through GPS. This would allow for experimentation when the benefit of GPS is uncertain while allowing for tax revenue should benefits occur. However, this approach is likely to have high transaction costs in acquiring productivity information, create cheating incentives, and begin to duplicate the role of corporate income taxes already in place.

Questions of policy motivation for, and the costs of, taxes and fees are central to their use. GPS was built as a government program to gain national security benefits; it could not be justified by market forces alone. If GPS could have been built as a private venture, arguably it should have been. Taxes and fees deter the use of a system built to serve the public interest and lessen the secondary, but important, commercial benefits now being derived.

International Standards and Spectrum Management

Use of the electromagnetic spectrum is vital to GPS, and intentional or unintentional interference can be a serious threat to all GPS applications. Interference can occur when unwanted signals enter the 1.57 GHz–1.58 GHz passband allowed into GPS receivers. These unwanted signals may arise from direct inband or suppressive interference, as for example, by intentional jamming or illegal radio emitters. Unwanted signals can also arise as a result of harmonic, side-lobe, and intermodulation interference from emitters operating near the GPS passband.[100]

GPS signals are relatively weak and receivers typically require a line-of-sight path to the satellites. GPS receivers do not function well, if at all, inside buildings or cars without an external antenna. There can be gaps in GPS reception on the ground caused by structures and at higher altitudes by interference from ground-based transmitters. Gaps in GPS coverage at aircraft altitudes have been observed in widely separated areas such as Northern Italy, Hawaii, Florida, and the American Midwest.[101] It has been speculated that a potential source of interference is the third harmonic of UHF TV Channel 23 and that

---

[100]Intermodulation interference occurs when two or more out-of-band signals interact to create a product in the passband. Suppressive interference can occur when a strong signal outside of the passband saturates the preamplifier in a GPS receiver.

[101]"'Worm Holes' in GPS Coverage Raise Interference Concerns," *Aviation Week and Space Technology*, June 5, 1995, p. 32.

problems in Northern Italy may be attributed to a number of illegal TV transmitters.[102]

The Russian GLONASS system operates near the GPS frequencies, as will proposed mobile satellite systems (MSS) operating in low earth orbit (see Figure 4.13). GLONASS operations in the 1.6 GHz band have caused interference with radio astronomers, and there has been concern that operations at the lower end of the MSS band (1.61–1.6265 GHz) could experience interference as well. The Russians have agreed to move their operations to stay below 1.61 GHz by the year 2005, with an interim plan to be implemented by 1998.[103] While there does not appear to be interference between GPS and GLONASS at present, this case highlights how international decisions on spectrum allocation might affect GPS.

Many GPS applications require radio spectrum in addition to that of the GPS signal itself; an example is communication links to provide differential GPS corrections or value-added services dependent on GPS. As commercial firms seek to expand into global markets, adequate spectrum allocations and global, interoperable standards for GPS applications become of interest. GPS manufacturers would prefer to build a single product that is exportable to all markets, rather than having to differentiate frequencies and standards by market. Similarly, GPS equipment buyers who travel internationally, such as aviators and surveyors, want to be able to easily use their equipment in different countries. Global, interoperable standards have not been established for cellular phones and as a result, one cannot use a U.S. cell phone in Europe or a European phone in the United States. Ironically, this fragmentation of the market is one reason mobile satellite phones may have a competitive advantage in being usable anywhere.

Spectrum will be needed to exploit applications in which communication links are used in conjunction with GPS. Allocated frequencies help minimize interference problems, and some countries, notably Japan, are assessing the merits of national allocations for GPS data communications. A commercial frequency allocation seems to be a particularly pressing issue for RTK applications because of relatively high bandwidth requirements.[104] There are competing arguments for all the spectrum, however, and non-GPS techniques can provide location information. An example of technical competition is "911" service for mobile phones. The FCC has proposed that mobile radio services (e.g., cellular

---

[102]Ibid.

[103]"Status of GPS/GLONASS Compatibility Testing," briefing by the Aerospace Corporation at the GPS Joint Program Office, Los Angeles AFB, June 16, 1994.

[104]One industry estimate of the need for potential RTK spectrum was for 25 kHz channels at 5–10 Watts of power and capable of 9600 baud transmission rates. This would be sufficient for ranges of 20–50 km.

phones) be required to furnish information necessary for emergency services to locate a 911 caller.[105]   Instead of using GPS, the mobile phone user could calculate his position by triangulating off of FM radio beacons or cellular phone towers.   While both approaches may work for urban areas, neither has the remote area coverage of GPS. The use of GPS in this case may conserve spectrum.

Inefficient spectrum allocations and incompatible standards can manifest themselves as problems for commercial GPS firms in many ways. The imposition of proprietary national standards (e.g., for safety reasons or to protect local firms) can limit market access by U.S. firms. Split-spectrum allocations in different regions of the world can force manufacturers to build different versions of the same product, thus forgoing economies of scale. The cost to access and use additional spectrum can involve perceptions of convenience as well. The lack of a universal radio product with some GPS applications can constrain users from moving easily from country to country, thus limiting their productivity and ability to buy future products. In the case of local-area DGPS, some UHF and VHF bands can be technically useful, but surveyors may be unwilling to go through the trouble of getting a license to operate at the necessary power levels. On the other hand, radio equipment that does not require a license may be subject to local interference and thus be unattractive for use with GPS.

The rapid growth of DGPS applications has resulted in the deployment of DGPS base stations and networks at many different operating frequencies. These include the U.S. Coast Guard and civil agency LF and MF beacon systems, commercial DGPS services on FM subcarrier bands, and private DGPS stations operating at HF, VHF, and UHF frequencies. Each of these frequencies has limitations: VHF and UHF require line-of-sight transmissions, whereas the LF, MF, and HF systems have noise and propagation problems (e.g., multipath errors). These ground-based system limitations have fed interest in satellite-based transmission of DGPS information. In the case of international aviation, for example, there are several mobile satellite communication systems that could deliver wide-area GPS augmentation information. INMARSAT is one possibility, as are dedicated national satellites or commercial satellites providing mobile services.

American Mobile Satellite Corporation (AMSC) is a U.S. venture to provide mobile communications services via geosynchronous communication satellites. As part of their license from the FCC, they have the exclusive right to serve domestic land-mobile and aeronautical commercial users, and there seems to be a

---

[105]"Action in Docket Case—FCC Takes Actions to Ensure Accessibility to 911 Services," Press release by the Federal Communications Commission, Washington, D.C., September 19, 1994.

preference for AMSC when the U.S. government needs such services.[106] The FAA may be asked to select AMSC as a preferred provider for WAAS information in the United States, although it has usually discussed using INMARSAT services. A serious issue might arise if an international flight arriving in the United States wants to make another domestic stop and has to shift from using an INMARSAT-link to an AMSC-link in the United States. It is unlikely that the airlines would want to carry duplicate equipment; they would prefer the equipment be interoperable. Interoperable standards between AMSC and INMARSAT have not yet been developed for GPS augmentations. International coordination will also be needed if encryption is to be used for the wide-area accuracy signals, whatever the communications carrier.

International Legal Issues

The final area of potential threat to the commercial growth of GPS are international legal issues on its "acceptability." These issues affect the ability and willingness to buy and use GPS as opposed to other technologies. In some countries, it can be illegal to possess technologies such as satellite TV receiver encryption software. Barring local restrictions for security or cultural reasons, however, the legal acceptance of GPS is driven by civil government concerns over liability, national dependency, and admissibility in court.

Many countries, such as those in the European Community, have domestic laws that require navigation aids (e.g., those used for safety-of-life applications) to be under sovereign control. In the United States, private maritime aids are banned and private aviation aids are permitted under strict regulation.[107] This was a reasonable approach when navigation aids were lighthouses or radio beacons located at a fixed point. GPS signals, however, are emitted from space satellites owned by a single country. While sales of GPS equipment for navigation use is not a large market in itself, the use of GPS promises large benefits in terms of safety, reliability, and lower costs. This poses a dilemma for foreign countries whose laws on navigation aids were written before the advent of GPS. On one hand, they want the benefits of GPS; on the other, they are reluctant to allow use of a system that may impose liabilities on them without their having ownership or control of that system. The United States would be understandably reluctant to take full liability for global uses of GPS.

---

[106]Interview with Lon Levin, Vice President, American Mobile Satellite Corporation, April 20, 1995. Since the AMSC spectrum allocation came from a U.S. band set aside for aeronautical users, the U.S. government has a preemption right for aviation safety uses.

[107]See Chapter Five for a more extensive discussion of institutional and legal issues associated with GPS.

There are at least three possible steps that might help the international acceptance of GPS by governments (since acceptance by users has already been demonstrated). The first is the provision of global integrity monitoring in real-time to provide timely warning in the event of problems with GPS. Not only is such integrity monitoring a good safety practice, but it can supplement warning notices to airmen and mariners and help constrain potential U.S. liabilities. The second is the continuation of local or regional navigation aids to limit complete national dependence on GPS. The U.S. Coast Guard is in the process of turning over management of its global Loran-C radio beacon system to host nations as it transitions to GPS. Loran-C may be obsolete in the United States, but it may stay in international use for many years to come. Third, the United States can explore bilateral and multilateral agreements with countries that have legal concerns over the use of GPS for navigation. While preserving its national security interests, the United States may be able to make more formal diplomatic commitments on the maintenance of GPS according to the Federal Radionavigation Plan. A foreign country could, in turn, modify its laws to allow use of a space-based navigation system that is subject to an international agreement to which the state is a party.

GPS legal acceptance has domestic as well as international aspects. How should GPS-based evidence be treated in court? When should GPS data be allowed in court? The European Commission has been using GPS to enforce fishing fleet regulations, and GPS data were used in a fishing conflict between Canada and Spain. This has raised the question of the admissibility of GPS data in court. European courts are not familiar with GPS (many U.S. courts are not much more aware) and how much trust should be placed in GPS data. GPS technology has been proposed for use in "intelligent vehicle highway systems" in which GPS data are provided to cars from central locations. While most people like the idea of GPS as a car navigation aid, they become uncomfortable with the idea that their car is being tracked by a government agency, no matter how benign the motivation. Thus the use of GPS may raise privacy issues depending on who controls use of the technology. Both commercial fishermen and car drivers require licenses and must obey certain regulations. The legal difference between how each is affected by GPS technology is likely to be an ongoing debate.

COMMERCIAL FINDINGS

This section summarizes the principal findings on commercial applications of GPS and related technologies.

Commercial and Civil Uses of GPS

- The availability of GPS signals to civil and commercial users has, along with supportive policy and management decisions, enabled the growth of many diverse commercial applications of GPS. Users have varying needs for accuracy, with increasing commercial interest in submeter, real-time applications. The role of precision timing for mobile communications and computing will increase with the growth of global wireless applications. GPS technology is becoming increasingly embedded in national and international infrastructures—from civil aviation and highways to telecommunications and the Internet. This is creating opportunities for improved productivity as well as potential vulnerabilities.

Commercial GPS Markets

- According to the U.S. GPS Industry Council projections, world sales of commercial GPS equipment alone (not including related services and multiplier effects) are expected to be about $8.5 billion in the year 2000. The U.S. practice of providing the SPS service free of direct or indirect user charges has encouraged the growth of commercial GPS applications. The no-fee approach is a technical necessity because enforcing payments today would be virtually impossible given the nature of the civil GPS signals and the large installed base of GPS equipment.

GPS Technology Patents and International Competition

- The United States enjoys a leading position in the manufacture of GPS equipment and the development of new applications, particularly those requiring advanced software. Japan is the nearest competitor to the United States, followed by Europe. U.S. industry tends to see GPS technology as something that adds an "embedded capability," whereas Japanese industry tends to see GPS as another form of consumer electronics. European firms, with the exception of DGPS suppliers to the North Sea oil industry, tend to see GPS in terms of potential government contracts for improving domestic infrastructure. There is increasing interest in consumer automotive applications, however, in Europe as well as the rest of the world.

Potential Changes to Civil GPS Services

- Selective availability is a controversial topic for some civil and commercial GPS users, and it is unclear whether leaving SA on or off in peacetime would have any significant impact on commercial growth or the development of new applications. Technical "workarounds" in the form of DGPS and RTK techniques are increasingly available and many users need accuracies better than GPS alone can provide.

- Industry access to the Precise Positioning Service is unlikely to be of significant commercial benefit. In part, this is because of the policy requirements of showing that a specific request for access is in the national interest, and in part because there are no reasonable alternatives. In addition, requirements to protect necessary security devices for PPS access tend to make PPS unattractive to commercial users compared to commercial techniques already available.

Augmentations to GPS

- The U.S. government intends to provide wide-area augmentations of GPS accuracy for aviation and maritime navigation. DGPS service providers are concerned that these government services will compete with their enterprises. The economic harm from competition may be small relative to the benefits of wide-area GPS augmentations, but nevertheless U.S. government policy needs to find a balance between public safety requirements and competition with industry. We did not reach any conclusion on whether public or private provision of GPS augmentations would be more cost-effective in meeting government requirements.

- There are and will be multiple regional and national GPS augmentations of varying size. From a commercial perspective, the most important policy consideration is that there be open, interoperable standards that allow GPS users to operate easily anywhere in the world. Such systems can help promote international acceptance of GPS by providing a form of local control over some air, sea, and land applications.

- In deciding whether civil GPS accuracy augmentations should be selectively deniable, the primary concern should be to balance national security and public safety, and to foster international acceptance. Commercial concerns are important, but of lesser national priority. International discussions are necessary to determine what types of selective denial would be both effective and broadly acceptable. Encryption is only one means of selective denial and need not be implemented if other means meet national security purposes.

- The ability to impose direct user fees on GPS augmentations depends on being able to selectively deny service, usually with some form of encryption. The United States might decide not to employ encryption for civil GPS augmentations. Alternatively, it could have encryption for national security reasons but choose not to impose user fees for public safety considerations. Again, while commercial concerns are important, they are secondary to those of public safety. Government competition with commercial DGPS providers may be an unavoidable consequence in areas where both services overlap.

Potential Threats to Commercial GPS

- Government policy decisions can create risks to commercial GPS in many ways. New taxes and fees can be imposed, spectrum licenses may be difficult or impossible to get, international trade disputes can harm access to foreign markets, and governments may impose standards that fragment global markets into less attractive sizes. The problem of standards is particularly pervasive because it cuts across civil, commercial, and military concerns in areas such as encryption, safety certification standards, and international spectrum allocations.

- GPS accuracy, reliability, and availability are quite good and various augmentations are available to meet needs beyond the SPS or even PPS level of service. Competitors to GPS could arise, however, if the United States fails to maintain the GPS constellation, fails to provide a continuous, stable signal, or imposes unilaterally initiated changes to the civil signal, such as encryption or user fees, so that other countries felt they could not depend on GPS or needed a complementary system. Commercial interests, foreign governments, and international organizations have the resources to create alternative or complementary systems to GPS if conditions warrant.

- As commercial GPS firms evaluate the various forms of risk they face— technical, market, financial, and political—they appear confident in managing the first three. This leaves political risk. Past cooperation between the U.S. Department of Defense, U.S. civil agencies, and industry indicates that political risk to commercial growth should be minimal. Nonetheless, rapid changes in GPS since the Persian Gulf War have created a strong commercial interest in a formal national GPS policy that provides a predictable environment for future business decisions.

- Critical to the system's future commercial growth is whether GPS becomes an accepted global standard for position location, navigation, and precision timing. GPS is well on its way to de facto acceptance, but official acceptance depends on international decisions about using GPS in safety applications, especially civil aviation. This is not just a political question, but one that can affect technical standards, spectrum allocations, export sales, and even military cooperation. International concerns over U.S. intentions with regard to GPS can be lessened by U.S. policy statements, but direct discussions and explicit agreements are likely to be more effective in addressing such specific concerns as legal liabilities and regional security.

Chapter Five

INSTITUTIONAL AND LEGAL ASSESSMENT

This chapter discusses institutional and legal issues that can affect how GPS signals and signal augmentations are provided, including alternatives for managing and funding these services. It first identifies the basic institutional capabilities necessary for managing, operating, and funding GPS and uses them to define criteria for assessing management and funding options. It then assesses a range of institutional arrangements for GPS that address possible funding and cost-recovery mechanisms. It also addresses recurring themes—often presented as criteria for preferring one set of options to others—in GPS policy debates, and attempts to inform the debate with relevant legal and historical background. This chapter provides a framework for thinking about the advantages and disadvantages of the various institutional options and clarifies terms in the policy debate.

Here, we assume that the domestic benefits of making GPS available for non-military uses exceed the risks of misuses of GPS and the cost of countermeasures against the misuse of, or interference with, GPS signals by terrorists, smugglers, or hostile military forces. These countermeasures could conceivably include converting the GPS system to one with greater control over usage or access. Today, the only barrier to the use of the GPS Standard Positioning Service is the retail-taxed price of GPS receivers. Although it might seem that the marginal cost of delivering GPS to any new user in its broadcast range is zero (like any radio broadcast), the expanding use of GPS can create additional costs and risks in the need to protect GPS signals that are not reflected in current equipment prices. A larger percentage of the benefits that are derived from GPS might need to be devoted to ensuring the continued reliability of GPS-dependent systems, whether through taxes, fees, or private investments.

GPS MANAGEMENT, OPERATION, AND FUNDING OPTIONS

As policymakers evaluate the implications of increasing civil, commercial, and military uses of GPS, institutional questions on its future can be reduced to two key questions: (1) Who should manage and operate GPS? and (2) How should GPS be funded? Different "visions" for the institutional future of GPS can be summarized as:

- GPS continues as a U.S. military system
- GPS becomes jointly or exclusively governed by one or more U.S. civilian agencies
- GPS is privatized and managed by a U.S. entity
- GPS is privatized and internationally managed
- GPS is augmented by civil/private/foreign elements (space-based or ground-based)
- GPS is gradually displaced by private space systems or other technologies.

These visions are not all mutually exclusive. A GPS that continues to be a U.S. military system may be augmented by elements from foreign countries or international consortia, such as INMARSAT. Similarly, a GPS under the control of a private U.S. entity may be part of a broader international venture in related space-based communication services. There can be hybrids of privatization and international management whereby governments enforce fee payments to a private international entity. In any event, ensuring continued benefits from GPS will require competent and stable operations and protection of interests of the United States (as the country likely to be most dependent on GPS).

Each of the institutional visions has different funding options associated with them. In the status quo case of GPS continuing as a U.S. military system, the Department of Defense pays for the space and control segments, as well as the military user equipment. All other users buy their own ground equipment. Civil U.S. government agencies are responsible for paying for any GPS augmentations that they might require, as is being done by the FAA and the U.S. Coast Guard. If U.S. civil agencies were to become more responsible for GPS, then they may be asked to share in the cost of maintaining the basic system.

If GPS is to be funded in some way other than with U.S. tax dollars, then private and international (perhaps foreign government) sources of payment are needed. Private sources could include special taxes on GPS receivers or fees for the use of GPS signals, assuming payment could be enforced. Being able to charge for equipment and/or services is central to any proposal to privatize GPS. Whether GPS is under government or private control, it may be displaced by private systems such as space-based communications that could offer competing services. Like a privatized GPS, such systems would need the ability to charge, exclude users, lower costs, or offer better services to compete effectively with it.

NECESSARY CONDITIONS FOR GPS

Theoretically, there are several possible options for organizing the management, operation, and funding of GPS, although these options usually assume the existence of other institutions and mechanisms. Necessary institutional conditions for the operation of the GPS include:

1. The continued cooperation of the International Telecommunication Union in allocating an exclusive worldwide "easement" to a frequency range or ranges;

2. The continued cooperation of the United Kingdom and the Republic of the Marshall Islands for easements to the territory on which three of the five ground stations that communicate with the satellites have been established, as well as the cooperation of the United States for access to the two ground stations on U.S. territory (or substitute control stations must be established);

3. A group of skilled engineers and technicians who know how to manage satellite operations;

4. A source of funding for the maintenance of the system;[1] and

5. A highly reliable organization disciplined to follow operational procedures, especially emergency procedures.

In aggregate, these conditions are sufficient for the continued operation of GPS. Given the proof of the technical feasibility of satellite-based navigation, as demonstrated by GPS, one might argue that the only really necessary and sufficient condition for its continued operation is a source of funds—whether from public or private sources. Not surprisingly, funding is a central institutional issue.

Debates over whether a public or private organization should operate a particular system, whether garbage collection or telephone service, often focus on who can best reduce operating expenses. In the case of GPS, however, payment collection techniques and procedural discipline (conditions 4 and 5) are more important factors than operating-expense reduction for several reasons. Although we care about measurable results (e.g., GPS accuracy, availability, and reliability), which can be well-served by private, profit-seeking organizations, we also care very much about procedures to be followed during national secu-

---

[1]Whether the United States should and can recover its capital investment in the GPS can be separated from the maintenance question.

rity emergencies.[2] Second, it is not clear whether it would ever be technolog-
ically cost-effective to collect from nongovernmental users for the provision of
GPS signals in ways other than those available to a government (e.g., taxes).
Third, given the need to service military as well as nonmilitary users, there does
not appear to be much opportunity to drastically reduce the GPS operating
budget, which goes primarily toward satellites and launch services.[3] There may
be ways of reducing military and civilian personnel costs for functions not
directly related to the operation of GPS, and these can be explored
independently in any case.

Although it might have been difficult for a private company to obtain the necessary easements (conditions 1 and 2) in the first place (that is, the military utility
of the GPS, as originally conceived in the 1970s, might have been the reason the
easements were granted), we can assume that a private company, a civilian
agency, or an international governmental organization might be assigned the
existing easements. We also assume that any organization made responsible for the GPS can hire engineers who know how to fly satellites (and contract
with others to design and build replacement satellites).

The question of who should provide the GPS, if not the DoD through the U.S.
Air Force, thus seems to reduce to funding capabilities and procedural discipline: What payment-collection methods do potential GPS operators have?
Who can be most trusted to follow procedures, both for evaluating user requirements and for emergencies? U.S. and international user groups are becoming very large now that commercial GPS receivers can be obtained for less
than $300. As these groups come to depend on GPS, they seek assurance that it
will be available and reliable. At the same time, changing the availability or
reliability of the signal might be necessary to counteract an undesired use of the
system, and the government seeks assurance that GPS operators will
predictably execute emergency procedures.

ASSESSING INSTITUTIONAL OPTIONS

Table 5.1 ranks how well each institutional GPS option meets the necessary
conditions for GPS operation. A minus (–) means that the option cannot

---

[2]See John D. Donohue, *The Privatization Decision: Public Ends, Private Means,* Basic Books, New
York, 1989, pp. 37–56. Nearly half of all public-sector spending on goods and services went to outside organizations in 1988 (see p. 34).

[3]U.S. Government, Joint DoD/DoT Task Force on GPS, *The Global Positioning System: Management
and Operation of a Dual-Use System,* December 1993, p. 3. The operation of the ground-control
stations might be quite efficient right now, and contracting to (or selling to) a profit-seeker might
not reduce the $30 million per year price tag. The bulk of the $400 million per year cost of GPS
already goes for privately produced goods such as satellites and rockets.

Table 5.1

Ability of Institutional Options to Meet GPS Conditions

Institutional Option	Condition 1, Frequencies	Condition 2, Sites	Condition 3, Personnel	Condition 4, Funding	Condition 5, Discipline
1. Military	+	+	+	+	+
2. U.S. civil	+	+	+	?	+
3. Private	?	?	+	–	?
4. International	?	?	+	?	–
5. Augmented	?	?	+	?	?
6. Displaced	?	?	+	?	?

NOTES: Options
1.   Continue as a U.S. military system
2.   Jointly or exclusively governed by U.S. civilian agencies
3.   Privatized and managed by a U.S. entity
4.   Privatized and internationally managed
5.   Augmented by civil/private/foreign elements
6.   Gradually displaced by private systems or other technologies

Conditions
1.   Frequency allocations
2.   Ground station sites
3.   Skilled operators
4.   Funding
5.   Procedural disciplines, especially for security

meet— or is very unlikely to meet—an operating condition. A question mark (?) means that the option may be able to meet the condition, but that there is some uncertainty. A plus (+) means that the option already meets the operating condition or there is no major barrier to doing so.

As a military system, GPS today meets all of the necessary operating conditions. While it can be argued that there are areas of national interest that GPS does not support as well as it might, the system nonetheless meets the minimal conditions to operate successfully. GPS could also operate with the participation of U.S. civil government agencies, such as the Department of Transportation (DoT), but the key uncertainty is whether DoT would be able to provide adequate or stable funding as more congressional committees became involved.

Some form of international GPS is possible, but the uncertainties are much greater than for a U.S. system. Aside from obtaining frequencies and ground control sites, the key uncertainties are how the systems would be funded and what procedural disciplines would apply. An international system may be able to use the power of government to secure funding, whereas a private operator of the current GPS would have no way of enforcing payment. The alternatives would be to make some arrangement to use governmental power to collect taxes or to encrypt the signal so as to enforce payment. The latter is likely to be so disruptive—especially given the large installed base of GPS equipment—as to be impractical.

Procedural disciplines in national or regional security emergencies are likely to constitute a major problem for any private or international GPS system. The 1992 Federal Radionavigation Plan declares that

> civil users worldwide may rely upon the availability of GPS signals and services at specified accuracy levels. Only in the event of national emergency would the U.S. degrade the accuracy and availability of GPS-SPS signals. Any such degradation would be undertaken only at the direction of the President of the United States.[4]

U.S. military forces are increasingly reliant on GPS in ways that potential adversaries are not. It is unlikely that the United States would willingly give up that advantage to an international organization. If GPS were managed by a private entity under U.S. jurisdiction, it would be subject to national security regulations, as are commercial satellite communications and remote sensing.[5]

The following sections address more specific arguments and alternative assessments made in the course of the study.

Collective and Individual Payments

In a financial accounting sense, the GPS program is a distinct operation. The projected cost to maintain GPS over the next several years is about $400 million per year.[6] What kind of organization is most likely to accrue enough payment to meet ongoing expenses?

The overall cost of DoD procurement may be as much as 18 percent higher than the cost of comparable commercial procurement.[7] In looking at the GPS space and ground segments, however, there seems to be little opportunity for major cost savings.[8] It does not seem likely that a different organization could significantly reduce direct costs—much of the budget already goes to contractors, rather than to government employees, for the production of GPS satellites and related support equipment. In addition, GPS satellite operations at the master

---

[4]Joint DoD/DoT Task Force on GPS, op cit., p. 46.

[5]For example, commercial remote sensing systems licensed by the United States may have operations suspended in the event of threats to U.S. national security. 15 U.S.C. § 82 (5621–5625).

[6]Joint DoD/DoT Task Force on GPS, op. cit., p. 3.

[7]*Directions for Defense*, Report of the Commission on Roles and Missions of the Armed Forces, advance copy, May 24, 1995, p. 3-23.

[8]We did not look closely at GPS Joint Program Office activities such as the procurement of military user equipment.

control station are increasingly in the hands of skilled enlisted personnel, rather than officers, both of whom are already paid less than their private-sector counterparts. One might ask whether operating costs could be reduced if a commercial entity operated the system without DoD regulations. This step could conflict, however, with one of the other necessary conditions for GPS— the existence of procedural disciplines for national security and public safety.

GPS can be thought of as a super-lighthouse that delivers its signal like a broadcast radio or television station. But unlike radio and television, payment for these helpful beacons[9] cannot come from the sale of advertising ("sender-users"), which leaves receiver-users as the only possible paying customers.[10] In addition to general tax receipts, one might imagine excise taxes on receivers, indirect fees for GPS-specific trust funds, patent royalties, and direct usage-metering (e.g., encryption keys or prepaid cards similar to telephone cards).[11]

The GPS program, like other defense activities, is financed through collective payment by U.S. taxpayers and provided by the public sector. If the system were sold or turned over to a private corporation, it would then be delivered by the private sector and could be funded by individual or collective payments. See Figure 5.1.[12]

Government agencies (e.g., the Department of Defense), that need navigation aids could become customers of a commercial GPS, so part of the firm's revenue would come from government funds, as shown by (a) in Figure 5.2.

This complication suggests that the representation of government-provided GPS should not be a single point. Indeed, most GPS expenses are payments for privately-supplied goods and services, such as satellites and launch services as represented by (b) in Figure 5.2.

---

[9]According to definitions in the Code of Federal Regulations, the GPS seems partly a beacon and partly a buoy: Beacons are aids to navigation structures that are permanently fixed to the earth's surface; buoys float. 33 C.F.R. § 62.23(b)–(c) (1990). Although GPS satellites are not geostationary, their positions in orbit are nevertheless precisely known, so that at each moment they transmit, they are indeed "fixed" relative to the earth's surface. Thus they should be considered a kind of beacon.

[10]Unless, for example, an FM station that sublicenses part of its subcarrier capacity to a DGPS supplier chooses to do so as a public service, much like time and temperature information is provided via toll-free telephone numbers. Advertising, of course, can also be considered to be an indirect user charge, paid for by the subset of listeners who become customers of the advertiser.

[11]Encryption keys might be good for a set or indefinite period of time, whereas a prepaid card would be good for a set amount of usage.

[12]Although in each case we might say that the system is being provided "to the public," the word "public" is best used as an adjective to describe a government organization; it reduces confusion not to use "public" as a noun and instead to say "to private persons and commercial organizations."

RAND*MR614-5.1*

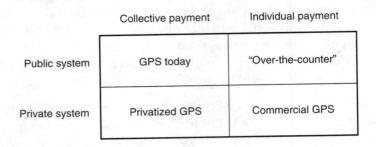

	Collective payment	Individual payment
Public system	GPS today	"Over-the-counter"
Private system	Privatized GPS	Commercial GPS

Figure 5.1—Public and Private Payment Categories

RAND*MR614-5.3*

	Collective payment	Individual payment
Public providers	GPS now DoD	
Private providers	(b) Contractors	(a) Commercial GPS

Figure 5.2—Flow of Funds for Public and Private Providers of GPS

A civilian government program can be paid for by general funds, but it might also be funded through excise taxes that support a GPS trust fund. Airline ticket taxes and gasoline taxes are used to support trust funds for the maintenance of air transportation and highway infrastructures, respectively. In Figure 5.3, the horizontal axis of the diagram is modified to include this possibility, which is more focused than a general tax yet may not reach every individual GPS user, much as the government charges over-the-counter fees for passports, national park entrances, political risk insurance on overseas investment loans, and postal services.

As the experience of the U.S. Post Office suggests, however, when it is possible to charge individuals for services, the American economic system creates private alternatives to government provision of public goods and services.

RAND*MR614-5.3*

	Collective payment		Individual payment
	General taxes	Excise tax	Over-the-counter charges
Public providers	GPS now	"Civil GPS"	
Private providers			

Figure 5.3—Excise Taxes as a Payment Choice

Private Conditions to Operate GPS

Each of the possible means of funding GPS has its own associated collection costs. Although numerical estimates of collection costs have not been made (and seem difficult to make), it is usually asserted or implied that funding from the general treasury or from government trust funds is the most efficient approach. Let us assume that a private company invents a feasible method of collecting payments from GPS users that is cost-effective enough to overcome the costs of transition to a fee system and meet operating expenses, without interrupting the supply of the GPS signals.[13] What other factors might influence the price that the private firm would bid for the GPS?

The firm would probably want governmental assurances (from the United States and as many others as possible) that unauthorized GLONASS receivers would be banned. In effect, the company would ask for a monopoly, since its collection method is moot if another supplier charges nothing for its signals. Could the private GPS supplier stay in business if the United States were its only market? It would likely be subjected to cost-of-service rate regulation, similar to a public utility, although there would be none of the usual issues of capacity problems or adequacy of service to remote customers for regulators to solve.[14] If this reduction in profit potential makes a private company decline to bid for

---

[13]Although the United States has declared its intention to deliver GPS signals worldwide without direct user charges, this does not require the domestic payment to continue to be from general federal funds if a cost-effective way to charge users is found.

[14]The "public utility"—a privately owned firm regulated by public agencies—has been the United States' solution, beginning in the 19th century, to the problem of dealing with goods and services that complicate the functioning of competition because they seem so essential to all persons that delivery should be ensured for all who ask for them. Roger Sherman, *The Regulation of Monopoly*, Cambridge University Press, New York, 1989, p. 3.

GPS, a nationalized GPS is still possible, since GPS does not have the allocation and efficiency problems often associated with nationalized services. In any event, the viability of the private GPS operator would still depend on active use of governmental power, even with a feasible individual payment method.

GPS as a Civil Function Within DoD

It is sometime argued that since there are fewer military users than civil or commercial users, U.S. civil agencies should have a greater role in the policy, management, and funding of GPS. On the other hand, the DoD has demonstrated its stewardship of GPS to date and supports GPS for the benefits it provides to U.S. forces worldwide. At present, there is no clearly viable alternative home for GPS other than the U.S. Department of Defense. U.S. civil agencies may want to have a larger direct role in GPS management and operations, but they have limited budgets to sustain large financial contributions. Excise taxes may be increased or imposed, but the associated transaction costs and dis-benefits are unclear.

A hybrid option for continuing GPS operations within the federal government would be to create a civil function within the Department of Defense. Its purpose would be to maintain military involvement for the institutional conditions of funding and procedural discipline, but to allow a greater role for civil agencies in advocating the interests of civil, commercial, and international users. A well-known example of a civil DoD function is the U.S. Army Corps of Engineers, which uses civilian contractors under the direction of uniformed military personnel. GPS operations could be delegated to the Air Force and continue to be subject to the Federal Radionavigation Plan. Making GPS civilian, but leaving it within DoD (like the Corps), would significantly dilute the "military" nature of the activity, which could benefit international cooperation and attract greater civilian participation without jeopardizing the critical connection of GPS to military operations.

The flows of funds to and from a civil GPS function within the DoD (CF) are shown in Figure 5.4. The civil function could receive funding from general tax funds, from user community excise taxes, as well as from interagency transfers from user agencies such as NASA and the Department of the Interior. These agencies could in turn decide whether to institute charges of their own or pay from their appropriations. Thus funds from multiple sources could support Air Force operations and their contractors. The Air Force and other DoD elements could negotiate the level of support they would provide to the civil function or agree to mutual support with no transfer of funds. In principle, this structure could also allow for payments from foreign user agencies, such as civil aviation authorities.

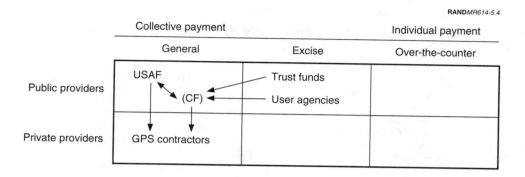

Figure 5.4—Flow of Funds for a Civil Function in DoD

In the civil function option, GPS funding would no longer come from DoD military appropriations and compete with more traditional weapon system procurements. Appropriations would become the responsibility of the Transportation Subcommittee of the Appropriations Committee, a subcommittee that can more easily receive input from nonmilitary government, industry, and other user groups.[15] Nonmilitary user groups' requirements for GPS design and operations could also be incorporated through appropriate agencies within the Departments of Transportation and Commerce. While this would lower the burden on DoD, it would also increase the voice of non-DoD agencies in setting GPS policy and priorities. Whether the new system of funding would be more stable than the current reliance on DoD is unknown.

How much should identifiable civilian, commercial, and private users pay for the GPS to reduce the collective-payment burden that up to now has been justified by the national-defense function of the GPS?[16] Perhaps nothing at all. The GPS could continue to be funded through general funds. Compared with private expenditures on other commonly available goods and services, the GPS budget does not seem a large burden on the economy. Compared with the entire budgets of U.S. civil agencies involved with navigation, however, it does indeed seem large, and significant contributions would be a major burden on those agencies.[17] See Table 5.2.

---

[15]The Army Corps of Engineers is similarly funded through a nonweapons Appropriations Committee, the Water and Energy Subcommittee (inland waterways); yet it too is managed by uniformed military personnel.

[16]The intention of the United States not to impose direct user fees for GPS on the international aviation community is independent of the domestic funding burden.

[17]Estimated budgets are from *Budget of the United States Government,* Fiscal Year 1995.

Table 5.2

U.S. Expenses for Traditional Utilities and Major Civil Agencies

Personal U.S. consumption of		
Electricity	$75 B	(1991)[a]
Communications	$54 B	(1991)
Gas	$28 B	(1991)
Water/sewer	$28 B	(1991)
Annual GPS maintenance	**$0.4 B**	**(1993)**
GPS receiver purchases	**$0.9 B**	**(1994)[b]**
Civil agency budgets		
FAA	$9 B	(1995 est.)
Corps of Engineers	$7 B	(1995 est.)
Coast Guard	$4 B	(1995 est.)

[a]Charles F. Phillips, *The Regulation of Public Utilities: Theory and Practice*, Public Utilities Reports, Arlington, VA, 1993, p. 9.

[b]U.S. GPS Industry Council, March 1995.

The alternative to having civil agencies pay for GPS out of their appropriations is to allow them to impose excise taxes. Revenues from excise taxes can be considerable, as shown in Table 5.3. Possible domestic excise-tax sources include transportation fuels, receiver equipment (it is too late to enforce U.S. government GPS patents, as discussed in Chapter Four), vehicle/vessel registration, passenger tickets, surveyor's licenses, map publishers, exploration companies, and DGPS services. Some fees for navigation aids are also levied on foreign vessels.[18]

Table 5.3

Example Revenues from U.S. Excise Taxes, 1994

	$ Billion
Highway (trust fund)	16.7
Transportation fuels	9.4
Alcohol	7.5
Tobacco	5.7
Airport (trust fund)	5.2
Telephone	3.5

SOURCE: *Budget of the United States Government*, Fiscal Year 1996, Table 2.4.

---

[18]For example, see the House Ways and Means Committee report, *New Tonnage Fees at U.S. Ports, Passenger Excise Taxes for Voyages Departing the United States, and Excise Tax on Liquid Fuels Used by Vessels Engaged in Foreign Transportation*, for USCG Maritime Safety and Navigation Services (Maritime Administration and Promotional Reform Act of 1994), 25 CIS/Index (July 9, 1994) H783-8.

If the GPS does not fully displace other civil navigation systems, an increase of a few percent in the pertinent excise tax revenues would seem to be required to cover its costs (even if DoD appropriations continued to pay for part of the annual expense). Such increases can be expected to be resisted by the user communities asked to bear them. As discussed in Chapter Four, additional taxes and fees are a threat to the continued growth of GPS. A full assessment of the merits of such taxes would have to balance not only collection costs but the potential decline of general tax revenues from slower adoption of GPS-based applications in the economy.

The primary motivation for creating a civil function for GPS would be budgetary. One could argue that as long as GPS is included in the military portion of DoD's budget, it is in jeopardy of losing the increasing competition for DoD dollars, dollars that will not be supplemented by civilian agencies because of GPS's location in the budget (under OMB Function 050). By converting GPS into a DoD civilian program, the Congressional Appropriations Committee jurisdiction would also change, most likely to Transportation, which would open the possibility of using transportation-related trust funds. Once the funding of GPS was officially shared or transferred between DoD and civilian agencies, neither would be likely to think of it as "free," which is how the civilian agencies now view it.

The major concern for GPS users is that the signal continue to be supplied in a stable, competent, and fair manner. Any movement of GPS toward more civil involvement could raise concerns that military support, particularly from the Air Force, would decline. While we acknowledge the budget constraints felt by the Air Force, a decline in support seems unlikely given both the military importance of GPS to national security and the popularity of GPS, compared to other military space activities, among conventional force commanders.

DIFFERENTIAL GPS ISSUES

Better GPS accuracy and reliability can be achieved by installing known, fixed-reference receivers that can send differential GPS (DGPS) corrections to remote or mobile GPS receivers. The relation of DGPS to GPS is similar to the original relation between community-access television (CATV) and broadcast television—it is an added-value service that improves the quality of the signal received directly from distant broadcast transmitters. Like CATV, persons who want DGPS data can be charged for it and others can be excluded by the DGPS supplier through encryption or activation by a prepaid card.

One of the reasons most countries have provided lighthouse services and other navigation aids out of general funds, or from ship tonnage fees and airport and excise taxes, is that private operators cannot overcome the problems of small numbers of customers and free-ridership (non-excludability) without government assistance.[19] DGPS is different because there are several ways to deliver (or exclude) DGPS signals. Private companies already collect for the provision of DGPS data around the world and the industry can support price and service-level competition. Although some refereeing might be needed for frequency assignments, neither cost-of-service rate-making nor nationalization is a necessary requirement.[20]

The first use of DGPS receivers to be required by federal regulation are in Prince William Sound, Alaska.[21] Other U.S. Coast Guard DGPS locations are being assessed.[22] DGPS services can be delivered by either the government or private companies, but the government can charge user fees for the DGPS data it provides or restrict access to it to prevent preemption of private providers.[23] OMB Circular A-25 provides guidance on the scope and types of government activities for which the government may assess user charges. One of its objectives is to "allow the private sector to compete with the government without disadvantage in supplying comparable services, resources, or goods where appropriate."[24] If a private company can charge for a service, then the government should not provide the same service for free. There are some important exceptions, however, such as providing the service for national security, foreign policy, or public safety reasons. Thus, the United States can provide a free service for its forces, as part of an international agreement, or as necessary for safety-of-life purposes such as air and sea navigation. The latter is a key reason for the installation in Prince William Sound, which has already suffered from the oil spill of the *Exxon Valdez*.

Individual charges to persons needing DGPS signals can be used in conjunction with incremental increases in excise taxes to pay for the use of GPS. For example, the U.S. government might collect a value-added tax from private DGPS providers and users. The fundamental difference between DGPS and CATV involves sources of revenue. Broadcast television companies (the "networks") were not allowed by the FCC to collect fees from CATV companies because

---

[19]David E. Van Zandt, *The Lessons of the Lighthouse: "Government" or "Private" Provision of Goods*, 1993, 22 *J. Legal Studies*, pp. 47–72, at 56.

[20]For a discussion of choosing government intervention to match the market problem, see Stephen Breyer, *Regulation and its Reform*, Harvard University Press, Cambridge, MA, 1982, p. 149.

[21]33 C.F.R. § 161.376(a)(5).

[22]For example, see 60 F.R. 5453 (Atlantic Intercoastal Region)(January 27, 1995); 59 F.R. 59816 (Hawaii Region)(November 18, 1994).

[23]The U.S. charges fees for other navigation-related services, even where there is no parallel private provision (e.g., light dues/tonnage dues, 14 C.F.R. 4.20–22; harbor maintenance, 14 C.F.R. §§ 24.24; navigation fees, 14 C.F.R. § 4.98; and aircraft arrival fees, 14 C.F.R. § § 24.22, 111.96, 122.29).

[24]Office of Management and Budget, Circular No. A-25, Revised, Transmittal Memorandum no. 1, ¶ 5.c, July 8, 1993.

CATV increased the reach of the sponsors' advertising messages, which made the broadcast time more valuable. GPS is not funded by advertising and thus can be paid for only by "subscription" or taxes.

NAVIGATION USES OF DGPS

The U.S. government seems to have little interest in competing with private DGPS suppliers in commercial markets such as survey and mapping. The government does, however, have a strong interest in ensuring that reliable, effective navigation aids exist for public safety and commerce. As discussed in Chapter Four, it is the overlap between public and private interests in DGPS navigation that has stimulated conflicts over FAA and U.S. Coast Guard plans for DGPS services. Furthermore, the U.S. government places special burdens on private providers of navigation aids, as described below.

Water Navigation

The United States has a long history of supporting aids to navigation for both military and commercial reasons. Aids to water navigation have been provided by the federal government since 1789, for two basic reasons.[25] First, by directing the states to cede their lighthouses and beacons to the United States and by putting the federal government in the business of constructing, operating, and financing a nationwide system of aids to navigation, Congress could assert a national authority and a national responsibility, and begin to bind the states to the idea of a common enterprise.[26]

Lighthouses and beacons were brought under control of the Secretary of the Treasury, which suggests a second reason for Federal jurisdiction. Coastal lights were not only part of a nation's internal identity, but also a part of a nation's stance toward other nations. Ships in harbors were one of the few sources of collectible revenue for the young U.S. government.[27] Other countries, of course, charged import duties, but Great Britain also charged light

---

[25]An Act for the Establishment and Support of Lighthouses, Beacons, Buoys, and Public Piers, 1 Stat. 53 (1789)(enacted August 7, 1789).

[26]The cession of jurisdiction is still a requirement: "No lighthouse, beacon, public pier, or landmark shall be built or erected on any site until cession [by the State] of jurisdiction over the same has been made to the United States." 33 U.S.C. § 727 (1986) (codified R.S. § 4661).

[27]A whiskey tax and a domestic ship-licensing fee were others. An Act for laying a Duty on Goods, Wares, and Merchandises Imported into the United States. 1 Stat. 24 (1789) (enacted July 4, 1789); An Act imposing Duties on Tonnage, 1 Stat. 27 (1789) (enacted July 20, 1789). {Whiskey Tax} 1 Stat. 202–03, §§ 14–15 (1791); {Ship Licensing} 1 Stat 55, § 1 (Sept 1, 1789).

dues.[28] Thus it seems that the United States set up tonnage duties and, soon after, a "light money" duty, to reciprocate Great Britain's practice.[29]

Today, the U.S. Coast Guard is specifically empowered to

> establish, maintain, and operate electronic aids to navigation systems required to serve the needs of the armed forces of the United States peculiar to warfare and primarily of military concern as determined by the Secretary of Defense or any department within the Department of Defense[30]

or as required to

> serve the needs of the maritime commerce of the United States.[31]

In addition to empowering the Coast Guard, private DGPS providers are correspondingly limited by federal regulations. Commercial DGPS services are not authorized for use by the armed forces or for maritime commerce. The only kind of private electronic aids to water navigation that are authorized are "radar beacons and shore-based radar stations."[32] This leaves open the possibility of a noncommercial maritime navigation market for private DGPS providers. GPS equipment is increasingly popular on recreation boats, and DGPS systems could find favor with current users of Loran-C radio beacons. One of the familiar barriers, however, is the fact that Loran-C is free of direct user charges.

Air Navigation

Provision of air navigation facilities and services is the duty of members of the International Civil Aviation Organization (ICAO) within the limited range set forth in Article 28(a) of the 1948 Chicago Convention. Each signatory undertakes, so far "as it may find practicable," to provide in its territory radio services, meteorological services, and other air navigation facilities for international air navigation. In 1987, a commentator on the work of the Future Air Navigation Systems (FANS) committee of the ICAO asserted that nothing in the Chicago Convention "prevents the States from delegating their functions to a specific

---

[28]Britain had consolidated ownership of lights in 1679 into the Trinity House, which began as an association of seafarers in 1514 to control pilots in harbors and to accumulate funds for old seamen, their widows, and orphans. Trinity House either exploited the exclusive licenses itself or leased the "patents" to individuals. Most holders employed local collectors provided by Trinity House who were paid commissions on the amount collected from ships that entered port.

[29]Act March 27, 1804, c. 57, § 6, 2 Stat. 300. See also Lawrence A. Harper, *The English Navigation Laws*, Columbia University Press, New York, 1939, p. 276.

[30]14 U.S.C. § 81(3)(a).

[31]14 U.S.C. § 81(3)(b).

[32]33 C.F.R. § 66.01-1(d).

entity, public or private, within their jurisdictional limits."[33] This could be taken as allowing an international organization to provide navigation services based on GPS.

The U.S. Secretary of Transportation prescribes the regulations on standards for installing navigational aids for air commerce, including airport control towers.[34] The Federal Aviation Administration is responsible for locating, constructing or installing, maintaining, and operating federal aids to air navigation.[35] In contrast to the practice with maritime aids, many kinds of privately operated air navigation aids are permitted by the FAA.[36] The FAA could also permit private DGPS companies to compete in air navigation markets under suitable regulation for signal accuracy, reliability, availability, and integrity.

Land Navigation

The Global Positioning System has, of course, stimulated the market for land-navigation DGPS services, and neither the Coast Guard nor the FAA seems to have jurisdiction over that user segment. Private providers of DGPS signals already serve the land-navigation user segment. As GPS technology develops, there may be interest in regulating the use of DGPS for land navigation—for example, for use on public highways, where public safety may be affected.

INTERNATIONAL CONTROL AND MANAGEMENT

By the middle of the 19th century, most nations were providing maritime and inland-waterway navigation aids, such as lighthouses, as a public service to their own merchant marine as well as foreign ships. These aids were paid for from general funds and without direct user fees. (Customs duties and tariffs were designed to achieve other purposes.) Most countries had recognized the provision of lighthouses and harbor markings as a mutual service, and had decided not to charge navigation-aid fees.[37] Radionavigation aids, made possible

---

[33]Michael, Milde, "Legal Aspects of Future Air Navigation Systems," 12 *Annals of Air and Space Law,* 1987, pp. 87–98, at p. 92.

[34]49 U.S.C. 44719.

[35]49 C.F.R. § 1.4(c)(4).

[36]C.F.R., Title 14—Aeronautics and Space, Chapter I—Federal Aviation Administration, Department Of Transportation, Subchapter J—Navigational Facilities, Part 171—Non-Federal Navigation Facilities.

[37]See David E. Van Zandt, "The Lessons of the Lighthouse: 'Government' or 'Private' Provision of Goods," 22 *J. Legal Studies* 1993, 47–72, at p. 70. England seems to have been a hold-out. In the late 19th century, Britain continued to refuse to eliminate the light dues. Even today, 46 U.S.C. 128 declares "a duty of 50 cents per ton, to be denominated 'light money', shall be levied and collected on all vessels not of the United States. . . ." The Customs Service of the U.S. Department of Treasury ex-

by the development of radar during World War II, might not be as palpable or as romantic as lighthouses, but they are a traditional government responsibility. Since the formation of the ICAO in 1947, nations have been responsible, so far as each "may find practicable," for providing air navigation systems in their territories.[38] Radio-based aids for water navigation have been developed during the past 50 years.

By design, GPS signals extend beyond U.S. territory and can be received anywhere on the earth's surface or in its atmosphere. The decision not to exclude use of a "civilian" signal outside the United States had been made by the time of a 1981 notice in the *Federal Register*, but the decision was more dramatically announced soon after an off-course Korean airliner (flight KAL 007) was shot down by the Soviet Union in 1983.[39] President Reagan declared that GPS would be made available to international civilian aviation to help prevent such tragedies in the future. The general availability of the system, however, was not expected to occur until 1987 or 1988.

The declaration of GPS availability was repeated, and in some ways expanded, to ICAO by the FAA administrator, in 1991, 1992, and 1994, and by President Clinton in 1995. It was stated that the United States intends to deliver GPS signals on a continuous, worldwide basis, subject to the availability of funds (as required by U.S. law) while not charging direct user fees, for ten years, and will give six years notice if it is going to discontinue the service. Today, this policy might strike some as overly generous, but it probably would have proven expensive or impossible to collect direct user fees for a system that (a) was not asked for, (b) could displace national radionavigation systems, (c) was subject to U.S. national control, and (d) was already available without encryption to U.S. users. Short of creating some kind of signal "shadow" over a country (which would overlap neighboring areas), or changing the signal so that new re-

---

empts 116 nations from paying this "light money" and the United Kingdom is not on the list.   19 C.F.R. § 4.22 (4-1-94 edition).

[38]Chicago Convention 1944 Art. 28(a).

[39]46 F.R. 20724 (April 7, 1981): Notice by the Secretary of Defense re NAVSTAR GPS Navigation Satellite Systems Status: "Notice is hereby given that the Department of Defense's NAVSTAR GPS program is now in the Full Scale Development phase . . . the satellites may transmit both the precise (P) and coarse acquisition (C/A) signals which are intended only for military or other Federal agency testing purposes. Other possible users are cautioned that the system is developmental and that availability of the signals, or the accuracy possible, are subject to change without advanced warning. *The latest DoD policy concerning NAVSTAR GPS is that when the system is declared operational, the highest possible level of C/A signal accuracy will be made available to the worldwide civil/commercial community within the limits of national security considerations.* It is projected that this will be an accuracy of 200M Spherical Error Probable (SEP). This level of accuracy will be reviewed by DoD annually and the level modified to accommodate any changes commensurate with our national security posture. It is anticipated that this non-military accuracy may be increased as time passes. The DoD is also considering the possibility of charging users of the NAVSTAR GPS worldwide positioning/navigation system for the service provided." [Emphasis added.]

ceivers would have some kind of metering system, the United States did not have much leverage to induce payment. Yet it is precisely because these acts are thought possible, at the option of the system operator, that other countries are reluctant to rely on GPS for domestic civil aviation or maritime navigation.

The United States seeks international acceptance of GPS for many reasons, including enabling allied and U.S. forces to work more easily together and promoting economic growth through use of GPS applications and sales of U.S. equipment and services. Given that seeking payment is not a U.S. objective, U.S. economic interests could be pursued even if other systems, such as GLONASS, became the world standard. Assuming U.S. manufacturers are allowed to build GLONASS-capable receivers, the key condition enabling the United States to compete is whether the signal structures of the others systems are published. The fact that U.S. industry led in developing GPS equipment and applications means that it is in the economic interest of the United States to see GPS as a global standard now. However, the ability to compete depends on the availability of open, international standards that can be used by anyone.

The United States would like other countries to install DGPS reference receivers and correction-data transmitters at their airports and harbors because GPS signals alone do not give sufficient approach accuracy. Since the United States is planning to use DGPS for its domestic airports and harbors, it seeks international acceptance of GPS "to limit the amount of expensive equipment that U.S. ships and aircraft must carry and to prevent duplication of systems at U.S. airports and harbors."[40] Although other nations might install DGPS systems with their own funds, the United States could consider other means of achieving widespread DGPS availability and standardization, including (a) installing both GPS and "GLONASS-capable" radionavigation receivers on U.S. aircraft and ships when they are refitted for DGPS, or (b) paying for DGPS equipment to be installed and operated at foreign airports and harbors (which would of course displace the expense of installing the GLONASS equipment on every U.S. aircraft and ship).[41] Given the wide availability of GPS equipment and the relative lack of comparable GLONASS equipment, a decision to use GLONASS would likely be a political rather than an economic or technical decision.

---

[40]Joint DoD/DoT Task Force on GPS, 1993, p. 45.

[41]If there are multiple DGPS and D-GLONASS data formats possible, then (b) seems the better choice, to ensure that differential equipment sending the same format is installed everywhere. The (b) option would also eliminate the problem of having to install still other types of radionavigation equipment in aircraft for airports that use neither DGPS nor D-GLONASS. In each of these plans, the problem of what equipment gets installed on foreign craft that might travel to the United States could be overcome by allowing U.S. GPS receiver manufacturers to build and sell "GPS and GLONASS-ready" models (similar to television sets that are capable of making sense of feeds from NTSC, PAL, SECAM, HDTV, CATV, and VCR sources). This would seem to satisfy another ostensible objective of "international acceptance" of the GPS, which is to foster export sales by U.S. manufacturers of GPS receivers, who currently have a product-design lead and a strong market share.

Like all radio broadcasts, GPS can be seen as an intrusion into the sovereign territory of a nation. Aids to navigation are landmarks and inland-waterway marks, and thus represent claims to territory and jurisdiction. The resistance to quick acceptance of the GPS (or GLONASS) might be best explained by this disturbance of sovereign identity and power as states realize the commercial and military benefits of satellite-based navigation.

By making superfluous some existing aids to a nation's navigation, GPS over-laps with the power of other sovereigns to provide aids to navigation within their territories and at their frontiers, and with the missions of some interna-tional civil governmental organizations (IGOs) and some long-established in-ternational nongovernmental organizations (INGOs); see Table 5.4. It seems likely that a civil agency or a private venture to build a GPS would have been blocked, or at least boycotted, by various interest groups. The national security purpose of the GPS and the commitment of the United States were vital to overcoming historical inertia. It is understandable, now that the GPS is op-erational and available for civilian purposes, that some of these groups would suggest that other nations should not become dependent on a system con-trolled by the United States, but instead should develop and operate a separate system, unless control of the GPS (and GLONASS) were somehow moved to an international organization. Potential homes include existing satellite operators (INMARSAT, INTELSAT, EUTELSAT), and others without current specific authority in their charters to operate navigation systems (IMO, ICAO, IALA, the European Space Agency).

Table 5.4

Sample International Civil Organizations Affected by GPS

IGO (International governmental organization):
  ICAO —International Civil Aviation Organization (171 UN members)
  IMO—International Maritime Organization (137 UN members)
  INMARSAT—International Maritime Satellite Organization
  INTELSAT—International Satellite Organization
  Eutelsat—European Telecommunications Satellite Organization
  Eurocontrol—European Organization for the Safety of Air Navigation
  Loran-C Operating Authority in six European states
INGO (International nongovernmental organization):
  IOC—Intergovernmental Oceanographic Commission
  IATA—International Air Transport Association
  IALA—International Association of Lighthouse Authorities
  IAIN—International Association of Institutes of Navigation
  IFSMA—International Federation of Shipmasters' Associations
  ICS—International Chamber of Shipping
  OCIMF—Oil Companies International Marine Forum

There are few advantages to be gained by the United States from selling or transferring GPS to an international organization and some distinct risks. In the first place, economic benefits from the sale would depend on maintaining or increasing international use of GPS equipment and services. An international organization would be unlikely to be able to positively affect voluntary economic choices save indirectly through maintaining stable, high-quality GPS signals. Second, the United States would continue to be a major, if not primary, user of GPS and would probably continue to pay a large share of the operating budget. The United Nations could not afford to pay very much for GPS, unless it found a collection system to allow it to recover costs over several years with income from operations. Even if the UN could give a credit toward the annual U.S. assessment of about 25 percent of the total regular UN administration budget, the amount would be less than the annual GPS maintenance budget.[42] Third, and perhaps most important, the United States could not have the same level of control over procedural disciplines for GPS in an international organization. Given the national security importance of GPS to the United States, this is likely to be a decisive factor in keeping GPS under U.S. jurisdiction.

If the United States wishes to gain economic benefits from GPS and protect its national security interests, then it should retain ownership and operational control. This does not preclude, however, an international effort to make individual agreements with major trading nations that address concerns of availability, reliability, emergency procedures, liability, and payment. Other nations do have legitimate technical, legal, and political concerns with relying on GPS—as would the United States if positions were reversed. No existing international organization can address the full range of international security and economic concerns found in GPS. Thus, direct discussions between the United States and its traditional friends and allies would be more effective than specialized, multilateral negotiations.

INFORMING THE POLICY DEBATE

Many kinds of justifications for preserving or changing the GPS governance and funding arrangements are advanced in public policy debates. The remainder of this chapter examines some of these themes in order to explore underlying assumptions and premises sometimes relied on by advocates. We argue that the criteria for deciding how GPS should be governed, managed, and funded can be reduced to two questions: (1) Who can be most trusted to follow particular procedures, both for evaluating user requirements and for emergencies? (2) What effective payment collection methods are available to potential GPS operators?

---

[42]Werner J. Feld, Robert S. Jordan, and Leon Hurwitz, *International Organizations: A Comparative Approach*, Praeger Press, New York, 1994, p. 50–51. Total United Nations assessments in 1991, for regular budget and peacekeeping combined, were approximately $1.3 billion.

GPS has been an occasional subject of speculation for potential "privatization," transfer to a civil agency, or transfer to an international organization. In varying forms, there are at least four recurring reasons for this interest:

1. GPS is seen as a natural monopoly, a public good, or a utility.

2. GPS is seen as a dual-use technology and should therefore be managed jointly by civil and military authorities.

3. The United States needs to change the way it provides GPS in order to earn international "good will."

4. Governance of GPS should naturally fall to the U.S. government because it performs a "government function," or because the liability issues preclude private-sector control.

GPS as a "Natural Monopoly," "Public Good," or "Utility"

Proponents of keeping the U.S. government in control of GPS frequently assert that GPS is more efficiently run by the U.S. government because it is a "natural monopoly," "public good," or a "utility." Yet these terms beg the question of how GPS should be managed. In fact, their use assumes that a particular model of management and funding is natural for GPS or has already been determined.

The delivery of some goods is labeled "a natural monopoly" not because of company behavior, but because of "natural" constraints on competition. These constraints are not necessarily legal ones, but rather the result of larger production plants or distribution networks being dramatically more efficient than smaller ones. These economies of scale then create competitive barriers to entry. Examples of natural monopolies include the delivery of natural gas, electricity, and water, all of which require physical connections to customer sites and which seem to be most efficiently supplied by one big (local) supplier. A satellite-based navigation aid would seem to qualify as a "natural monopoly" because it requires a large initial investment and it can be provided efficiently by a single system. Thus, we should simply consider the two traditional institutional solutions for a natural monopoly—nationalization or a private company regulated with cost-of-service ratemaking.[43]

One must be careful not to label something a natural monopoly too quickly, however, because "once a service is labeled a natural monopoly the urge takes hold to enshrine in law what reality seems to have ordained and to forbid com-

---

[43]Cost-of-service ratemaking, of course, presupposes a payment-from-individuals collecting method.

petition in that market as wasteful and harmful to the public interest."[44]   It would be misleading to label the GPS a natural monopoly, both because competition is possible without redundancy and because the label presupposes that all nations have granted the GPS a franchise to operate in their countries.

To an economist, "single-firm efficiency" means that the average cost of providing the service declines indefinitely as output (or usage) grows, so that the larger firm is more efficient than the smaller one.   In the case of a satellite broadcast, the marginal cost (leaving aside any effect on military utility) of serving additional users is zero.   However, the economy of scale for the satellite system is not in the size of its plant, but in the range of its signal and its availability and reliability.   A satellite navigation system does not have the easement problems that traditional natural monopolies have.   Unlike gas and electric lines, and the waste that multiple pipe and wire pathways seem to create, radio spectrum and orbital space, although finite, are not yet so crowded as to foreclose other satellite-based navigation systems.   It remains possible for there to be competition in terms of availability, reliability, and the accuracies achievable from different operators' signals.

The United States may prefer to minimize the number of "GPS-like" systems for reasons unrelated to easements (such as frequency licenses) or economies of scale, but rather for national security and foreign policy objectives.   Even if GPS is treated as a natural monopoly from one country's perspective—that is, a second system seems superfluous—it is not necessarily a natural monopoly from another's perspective.   The United States cannot stop another country from putting up a GPS-like constellation of satellites.   Although the redundancy might seem wasteful, there could be competitive—not just military—reasons for such an investment.

GPS is sometime referred to as a "public good," with the implication that it should continue to be made available by government.   The term "public good" is formally applied to things which are nonrivalrous and non-excludable in use. (National defense is the archetypal example of a public good.)   Nonrivalrous means that one person's benefit does not preempt another's benefit.   For example, if I benefit from GPS, that does not prevent you from benefiting from GPS.   Non-excludable means that it is difficult to deny the benefit to particular persons.   For example, if I am using GPS, I cannot prevent you from using GPS.

Although GPS is nonrivalrous, it need not be non-excludable, and thus GPS need not be a public good.   Excludability is a function of the costs of fee-collection methods, and these costs can vary with time.   The United States

---

[44]Charles H. Kennedy, *An Introduction to U.S. Telecommunications Law*, Artech House, Norwood, MA, 1994, p. xiv.

could have chosen to deny the GPS signal to all but military users, limited use to those with "registered" decrypting receivers, or imposed an excise tax. Even if we treat GPS as a public good, labeling it as such does not resolve the question of whether a private company should be paid by the U.S. government to operate it, or questions of international use, mutual benefits, and competition.

In contrast to "public good," GPS is sometimes referred to as a "utility," with the implication that it be made available by a private firm as are public utilities. The imagery may be understandable, but the analogy is not accurate when applied to GPS. In the United States, a public utility is a

> privately owned and operated business whose services are so essential to the general public as to justify the grant of special franchises for the use of public property or the right of eminent domain, in consideration of which the owners must serve all persons who apply, without discrimination . . . . To constitute a true public utility, the devotion to public use must be of such character that the public generally, or that part of it which has been served and which has accepted the service, has the legal right to demand that service shall be conducted, so long as it is continued, with reasonable efficiency under reasonable charges.[45]

Aside from the obvious fact that GPS is a DoD-owned and -operated system, there are other differences between GPS and a public utility. The most important one is the inability to collect payment for the Standard Positioning Service. Although it is possible to collect payment for access to the Precise Positioning Service, current U.S. policy clearly opposes making that service available to all person who apply. National security concerns are another barrier to allowing users to legally demand GPS service at specified terms and conditions.

If the United States were willing to allow legal recourse to users, say in the context of an international agreement, that would be a significant change in U.S. policy. To become a public utility, a method of enforcing payment would have to be imposed and national security concerns would have to be resolved. The same technology may serve both ends, leaving a policy judgment as to whether government management or private management best serves the public interest.

GPS as a Dual-Use Technology

Although GPS was not originally designed to meet commercial or private requirements, position and velocity information is useful to nonmilitary activities such as civil aviation, merchant marine shipping, city bus fleet monitoring, am-

---

[45]Henry Campbell Black, *Black's Law Dictionary*, Fifth Ed., West Publishing, St. Paul, MN, 1979, pp. 1108–1109.

bulance dispatch/routing, land surveying, farming, and navigating city streets by automobile. Some GPS applications might improve upon and thus displace other aids to navigation and their costs. Other applications were not feasible before GPS and are thus dependent on GPS continuing.

It can be confusing to call GPS a "dual-use technology" in the same sense as radar, jet propulsion, or night-vision devices, because it is not just the technology of satellite radionavigation signal-making that is sought by other groups, but access to the system. In this sense, the GPS is similar to the 42,795-mile Dwight D. Eisenhower System of Interstate and Defense Highways, a program whose original military function likewise helped overcome obstacles to obtaining easements and funding that a private company or even a civilian agency might not have overcome.[46] The major commercial and private benefits of the interstate highways were not derived from new road-building technology that could be sold or exported; it was the direct use of the system itself.

Like the interstate highway system, GPS signals are shared by the military because of their commercial and private utility. The additional usage provides supporting justification the DoD might need to sustain funding for the system. These additional benefits also introduce additional costs. In the case of the highway system, sharing the system reduced the military utility of the system by reducing its availability. This reduction in military utility has not proved to be a problem because the military need for the interstate system has been small relative to its total capacity. In the case of the GPS, which is "nonrivalrous"— one user does not preclude any others—the sharing of the system reduces its military utility because the accuracy and reliability required for some commercial applications are equal to or greater than some military requirements, and therefore hostile uses of GPS cannot be reduced by simply denying access to military-level accuracy. In addition, if commercial and private users do not keep or install local, alternate navigation systems as backup to the safety-of-life uses of the GPS, then turning off the "civilian signal" will be a politically difficult option to exercise. Clearly, military users will need other means of countering potential hostile users of GPS than simply turning the system off.

The problem of commercial and private dependency, which hostile users can exploit, would exist even if the GPS was not shared and a similar, separate system were established for commercial uses. To block the access of hostile users to the GPS, while at the same time enabling one's own military users, means blocking the access of commercial and private users. Thus there seem to be no

---

[46] *U.S. Government Manual,* U.S. Government Printing Office, Washington, D.C., 1993/4, p. 466 (Federal Highway Administration).

domestic advantages, for national emergency purposes, in having a second, somewhat redundant, GPS, even if the price of the second system were affordable.[47] The military must develop countermeasures whether it directly operates the GPS or not. These countermeasures can operate at the GPS reception site (e.g., jamming), act against the use of GPS (e.g., defenses against GPS-aided weapons), or be emergency institutional procedures. In the case of U.S. air navigation aids, emergency procedures were developed between the DoD and the Federal Aviation Administration to prevent their use by hostile aircraft during wartime.[48]

It is unlikely that U.S. commercial and private users will agitate for the transfer of GPS operation and control from DoD to a civil agency, let alone a private corporation, if their accuracy, reliability, and availability requirements are being met. From a historical viewpoint, other civil works, especially those related to transportation and navigation, have long been provided by military or hybrid-military organizations. The Naval Observatory is the keeper of the nation's time standard; the Army Corps of Engineers builds dams and bridges and maintains interior navigable waterways; the interstate highway system was originally conceived and funded as a troop and weapons transport network; the Coast Guard serves private boaters and commercial shipping, but becomes part of the Navy in military emergencies; and, as mentioned earlier, the country's civil aviation navigation aids come under military control during defense emergencies (SCATANA).[49]

In 1789, lighthouses could be as useful to naval vessels as they were to commercial vessels. Thus it could be argued that lighthouses were "necessary and proper"[50] for providing and maintaining a (future) navy, or that, because navigation aids were important to commerce, they were "necessary and proper" to the regulation of commerce.[51] Unfortunately, the legislative record does not make clear what authority the first Congress used for the Act that

---

[47]This is in contrast to, for example, the Virginia state toll road that parallels the Washington-Dulles Airport access road, which serves both "emergency" (access to Dulles) and toll-collecting purposes.

[48]One of the first steps that Executive Departments take in deciding whether an activity should be performed under contract with commercial sources or in-house, using government facilities and personnel, is to apply the following two tests: (1) If activity is a governmental function, retain in-house; (2) if in-house performance is required for national defense, retain in-house. See the "Flow Chart, Implementation of OMB Circular No. A-76, Existing government activities and expansions," August 1983, Supplement, OMB Circular No. A-76 (Revised), *Performance of Commercial Activities*, Part 1 (Policy implementation), Exhibit 1, p. 4–5.

[49]Plan for the security control of air traffic and air navigation aids (Short title: SCATANA), 32 C.F.R. § 245, 12 p.

[50]U.S. Const., Art. I, § 8. cl. 13.

[51]U.S. Const., Art. I, § 8. cl. 3.

brought lighthouses under the control of the Treasury.[52] The construction and operation of lighthouses is not itself regulation of commerce, and the states, though prohibited from levying any of their own duties on imports or exports, or on tonnage, without the consent of Congress,[53] could have nevertheless continued to operate their lighthouses and get paid for doing so by Congress. Congress has the power to "provide," which is not necessarily to "supply," for the general welfare of the United States and a state or private role is not precluded.[54]

In short, there is no compelling historical or legal argument for preferring civil or military federal control of GPS as a navigation aid—or any preference for government or private providers. The choice is essentially one based on U.S. national interests and the availability (or inability) to charge for services provided.

International Good Will

It is sometimes argued that GPS should be transferred to a civil agency or an international organizations in order to generate international "good will." While acknowledging that providing free GPS signals to users worldwide is already a major gift on the part of the United States, some say the fact that the system is controlled by one country and operated by its military is unwelcome. Thus, GPS should be placed under civilian control, preferably an international organization in which all users could share in decisions about GPS operation, management, and funding. What the United States would presumably gain is additional good will, enhanced international standing, and the satisfaction of seeing GPS more rapidly adopted as a global standard with concurrent economic benefits.

In the past, the United States has led the development of international technical systems such as the Internet, weather satellites, and INTELSAT. In the case of the Internet, which was initially developed as a military research program, there was no hardware system to transfer. Instead, there is a series of interface standards and protocols that allow anyone to use this global communications system. In the case of weather satellites, space-faring countries deploy weather satellites on their own and exchange data internationally through the World Meteorological Organization (WMO). Space and ground elements are paid for

---

[52]See David P. Currie, *The Constitution in Congress: Substantive Issues in the First Congress, 1789–1790,* 1994. The fact that states, rather than private parties, had been operating the lighthouses, however, indicates that the provision of navigation aids is in part a function of available payment-collection methods.

[53]U.S. Const., Art. I, § 10. cls. 2, 3.

[54]U.S. Const., Art. I, § 8. cl. 1.

by states, but the data (with some exceptions) are shared globally. In the case of INTELSAT, the United States led an effort to create an international organization that would own, operate, and manage a global communications system. The INTELSAT model is most often brought up as a desirable future institutional structure for GPS in terms of international funding and control.

Notwithstanding how previous examples of U.S. technical leadership have earned international good will, the case for securing good will through the transfer of GPS operations away from DoD is not compelling. First, while DoD may operate GPS, policy is set at a national level through the Federal Radionavigation Plan and the Office of the President. A country may say it does not trust GPS in the hands of the United States, but it is not accurate to blame that mistrust on the DoD alone. Second, GPS is well on its way to becoming a global standard as a result of the compelling productivity benefits from its use. It is not clear that this pace would quicken with changes in the institutional home of GPS.[55] Third, the INTELSAT comparisons are inaccurate in that GPS does not have a feasible mechanisms for collecting payment in the way that two-way communications do. Conversely, GPS does not require "landing rights" in the areas it serves but broadcasts its signals uniformly and globally. Finally, international civil organizations by their nature cannot address the military risks associated with the potential misuse or denial of GPS to U.S. armed forces. Providing a greater role for U.S. civil agencies in GPS would not necessarily risk U.S. security interests, but the potential for earning goodwill would seem to be limited to those countries with a prejudice against the DoD but not the United States as a whole.

Government Functions and Liability

Aids to navigation in the United States have been provided by the federal government since 1789, first administered by the Treasury, later by the Department of Commerce, and since the 1960s by the Department of Transportation.[56] This tradition is reflected in current federal statutes and regulations. Aids to navigation in the United States are provided by the Coast Guard, the Federal Aviation Administration, and the Army Corps of Engineers. The Department of Defense may also, of course, establish aids to navigation for its own use.

Private navigation aids can cross the boundaries between civil, commercial, and military interests, and their regulation is a bit more complex. The statutes

---

[55]What could change is the pace of international acceptance by governments to catch up with international public acceptance of GPS.

[56]An Act for the Establishment and Support of Lighthouses, Beacons, Buoys, and Public Piers, 1 Stat. 53 (1789)(enacted August 7, 1789). See also Historical Note to 33 U.S.C. §§ 711–715, and *U.S. Government Manual*, 1993/4, pp. 454, 460.

and regulations could be changed to make an additional exception for private GPS operation, which serves users on land, water, or in the air.[57] At present, private aids to water navigation may be established and maintained only if the Coast Guard authorizes them.[58] Operation of private electronic aids to water navigation will not be authorized at all, except for radar beacons and shore-based radar stations, which may be operated if authorized.[59] The Federal Aviation Administration is responsible for locating, constructing or installing, maintaining, and operating federal aids to air navigation, wherever necessary.[60] Many kinds of privately operated air navigation aids are permitted by the FAA, such as:

- VOR facilities

- Nondirectional radio beacon facilities

- True lights

- Simplified directional facility (SDF)

- Distance measuring equipment (DME)

- VHF marker beacons

- Interim Standard Microwave Landing System (ISMLS)

- Microwave Landing System (MLS).[61]

Some attempts at defining "government functions" have addressed the question of who should manage and operate GPS. The Office of Management and Budget Circular A-76 definition of governmental functions includes the "regulation of the use of space, oceans, navigable rivers and other natural resources."[62] Whereas "regulation" is usually thought of as meaning "rule-making" and not "operation of an electronic system," one could try to construe regulation to include the actual operation of a traffic management system. As an example, consider the Federal Reserve's operation of an electronic transfer

---

[57]GPS has created a market for land-navigators; neither the Coast Guard nor the FAA seems to have jurisdiction over that user segment.

[58]33 C.F.R. § 66.01-1(a).

[59]33 C.F.R. § 66.01-1(d).

[60]49 C.F.R. § 1.4(c)(4); *U.S. Government Manual*, 1993/4, p. 464: "Location, construction or installation, maintenance, operation, and quality assurance of Federal visual and electronic aids to air navigation."

[61]C.F.R., Title 14—Aeronautics and Space, Chapter I—Federal Aviation Administration, Department Of Transportation, Subchapter J—Navigational Facilities, Part 171—Non-Federal Navigation Facilities.

[62]OMB Circular A-76, *Performance of Commercial Activities*, August 4, 1983, ¶ 6e(1); see also OFPP Policy letter, 57 Federal Register No. 190, Wed 30 Sept 1992, p. 45096.

system, through which all transfers of funds, including all personal checks, are executed. This raises the possibility that government operation of a satellite-based navigation system, for its own use as well as private use, could be construed as part of the act of governing.[63]

Likewise, questions of liability have sometimes been raised by opponents of privatization, claiming that the government has a special role in providing transportation safety systems. Yet the liability rule for the government maintenance of aids to navigation (at least for buoys), seems to be the same as what the rule would be for a private organization. Once an aid is established, the government has a duty to maintain it.[64] The government neither invokes sovereign immunity nor offers private persons a higher standard of care than a private organization might agree upon.

An important consideration in assessing the magnitude of liability is whether notices of reliability and availability of a navigation aid were adequate.[65] For GPS, the U.S. government is already delivering service-level information and operational notices, via the Federal Radionavigation Plan, *Federal Register* notices, FAA Notices to Airmen, USCG Notices to Mariners, and the Coast Guard's GPS Information Center.[66] A private company could deliver similar forms of notification about its services to insulate itself much as the U.S. government already does.

Liability is not a strong criterion for choosing between government and private providers of GPS, and liability considerations do not preempt the possibility of private provision. The liability argument against privatization is sometimes extended to say that while private companies may have the same exposure as governments, their ability to pay is less. Thus private companies cannot economically assume the large potential liabilities inherent in some safety-of-life

---

[63]The OMB also says that the Secretary of Defense can decide that the government performance of a commercial activity is required for national defense reasons, based on criteria that the Secretary shall furnish to the Office of Federal Procurement Policy, OMB, upon request. OMB Circular A-76, *Performance of Commercial Activities*, August 4, 1983, ¶ 8b(1). For the purposes of this chapter, we assume that DoD has not exercised this option.

[64]Dion C. Raymos, "Liability of the Government for Improper Placement of Aids to Navigation," 17 *J. Maritime Law and Commerce*, 1986, pp. 517–530.

[65]We did not find a case involving the Loran radionavigation system that also involved the reliability or availability of the Loran signals themselves. Tringali Bros. v. U.S., 630 F.2d 1089 (5th Cir.(La.), 1980) (buoy maintenance; the person did not use the Loran system on board); Greer v. U.S., 505 F.2d 90 (5th Cir.(Fla.), 1974) (buoy maintenance); U.S. v. Sandra & Dennis Fishing Corp., 372 F.2d 189 (1st Cir.(Mass.), 1967) (while USCG was towing a vessel, its Loran receiver stopped working; the error was in not using the other vessel's Loran); Universe Tankships, Inc. v. U.S., 336 F.Supp. 282 (E.D.Pa., 1972) (buoy maintenance).

[66]See, for example, U.S. Coast Guard, "Announcement of Global Positioning System (GPS) Initial Operational Capability (IOC) and its impact on vessel carriage requirement regulations," 59 *Federal Register*, 13757 (Mar 23, 1994).

applications. Whether a private organization would be willing to provide a GPS is a separate question, one that involves the aviation and marine insurance industries, and the existence of profits commensurate with the risks.[67]

INSTITUTIONAL AND LEGAL FINDINGS

- Current legal structures and historical precedents that may be applicable to GPS are more descriptive than prescriptive. There is no compelling historical or legal argument for preferring civil or military federal control of GPS as a navigation aid, or any preference for government or private providers. The choice is essentially one based on U.S. national interests and the ability (or inability) to charge for services provided.

- The two most important criteria for selecting among various institutional options for GPS are (1) the existence of procedural disciplines to deal with emergencies (e.g., wars and crises) and user requirements, and (2) the existence of an effective funding mechanism, whether taxes or fees.

- Although the terms are often used, GPS is not a natural monopoly or a utility. Its characterization as a public good arises more from the lack of an effective means of charging individual users—given the current state of technology—than any legal or policy decision.

- A private GPS system does not appear feasible because of the lack of an enforceable funding mechanism that can deny access to non-authorized users. An internationalized GPS does not appear desirable because of potential risks to U.S. security and the lack of compensating benefits.

- If the United States wishes to gain economic benefits from GPS and protect its national security interests, then it should retain ownership and operational control of the GPS.

- A civil function for GPS could be created within the Department of Defense to receive funds from user agencies. The major benefit of this step would be to shift the competition for GPS funding outside of the Armed Services Appropriations Committees. U.S. civil agencies could play a larger direct role in GPS management and operations, but they have limited budgets to sustain significant financial contributions to GPS. Excise taxes may be increased or imposed, but the associated transaction costs and disbenefits are unclear.

---

[67]The U.S. government has acted as an insurer in market niches that the commercial insurance industry does not serve. For example, the FAA Act of 1958 allowed the Secretary of Transportation, with approval from the President, to provide insurance and reinsurance for aircraft used to carry out the foreign policy of the United States. See Rod D. Margo, *Aviation Insurance*, Butterworths, Boston, MA, 1989.

- There does not appear to be any international organization that can address the full range of international security and economic concerns found in GPS. Thus, direct discussions between the United States and its traditional friends and allies would likely be more effective than specialized, multilateral negotiations.

Chapter Six

CONCLUSIONS AND RECOMMENDATIONS

The four major sections of this chapter build on previous chapters to reach final recommendations. Special factors that affect decisions about GPS technology make GPS policy a unique case in many ways; however, other dual-use technologies share some of these factors. The first section discusses these special factors and how GPS may serve as a broader instructive model.

The second section summarizes the study findings on national security, commercial, and institutional and legal issues. This leads to conclusions in the third section that identify key GPS policy decisions that should be made. Additional conclusions are drawn with respect to how GPS can affect national and regional security, the role of selective availability, the importance of international acceptance, and preferred modes of governance for GPS and GPS augmentations.

Finally, the last section contains recommendations that respond to the fundamental questions being faced by national decisionmakers.

SPECIAL FACTORS AFFECTING GPS TECHNOLOGY POLICY DECISIONS

GPS is a difficult policy problem for at least three distinct reasons that are independent of particular applications and interest groups. In the first place, GPS originated as a military system, which has encouraged a risk-averse view of the technology within the U.S. government. Second, GPS is a technology that lends itself to an extremely wide range of possible applications. Third, GPS is an information technology whose impact depends not only on specific hardware and software but the exploitation of time and ephermeris information. Each of these reasons is discussed in the following section.

The Origin of GPS and Some Consequences

GPS had a military origin, and its technology arose from projects designed to support strategic nuclear and tactical military missions. The military is necessarily risk averse in its approach to technology. The collective mission is narrow; the objective is a unilateral advantage on the battlefield. The military thus tends to restrict technologies that affect operations, such as time and position data, for as long as possible to keep a unilateral military advantage for the United States.

If GPS had originated outside of the national security community and outside of the Cold War, the pressures would have been different. In that alternative world, it is likely that GPS would have been advanced as an international standard and its dissemination given a higher priority than protecting the system itself. There might have been provisions for disabling the system in wartime, but few concerns of system preemption by a potentially hostile power.

In evaluating GPS today, current and projected circumstances, rather than the heritage of the program, should be the basis for decisions. As a practical matter, this means reevaluating basic assumptions concerning the user communities, the threats posed by system preemption by adversary nations, benefits from its use in broader society, and the possibility of competing systems. Questioning some well-established assumptions is better than being artificially constrained by past history and circumstances.

GPS as an Enabling Technology

A characteristic of an enabling technology such as GPS is that a wide variety of applications can be enhanced or made possible. Good, neutral, or perhaps undesirable outcomes are now possible.

From the space segment, GPS provides precision time and ephemeris data that the end-user might apply to various applications. In the hands of a scientist, GPS provides a low-cost distributed timing system for experiments; for the entrepreneur developing network hardware, it facilitates measurement of latency in very-high-speed networks; for the civil community, it provides a precision-location service for ships and aircraft; and for the military, it allows a precision weapon to guide to its target. In the hands of the United States, GPS is a great boon, but it can also represent a hazard if it helps potentially hostile military forces find their positions or aids en route navigation of their missiles.

Tension arises between some of the civil/commercial applications and the desire to preclude an adversary's use of GPS. It is extremely difficult (technically, institutionally, politically, and economically) to combine the nonmilitary benefits of the system that require universality of access, ease of use, and low cost with military requirements for denial of the system to adversaries. Practical considerations require civil/commercial applications to have relatively easy access.

GPS as an Information Technology

GPS can be thought of as a system of hardware, software, and information (time and ephemeris) transmitted from satellites. GPS-derived information (time, position, and velocity) may be combined with other systems such as communications devices and computers (GIS systems, for example) to perform a variety of tasks. Figure 6.1 illustrates how various information technologies can be combined with GPS. The ultimate application (desirable or undesirable) of GPS's contribution to such technologies may be relatively small but is vital in the process.

Emerging information technology trends include the wide-scale use of cryptography, growing commercial use of traffic analysis techniques and database systems, powerful GIS systems and imagery workstations, and other capabilities that allow information to be combined and utilized in new ways. Like GPS, the character of these technologies is determined by how and to what end they are applied. Because these technologies are of a class that do not pose obvious, immediate dangers, it is difficult to see how controls can work or find political support. Further compounding the problem is the nonphysical nature of many of these technologies, which makes controlling them difficult.

Information technologies such as GPS represent a serious challenge to government control. In addition to the difficulties of restricting the technology, it may not serve overall U.S. interests to do so—any restriction may simply foster foreign competition and shrink U.S. advantages. In general, the United States has followed a pattern of allowing free dissemination and use of technology unless it posed an *immediate and serious* safety hazard, or a *direct* national security threat.

Decisionmakers must find an appropriate approach to handling technological issues in the information age, and address enabling technologies within a context of joint civil, commercial, and military use. If the maximum benefits of these technologies are to be realized, we must balance the benefits and risks of technologies that do not fit the mold of older physical technologies. GPS is only one information technology to hit the policy frontier. Lessons learned and policies established for GPS will likely endure in other areas.

**Figure 6.1—A Combination of Information Technologies
(GPS Receiver, Cell Phone, and Laptop Computer)**

STUDY FINDINGS

National security, commercial, and institutional/legal issues affected by national GPS policy interact and are not cleanly separable. Nonetheless, the major findings of this report can be summarized as follows.

National Security

GPS has become an integral component of U.S. military systems, and U.S. forces are increasingly reliant on access to GPS signals. GPS provides accurate positioning and navigation for all types of military equipment, including land vehicles, ships, aircraft, and precision-guided weapons. The DoD degrades the civilian GPS signal (through selective availability) and encrypts the military GPS signal (through anti-spoofing) to prevent potential adversaries from gaining access to high accuracies. However, the introduction of domestic and foreign local- and wide-area differential GPS systems is effectively circumventing the immediate effects of SA for most civil and commercial applications.

The wide-scale availability of highly accurate (below 15 m) positioning has many national security implications, although it is not a significant factor in nuclear threats. Potential nuclear adversaries are not likely to be capable of a strategic nuclear counterforce strike and do not need GPS-level accuracies to use nuclear weapons for lesser efforts.[1] At present, it is highly unlikely that nuclear weapons will be delivered by GPS-guided cruise missiles, although such platforms might deliver chemical and biological weapons. The situation may change if advanced cruise missiles become readily available to less-developed countries.

Second, GPS-aided conventional weapons represent an air defense challenge to the United States and its allies. Conventionally armed GPS-aided cruise missiles, in particular, may pose a significant threat to large fixed targets, although they do not threaten most mobile targets. GPS-aided weapons that evade U.S. defenses will have a greater potential for causing significant damage. The spread of low-observable technologies can increase the number of hostile aerial weapons leaking through U.S. defenses. However, the hostile use of low observable technologies is an independent concern distinct from the hostile exploitation of GPS.

Third, selective availability has little effect on the accuracy of short- and medium-range GPS-guided ballistic missiles. Third World missiles such as the Scud and No Dong 1 can improve their overall accuracy by 20–25 percent but to no appreciable affect. Missile accuracy cannot be increased simply by reducing the burnout velocity measurement errors. Vernier engines are needed to minimize cutoff control uncertainties and, more important, thrust termination control and reentry dispersion errors need to be minimized. The latter can be accomplished by spin-stabilizing the reentry vehicle or designing it to have a high ballistic coefficient, greater technical challenges than being able to access GPS signals.

---

[1]Counterforce strikes have traditionally been thought of in terms of fixed installations such as airfields and ICBM silos. As SLBMs make up a greater share of the U.S. nuclear arsenal, U.S. vulnerability to a counterforce attack will diminish.

Access to GPS can allow modern ICBMs to improve their accuracies through the use of low-cost inertial instruments for initial azimuth alignment and by minimizing the effects of boost-phase inertial instrument errors. Thus there is the risk that the availability of highly accurate positioning data may provide incentives for the proliferation of ICBM-class ballistic missile technologies. Most of the advantages of GPS can be achieved with SPS-levels of accuracy, however, and DGPS is probably not required.

It is important to remember that missile proliferation—especially the spread of ballistic missiles—is (and has been) a serious problem independent of GPS.[2] There is no question that use of GPS may allow Third World nations to develop accurate cruise missiles, but GPS is a facilitator, not a driver, of missile proliferation.[3] Any potential solution to the problem of missile proliferation will require military, political, and economic components and cannot be effectively addressed by GPS policy decisions alone.

Fourth, denying access to GPS signals and GPS-related augmentations should not be done to the neglect of other countermeasures such as passive defenses, mobility, and avoidance of single-point failure modes, which can greatly reduce the effectiveness of attacks. In particular, electronic combat against GPS must be integrated into U.S. planning and routine operations. A major jamming threat arises from the proliferation of low-power, wide-band jammers, and U.S. forces must acquire P-code before entering a jamming environment. An aided military receiver can be designed to achieve a jamming resistance of about 70 dB, and special antennas can provide an additional anti-jam margin of from 10 to 30 dB. In all cases, GPS-guided weapons will require low-cost inertial navigation systems if they are to maintain high accuracies once they are jammed near a target. If the adversary employs a large jammer, it will be a ripe target for attack by precision-guided munitions such as an anti-radiation missile.

Although any threat associated with hostile use of GPS is minor at present, future threats may be greater.[4] The U.S. military must anticipate these threats and act to counter them today. To cope with the wide range of possible future threats, selective GPS denial techniques should be developed for future theaters

---

[2]See, for example, Janne E. Nolan, *Trappings of Power: Ballistic Missiles in the Third World*, The Brookings Institution, Washington, D.C., 1991, and Center for International Security and Arms Control, *Assessing Ballistic Missile Proliferation and Its Control*, Center for International Security and Arms Control, Stanford, CA, 1991.

[3]See W. Seth Carus, *Cruise Missile Proliferation in the 1990s*, The Washington Papers #159, Praeger, Westport, CT, 1992; K. Scott McMahon and Dennis M. Gormley, *Controlling the Spread of Land-Attack Cruise Missiles*, American Institute for Strategic Cooperation, Marina del Rey, CA, 1995.

[4]GPS-guided cruise missiles are likely to be the most significant threat from the hostile exploitation of GPS. It is the marriage of GPS with other technologies such as low-observable materials, efficient turbofan engines, accurate inertial navigation systems, and weapons of mass destruction that poses the greatest threat to U.S. and allied forces.

of operations. In the near term, this includes DoD development of tactical jammers to deny positioning and navigation information from GPS, DGPS, GLONASS, and commercial position-location services. In addition, the United States should explore both active and passive defense programs against theater-area cruise missiles and ballistic missiles that may carry either conventional warheads or weapons of mass destruction.

Finally, the United States needs to think about how it can and should shape the international environment for space-based navigation services. For example, a stable and predictable GPS policy in the United States can promote GPS as a global standard. In the case of DGPS services that cross international boundaries, it is in the security interests of the United States to have such systems under the direct control of allies, as opposed to potential adversaries or international civil organizations. Direct control can encompass a spectrum of techniques from using encryption of the DGPS communications link to ensure access only by authorized receivers through diplomatic agreements to limit areas and times of operation when international conditions warrant.

The United States cannot count on maintaining a monopoly on precision time and location services forever. Indeed, because of the relative simplicity of GPS-like technologies, the United States must begin preparing to operate in a world where access to GPS-type and augmented GPS services are the norm. The economic and technical barriers to entry for a competing satellite navigation system are shrinking with the creation of low-earth-orbit communication satellite networks (which may lower the costs of building and launching satellites). Thus, it will become increasingly risky to assume that no other party will introduce a competing system should GPS become unavailable or unreliable.

Commercial

The availability of GPS signals to civil and commercial users has, along with supportive policy and management decisions, enabled the rapid growth of commercial applications of GPS. According to U.S. GPS Industry Council projections, sales of commercial GPS equipment alone (not including related services and multiplier effects) are expected to be about $8.5 billion in the year 2000. The important practice of providing civil GPS service free of direct or indirect user charges is a technical necessity today because enforcing payments would be virtually impossible due to the unencrypted nature of the GPS Standard Positioning Service and the large installed base of GPS equipment.

The commercial uses of GPS are diverse, with applications across many industries. Some applications are simple, such as determining a position; some are complex in combining GPS with communications and other technologies. Commercial users have varying needs for accuracy, with increasing interest in submeter, real-time applications. GPS technology is becoming increasingly embedded in national and international infrastructures—from civil aviation and highways to telecommunications and the Internet. This is creating opportunities for improved productivity and potential vulnerabilities. The role of precision timing for mobile communications and computing will increase with the growth of global wireless applications.

The United States enjoys a leading position in the manufacture of GPS equipment and the development of new applications, particularly those requiring advanced software. Japan is the nearest competitor to the United States, followed by Europe. U.S. industry tends to see GPS technology as something that adds an "embedded capability," whereas Japanese industry tends to see GPS as another form of consumer electronics. European firms, with the exception of DGPS suppliers to the North Sea oil industry, tend to see GPS in terms of potential government contracts for improving domestic infrastructure. There is increasing interest in consumer automotive applications, however, in Europe as well as the rest of the world.

The U.S. government intends to provide wide-area augmentations of GPS accuracy for aviation and maritime navigation, which creates concerns among DGPS service providers that these government services will compete with them. The economic harm from competition may be small relative to the benefits of wide-area GPS augmentations, but U.S. government policy must balance the requirements of public safety with avoiding competition with industry. We did not reach any conclusion on whether public or private provision of GPS augmentations would be more cost-effective in meeting government requirements.

In deciding whether civil GPS accuracy augmentations should be selectively deniable, the primary concern should be to balance national security and public safety, and should include international acceptance. Commercial concerns are of lower national priority. International discussions must determine what types of selective denial would be both effective and broadly acceptable. Encryption is only one means of selective denial and need not be implemented if other means are available for national security purposes.

The ability to impose direct user fees on GPS augmentations depends on being able to selectively deny service, usually with some form of encryption. The United States could have encryption for national security reasons, but no user fees for public safety reasons. Again, while commercial concerns are important, they are secondary to those of public safety.

Although GPS accuracy, reliability, and availability are quite good, competitors to GPS could arise if the United States fails to maintain the GPS constellation, fails to provide a continuous, stable signal, or unilaterally initiates changes to the civil signal, such as encryption or user fees. If other countries feel they cannot depend on GPS or need a complementary system, commercial interests, foreign governments, and international organizations have the resources to create alternative or complementary GPS systems.

As commercial GPS firms evaluate the various forms of risk they face—technical, market, financial, and political—they are probably confident in managing the first three. This leaves political risk. Government policy decisions can create risks to commercial GPS in many ways. New taxes and fees can be imposed, spectrum licenses may be difficult or impossible to get, international trade disputes can harm access to foreign markets, and governments may impose standards that fragment global markets into less attractive sizes. The problem of standards is particularly pervasive. Standards cut across civil, commercial, and military lines in areas such as encryption, safety certification standards, and international spectrum allocations. Rapid change in commercial GPS since the Persian Gulf War has created a strong industry interest in having a formal national GPS policy in order to provide a predictable environment for future business decisions.

Institutional and Legal

Current legal structures and historical precedents that may be applicable to GPS are more descriptive than prescriptive. There is no compelling historical or legal argument for preferring civil or military control of GPS as a navigation aid, nor is there any preference for government or private providers. The choice is essentially based on U.S. national interests; procedural disciplines to deal with emergencies (e.g., wars and crises) and user requirements; and the existence of an effective funding mechanism, whether taxes or fees. A private GPS system does not appear feasible without an enforceable funding mechanism that can deny access to non-authorized users. An internationalized GPS does not appear desirable because of potential risks to U.S. security and the lack of compensating benefits.

Future commercial growth of GPS will depend on whether it becomes an accepted global standard for position location, navigation, and precision timing. GPS is well on its way to de facto acceptance, but official acceptance depends on international decisions to use GPS in safety applications, especially civil aviation. This question can affect technical standards, spectrum allocations, export sales, and even military cooperation. At the same time, there will be multiple regional and national GPS augmentation systems. From a commercial perspective, the most important factor is that there be open, interoperable standards that allow GPS users to operate easily anywhere in the world.

International concerns over U.S. intentions with regard to GPS can be eased by U.S. policy statements, but direct discussions are likely to be more effective in addressing such specific concerns as legal liabilities and regional security. There does not appear to be any international organization that can address the full range of international security and economic concerns arising from GPS. Thus, discussions between the United States and its traditional friends and allies would likely be more effective than specialized, multilateral negotiations (e.g., in forums like ICAO) on the overall international regime for GPS. Allowing for multiple augmentation systems with common agreements on security concerns, technical standards, and spectrum usage may help international acceptance by providing a form of local control over air, sea, and land uses of GPS as well as DGPS.

CONCLUSIONS

The Global Positioning System is a simple idea that has some complex results. GPS satellites may be thought of as "clocks in space" that broadcast a uniform time. Their signals can be processed to tell a passive receiver what his location is, combined with communications to tell where someone else is, or linked into vast networks tracking the locations of physical objects or packets of data. The military applications of GPS have already been profound and promise to become more so, as both U.S. and foreign forces exploit the availability of precision time and location data. Although commercial applications were initiated many years after the first GPS satellite launch, commercial users of GPS now vastly outnumber and outspend military equipment users. Begun as a military system that allowed for civil access, GPS has become a necessity to civil, commercial, and military infrastructures around the world.

In many respects, GPS applications and their impacts have run ahead of policy. Stable, clear policy is key to the future exploitation of GPS and the development of countermeasures to the vulnerabilities and risks created by this technology. Military force structure decisions involving electronic warfare and theater air defenses are affected by GPS policy (or its lack). Similarly, industry business plans and strategies depend on U.S. and international policies involving GPS. In both cases, policy provides the framework within which military and industry leaders can plan for the future—something which they need to do irrespective of the specific policy decisions themselves.

Key GPS Policy Decisions

Key GPS policy decisions can be divided into three categories: U.S. policy decisions, foreign government decisions, and international decisions (those requiring cooperation between one or more countries). The most important long-term policy decision is the U.S. commitment to stable funding and management for GPS to serve both national security and economic interests. In the near term, the most pressing U.S. policy decisions involve government-supported GPS augmentations such as the FAA's Wide-Area Augmentation System (WAAS) and the Coast Guard's radio beacon system. Decisions on how to proceed with these systems are significant not only for the money involved, but for what safeguards are put in place to deter hostile misuse while meeting public safety requirements. U.S. decisions on the accuracy, availability, and integrity of GPS signals and related augmentations also need to be made for the biennial Federal Radionavigation Plan (the last edition was in 1994). These decisions create expectations and political pressures in the international community as well as in private industry to maintain or perhaps increase those commitments.

The most important policy decision to be made by foreign governments is whether to accept GPS as a navigational aid within their borders. Foreign nationals have already voted for GPS with their extensive purchases, but certification of GPS for safety-of-life applications is another matter. Decisions on foreign government acceptance of GPS will be influenced by their perceptions of U.S. policy and whether the United States will be a trustworthy steward of the system, as well as their own internal political and technical assessment of alternatives to relying on GPS. In general, efforts to promote acceptance of GPS internationally are in the interests of the United States, provided appropriate protections are provided for U.S. security.

The most important international safeguards for GPS involve preventing or deterring the hostile misuse of high-accuracy GPS augmentations. With the proliferation of long-range precision strike weapons, more of our allies are facing the kind of homeland strategic threat that the United States faced for decades. The U.S. response in the case of air navigation aids was to create the SCATANA system, which provides for military control of air traffic control radars and other air navigation aids in times of war.[5] Traditional channels within NATO and the U.S.-Japan Treaty of Mutual Cooperation and Security might be used to create international SCATANA-type procedures with respect to wide-area GPS augmentations. In the event of war or a regional crisis, the operation of GPS-based navigation aids could be modified or suspended in an orderly way to mitigate the impact on commercial users.

Other international policy decisions will likely involve standards for GPS and related technologies, particularly in commercial applications. Government in-

---

[5]Plan for the security control of air traffic and air navigation aids (Short title: SCATANA), 32 C.F.R. § 245, 12 p.

terventions can either help maintain an open environment for commercial development or raise protectionist barriers. Along with technical standards, the international acceptance of GPS for transportation and information applications will require agreement on allocating liability for GPS-related losses. The United States is unlikely to accept unlimited liability for all uses of GPS, but may be willing to support international integrity monitoring to provide timely warnings to aircraft and ships in event of malfunctions.

National and Regional Security

Mitigating the national security problems raised by the spread of GPS technology will require more than policy statements alone. U.S. forces are increasingly reliant on GPS and must have ensured access to the signal. The potential for hostile use of GPS against the United States and its allies is increasing with the spread of long-range, precision-strike weapons. Policy statements can provide a predictable environment for force planning decisions and can facilitate regional military cooperation, but they cannot substitute for appropriate doctrine, operational concepts, and trained, well-equipped forces.

In the immediate future, U.S. forces will likely derive more military advantages from GPS than will foreign forces—because of how U.S. forces are organized, trained, and equipped, as well as their longer operational experience with GPS. Thus, ensuring reliable access to GPS is a higher priority for the United States than preventing hostile exploitation of GPS by others. The DoD should take steps to resist enemy electronic countermeasures such as jamming and spoofing. In particular, the DoD should continue its efforts to lessen its dependence on the C/A-code to acquire PPS and should seek an operational capability to acquire the P(Y)-code directly. The DoD should also ensure that it integrates electronic warfare with (and against) GPS, GPS augmentations, and GLONASS into planning, training, and operations at varying levels of conflict. The United States needs a low-cost, effective means of selectively denying access to GPS and GPS augmentations, especially in situations where ground-based reference stations are located in nearby neutral countries. This denial could be accomplished by DoD actions as well as through positive control over access to GPS augmentations by foreign system operators.

Hostile cruise missiles and ballistic missiles may seek to exploit GPS, GPS augmentations, and GLONASS. The potential contribution of a satellite-based navigation aid to weapon effectiveness is much greater for cruise missiles than for ballistic missiles. In either case, air defense and suppression capabilities and theater missile defenses, not GPS policy, will drive force structure responses and budgets. The United States can, however, help stabilize the international environment by ensuring GPS is accepted as the primary (if not only) satellite-based navigation aid, with GPS-related augmentations under the national control of friends and allies.

Differential GPS-based networks, some with quite broad coverage areas, have spread around the world. Many nations and regions have their own DGPS networks for civil transportation and commercial purposes. In such an environment, potentially hostile weapons systems using GPS could emerge relatively rapidly (e.g., in 12–18 months). Thus, the United States and its allies need to plan for the possible emergence of DGPS weapons, even if widely acknowledged evidence of such systems is lacking. The threat posed by accurate GPS-aided weapons—aerial weapons in particular—is most acute when the defender lacks air superiority. U.S. air power, when generated in the theater, is formidable against any foreseeable threat.[6] U.S. allies can be at greater risk than the United States itself—for example, in the opening period of conflict before U.S. air power can be brought to bear. Thus, U.S. regional allies should have greater incentives to deter or prevent the hostile exploitation of DGPS networks.

Selective Availability

We did not find a compelling economic or national security reason for keeping SA on or turning it off in peacetime. The amount of attention paid to this aspect of GPS policy seems to have obscured underlying issues that we believe are more important, such as the development of electronic countermeasures and shaping the international environment for GPS. We did conclude that SA should not be turned off without warning and a transition period, but in the future, turning SA off in peacetime could be acceptable under the right international conditions. In any event, SA should be retained as a wartime option for the United States. Since the definition of what constitutes "wartime" and "peacetime" can be debatable, we concluded that decisions about SA should remain with the National Command Authority and not lower-ranking organizations.

Selective availability is a controversial topic for some civil and commercial GPS users—who would like to see it turned off in peacetime—but the net effect of any SA decision on commercial growth and new applications is unclear. Technical alternatives in the form of DGPS and RTK techniques are increasingly available to users who need accuracies better than GPS alone can provide, even if SA were off. Although virtually all users would like better accuracy if it was costless, the commercial GPS market is driven much more strongly by declining prices.

---

[6]Christopher Bowie et al., *Trends in the Global Balance of Airpower*, RAND, MR-478/1-AF, 1995.

The ability of SA to degrade the quality of civil GPS signals can be useful in wartime, assuming U.S. forces are not reliant on civilian GPS receivers. However, the military utility of leaving SA on in peacetime is not so clear.[7] The central argument for leaving SA on in peacetime is that doing so discourages foreign military exploitation of GPS by making the signal less accurate and reliable than military users would want. Also, turning SA back on would be politically difficult, even in war or crisis, because of the high degree of civil and commercial dependence accrued while it was off. However, these arguments are being overtaken by the spread of DGPS techniques that can circumvent SA, initially by the use of ground-based reference beacons and potentially over wide areas by the use of reference beacons on geosynchronous satellites.

These arguments highlight the importance of regional and international agreements on how GPS and especially GPS augmentations should be managed in times of war or crisis. The most difficult questions about whether or when to turn SA on arise in the event of attacks on allies or third party conflicts in which U.S. interests are unclear. In regional crises the United States would want a range of options, from working with allies to limit the performance of GPS augmentations, to turning SA on, to actively jamming GPS signals or attacking local DGPS ground stations. These options would be facilitated by agreements that provided a mechanism to address regional GPS security concerns and are likely to be more important than the single decision to have SA on or off in peacetime.

A related issue is whether the United States should proceed with or even encourage wide-area GPS augmentations that provide even greater accuracies than the GPS SPS signal without SA. The wide coverage of these systems and their intended usage for international air and sea transportation will make decisions to suspend operations politically even more difficult. This in turn could encourage the proliferation of GPS-aided weapons under the belief that the signals will be available even during regional conflicts. Again, the United States should be sure it has both military countermeasures and international mechanisms in place to deal with the potential misuse or hostile denial of GPS-related signals upon which civil, commercial, and possibly military users will depend. Other countries may want the United States to keep SA on to encourage use of local and regional DGPS networks that are under their own control.

Time is needed both to develop electronic countermeasures and negotiate international agreements. In 1995, for example, the U.S. Senate called for SA to be turned off in one year unless the Secretary of Defense submitted a plan for of-

---

[7]A more compelling case for leaving SA on could be made if the United States faced a significant mobile strategic nuclear threat that could exploit GPS for geolocation in a first strike, as it did with Soviet SLBMs.

fensive and defensive GPS electronic countermeasures.[8] Electronic warfare is not the only consideration for SA decisions. The risk of encouraging the proliferation of GPS-aided weapons must be balanced against the benefits of GPS as a global standard for satellite-based navigation. In this balancing, a decision on SA policy must consider U.S. interests in shaping the international environment for GPS and not just individual military risks and uncertain economic benefits.

International Acceptance

The dual-use nature of GPS and its challenges to U.S. policymaking have resulted in extensive dialog among the U.S. military, civil government, and commercial communities on common policy and technical problems. In contrast, foreign discussions of GPS tend to be segregated in separate communities depending on particular applications, both because of the origins of GPS as a U.S. military system and because of domestic political constraints. For example, the Japan Defense Agency is highly constrained in its interactions with civilian ministries, and it is difficult to forge a common Japanese government approach on theregional security and economic concerns arising from the spread of DGPSnetworks, including DGPS services provided by Japanese civil government agencies. In Europe, the European Community is interested in GPS for transportation infrastructure applications, but the EC does not have jurisdiction over military matters. Similarly, NATO and the Western European Union are interested in the military benefits and risks of GPS, but have difficulty addressing civil and commercial applications in a common forum. The United States can thus have a unique role in creating and shaping an international dialog on this dual-use technology.

There is no international organization that can address all GPS-related issues at a government-to-government level. Multilateral organizations such as ICAO and IMO can address certain categories of GPS applications, but not broader international security and trade matters associated with the technology. Different regions of the world have differing interests in GPS; for example, the

---

[8]U.S. Senate, *National Defense Authorization Act for Fiscal Year 1996,* S.1026, placed in the Senate July 1995. Section 1081 of the Senate bill, "GLOBAL POSITIONING SYSTEM," reads: "The Secretary of Defense shall turn off the selective availability feature of the global positioning system by May 1, 1996, unless the Secretary submits to the Committee on Armed Services of the Senate and the Committee on National Security of the House of Representatives a plan that (1) provides for development and acquisition of (A) effective capabilities to deny hostile military forces the ability to use the global positioning system without hindering the ability of United States military forces and civil users to exploit the system; and (B) global positioning system receivers and other techniques for weapons and weapon systems that provide substantially improved resistance to jamming and other forms of electronic interference or disruption; and (2) includes a specific date by which the Secretary of Defense intends to complete the acquisition of the capabilities described in paragraph (1)."

economic and security situation for Japan is quite different from that of Europe or the Middle East. In addition, a single international civil organization for GPS or GPS augmentations is unlikely to be desirable from a U.S. perspective. Such an organization may be welcomed by users who want access to high-accuracy signals at all times, but it would lead to a decline of U.S. influence in deterring the misuse of GPS in regional conflicts. The spread of GPS equipment technologies may be almost inevitable, but loss of U.S. influence and leadership is not. The United States should seek direct talks with its traditional friends and allies, especially Japan and Europe, which have economic and military importance.

Foreign government concerns with relying on the United States for GPS include public safety in air and sea transportation. Statements of U.S. intentions regarding GPS, as in the Federal Radionavigation Plan or by the FAA to ICAO, are unlikely to be sufficient, and more formal mechanism commitments are needed. Such commitments are not vital to private-sector acceptance, as demonstrated by current GPS export sales, but they can help accelerate commercial usage. International agreements other than treaties are feasible and perhaps the most effective means of overcoming foreign government objections to the official use of GPS and related augmentations.

A U.S. commitment to provide a specific level of GPS service can be verified by international integrity monitoring. Such monitoring can also limit liability for accidents because timely warnings can be considered a form of real-time notice (especially important to international civil aviation). International integrity monitoring would not appear to compromise U.S. security interests, and the United States could agree to refrain from actively interfering with such monitoring.

To help bring about international agreement, the United States might turn SA off in peacetime. On the other hand, U.S. allies may wish SA kept on so that they are able to control access to higher-accuracy signals via their own GPS augmentations. This question should be addressed in international fora; the answer is not obvious from a U.S. perspective alone.

The United States can draw on its Federal Radionavigation Plan as well as the SCATANA emergency plan in drafting clauses related to service levels, regional security measures, and third-party monitoring of GPS signal health. It should also be possible to craft, within an agreement, some quid pro quo for the provision of GPS, and the United States should carefully consider what it would want. For example, it would be unwise to require direct foreign payments for GPS because that creates a contractual relationship that would lead to an unnecessary degree of foreign influence over GPS. On the other hand, international agreements commonly seek mutual benefits without exchanges of funds, and notional benefits to the United States could include reduced landing fees for aircraft equipped with GPS, tariff reductions, waiver of local content or off-set requirements for GPS equipment, and agreement on technical standards and spectrum allocations for GPS and DGPS applications, as well as expedited foreign military sales of GPS equipment and enhanced military-to-military co-operation.

Governance of GPS and Augmentations

Given the worldwide popularity of GPS applications, the future governance of GPS is of interest to users in the United States and overseas. Aspects of governance include ownership, control, funding, and management decisionmaking. The pursuit of U.S. national security and economic interests in the use of GPS does not necessarily require U.S. control over all GPS aspects and its technologies, even if that were possible. Pursuit of such interests does, however, require the United States to make policy decisions about how it will deal with international GPS cooperation and competition.

The United States should ensure that GPS itself remains subject to its control to protect its national security interests. By GPS itself, we mean the space segment and the control segment, consisting of the satellites and the master control station, and access to overseas monitoring stations. It does not preclude larger roles for government agencies other than the Department of Defense in poli-cymaking, management, or even funding. Nor does it preclude international agreements to which the United States becomes a party. It does say that the space and control segments should continue to be funded by the U.S. govern-ment. The user segment—and the associated burgeoning market for GPS-related equipment, applications, and services—is effectively in the hands of the private sector.

The possibility is sometimes raised of there being a competitor to GPS. This seems to be an unlikely possibility provided the United States is able to sustain key elements of current GPS practices, such as providing a reliable GPS signal with no direct user charges. The United States could create strong incentives for an alternative to GPS if it were to fail to sustain the GPS constellation (e.g., as a result of funding instability), fail to operate GPS in a competent, reliable way (which would also put U.S. forces at risk), or attempt to charge users for access to currently available signals, thus creating an economic niche for a competing system. GLONASS may be used as a supplement to GPS by some users, like other GPS augmentations, but it is unlikely to become a true alternative to GPS unless U.S. support of GPS falters.

Of greater importance than a GPS competitor is the nature of the international regime for GPS augmentations such as WAAS and local-area DGPS networks.

Local-area networks are already under the control of the private sector and national governments. The limited range, strong national interest in retaining local control, and the lack of a means for enforcing international control make such networks unlikely candidates for international control. Wide-area augmentations, particularly those using space-based reference stations, are another matter.

Wide-area augmentations to GPS can provide at least three major enhancements to GPS—improved integrity, improved availability, and improved accuracy. The public safety and commercial benefits of improved GPS integrity and availability would be of global benefit, and international, regional, or national governance would not harm U.S. security interests while enhancing international acceptance of GPS. It is likely that international organizations such as ICAO and IMO, as well as individual nations, would want independent oversight of augmentations to GPS integrity and availability, which may be accommodated in international agreements on GPS.

Accuracy augmentation governance should remain under the national control of the country providing the service. At present, the United States, Japan, Europe, and potentially Russia have the capability to provide wide-area accuracy augmentation. As argued previously, high levels of accuracy can pose risks to U.S. and regional security and require the development of military countermeasures. Wide-area accuracy augmentation should first be subject to bilateral agreements among the providers to address security and economic interests before considering multilateral agreements. Table 6.1 summarizes the various preferred forms of GPS governance.

The international environment for GPS can evolve in different directions depending on the nature of U.S. policy. If the United States makes active efforts to promote GPS as a global standard, then it will necessarily need to address the

Table 6.1

Preferred Forms of GPS Governance

Regime	International	Regional	National/ Bilateral	Local/Private
GPS segment				
Space/control			X	
User equipment				X
Wide-area GPS augmentation				
Integrity	X	X	X	
Availability	X	X	X	
Accuracy			X	
Local-area GPS augmentation			X	X

dual-use nature of the technology through international agreements. If the United States does not actively support GPS, or becomes an unreliable steward, GPS augmentations will move forward independent of U.S. interests. This will encourage the entry of foreign alternatives to GPS (e.g., GLONASS or an INMARSAT service). The United States could still have GPS for its own national security purposes, but it would risk losing the economic and diplomatic benefits from its past investments in GPS.

RECOMMENDATIONS

GPS is a unique and valuable system that enables unique military, civil, and commercial capabilities. The United States has before it an opportunity to shape the direction of GPS applications and mitigate the risks of this new technology. The window for leadership is, however, likely to be brief before foreign capabilities to field GPS augmentations and even autonomous space systems increase.

In the Introduction, we listed four major questions facing national decision-makers with regard to GPS:

- How should the United States integrate its economic and national security objectives into GPS policy decisions?

- How should the Department of Defense respond to the existence of widely available, highly accurate time and spatial data?

- What approach should the United States take toward international cooperation and competition in global satellite navigation systems?

- How should GPS and associated augmentations be governed?

The study recommends actions that address these questions in terms of how the United States can best promote its broad interests in GPS.

Integrating Economic and National Security Objectives

- The United States should issue a statement of national policy, perhaps a Presidential Decision Directive, on the Global Positioning System to provide a more stable framework for public- and private-sector decisionmaking. This statement should identify U.S. interests and objectives with respect to GPS, address GPS management and acquisition issues, and provide guidance for the development of GPS augmentations and future international agreements.

- The United States should initiate discussions with Japan and Europe on regional security and economic issues associated with GPS that will potentially lead to international agreements. These agreements should be mutually beneficial to all parties but not involve the exchange of funds. The United States should be prepared to commit itself to providing the levels of GPS service defined in the Federal Radionavigation Plan.

Department of Defense Responses to the Availability of GPS Signals

- The DoD should reduce its reliance on civilian GPS receivers and the C/A-code for military purposes. The DoD should develop and introduce into operation, as rapidly as practicable, GPS equipment capable of rapid, direct P-code acquisition.

- The DoD should ensure that it can acquire GPS signals even in a challenged environment and should develop and field anti-jam receivers and antenna enhancements. The DoD should also ensure it has adequate electronic countermeasures to selectively deny GPS, GPS augmentations, and GLONASS signals to an adversary.

- Selective availability should be retained as a military option for the United States and not be turned off immediately ("right now"). A decision on whether to turn SA off in the future should be made by the National Command Authority after international consultations and the demonstration of appropriate GPS and GPS augmentation countermeasures.

- The United States should not preclude or deter private DGPS services except for reasons of national security or public safety. In deciding whether civil GPS accuracy augmentations should be selectively deniable, the primary concern should be to balance national security and public safety, while taking international acceptance into account. Commercial concerns are of lower national priority.

Approach to International Cooperation and Competition

- The United States should work to minimize international barriers to commercial GPS-related goods and services, such as proprietary standards and inadequate spectrum allocations.

- However, the United States should refrain, and encourage others to refrain, from providing wide-area augmentations of GPS accuracy until appropriate mechanisms (e.g., military countermeasures, diplomatic agreements) are identified to deal with the potential misuse or denial of high accuracies.

Subject to international agreements, the United States should encourage international integrity monitoring of GPS for purposes of public safety.

Governance of GPS and GPS Augmentations

- The United States government should ensure that the GPS is funded and maintained in a stable manner, free of direct user charges, to promote the adoption of GPS as a global standard for position location, navigation, and timing. The GPS space and control segments should remain under U.S. jurisdiction for the foreseeable future.

- In the case of DGPS services that cross international boundaries, it is in the security interests of the United States to have such systems under the direct national control of allies, as opposed to potential adversaries or international civil organizations.

GPS TECHNOLOGIES AND ALTERNATIVES

This appendix contains technical background material on GPS and describes the Global Orbiting Navigation Satellite System (GLONASS) and inertial navigation systems (INSs).

A DESCRIPTION OF GPS

The Global Positioning System consists of three separate elements: the space segment, the control segment, and the user segment (Figure A.1).

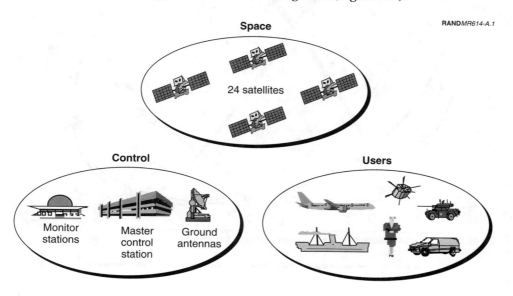

RAND*MR614-A.1*

Space

24 satellites

Control

Monitor stations

Master control station

Ground antennas

Users

Figure A.1—Three Segments of GPS

Space Segment

The complete GPS constellation consists of 24 NAVSTAR satellites in six orbital planes. The satellites orbit the earth with a period of 12 hours in circular 10,900 n mi orbits at an inclination of 55 degrees with respect to the equator. Each satellite passes over the same location on earth about once every day (or every 23 hours and 56 minutes). The spacings of the satellites in orbit are arranged so that a minimum of five satellites are in view to users worldwide with a Position Dilution of Precision (PDOP) of six or less.[1]

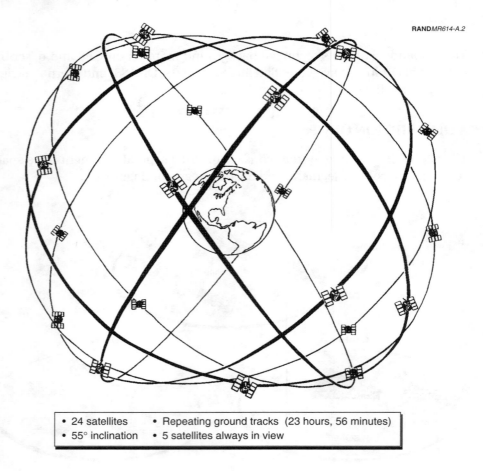

RAND*MR614-A.2*

- 24 satellites
- 55° inclination
- Repeating ground tracks (23 hours, 56 minutes)
- 5 satellites always in view

Figure A.2—GPS Constellation

[1]U.S. Department of Defense and U.S. Department of Transportation, *1994 Federal Radionavigation Plan*, National Technical Information Service, DOT-VNTSC-RSPA-95-1/DOD-4650.5, Springfield, VA, May 1995 (Appendix A, p. 34).

Several types of GPS satellites are currently in use. The first ones, called Block I satellites, were launched in the early to mid-1980s. Of the eleven Block I satellite vehicles (SVs) launched, three remained in orbit and one was functioning as of April 1994. The follow-on SVs to the Block I, called Block II satellites, were launched beginning in 1989. As of April 1994, 24 Block II satellites were still in orbit. All Block IIs are functioning properly; hence, the U.S. Air Force has issued a "full operational capability" designation to the system.

Another GPS satellite, called the Block IIR (replenishment), is in production. Twenty of the Block IIRs will be launched beginning in 1996 to replace the Block II satellites. The Block IIF (follow-on) satellites will start replacing the Block IIRs in about 10 years.

GPS satellites transmit two codes: the Precision or P-code and the Coarse Acquisition or C/A-code.[2] The codes are modulated onto spread-spectrum transmissions (direct-sequence pseudorandom binary codes) at two different frequencies: The L1 band transmits both the C/A- and P-codes at a frequency of 1575.42 MHz; the L2 band transmits the P-code only at a frequency of 1227.6 MHz.

Designed for military users, the P-code is a week-long pseudorandom number (PRN) sequence, approximately 6×10^{12} bits long, with a bandwidth of 10.23 MHz. The long length of the code makes it hard to acquire and difficult to spoof.[3] The P-code is also more accurate than the civilian code and is more difficult to jam because of its wider bandwidth.[4] To ensure that unauthorized users do not acquire the P-code, the United States can implement an encryption segment on the P-code called anti-spoofing (AS). The P-code with AS, designated the Y-code, is available only to users with the correct deciphering chips.[5]

The C/A-code, designed for nonmilitary users, is a 1023-bit Gold Code (a type of PRN code) with a bandwidth of 1.023 MHz. Less accurate and easier to jam than the P-code, the C/A-code is also easier to acquire, so many military receivers track the C/A-code first and then transfer the P-code. The U.S.

---

[2]Much of the following information is found in Spilker, "GPS Signal Structure."

[3]A receiver is spoofed when it processes fake signals (e.g., those produced by an enemy) as if they were the desired signals. Users of GPS who are spoofed can be made to believe they are on course when they could actually be very far from their desired position.

[4]Spread-spectrum signals are resistant to jamming because of the spreading/despreading process they undergo. The amount of jamming resistance is a function of the bandwidth of the signal (also called the spreading function). Thus, the P-code gains 70 dB of jamming resistance while the C/A-code gains 60 dB of jamming resistance relative to 1 Hz.

[5]AS was officially implemented January 31, 1994. See "Newsfront," *GPS World*, March 1994, p. 21.

military can degrade the accuracy of the C/A-code by implementing something called selective availability (SA), as described below.

GPS works by timing how long it takes coded radio signals to reach the earth from its satellites. A receiver does this by generating a set of codes identical to those transmitted by the system's satellites. It calculates the time delay between its codes and the codes received from the GPS satellites by determining how far it has to shift its own codes to match those transmitted by the satellites. This travel time is then multiplied by the speed of light to determine the receiver's distance from the satellites. A GPS receiver could, in theory, calculate its three-dimensional position by measuring its distance from three different satellites, but in practice a fourth satellite is necessary because there is a timing offset between the clocks in a receiver and those in a satellite. The fourth measurement allows a receiver's computer to solve for the timing offset and eliminate it from the navigation solution (see Figure A.3).

GPS velocity measurements are made by taking the rate of change of pseudorange measurements over time. These pseudorange rate measurements are performed by noting the difference in phase measurements (i.e. the average Doppler frequency) over a given time interval.[6]

RAND*MR614-A.3*

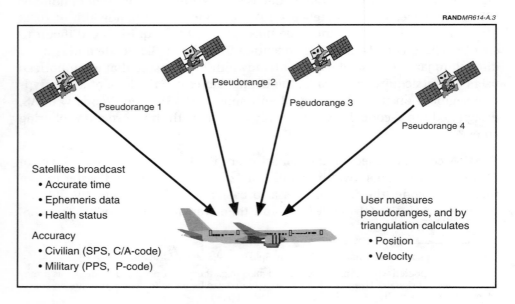

Figure A.3—How GPS Works

---

[6]The measured quantity is called a delta range (ibid., p. 62). Thus, uncorrected velocity measurements are often referred to as pseudo-delta-ranges.

GPS satellites transmit a 50-bit-per-second data stream which is superimposed on the C/A- and P-codes via modulo-2 addition. Once a receiver has matched its code to the code of a satellite, it can begin to decipher that satellite's data message. A satellite's entire data message lasts 12 1/2 minutes; it consists of a 30-second frame repeated 25 times. The 30-second frame contains five subframes, each lasting 6 seconds (i.e., each having 300 bits of information). The subframes are further subdivided into ten mini-subframes lasting 0.6 seconds (30 bits).[7]

Two factors affect a user's overall position accuracy: the errors inherent in the GPS signals themselves, and the geometry of the four NAVSTAR satellites whose signals are used to perform the navigation solution. The inherent errors make up what is known as the user equivalent range error (UERE). The primary contributors to a receiver's UERE are SV clock and ephemeris errors, atmospheric delays, multipath, and receiver noise (including that due to receiver kinematics).

The other factor, satellite geometry, is important because a GPS receiver determines its position via a triangulation; hence, the farther apart four satellites are, the better accuracy a receiver will have. The terms developed to measure the contribution of satellite geometry to the accuracy of a navigation solution are called geometric dilution of precision (GDOP) parameters. They are defined below:[8]

PDOP: Dilution of precision in three-dimensional positioning. Relevant for airborne receivers.

HDOP: Dilution of precision in horizontal position only. Relevant for maritime receivers.

VDOP: Dilution of precision in vertical position only. Relevant for airplanes attempting precision landings.

TDOP: Dilution of precision in time. Relevant for scientists, engineers, and military personnel who are attempting to synchronize clocks using GPS.

---

[7]A detailed description of the contents of each subframe is found in *Global Positioning System Standard Positioning Service Signal Specification,* Department of Defense, November 5, 1993, pp. 20–33.

[8]Tom Logsdon, *The NAVSTAR Global Positioning System,* Van Nostrand Reinhold, New York, 1992, p. 59.

A user's PDOP depends on which satellites can be seen. That, in turn, depends on a user's mask angle[9] (the angle above the horizon below which GPS signals will not be used). Depending on the applications, mask angles typically range between 5 and 15 degrees. The overall accuracy obtained by a user of GPS is a product of the system UERE and the user's GDOP.

Selective availability[10] also affects a user's accuracy. First, it introduces errors into the clock of each satellite (this process is called dithering). These errors have components that vary both rapidly and slowly over time. Dithering the satellite clock introduces errors into the UERE. SA also introduces slowly varying errors into the orbital parameters which are part of the GPS data message. These errors misrepresent the position of a given satellite, which also increases a user's UERE. Because both components of SA have slowly varying errors, it is difficult to distinguish between them.

Control Segment

The control segment tracks the GPS satellites and provides them with periodic updates, correcting their ephemeris constants and clock-bias errors.[11] The United States operates five unmanned monitor stations located at Hawaii, Ascension Island, Diego Garcia, Kwajalein, and Colorado Springs to pick up the NAVSTAR satellites' signals (Figure A.4).

The locations of the monitor stations are known with a high degree of accuracy and each station is equipped with a cesium atomic clock. Each satellite's signals are read by four of the five stations (the station in Hawaii does not have a ground antenna). Because the stations' positions and time coordinates are known, the pseudorange measurements made by each station for a given satellite can be combined to create an inverted navigation solution to fix the location and time of that satellite.

---

[9]If a user could see all satellites above the horizon, the optimal PDOP would occur when 1 SV was directly overhead and the others were on the horizon 120 degrees apart. In that case, the PDOP would be about 1.6. See ibid., p. 59.

[10]In the 1970s, tests of GPS by the GPS Joint Program Office (JPO) found that the low-cost C/A-code unit proved much better than expected. Although it was predicted to provide position accuracies of no better than 100 meters, its actual performance was at the 20- to 30-meter level. This discovery of the C/A-code unit as a precise navigational tool caused a rethinking of the strategy for high-accuracy availability. The DoD invited the Office of the Joint Chiefs of Staff, the Office of the Secretary of Defense, and the National Security Council to establish a national policy regarding availability of GPS to the general public. This was the beginning of selective availability. (Yale Georgiadou and Kenneth D. Doucet, "The Issue of Selective Availability," *GPS World*, September/October 1990, p. 53).

[11]The following discussion is based on information provided in Logsdon, pp. 30–32. A more detailed description is found in S. S. Russell and H. J. Schaibly, "Control Segment and User Performance," *Global Positioning System Volume I*, Institute of Navigation, Washington, D.C., 1980.

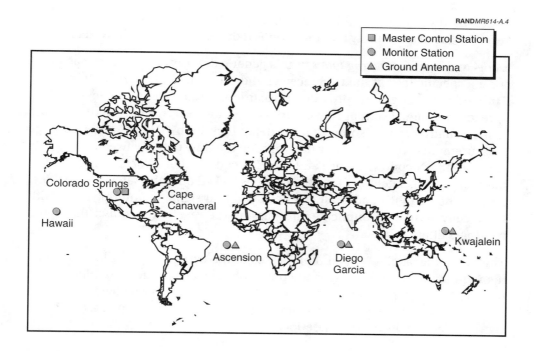

RAND*MR614-A.4*

☐ Master Control Station
● Monitor Station
△ Ground Antenna

Colorado Springs
Hawaii
Cape Canaveral
Ascension
Diego Garcia
Kwajalein

Figure A.4—GPS Control Segment

The measurements are then sent to a master control station called the Consolidated Space Operations Center (CSOC) in Colorado where they are processed to determine each satellite's ephemeris and timing errors. That information is then relayed to the satellites themselves once per day via ground antennas located around the world.

User Segment

The GPS user segment consists of GPS receivers and their auxiliary equipment such as antennas. This section describes how the receivers work, and examines two specific components: code- and carrier-tracking loops. Figure A.5 is a block diagram of a single-channel GPS receiver. Some elements shown in the figure are described below.

Generally speaking, a *tracking loop* is a mechanism that enables a receiver to track a signal that is changing either in frequency or in time. It is a feedback device that basically compares an incoming (external) signal against a locally produced (internal) signal, generates an error signal that is the difference between the two, and uses this signal to adjust the internal signal to match the external one in such a way that the error is reduced to zero or minimized.

Code- and *carrier-tracking loops* fit this generic description, but they each perform a specific task in the GPS receiver and they are implemented differently. The code-tracking loop provides measurements of pseudorange and "despreads" the signal so that satellite messages can be retrieved. To do this, the loops usually employ some type of delay-lock loop (DLL).[12] Pseudorange measurements are obtained by determining the time delay between the locally generated PRN code sequence and the PRN code (either P- or C/A-code) arriving from a given satellite. Once the DLL has locked onto the satellite signal (i.e. aligned the two PRN codes), it can despread that signal by multiplying it with the locally generated duplicate and passing the resultant product through a bandpass filter.

The incoming satellite signal then passes to the carrier-tracking loop for data demodulation. The loop aligns the phase of the receiver's local oscillator with the phase of the despread satellite signal (known as the Intermediate Frequency or IF signal). Because carrier-tracking loops need to follow the phase of the two signals, they usually utilize phase-lock loops (PLLs).

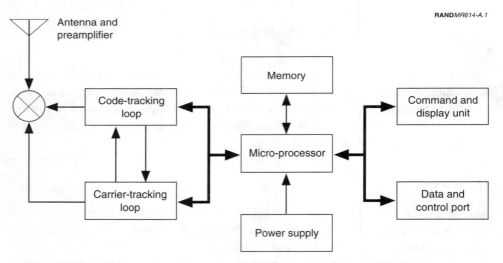

RAND*MR614-A.1*

SOURCE: Richard B. Langley, "The GPS Receiver: An Introduction," *GPS World*, January 1991, p. 51.

Figure A.5—Block Diagram of a Single-Channel GPS Receiver

_____

[12]See J. J. Spilker, *Digital Communications by Satellite*, Prentice-Hall, Englewood Cliffs, NJ, 1977, pp. 528–608.

PLLs work much like DLLs except that they match phases instead of PRNs. For example, if the local oscillator's phase is not correctly matched with the IF signal's phase, the demodulator in the phase-lock loop detects it and applies a correction signal to the oscillator.[13] (In much the same way, a DLL shifts a local PRN sequence when the local and incoming signals are not correctly matched.)

Once the oscillator locks onto the satellite signal, it will continue to follow the variations in the phase of the carrier as the range to the satellite changes. By tracking the rate of change of the carrier phase over time, one can obtain estimates for the velocity of a moving GPS receiver. Finally, once the PLL has locked onto the phase of the satellite signal, the incoming data message can be decoded using standard techniques of bit synchronization and a data detection filter.[14]

The operating states of a GPS receiver are defined as follows:[15]

State 1: Normal Acquisition. The receiver tries to acquire the C/A signal using Doppler estimates derived from satellite almanac data plus present position, velocity, and time inputs from the host vehicle. Subsequent to reading and verifying the hand-over-word (HOW) in the GPS data message, the receiver will acquire and track the P-code.[16]

State 2: Direct Acquisition. The receiver acquires the P-code directly without first acquiring the C/A code. Precise time inputs, as well as position, velocity, frequency, and phase estimates are required.

State 3: Code Lock. The receiver maintains code lock but is unable to maintain precise carrier tracking. In addition, pseudorange measurements are coarse. The receiver reverts to State 4 or 5 when dynamic excursions or jamming levels do not exceed the carrier tracking thresholds.

State 4: Carrier Lock. The receiver maintains carrier lock. Both pseudorange and pseudo-delta-range measurements will be less than full accuracy. Data may be demodulated.

State 5: Carrier Track/Data Demodulation. The receiver precisely tracks the carrier and is able to demodulate system data from the carrier. Pseudorange and pseudo-delta-range measurements are made to full accuracy.

---

[13]Ibid., p. 52.

[14]Langley, "The GPS Receiver," p. 52.

[15]The following definitions, which are universally accepted, were taken from Major Elio Bottari, "User Equipment Overview," *The NAVSTAR GPS System,* Advisory Group for Aerospace Research and Development (AGARD) Lecture Series No. 161, NATO, Neuilly Sur Seine, France, 1988, p. 6-6.

[16]The HOW contains synchronization information for the transfer of receiver tracking from the C/A- to the P-code.

State 6: Sequential Resynchronization. The receiver serially measures pseudo-range and pseudo-delta-range to the GPS satellites. Receivers with continuous tracking do not have this state.

State 7: Signal Reacquisition. This state is reached only when a receiver has been in a tracking state (e.g. State 5) but has subsequently lost the lock of the GPS signal. A receiver in State 7 is in search mode while it tries to reacquire the signal it has lost.

Thus, a receiver that has locked onto GPS signals fully is in State 5. A receiver in State 3 can still function, but its performance will be degraded unless it obtains velocity aiding from an INS (to replace the carrier-derived pseudo-delta-range measurements).

DIFFERENTIAL GPS

The differential GPS (DGPS) method allows a user to obtain extremely high accuracies while circumventing the effect of SA. The concept behind DGPS is illustrated in Figure A.6.

For example, a reference receiver is placed at a surveyed location. The GPS signals arriving at that location contain errors that misrepresent its position. These errors can be estimated by comparing the site's known position with its

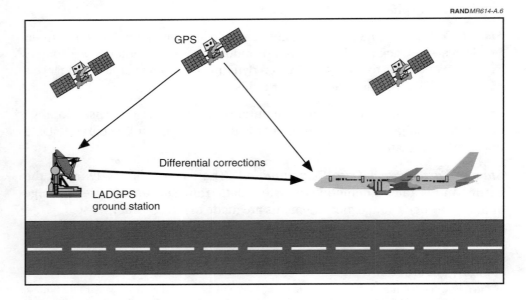

Figure A.6—Differential GPS

position according to GPS. Once the errors are identified, correction terms can be communicated to nearby users with other "roaming" GPS receivers. Each satellite monitored and in view of both the reference and roaming receivers will generate its own error corrections. Those correction terms allow the roaming user to eliminate the bias errors (e.g., atmospheric delays, and satellite clock errors) in the GPS signals from the satellites they are using.

The accuracy of DGPS positioning varies, depending on a user's range from the ground station, the timeliness of the corrections, the geometry of the satellites, the user's equipment, and the technique used. Most sources in the literature report accuracies in the 1–5 meter (1σ) range, which corresponds to 3–14 meters (2 drms). Since SA works by introducing artificial bias errors into the satellite signal, DGPS is successful at canceling out the effects of SA.

Several DGPS techniques exploit various aspects of the GPS signal to achieve high-accuracy measurements. The simplest technique, code-based DGPS, corrects the basic GPS signal by sending pseudorange and pseudorange rate corrections to a user from a base station as described above. The C/A-code pseudorange errors are caused primarily by atmospheric delays, dithering of the satellite clocks, and false orbital parameters information due to SA. The base station has been surveyed, so its position is known with a high degree of accuracy. Because most pseudorange bias errors have a similar effect at both the reference station and the user's position (i.e., the effects are correlated), these errors can be corrected, assuming that the base and user locations are not more than 100–200 km apart. The differential corrections are sent at a fairly low data rate of about 100 bits/sec. After applying the differential corrections, the user can estimate his or her position to 1–5 meters (2 drms). The remaining position uncertainty is due to user receiver and multipath effects.

The carrier-based DGPS method is based on measurements of the GPS signal carrier phase rather than on the code signal. This method achieves high-accuracy positioning since the carrier wave is about 20 cm (the length of the C/A-code is about 300 meters). Therefore, the accuracy that can be achieved with carrier phase measurements is a few centimeters as compared with a few meters for code-based measurements. Carrier-based DGPS requires high-end receivers, which can measure a fractional part of the wavelength for both the base station and the user. The differential correction link needs to be capable of transmitting high data rates (9600 bits/second or more). The key problem is tracking the correct carrier wave, which means that the carrier wavelength ambiguity needs to be resolved at both the reference and user stations. One way to solve this problem is to use differences between carrier phase measurements of both the L1 and L2 carrier frequencies to help narrow the space of possible solutions.

The *static positioning* technique usually involves one, two, or several points, where the solutions are normally post-processed since the results are not needed in real time. While most positioning applications in the survey community use GPS carrier phase measurements, static positioning yields the highest accuracy due to data redundancy and reliability of observations. In an extension of this technique, *kinematic positioning*, a trajectory is determined. The trajectory could be a moving vehicle, such as a ship or aircraft, tectonic plate, or a survey traverse loop. This technique can be performed in many different ways, using single or multiple GPS receivers, and with other sensors such as an inertial navigation system. The key tradeoff is the number of observation epochs needed to guarantee a required level of accuracy. Approaching real-time solutions requires algorithms that quickly resolve the carrier phase ambiguity. Positioning by the survey community has progressed from using static, rapid-static, to near-real-time techniques. The real-time solutions are termed on-the-fly (OTF) or real-time kinematic (RTK).

Despite its benefits, DGPS has some limitations. For example, both the user receiver and the DGPS reference receiver must be looking at the same set of satellites, which limits the range of differential corrections to less than about 500–600 km.[17] Also, corrections are limited by the ability of the reference sight to communicate with a user. In some cases, the range limit will be driven by the "line-of-sight" between the user and the reference station transmitter. Depending on the altitude of the user, this line-of-sight limit can be much shorter than the range limit discussed above. For example, a cruise missile flying at an altitude of 100 meters can see a ground-based transmitter only at a range of about 40 km. These line-of-sight limits can be overcome by using low-frequency transmissions which "bounce" off the ionosphere. However, low-frequency signals require more power than high-frequency transmissions. In addition, low-frequency (1.6–2.5 MHz) waves are limited to ranges of approximately 100 km over land at high latitudes (i.e., above 50 degrees) due to ionospheric disturbances. The range of such transmissions over water can be greater than 400 km.

A potential solution to the problems discussed above is known as wide-area DGPS (WADGPS). It is basically a networked DGPS system as shown in Figure A.7.

---

[17]Earl G. Blackwell, "Overview of Differential GPS Methods," *Global Positioning System, Volume III*, Institute of Navigation, Washington, D.C., 1986, p. 91.

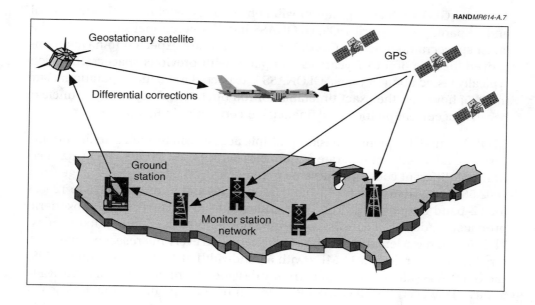

Figure A.7—Wide-Area Differential GPS

With WADGPS, a number of reference sites over a given area are connected to a central facility, which processes the corrections from each site and sends the information to communication satellites in orbit around the earth. The satellites can then transmit the differential corrections to users over a large area. The users select the corrections appropriate for the specific GPS satellites they are using. This eliminates the spatial and temporal limits described above.

GLONASS

The Global Orbiting Navigation Satellite System (GLONASS) is the Russian counterpart to GPS. GLONASS satellites are placed in near semisynchronous circular orbits at a mean altitude of 19,100 km and at an orbital inclination of 64.8 degrees. The GLONASS constellation consists of three orbital planes separated by 120 degrees along the equator. Each plane will eventually contain eight satellites, which have an in-plane separation of about 45 degrees. Satellites in one plane are out of phase by 15 degrees with satellites in the adjacent plane.

The final GLONASS configuration will consist of 24 satellites: 21 operational and 3 spares. As of April 1995, GLONASS has 19 operational satellites.[18] The latest spacecraft, known as GLONASS-M Block 1, are expected to have an improved lifetime of 5 to 7 years as compared with previous spacecraft, which typically lasted about 3 years. GLONASS is expected to be fully operational late in 1995; however, the exact timetable for full operational capability is unclear because of current political and financial uncertainties in Russia.

GLONASS uses frequency division multiple access, where each satellite broadcasts a similar code on separate frequencies (as opposed to GPS satellites which transmit different codes on the same frequencies). The frequencies range from 1602.5625 to 1615.5 MHz for L1-band frequencies and from 1246.4375 to 1256.5 for L2-band frequencies. The two bands are used to correct for ionospheric propagation delays. Like GPS, GLONASS has both civilian and military codes. The civilian has a length of 511 bits and is repeated every microsecond; the military has a code rate of 5.11 MHz with a bandwidth of 10.22 MHz. Unlike GPS, the GLONASS satellites are not currently designed to implement selective availability. However, the GLONASS P-code can be encrypted. Accuracies associated with GLONASS are somewhat better than those obtained with the GPS Standard Positioning Service (SPS) but not as accurate as with the Precise Positioning Service (PPS).

GLONASS operating frequencies are currently being shifted downward because of concern that there could be future interference problems with the worldwide mobile satellite service (MSS). The frequency band of 1610 to 1626.5 has been set aside for MSS users under the International Telecommunications Union (ITU), which is part of the United Nations. In addition, GLONASS is currently experiencing interference problems with the international radio astronomy band at 1610.6 to 1613.8 MHz. For these reasons, Russia recently began reducing the number of GLONASS transmission frequencies. By transmitting 12 different frequencies on one side of the earth and the same 12 frequencies on the other side (antipodal method) for each orbital plane, Russia preserves bandwidth and reduces the amount of in-band interference with other users.

GEOSTAR

At one time, there was a private-sector alternative to the GPS space and control segments. The U.S. firm Geostar provided satellite-based positioning and communications services from 1983 to 1991. The original concept of Geostar's founders was to provide accurate navigation service for air traffic control via what was called a Radio Determination Satellite Service (RDSS). Satellites in

---

[18]"Newsfront," *GPS World*, April 1995, p. 18.

geosynchronous orbit would communicate with aircraft and a ground station, which would actively calculate the position of the aircraft at any time via active ranging measurements. In contrast to GPS, the RDSS system depended on two-way communications, and position calculations were done at a central site, not within the user equipment itself.[19] The communication links also allowed for limited message traffic, and it was thought that a modest combination of mobile communications and positioning services would prove financially viable.

After encountering FAA resistance to satellite-based navigation,[20] Geostar sought to enter the commercial market by serving railroads and trucking companies. In the late 1980s, Geostar was providing limited two-way communication and positioning services using Loran-C receivers and satellite transponders in geosynchronous orbit. The firm hoped to build a system that could support 5–10 meter accuracies and messages of up to 100 characters by 1992. But a series of payload failures and launch delays created numerous setbacks, and the firm could not raise the $100 to $200 million necessary to complete its desired system.[21] The capabilities promised by Geostar were attractive at the time and arguably helped identify a market for accurate positioning information in vehicle fleet management. Geostar was overtaken by a mixture of financial setbacks and rapidly evolving technology. Not only did commercial GPS receivers arrive at competitive prices, but mobile communications technology, such as nationwide paging and cellular phones, overtook RDSS services. Ironically, GPS technology is increasingly being combined with communications, and the original Geostar packaged service concept is becoming a reality, but with a much greater degree of sophistication and power.

INERTIAL NAVIGATION TECHNOLOGIES

Inertial navigation systems (INSs) based on electromechanical technologies have proved extremely successful in the fields of navigation, guidance, and control since the 1950s. The INS provides the positioning signals to guide the vehicle to its intended destination or target. Electromechanical INSs have been used on a variety of platforms including strategic and tactical missiles, space vehicles, aircraft, land vehicles, ships, and submarines. Electromechanical inertial sensors based on mature technologies are typically required for missions where high performance is mandatory, such as ICBM guidance. Although these systems provide high performance, they carry some significant drawbacks, in-

---

[19]Both of these characteristics were considered unacceptable for military combat requirements in the design of GPS.

[20]The FAA supported ground-based radar.

[21]For a discussion of the Geostar corporate history, see U.S. Department of Commerce, *Commercial Space Ventures—A Financial Perspective*, Washington, D.C., April 1990, pp. 25–31.

cluding high production and life cycle costs, difficulties in maintaining accurate calibration and alignment, and extensive maintenance requirements. Because of these drawbacks, the trend is toward replacing electromechanical inertial sensors with solid-state devices, which are smaller, less expensive, and more reliable. For example, ring laser gyros (RLGs) are currently being used in many aviation navigation applications.

The rapid development of GPS during the last decade has provided both commercial and military users a low-cost, highly accurate positioning and navigation system. The quality and decreasing cost of GPS receivers have resulted in the gradual replacement of the INS as the primary means for positioning and navigation in many platforms. However, the integration of these two independent navigation systems will become the navigation solution of choice in the next decade.

GPS and INS navigation systems balance each other: Each technology compensates for the other's weakness. GPS provides long-term stability and bounds INS drift errors, while an INS can track high-vehicle dynamics, has increased jamming resistance, and allows for GPS reacquisition in case of GPS loss-of-lock. In addition, an INS can provide a backup navigation solution if GPS signals are unintentionally or intentionally jammed. Solid-state INSs are well-suited for integration with GPS receivers. Enhanced system accuracy and integrity can be obtained by the physical and functional integration of INS with GPS.

 In the future, GPS is planned to be the primary navigation means for the commercial aviation community. Integrating GPS with INS can provide improved system integrity for this application. GPS signals can be lost due to physical obstructions and interference from other radio signals such as mobile satellite service transmissions, and harmonics of high-power television stations. In addition, intentional jamming can be accomplished by low-power jammers. GPS/INS guidance packages can be 20 to 30 times more jam-resistant than GPS receivers alone and can provide high-accuracy navigation information for several minutes after GPS loss-of-lock.

PROJECTED INERTIAL SENSOR APPLICATIONS AND PERFORMANCE

Future trends in gyros and accelerometer performance and applications are shown in Figures A.8 and A.9.[22] The performance of these inertial sensors is measured in terms of (1) scale factor error, which describes how well an instrument measures the sensed inertial angular rate or acceleration, and (2) bias

---

[22]Neil Barbour, John Elwell, and Roy Sutterlund, *Inertial Instruments—Where To Now?* Draper Laboratory, CSDL-P-3182, Cambridge, MA, June 1992.

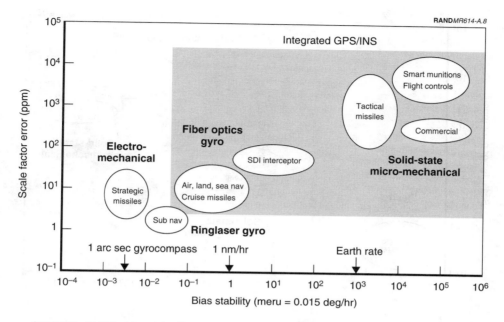

SOURCE: Neil Barbour, John Elwell, and Roy Sutterlund, *Inertial Instruments—Where To Now?* Draper Laboratory, Cambridge, MA, CSDL-P-3182, June 1992.

Figure A.8—Projected Gyro Applications and Performance

stability, which measures the sensor output under zero input conditions. The shaded zone in the figures illustrates some applications where high performance (accuracy and integrity) can be obtained for systems which integrate GPS with solid state micromechanical INSs. Military and civilian applications include tactical missiles, and commercial aviation navigation during en-route, approach, and landing operations.

Applications requiring extremely high performance, such as precision long-range ballistic missiles, will continue to rely on electromechanical inertial sensors because of their high accuracy and autonomous operations requirements. This is particularly true for today's fielded land- and sea-based IRBMs and ICBMs.

The medium performance region will be dominated by fiber optic gyros (FOGs) and solid-state vibrating beam or resonating accelerometers. The ring laser gyro will be useful where low-scale factor error is required; however, this sensor will continue to be relatively expensive because of the precision machining and alignment processes required for production.

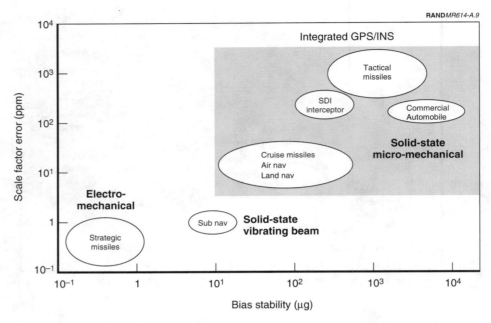

Figure A.9—Projected Accelerometer Applications and Performance

The low-performance end of the INS spectrum will be dominated by low-cost, solid-state quartz or silicon sensors. These micro-mechanical inertial sensors are produced by photolithographical processes, which result in low cost, small size, and high reliability. The solid-state sensors include gyros, accelerometers, or multi-sensors such as a complete IMU. For example, Rockwell International and Systron Donner have developed a low-cost digital quartz inertial measurement unit (IMU). The basic sensors are a quartz tuning fork device that operates on the Coriolis effect to measure angular rate, and a quartz vibrating beam for measuring acceleration.[23] Another interesting development is the growth of multi-sensor technologies, in which a sensor is designed to measure both angular rate and linear acceleration. For example, one multi-sensor technique measures the Coriolis acceleration of a rotating body with two pairs of piezo-electric ceramic sensing elements attached to a rotating drive. This sensor system provides measures of both angular rate and acceleration on two orthogonal axes.

---

[23]R. Silva and G. Murray, "Low Cost Quartz Rate Sensors Applied To Tactical Guidance IMUs," *IEEE PLANS—94*, Las Vegas, NV, April 1994.

Given their low cost, small size, and high reliability, it is not surprising that solid state quartz or silicon sensors are replacing the traditional electromechanical sensors in applications where high accuracies are not required.   Among the many commercial applications for solid-state micromechanical sensors are automotive dynamic functions, industrial robotics, and toys. The integration of GPS with INS will be in large demand for many military applications—for example, short-range stand-off weapons such as the Joint Direct Attack Munition (JDAM). Integration of the solid state INS with GPS will also open the door to applications that are currently challenging, such as low-cost, long-range standoff weapons.

GPS HISTORY, CHRONOLOGY, AND BUDGETS

This appendix provides an overview of the programmatic and institutional evolution of the Global Positioning System (GPS), including a history of its growing use in the military and civilian world, a chronology of important events in its development, and a summary of its costs to the government.

THE HISTORY OF GPS

Throughout time people have developed a variety of ways to figure out their position on earth and to navigate from one place to another. Early mariners relied on angular measurements to celestial bodies like the sun and stars to calculate their location. The 1920s witnessed the introduction of a more advanced technique—radionavigation—based at first on radios that allowed navigators to locate the direction of shore-based transmitters when in range.[1] Later, the development of artificial satellites made possible the transmission of more-precise, line-of-sight radionavigation signals and sparked a new era in navigation technology. Satellites were first used in position-finding in a simple but reliable two-dimensional Navy system called Transit. This laid the groundwork for a system that would later revolutionize navigation forever—the Global Positioning System.

The Military Evolution of GPS

The Global Positioning System is a 24-satellite constellation that can tell you where you are in three dimensions. GPS navigation and position determination is based on measuring the distance from the user position to the precise locations of the GPS satellites as they orbit. By measuring the distance to four GPS satellites, it is possible to establish three coordinates of a user's position

---

[1] The marine radionavigation aid LORAN (Long Range Aid to Navigation) was important to the development of GPS because it was the first system to employ time difference of arrival of radio signals in a navigation system, a technique later extended to the NAVSTAR satellite navigation system.

(latitude, longitude, and altitude) as well as GPS time. (See Appendix A for a technical explanation of how GPS works.)

Originally developed by the Department of Defense (DoD) to meet military requirements, GPS was quickly adopted by the civilian world even before the system was operational. This section describes the evolution of GPS, from its conceptualization to the present day, tracing its military development and its emergence in the civilian world.

The Forerunners of GPS. DoD's primary purposes in developing GPS were to use it in precision weapon delivery and to provide a capability that would reverse the proliferation of navigation systems in the military.[2] Beginning in the early 1960s, the U.S. Department of Defense began pursuing the idea of developing a global, all-weather, continuously available, highly accurate positioning and navigation system that could address the needs of a broad spectrum of users and at the same time save the DoD money by limiting the proliferation of specialized equipment that supported only particular mission requirements. As a result, the U.S. Navy and Air Force began studying the concept of using radio signals transmitted from satellites for positioning and navigation purposes. These studies developed concepts and experimental satellite programs, which became the building blocks for the Global Positioning System.

The Navy sponsored two programs which were predecessors to GPS: Transit and Timation. Transit was the first operational satellite-based navigation system.[3] Developed by the Johns Hopkins Applied Physics Laboratory under Dr. Richard Kirschner in the 1960s, Transit consists of 7 low-altitude polar-orbiting satellites that broadcast very stable radio signals; several ground-based monitor stations to track the satellites; and facilities to update satellite orbital parameters. Transit users determine their position on earth by measuring the Doppler shift of signals transmitted by the satellites.

Originally designed to meet the Navy's requirement for locating ballistic missile submarines and other ships at the ocean's surface, Transit was made available to civilian users in 1967. It was quickly adopted by a large number of commercial marine navigators and owners of small pleasure craft and is still operated by the Navy today.[4] Although it has proved its utility for most ship navigation,

---

[2]Bradford W. Parkinson, "GPS Eyewitness: The Early Years," *GPS World*, September 1994, p. 42.

[3]The concept for Transit evolved from observations of the Russian satellite Sputnik in 1957. Researchers at the Applied Physics Laboratory (APL) discovered that measurements of the Doppler shift as the satellite passed by were adequate to determine the entire satellite orbit. Dr. Frank T. McClure of APL noted that conversely, if the satellite orbit were known, position on the earth could be determined using these same Doppler measurements.

[4]The Navy plans to terminate operation of the system by the end of 1996 according to the 1994 Federal Radionavigation Plan (Draft).

the system has a number of drawbacks. It is slow, requiring a long observation time, provides only two-dimensional positioning capability, has limited coverage due to the intermittent access/availability of its signals (with periods of unavailability measured in hours), and requires users to correct for their velocities—all of which make Transit impractical for use on aircraft or other rapidly moving platforms. Nonetheless, Transit was important to GPS because it resulted in a number of technologies[5] that were extremely useful to GPS and demonstrated that a space system could offer excellent reliability.

Timation, a second forerunner of GPS, was a space-based navigation system technology program the Navy had worked on since 1964.[6] This program incorporated two experimental satellites that were used to advance the development of high-stability clocks, time-transfer, and two-dimensional navigation. The first Timation satellite launched in 1967 carried very stable quartz-crystal oscillators; later models orbited the first atomic frequency standards (rubidium and cesium). The atomic clocks had better frequency stability than earlier clocks, which greatly improved the prediction of satellite orbits (ephemerides) and would eventually extend the time required between control segment updates to GPS satellites. This pioneering work on space-qualified time standards was an important contribution to GPS.[7] In fact, the last two Timation satellites were used as prototype GPS satellites.

In the meantime, the Air Force was working on a similar technology program that resulted in a design concept called System 621B; it provided three-dimensional (latitude, longitude, and altitude) navigation with continuous service.[8] By 1972, the system had already demonstrated the operation of a new type of satellite ranging signal based on pseudorandom noise (PRN).[9] To verify the PRN technique, the Air Force ran a series of aircraft tests at White Sands Proving Ground in New Mexico using ground- and balloon-carried transmitters to simulate satellites. The technique pinpointed the positions of aircraft to within a hundredth of a mile.

---

[5]The satellite prediction algorithms developed for Transit were a significant contribution to GPS.

[6]Timation was developed by the Naval Research Laboratory (NRL) under the direction of Roger Easton.

[7]Parkinson, p. 34.

[8]The studies that led to System 621B originated at the Aerospace Corporation in 1963. Aerospace had begun looking at potential applications of space capabilities to meet critical military needs, one of which was the need for precise positioning of aircraft. In October 1963, the Air Force formally requested that Aerospace continue these studies, which later evolved into System 621B.

[9]The PRN technique had distinct advantages over other techniques, among them the ability to reject noise, which implies a strong ability to reject most forms of jamming or deliberate interference. With this technique, all satellites could transmit on the same frequency without interference. Also, a communication channel could be added which allowed the user to receiver ephemeris (satellite location) and clock information.

At that time, the Air Force concept envisioned a global system consisting of 16 satellites in geosynchronous orbits whose ground tracks formed four oval-shaped clusters extending 30 degrees north and south of the equator. This particular geometry allowed for the gradual evolution of the system because it required only four satellites to demonstrate its operation capabilities. That is, one cluster could provide 24-hour coverage of a particular geographic region (for example, North and South America).

However, no real progress was made toward full-scale development of System 621B until 1973. Part of the reason for this was that the Air Force work had stimulated additional work on satellite navigation, giving rise to a number of competing initiatives from the other services. By the late 1960s, the U.S. Navy, Air Force, and Army were each working independently on radionavigation systems that would provide all-weather, 24-hour coverage and accuracies that would enhance the military capabilities of their respective forces.[10] The APL had made technical improvements to Transit and wanted to upgrade the system, while the Naval Research Laboratory was pushing an expanded Timation system and the Army had proposed using its own system, SECOR (Sequential Correlation of Range). To coordinate the effort of the various satellite navigation groups, DoD established a joint tri-service steering committee in 1968 called the NAVSEG (Navigation Satellite Executive Group). The NAVSEG spent the next several years deciding what the specifics of a satellite navigation system should be—how many satellites, at what altitude, signal codes, and modulation techniques—and what they would cost.

Finally, in April 1973, the Deputy Secretary of Defense designated the Air Force as the lead agency to consolidate the various satellite navigation concepts into a single comprehensive DoD system to be known as the Defense Navigation Satellite System (DNSS). The new system was to be developed by a Joint Program Office (JPO) located at the Air Force's Space and Missile Organization, with participation by all military services. Colonel Brad Parkinson, program director of the JPO, was directed to negotiate between the services to develop a DNSS concept that embraced the views and needs of all services.

By September 1973, a compromise system was evolving which combined the best features of earlier Navy and Air Force programs. The signal structure and frequencies were taken from the Air Force's 621B. Satellite orbits were based on those proposed for the Navy's Timation system, but higher in altitude, giving twelve-hour instead of eight-hour periods. While both systems had proposed the use of atomic clocks in satellites, only the Navy had tested this idea. The

---

[10]Ivan A. Getting, "The Global Positioning System," *IEEE Spectrum*, Vol. 30, No. 12, December 1993, pp. 36–47.

system concept that emerged is what is known today as the NAVSTAR Global Positioning System. In December 1973, DoD granted the JPO approval to proceed with the first phase of a three-phase development of the NAVSTAR GPS.[11]

Testing the GPS Idea (1974–1979). The first phase of the GPS program was intended to confirm the concept of a space-based navigation system, demonstrate its potential for operational utility, and establish the preferred design.[12] The original program was funded at about $100 million and was supposed to cover four satellites, the launch vehicles, three types of user equipment, a satellite control facility, and an extensive test program.[13]

The very first NAVSTAR satellites were actually two refurbished Timation satellites built by the NRL. Known as Navigation Technology Satellite (NTS) numbers 1 and 2, they carried the first atomic clocks ever launched into space. Although these experimental satellites functioned for only short periods following their launches in 1974 and 1977, they proved the concept of time-based ranging using spread-spectrum radio signals and precise time derived from orbiting atomic clocks.

Soon after, the first developmental GPS satellites, known as Block Is, were launched and tested. This series of satellites supported most of the system's testing program. Between 1978 and 1985, a total of eleven Block I satellites built by Rockwell International were launched on the Atlas-F booster; one satellite was lost due to a launch failure. Others eventually failed due to deterioration of their atomic clocks or failures of their attitude control system. However, many of the Block I satellites continued to operate much longer than their design life of three years—in several cases more than 10 years longer.

Even before the first Block Is were launched, the military had begun planning a dual role for the GPS satellites. In addition to carrying the navigation and timing payload, GPS satellites would carry nuclear detonation (NUDET) sensors designed to detect nuclear weapon explosions, assess nuclear attack, and help in evaluating strike damage.[14] The system would also contribute to monitoring

---

[11]An earlier attempt to gain approval for the system was made in August 1973, but failed because the program presented to DoD at that time was not representative of a joint program, but rather a repackaged version of the Air Force's System 621B.

[12]The second phase of GPS was devoted to full-scale engineering development, and the third to production and deployment of the GPS segments.

[13]This funding was apparently just enough to cover the satellites but not enough for the other elements of the first phase of the program. Jeffrey A. Drezner and Giles K. Smith, *An Analysis of Weapon System Acquisition Schedules*, RAND, R-3937-ACQ, December 1990, p. 181.

[14]"GPS to Test Nuclear Detonation Sensor," *Aviation Week & Space Technology*, August 27, 1979, p. 51.

compliance with the nuclear test ban treaty. The first GPS satellite to carry a nuclear explosion detection sensor was the sixth Block I satellite, launched on April 26, 1980.[15] The use of satellites for detecting nuclear explosions dates back to the 1963 Limited Test Ban Treaty between the United States and the Soviet Union, which prohibited nuclear testing in the atmosphere, underwater, and in space. To monitor the ban, the U.S. Air Force and the Atomic Energy Commission (predecessor to the Department of Energy) jointly developed a series of nuclear detection satellites known as Vela. Since then, nuclear detection sensors have been orbited on a number of other DoD satellites, including the NAVSTAR satellites, in an effort to increase the number of detection satellites in space and to improve the existing detection network.[16] The sensors flown on GPS satellites are similar to those initially used on the Vela satellites. The satellites which currently make up the GPS constellation all have the capability to detect nuclear detonations and are presently an important component in the United States' capability to monitor compliance with the Nuclear Non-Proliferation Treaty of 1968.[17] According to DoD plans, future GPS satellites will continue to serve the nuclear detection mission.

Testing of GPS user equipment began in March 1977 before any satellites were in place. A system of solar-powered ground transmitters was set up on the desert floor at the Army's Yuma Proving Ground in Arizona to simulate GPS satellites. These transmitters, known as pseudolites (taken from the term pseudosatellites), broadcast a signal that has a structure similar to that of a GPS satellite.[18] Although the signals were coming from the ground rather than from space, they provided a geometry that approximated that of the satellites. By the time four Block I satellites were in orbit (1978), the JPO was running tests on several types of user equipment carried on aircraft, helicopter, ships, trucks, jeeps, and even by men using 25-pound backpacks.

The final segment of GPS—a prototype ground control system—was located at Vandenberg AFB, CA, during this period. With all the basic components of the

---

[15]The sensor carried on this satellite was called the Integrated Operational Nuclear Detonation Detection System (IONDS); later GPS satellites were fitted with a new sensor known as Nuclear Detonation Detection System (NDS).

[16]Other DoD satellites that have carried nuclear detection sensors include the Defense Support Program satellites used for early warning of missile launch and the Defense Meteorological Satellite Program. For further information, see Bhupendra Jasani, *Verification of a Comprehensive Test Ban Treaty from Space: A Preliminary Study*, United Nations, New York, Research Paper No. 32, 1994.

[17]The GPS Nuclear Detonation Detection System is managed as a joint program between the U.S. Air Force and the Department of Energy (DoE). The Air Force provides the "platform"—the GPS satellites—and operates the system; DoE provides the sensors through its national laboratories, Sandia and Los Alamos.

[18]The pseudolite concept has since become an important technique for improving accuracy and integrity for civil landing of aircraft.

system in place, the JPO was given the go-ahead to proceed with full-scale development of GPS in August 1979.

GPS Grows Up (1980–1989). Efforts to expand the fledgling GPS program suffered some growing pains during the development phase.

The first setback was brought on by a 1979 decision by the Office of the Secretary of Defense (OSD) to cut $500 million (approximately 30 percent) from the budget over the period FY81–FY86.[19] As a result, the GPS program was restructured and the scope of the program reduced. The final satellite constellation was cut from 24 to 18 satellites (plus three satellites serving as on-orbit spares); Block II development satellites were dropped; and the design was scaled down in terms of weight, power, and nuclear and laser hardening.[20] Plans for attainment of an early limited two-dimensional capability in 1981 were also dropped.

Funding for GPS was somewhat unstable during the early stages of the program even though it received support from many elements of the services. Because GPS is a support system and not a standard weapon system with a clear mission and a history of well-defined operational concepts, early understanding of the value of the system was less straightforward than with tanks or aircraft. This increased the need to sell the program, particularly to potential users. The JPO addressed this problem, especially during Phase I, by emphasizing one of the more tangible capabilities of the system: increased bombing accuracy. The fact that GPS was a joint program also increased the need to sell the program to multiple services. No one service was anxious to bear the entire financial load for a support system that was to be used by all services. As a result, GPS had service support difficulties. For example, the program was zeroed out in 1980 through 1982, but was reinstated by OSD.[21] It appears that OSD support contributed to the survival of the program.

GPS suffered another setback as a result of the Space Shuttle Challenger accident in 1986. As the only planned launch vehicle for GPS satellites at that time, the loss of the shuttle caused a 24-month delay in the scheduled launch of the second generation of GPS satellites, the Block IIs. Originally, the JPO planned to launch the first 12 satellites (Phase I) on refurbished Atlas F boosters and to use the McDonnell-Douglas Delta for the next series of launches (Phase II). Around 1979, the JPO had responded to DoD decisions which designated the Space Shuttle as the principal launch vehicle for Air Force missions. Although the

---

[19]Drezner, p. 184.

[20]The GPS constellation was later restored in 1988 to its original configuration of 24 satellites, including three spares, because the performance by 18 satellites was found inadequate.

[21]Drezner, p. 188.

Block IIs were built to be compatible with shuttle deployment, the JPO decided to switch back to the Delta II as the GPS launch vehicle following the Challenger disaster.

The first Block II satellite was eventually launched in February 1989 from Cape Canaveral AFS, and became operational for global use in April 1989. Since then, there have been 23 more Block II satellite launches. Like the Block I satellites, the Block IIs were produced by Rockwell International. The Block II satellites differ from the Block Is in shape and weight and incorporate design differences that affect security and integrity.[22] Significant Block II satellite enhancements include:

- Radiation-hardened electronics to improve reliability and survivability

- Full selective availability (SA) and anti-spoofing (AS) capabilities to provide system security

- Automatic detection of certain error conditions and switching to nonstandard code transmission or default navigation message data to protect users from tracking a faulty satellite and to maximize system integrity.

Block II satellites launched after 1989 have the additional capability of operating for up to 180 days without contact from the control segment. They are called Block IIAs. This represents a significant improvement over the earlier Block I and II satellites, which required updating from the control segment after only 3.5 days.

Further progress was made on the control and user equipment segments of GPS during this period. As part of the transition to an operational and sustainable system, the control segment was transferred to a new master control station located at Falcon AFB, CO. System testing was completed, and successful interoperability was demonstrated between the ground control stations, the satellites, and the "user" navigation equipment. Rockwell-Collins was chosen as the contractor for the production GPS user equipment. By the turn of the century, an estimated 17,000 U.S. military aircraft will be equipped with GPS, and 60,000 portable receivers will be in use by U.S. ground forces and on military vehicles.[23]

---

[22]*Security* refers to features built into GPS that can deny accurate service to unauthorized users, prevent spoofing, and reduce receiver susceptibility to jamming. These security measures, designed only with the military in mind, can cause difficulties for unauthorized users, i.e., anyone without a specific military need and/or mission. *Integrity* refers to the ability of the system to provide timely warnings to users when the system should not be used for navigation.

[23]The Aerospace Corporation, *The Global Positioning System: A Record of Achievement*, 1994.

Recent Military Use of GPS (1990–present). The 1990–1991 crisis in the Persian Gulf, the first major test[24] of GPS in a combat situation, proved beyond a doubt the importance and utility of the NAVSTAR. Some say that GPS revolutionized combat operations on the ground and in the air during Operation Desert Storm and was—as one Allied commander noted—one of two particular pieces of equipment that were potential war winners (the other was night-vision devices).[25]

Among the many uses of GPS in Operation Desert Storm, navigation proved to be a crucial technique for desert warfare.[26] GPS satellites enabled coalition forces to navigate, maneuver, and fire with unprecedented accuracy in the vast desert terrain almost 24 hours a day[27] despite difficult conditions—frequent sandstorms, few paved roads, no vegetative cover, and few natural landmarks. Although on average, each U.S. Army maneuver company (e.g., tank, mechanized infantry, or armored cavalry) had at least one GPS receiver, the demand for receivers was so great that more than 10,000 commercial units were hastily ordered during the crisis so that more coalition forces could benefit from the system.

Other operations made possible or greatly enhanced by GPS include precision-bombing, artillery fire support, the precise positioning of maneuvering troop formations, and certain special forces operations such as combat search-and-rescue missions. As well as being carried by foot soldiers, GPS receivers were attached, in some cases with tape, to vehicles and helicopter instrument panels and were also used in F-16 fighters, KC-135 tankers, and B-52 bombers.

Since the Persian Gulf War, the United States has employed GPS in several peacekeeping and military operations. During Operation Restore Hope in 1993, GPS was used to air drop food and supplies to remote areas of Somalia because of lack of accurate maps and ground-based navigation facilities. U.S. forces entering Haiti in 1994 also relied on GPS. During the present Balkan crisis, GPS has assisted in delivery of aid to the Bosnians by guiding U.S. Air Force trans-

---

[24]GPS played only a minor role in military operations of the 1980s. For example, the U.S. Navy used GPS to determine the position of minefields in the Persian Gulf in 1987–1988, and the U.S. Air Force used GPS during the intervention in Panama in December 1989 (Operation Just Cause) to overcome inaccuracies in maps that showed key bridges in the wrong position.

[25]Michael Russel Rip and David P. Lusch, "The Precision Revolution: The Navstar Global Positioning System in the Second Gulf War," *Intelligence and National Security*, Vol. 9, No. 2, April 1994, pp. 167–241.

[26]Rip, p. 171.

[27]Sixteen GPS satellites were active during the crisis. Block II satellites launched during Operation Desert Storm were adjusted to place them in an optimal position to provide maximum GPS coverage over the region.

port planes at night to their drop zones where food and medicine is then parachuted close to towns and villages.

Current Status of NAVSTAR GPS. The launch of the 24th Block II[28] satellite in March 1994 completed the GPS constellation. The NAVSTAR system currently consists of 25 satellites, including one Block I satellite.[29] Initial Operational Capability (IOC) was formally declared December 8, 1993, in a joint announcement by the DoD and the Department of Transportation (DoT).[30] The IOC notification means that the NAVSTAR GPS is capable of sustaining the Standard Positioning Service (SPS), the 100-meter positioning accuracy available to civilian users of the system on a continuous, worldwide basis.[31] Unlike IOC for other DoD systems, IOC for GPS has purely civil connotations.

In 1995, the U.S. Air Force Space Command formally declared tha GPS met the requirements for Full Operational Capability (FOC),[32] meaning that the constellation of 24 operational (Block II/IIA) satellites now in orbit has successfully completed testing for military functionality. While the FOC declaration is significant to DoD because it defines a system as being able to provide full and supportable military capability, it does not have any significant impact on civil users.

An additional 21 satellites called Block IIRs are being developed by Martin Marietta (formerly General Electric Astro Space division) as replacements for the current GPS satellites.[33] The Block IIR satellites will provide enhanced performance over the previous generation of GPS satellites, including the capability to autonomously navigate (AUTONAV) themselves and generate their own navigation message data. This means that if the control segment cannot contact the Block IIR satellites, the AUTONAV capabilities will enable these

---

[28]A total of 28 Block II satellites were built by Rockwell. There are four remaining Block II satellites in reserve, two of which are scheduled to be launched "on need" in 1995 and the other two during 1996. Glen Gibbons, "AF Says GPS Fully Operational," *GPS World Newsletter*, May 22, 1995, p. 5.

[29]The sole Block I spacecraft was taken off-line in June 1995 after nearly 11 years of service, due to declining performance.

[30]IOC requires a combination of at least 24 operating Block I and Block II satellites in orbit.

[31]Prior to IOC, GPS was considered a developmental system whose operation, including signal availability and accuracy, was subject to change at the discretion of DoD. Subsequent to IOC, any planned disruption of the SPS in peacetime will be preceded by a 48-hour advance notice to users through the Coast Guard GPS Information Center (GPSIC) and the FAA's Notice to Airmen (NOTAM) system. Unplanned system outages will be announced by the GPSIC and NOTAM systems as they become known.

[32]U.S. Air Force Space Command Public Affairs Office, "Global Positioning System Fully Operational," news release, July 17, 1995.

[33]The contract for the Block IIR satellites was awarded in June 1989.

satellites to maintain full system accuracy for at least 180 days.[34] The Block IIR satellites will be available for launch as necessary beginning in late 1996.

A follow-on set of replenishment satellites, known as Block IIFs, is planned to replace the Block IIR satellites at the end of their useful life. The Air Force intends to buy 33 Block IIF satellites[35] to sustain the quality of the GPS signal as a worldwide utility for the foreseeable future.[36] These satellites will have to meet even higher levels of performance than previous generations of GPS satellites, including a longer life cycle of 6.5 to 10 years. The IIF satellite will be launched on an Evolved Expandable Launch Vehicle (EELV).[37] The Air Force issued a draft request for proposals (RFP) on June 20, 1995, and plans to award a contract for the development and procurement of the Block IIF satellites in spring 1996.[38]

The Evolution of GPS in the Civilian World

This section examines the U.S. government's public responses to the growing number of civil users, the role of government agencies and other private-sector agents in fostering commercial GPS markets, and present GPS governance and management. With the proliferation of civil government and private-sector users and the widening array of commercial GPS applications, the U.S. government is having to juggle a growing set of civilian demands on the system along with the military demands.[39] This has given rise to a number of issues discussed here and in Chapter Two.

The United States Opens GPS Up to Civilians. The first U.S. pronouncement regarding civil use of GPS came in 1983 following the downing of Korean

---

[34]If the control segment lost contact with the Block I and Block II satellites, the satellites would continue transmitting the stored navigation message data previously uploaded by the control segment for 3.5 and 180 days, respectively. However, the system accuracy would degrade over time.

[35]Originally, the Air Force planned to buy 51 satellites. However, concerns over the legal and political ramifications of issuing such a large contract caused the service to scale back its planned buy to 33 satellites. "House Appropriators Cut GPS Block IIF, Add $100 Million For SBIRS," *Aerospace Daily*, Vol. 175, No. 17, July 27, 1995, pp. 129–130.

[36]The JPO also plans to procure six follow-on satellites as eventual replacements for the Block IIF satellites.

[37]EELV is a U.S. Air Force effort to develop by 2000 a new family of space boosters based on existing systems. The goal of this program is to lower the cost of launching medium and heavy U.S. government payloads into orbit. Warren Ferster, "Russian Rocket Engines Vie for Role in EELV Effort," *Space News*, May 8–14, 1995, p. 12.

[38]The value of the IIF contract is estimated to be in excess of $2 billion. Three teams are interested in bidding: Lockheed Martin, Loral Federal Systems, ITT; Rockwell International, Computer Sciences Corp., Rockwell Anaheim; and Hughes Space and Communications, National Systems & Research and Stanford Telecommunications and Space Applications. "Air Force Set To Release RFP on $2 Billion GPS Block IIF Contract," *C4I* via NewsPage, May 11, 1995.

[39]Parkinson, p. 44. Civil GPS receivers currently outnumber military receivers by more than 10 to 1.

Airlines Flight 007 after it strayed over territory belonging to the Soviet Union. At this time, President Reagan announced that the Global Positioning System would be made available for international civil use once the system became operational. In 1987 DoD formally requested the Department of Transportation to establish and provide an office to respond to civil users' needs and to work closely with the DoD to ensure proper implementation of GPS for civil use. Two years later, the U.S. Coast Guard became the lead agency for this project.

The Reagan announcement was followed by a U.S. offer to make available the Standard Positioning Service of GPS, which was announced at the International Civil Aviation Organization's (ICAO) Tenth Air Navigation Conference, September 5, 1991. The Federal Aviation Administration's (FAA) Administrator, James Busey, promised that GPS would be available free of charge to the international community beginning in 1993 on a continuous, worldwide basis for at least 10 years. This offer was extended the following year at the 29th ICAO Assembly, when the United States offered SPS to the world for the foreseeable future and pledged to provide at least six years notice prior to termination of GPS operations or elimination of the GPS SPS.

Both offers were formally reiterated in a 1994 letter from the FAA's chief, David Hinson, to ICAO, reaffirming the U.S. government's intention to provide GPS SPS free of charge for at least 10 years.[40] In 1995, President Clinton once again confirmed the government's commitment to provide GPS signals to international civil users in a statement that was released at an ICAO meeting in Montreal in March.[41]

The U.S. Government's Role in Fostering Commercial GPS Markets. The birth of one of the first GPS markets—surveying—was influenced by a 1984 decision by the Department of Commerce's National Oceanic and Atmospheric Administration (NOAA)[42] to publish the first draft standards in the Federal Register that allowed for the use of GPS data. This seal of approval of GPS data by a civil government agency helped jump start the expansion of the surveying market even while the GPS system was still in development.

By the mid-1980s, commercial GPS equipment aimed at the surveying profession appeared on the market even though only a small number of operating GPS satellites were in orbit. Surveying and time transfer were logical entry

---

[40]David Hinson, FAA Administrator, letter to Dr. Assad Kotaite, President of the Council, International Civil Aviation Organization, October 14, 1994.

[41]Bill Clinton, President of the United States, letter to the International Civil Aviation Organization, March 16, 1995.

[42]NOAA has historically chaired the Federal Geodetic Control Committee, which sets standards for mapping and geodesy.

points into the market because their applications could accept the limited availability of satellite signals.[43] Surveyors did not need to use their data in real time, but could make observations whenever sufficient satellite signals were available, day or night. GPS surveying offered greater productivity and cost savings over traditional survey methods. Tasks that normally required several weeks or months to finish could now be completed in a fraction of the time using GPS—at one-fifth to one-tenth of the cost of conventional surveying.[44] Satellite surveying also helped sustain the commercial market for GPS equipment after the Challenger disaster shut down operations and delayed satellite launches for several years.

The money generated by the survey market boom was also important to the overall development of GPS applications because it enabled U.S. manufacturers to invest in research and development (R&D) on GPS technology. The added R&D investment helped accelerate the development of GPS applications faster than would have been possible had the DoD been left to carry out this task on its own. In fact, surveyors were the first to employ some of the more advanced differential GPS techniques being used today, such as kinematic surveying and real-time carrier phase tracking. Now, ten years after the first standards were published, almost all geodetic standards are based on GPS data.

The growth in the GPS survey market opened the way for a number of GPS niche markets such as aviation. Even in these smaller markets, government agencies have contributed to their expansion. For example, the FAA issued performance standards for GPS receivers (Technical Standard Order C129) in 1992. This action allowed manufacturers to build GPS receivers as supplemental navigation aids for aircraft, thereby broadening the range of market opportunities for GPS suppliers. As evidence of this, Trimble, the first company to be awarded the GPS Technical Standard Order certification, signed an agreement with Honeywell in 1995 to cooperate in developing GPS products for the commercial, space, and military aviation markets. This alliance will allow both companies to tap into new GPS markets.

Government export controls have also affected GPS markets. Prior to 1991, most GPS user equipment shipped abroad required individual validated licenses to ensure compliance with various Department of Commerce (DoC) Bureau of Export Administration export control programs. On September 1, 1991, the DoC revised its export list of electronic equipment requiring licenses for shipment abroad. What the DoC essentially did was to make a clear delin-

---

[43]Frank Kuznik, "You Are Here: GPS Satellites Can Tell You Where You Are—Within Inches," *Air & Space*, June/July 1992, pp. 34–40.

[44]Cost estimates provided by the U.S. GPS Industry Council.

eation between military and civil GPS user equipment. Under the revised regulations, civilian GPS receivers, other satellite equipment, and telecommunications systems were freed of restrictions and were allowed to be shipped as "general destination items," although military receivers, GPS null steerable antennas, encryption devices, and certain other components were still treated as "munitions" with strict export restrictions.[45] This liberalization of export controls helped speed up the U.S. industry's entry into foreign markets. Today, export markets are important to U.S. GPS manufacturers, making up an average of 45 to 50 percent of overall sales.[46]

The export controls issue also served as a catalyst for the U.S. commercial GPS industry to organize itself. Prior to the 1991 revision of export controls, U.S. manufacturers were concerned that foreign competitors were gaining an unfair advantage because of fewer restrictions. Fearing that the United States would lose control over an American-made space technology, a group of GPS manufacturers began working together to tackle export problems and in the process formed the U.S. GPS Industry Council (USGIC). The USGIC now has a permanent office in Washington, D.C., and has incorporated as a nonprofit entity. The council monitors and addresses emerging regulatory, political, and global issues affecting the GPS industry and serves as an information resource for key policymakers.

By the time the GPS constellation neared completion in the early 1990s, domestic manufacturers were well aware of the commercial potential of GPS. Ironically, it was the military, through its involvement in the Persian Gulf conflict, that gave the commercial GPS market its biggest boost. The success of GPS in Operation Desert Storm sparked a surge in a growing multi-million-dollar market that had barely existed just a few years prior to the war. Desert Storm provided the setting for showing off all the military uses of GPS—from helping soldiers navigate across a featureless desert to enabling artillery and bomber units to target the enemy with unprecedented accuracy.

When the war broke out, there were a limited number of military receivers in the DoD inventory. This led the DoD to purchase thousands of GPS civilian receivers and the National Command Authority (NCA)[47] to turn off selective

---

[45]Prior to revision of export controls, approximately 50 to 60 percent of all exports by U.S. GPS manufacturers required validated export licenses in advance. Following changes in the export list, the percentage of GPS receivers and products shipped without a validated license rose to 80 percent.

[46]United States GPS Industry Council (USGIC), "GPS: A Dual-Use Technology Success," Washington, D.C., 1994, p. 3.

[47]The NCA is the President or the Secretary of Defense, with the approval of the President. The term NCA is used to signify constitutional authority to direct the Armed Forces in their execution of military action.

availability (SA) so that the troops could get better accuracy using the civilian receivers. The Pentagon bought most of the GPS receivers used in the Persian Gulf from Trimble Navigation and Magellan Systems. These two companies became emergency suppliers, selling the Pentagon 10,000 and 3,000 receivers respectively.[48] Close to 90 percent of the GPS receivers used in the war were of the commercial sort.[49]

In addition to precipitating a rise in demand for GPS commercial receivers, the war provided GPS technology and the suppliers of GPS receivers broad exposure. News coverage of the conflict served as free publicity for the two main wartime suppliers. Following the war, Trimble Navigation's sales to non-DoD customers went from a fraction of overall sales to a majority.[50] Desert Storm was also instrumental in helping manufacturers ramp up operations.[51] However, the war was also disruptive because manufacturing lines were turned to support DoD demand, and commercial GPS marketing efforts were slowed for the duration of the war. Nevertheless, in peacetime, the U.S. commercial GPS manufacturers continue to produce new and cheaper receivers.

While GPS markets have benefited from government policies and initiatives, the development in commercial markets has also contributed to the national security mission of GPS. The demand by civilian commercial users of GPS for smaller, better, cheaper receivers has directly benefited systems designed specifically for military use. For example, the precision lightweight GPS receiver (PLGR) used by U.S. military forces and designated a "non-developmental item" was built at a low cost and delivered on time in large part due to technical benefits derived from research and development being conducted for civilian commercial applications.[52]

GPS Management Today. The Global Positioning System management structure is currently undergoing a transition. Until recently, DoD was solely responsible for the management and operations of GPS as well as for policy formulation regarding the system and its uses. Although DoD and the Department of Transportation cooperated on those aspects of GPS policy affecting civil access to the system, much of the decision authority rested with DoD, and ultimately with the National Command Authority. However, now the civil govern-

---

[48]Kuznik, p. 39.

[49]Rip, p. 173.

[50]Andrew Jenks, "Bursting into Bloom After Desert Storm," *Washington Technology*, October 8, 1992, p. 17.

[51]Jenks, p. 18.

[52]USGIC, p. 1.

ment sector—primarily DoT—has been given a more active role in GPS management.

Many changes occurring are a result of recommendations made by a joint task force of the Departments of Defense and Transportation in 1993. The Joint DoD/DoT Task Force (JTF) was established after the Secretaries of Defense and Transportation agreed to examine the operational, technical, and institutional implications of increased civil use of GPS. The JTF was directed to (1) evaluate services derived from GPS signals; (2) evaluate the ability of GPS, as managed and operated by the DoD, to meet the needs of civil users; (3) assess the importance of GPS services to civil, commercial, and national security objectives; and (4) assess the long-term U.S. government sustainment of GPS as a national resource. The JTF recommendations, released in a report in December 1993,[53] point to seven core areas where GPS is not meeting civil user expectations or where alternate management strategies have been recommended. The GPS management structure was one of the core areas where the JTF saw room for improvement.[54] The JTF recommended that steps be taken to enhance civil participation in developing GPS policy and in managing the basic system and planned augmentations.[55] Thus the U.S. government is now involved in striking a balance between military and civil requirements and providing channels for both sectors to offer input to GPS management and policymaking.

The Domestic Military–Civil GPS Balance. The following overview of the current GPS management structure is intended to show how the United States balances the military and civilian roles domestically as well as in the international arena.

National Security. The Department of Defense is responsible for the day-to-day management and operation of GPS. Within DoD, the U.S. Air Force is in charge of carrying out these responsibilities. Research and development is managed by the GPS Joint Program Office (JPO), which is part of the Air Force Materiel Command in Los Angeles. Personnel from other military services, DoT, NATO, and other allied nations are also involved. Testing and evaluation are conducted jointly by the Air Force Operational Test and Evaluation Center and Air Force Space Command (AFSPACECOM), which also manages the operation and maintenance of the system.

---

[53]Joint Department of Defense/Department of Transportation Task Force, *The Global Positioning System: Management and Operation of a Dual Use System, A Report to the Secretaries of Defense and Transportation*, Washington, D.C., December 1993.

[54]The other core issues examined in the report are funding, accuracy, availability and integrity, regulation of GPS augmentations, international acceptance, and spoofing and jamming.

[55]Joint Department of Defense/Department of Transportation Task Force, p. 20.

Funding to support the basic GPS is appropriated in the DoD budget. The Assistant Secretary of the Air Force for Acquisition has budgetary oversight for all funding for procurement and launch of the GPS satellites and for the control segment. The Department of Energy provides additional funding to procure Nuclear Detection Detonation System (NDS) payloads. Federal civil agencies are responsible for providing their own resources to modify or enhance the capabilities of GPS to meet unique civil requirements.[56] Each agency is responsible for procuring user equipment to meet its mission needs.

Responsibility for policy formulation for GPS is now divided between DoD and DoT as a result of the JTF recommendations. The DoD is responsible for the military policy, the DoT for U.S. civil government policy. There is no single coordination of international policy on GPS; the international process is fragmented among several agencies described later.

DoD retains policy and decisionmaking authority for management of the basic GPS, the Precise Positioning Service (PPS), military uses of GPS, and funding requirements. Within DoD, GPS policy is set by the Office of the Secretary of Defense, with assistance from the DoD Positioning/Navigation (Pos/Nav) Executive Committee. The DoD Pos/Nav Executive Committee, chaired by the Under Secretary for Acquisition Technology, is supported by a Pos/Nav Working Group, which carries out the committee's decisions, identifies problem areas, assists in revising the Federal Radionavigation Plan (FRP), and provides recommendations to the committee. The Executive Committee also receives input from all the commands, departments, and agencies within DoD.

Civil Management. DoT is responsible for overseeing the civil uses of GPS. As the lead DoT agency for civil GPS service operations and the government point of contact for civil users of GPS, the Coast Guard manages and operates the Civil GPS Service (CGS) program, which consists of four main elements:

- The Civil GPS Service Interface Committee (CGSIC) serves as a forum for exchanging technical information and collecting information on the needs of the civil GPS user community. The committee, comprised of representatives from private, government, and industry user groups, both U.S. and international, meets semiannually.

- The Navigation Information Service (NIS) (formerly the GPS Information Center) provides GPS status information to all users of the system 24 hours a day.

---

[56]An example of this is the Coast Guard Differential GPS network currently being installed to meet a previously unsatisfied 8–20 meter harbor and harbor approach navigation requirement.

- The Precise Positioning Service Program Office (PPSPO) administers the program allowing qualified civil users access to the PPS signal.

- A differential GPS (DGPS) being developed by the Coast Guard augments the GPS Standard Positioning Service and will provide accuracies of 10 meters or better for civil users in the maritime regions of the United States once it becomes operational in 1996.

Oversight responsibility for GPS policymaking in DoT was recently assigned to the DoT Pos/Nav Executive Committee, established in 1994 as part of a DoT reorganization and in response to a JTF recommendation. Thus GPS responsibilities were consolidated within the office of the Assistant Secretary for Transportation Policy, who is also the designated chair of the DoT Pos/Nav Executive Committee. DoT was assigned responsibility for GPS policy relative to GPS augmentations, the SPS, all civil uses, and implementation of cost-recovery mechanisms. The committee, composed of policy-level representatives from 16 DoT offices and modal administrations including the FAA and Coast Guard, formulates coordinated policy recommendations for the Secretary of Transportation, provides policy and planning guidance to DoT's operating administrations on navigation and positioning issues, coordinates with similar committees in other government agencies, and provides unified departmental comments on the proposed rulemaking of other governmental agencies regarding navigation and positioning issues.

Two organizations provide input on civilian GPS activities to the DoT Pos/Nav Executive Committee:

- A GPS Interagency Advisory Council (GIAC) was recently established to identify and coordinate civil GPS positioning and timing issues for federal civil agencies.[57] GIAC serves as a policy arm to the DoT Pos/Nav Executive Committee, reporting policy issues relative to these GPS applications on behalf of federal agencies.

- The Civil GPS Service Interface Committee (CGSIC) (described above) has a more information-gathering and dissemination role. The CGSIC provides the DoT Pos/Nav Executive Committee information on GPS requirements from relevant private industry, government, and GPS civil user groups in the United States and overseas. Both the CGSIC chair and GIAC chair are members of the DoT Pos/Nav Executive Committee.

---

[57]Formed in response to a JTF recommendation, the GIAC is housed within the Federal Geographic Data Committee (FGDC) and is chaired by the FGDC's Federal Geodetic Control Subcommittee (FGCS). The FGCS is responsible for federal surveying, geodesy, and related spatial activities.

Although the Joint DoD/DoT Task Force anticipated that the DoD and DoT Pos/Nav Executive Committees would work closely together to facilitate routine coordination and management decisions, it is too soon to judge whether the joint management structure has been effective. The Task Force also recommended creation of a top-level GPS Executive Board, composed of an assistant secretary from each department, to resolve those conflicts about joint civil and military use of GPS that could be resolved between the Executive Committees. An Executive Board has been formed, but it has not held any meetings to date.

Other Civil Government Agencies. Several civil government agencies are leading initiatives which rely on GPS. They have no direct involvement in DoD's management of GPS, but their role in managing GPS applications is worth noting:

- The FAA is responsible for planning and managing the civil aviation usage of GPS and for implementing GPS in the National Airspace System (NAS). This entails publishing the FAA Satellite Navigation Program Master Plan[58] and developing requirements for the use of GPS in NAS, including a set of appropriate standards for GPS aviation receivers and methods for air traffic control handling of GPS aircraft operations. A recent example of this was the 1993 FAA approval of GPS for use as a supplemental navigation for en route through nonprecision approach phases of flight.[59] The FAA also leads the initiative to augment the GPS SPS with a Wide-Area Augmentation System (WAAS), intended to be the primary means of navigation for all phases of flight from en route to Category I approaches once the system is operational.

- The National Geodetic Survey (NGS), housed within the Department of Commerce's National Oceanic and Atmospheric Administration, leads an initiative to develop a high-accuracy GPS-based National Spatial Reference System (NSRS) to replace the existing National Geodetic Reference System (NGRS), a U.S. coordinate system established by classical survey methods. This effort should eventually result in a single, seamless, NSRS-based spatial data infrastructure that can be accessed by U.S. mapping, surveying,

---

[58]This plan presents the needs, scope, objectives, and other requisite planning information for the FAA's Satellite Navigation Program, including schedules for civil augmentation and operational implementation of GPS in the NAS. See U.S. Department of Transportation, Federal Aviation Administration, Satellite Program Office, *FAA Satellite Navigation Program Master Plan FY 94–99*, June 15, 1994.

[59]Supplemental use means that another navigation source such as a ground-based radio aid must be monitored while GPS is being used as the primary system. In 1994, the FAA authorized GPS as a sole means of navigation provided the GPS equipment meets the criteria of Technical Standards Order C129 and is capable of Receiver Autonomous Integrity Monitoring (RAIM). RAIM is a form of GPS integrity monitoring based on the principle that a GPS receiver can detect and isolate a failed satellite by calculating multiple position solutions.

transportation, geodetic studies, and geographic information systems users.

- The Federal Geographic Data Committee (FGDC) was assigned by Executive Order[60] the responsibility of coordinating the federal government's development of a National Spatial Data Infrastructure (NSDI), an electronic index to spatial data collected across the United States, including GPS-based data. The NSDI is intended to provide a pool of current and reliable data, partnerships among data producers and users, and standards for sharing data. Rather than centralize all the information in one place, the government will link all the sites across the country where data are produced or maintained in computers using the Internet. This approach enables users to access this network of information using the Internet and find out what data exist, the quality and condition of the data, and the terms for obtaining them. The FGDC will attempt to put together a comprehensive set of core geospatial data by 2000.

The Federal Radionavigation Plan—A Joint DoD/DoT Effort. The Federal Radionavigation Plan (FRP) is the official planning and policy document for all present and future federally operated common-use radionavigation systems (i.e., systems used by both the military and civil sectors), including GPS. The FRP, jointly drafted and issued biennially by DoD and DoT,[61] describes areas of authority and responsibility and provides a management structure by which the individual operating agencies can define and meet radionavigation requirements in a cost-effective manner.

The first edition of the FRP was released in 1980 in response to Congressional direction in the International Maritime Satellite (INMARSAT) Act of 1978 (P.L. 95-564), which instructed DoT and DoD to review their navigation needs and to select a mix of common-use systems that would meet requirements for accuracy, reliability, coverage, and cost while minimizing duplication of services. Since then, the FRP has served as a top-level plan for the joint coordination, implementation, and operation of all federally provided military and civil radionavigation systems used in air, space, land, and marine navigation. The primary objective of the FRP is to ensure that the DoD and the DoT work together to meet their needs and avoid unnecessary overlaps or gaps between military and civil radionavigation systems and services.

---

[60]On April 11, 1994, President Clinton signed Executive Order 12906, "Coordinating Geographic Data Acquisition and Access: The National Spatial Data Infrastructure." Published in the *Federal Register*, Vol. 59, No. 71, April 13, 1994, pp. 17671–17674.

[61]The federal government holds open radionavigation user conferences every two years to provide the public user community with the opportunity to comment on and provide input to the FRP.

Several formal structures within the DoD and DoT participate in the publication of the FRP. The DoD and DoT Pos/Nav Executive Committees handle the official staffing and coordination of the FRP, which is signed by both Department Secretaries. The latest edition of the FRP (the eighth) was published in May 1995.[62]

The Military–Civil GPS Balance in the International Arena. *The Military Side.* Since 1978, ten NATO nations and Australia have participated in GPS development, working with the U.S. military through cooperative development agreements signed with the nations to establish a flow of information among the participating nations in all GPS program activities. To this end, personnel from these countries were assigned to the GPS Joint Program Office to advise on and coordinate NATO applications, development, and testing. Additional NATO countries have since become involved, and the scope of international participation is being expanded to include nations such as Israel, Korea, and Japan. Recent agreements have tended to be more operationally oriented agreements for PPS security, availability, and access. Nevertheless, none of these countries participates directly in the DoD's management of GPS.

The Civil Side. International civil users are represented by several organizations that have a vested interest in global positioning, navigation, and/or timing. A focal issue for these organizations is the future Global Navigation Satellite System (GNSS), intended to be a worldwide position, velocity, and time determination system.[63] GPS will likely be the primary satellite constellation during early GNSS implementation.

The traditional major users of radionavigation aids—aviators and mariners[64]— are represented internationally on radionavigation matters through the following organizations:

- The International Civil Aviation Organization (ICAO), a specialized agency of the United Nations made up of 160 member countries, represents the world's aviation community. ICAO aims to develop the principles and techniques of international air navigation and to foster planning and developing international air transport. Although it serves as a mechanism for specifying and setting standards for the international use of aviation radionavigation aids, it has no authority for direct regulation. In recent years,

---

[62]The Department of Defense and Department of Transportation, *1994 Federal Radionavigation Plan*, National Technical Information Service: Springfield, VA, DOT-VNTSC-RSPA-95-1 or DOD-4650.5, May 1995.

[63]The GNSS will consist of one or more satellite constellations, end-user receiver equipment, and a system integrity monitoring function.

[64]There is no comparable international organization for land users.

ICAO's Future Air Navigation Systems (FANS) committee has been evaluating medium- and long-term options for a civil GNSS. ICAO's GNSS Panel continues to work on FANS findings, including institutional and legal matters, which should result in a set of recommendations for GNSS. The FAA represents the United States at ICAO.

- The International Maritime Organization (IMO) is the maritime counterpart to ICAO. Also a specialized agency of the UN, IMO now has 136 member states. While the IMO usually refers radionavigation questions to IALA, it recently became involved in GNSS issues and set up an Intersessional Working Group of the Maritime Safety Committee to study the requirements and implementation of GNSS.

- The International Association of Lighthouse Authorities (IALA), set up in 1865 by international agreements, has 78 members and is responsible for standardizing navigation facilities, including radionavigation, in the world's coastal waters. IALA has consultative status with IMO and also has a committee studying GNSS.

Another group involved in setting standards for GNSS is the U.S.-based Radio Technical Commission for Aeronautics, Inc. (RTCA), an association of aeronautical organizations from both government and industry. RTCA operates as a Federal Advisory Committee and develops consensus recommendations on major aviation-related issues, although it has no authority in and of itself. RTCA serves as the advisory arm to the FAA on GNSS and GPS matters. In 1991, the FAA asked RTCA to form a task force to develop a consensus strategy with recommendations regarding early implementation of an operational GNSS capability in the United States. A RTCA report outlining the transition and implementation strategy for accomplishing this task was issued the following year.[65] In addition, RTCA Special Committee 159 has been meeting for several years to develop minimum operational performance standards (MOPS) for GPS equipment, which will guide the FAA in adopting appropriate regulations.

Another forum available to international users for providing input to the U.S. government regarding GPS is the CGSIC's International Information Subcommittee. Because of the importance of international GPS issues to DoT, an international representative is assigned as the vice-chair of the CGSIC. The CGSIC reports civil GPS requirements and any concerns it identifies to the Office of the Assistant Secretary of Transportation Policy.

---

[65]RTCA, Inc., *RTCA Task Force Report on the Global Navigation Satellite System (GNSS) Transition and Implementation Strategy*, Washington, D.C., September 18, 1992.

Although the CGSIC is one avenue for GPS manufacturers to voice their concerns, in recent years the GPS industry in the United States and abroad has been organizing itself, forming associations to address its specific needs. In 1991, a group of U.S. GPS manufacturers established the USGIC initially to streamline export licensing requirements for GPS products in place at the time. Since then, the USGIC has placed emphasis on representing the industry before legislative and regulatory bodies, serving as a technical information resource to policymakers in government, and monitoring political and global issues affecting the GPS industry. USGIC membership consists of both private companies and government agencies.

A Japanese counterpart to the USGIC, the Japan GPS Council (JGPSC), was formed in 1992 primarily to avoid trade disputes between the United States and Japan.[66] Its membership is made up of private companies, associations, nonprofit corporations, and universities. Its purpose is to provide Japanese companies with a forum for exchanging information with each other and with U.S. counterparts. The council provides input to Japanese government agencies, works on standardization issues, and attempts to develop the market by organizing conferences and increasing public awareness of GPS applications.

European manufacturers and public agencies have expressed an interest in creating a counterpart to the U.S. GPS Industry Council and the Japan GPS Council, although currently there is no Europe-wide organization that specifically represents the GPS industry. However, the Norwegian GNSS Industry Foundation (NGIF), formed in 1995, shares aims and objectives similar to those of USGIC and JGPSC and plans to work closely with these two organizations. Efforts are also under way to establish a European GPS user forum.[67] The Tripartite Group, which intends to develop a European Geostationary Navigation Overlay Service (EGNOS) similar to the FAA's Wide-Area Augmentation System (WAAS),[68] is forming an ad hoc group to study the possible structure for this user forum and plans to survey the private sector regarding its user requirements.

---

[66]Kate Pound Dawson, "Japan Forms GPS Council to Avoid Tension with U.S. Firms," *Space News*, November 30–December 6, 1992, p. 6.

[67]Interview with Christopher Ross, Transportation Representative for the European Union, Delegation of the European Commission, June 16, 1995.

[68]The Tripartite Group consists of the European Space Agency, EUROCONTROL, and the Commission of the European Communities.

CHRONOLOGY OF GPS HISTORICAL EVENTS

Date	Event
1920s	Origins of radionavigation
Early WW II	LORAN, the first navigation system to employ time-difference-of-arrival of radio signals, is developed by the MIT Radiation Laboratory. LORAN was also the first true all-weather position-finding system, but is only two-dimensional (latitude and longitude).
1959	TRANSIT, the first operational satellite-based navigation system, is developed by the Johns Hopkins Applied Physics Laboratory (APL) under Dr. Richard Kirschner. Although Transit was originally intended to support the U.S. Navy's submarine fleet, the technologies developed for it proved useful to the Global Positioning System (GPS). The first Transit satellite is launched in 1959.
1960	The first three-dimensional (longitude, latitude, altitude) time-difference-of-arrival navigation system is suggested by Raytheon Corporation in response to an Air Force requirement for a guidance system to be used with a proposed ICBM that would achieve mobility by traveling on a railroad system. The navigation system presented is called MOSAIC (Mobile System for Accurate ICBM Control). The idea is dropped when the Mobile Minuteman program is canceled in 1961.
1963	The Aerospace Corporation launches a study on using a space system as the basis for a navigation system for vehicles moving rapidly in three dimensions; this led directly to the concept of GPS. The concept involves measuring the times of arrival of radio signals transmitted from satellites whose positions are precisely known. This gives the distances to the known satellite positions—which, in turn, establishes the user's position.

1963	The Air Force begins its support of the Aerospace study, designating it System 621B. By 1972, the program has already demonstrated operation of a new type of satellite-ranging signal based on pseudo-random noise (PRN).
1964	Timation, a Navy satellite system, is developed under Roger Easton at the Naval Research Lab (NRL) for advancing the development of high-stability clocks, time-transfer capability, and 2-D navigation. Timation's work on space-qualified time standards provided an important foundation for GPS. The first Timation satellite is launched in May 1967.
1968	DoD establishes a tri-service steering committee called NAVSEG (Navigation Satellite Executive Committee) to coordinate the efforts of the various satellite navigation groups (Navy's Transit and Timation programs, the Army's SECOR or Sequential Correlation of Range system). NAVSEG contracted a number of studies to fine-tune the basic satellite navigation concept. The studies dealt with some of the major issues surrounding the concept, including the choice of carrier frequency (L-Band versus C-Band), the design of the signal structure, and the selection of the satellite orbital configuration (a 24-hour figure 8s constellation versus "Rotating Y" and "Rotating X" constellation).
1969–1972	NAVSEG manages concept debates between the various satellite navigation groups. The Navy APL supported an expanded Transit while the Navy NRL pushed for an expanded Timation and the Air Force pushed for an expanded synchronous constellation "System 621B."
1971	L2 frequency is added to the 621B concept to accommodate corrections for ionospheric changes.
1971–1972	User equipment for the Air Force 621B is tested at White Sands Proving Ground in New Mexico. Ground and balloon-carried transmitters simulating satellites were used, and accuracies of a hundredth of a mile demonstrated.

April 1973

The Deputy Secretary of Defense determines that a joint tri-service program be established to consolidate the various proposed positioning/navigation concepts into a single comprehensive DoD system known as the Defense Navigation Satellite System (DNSS). The Air Force is designated the program manager. The new system is to be developed by a joint program office (JPO), with participation by all military services. Colonel Brad Parkinson is named program director of the JPO and is put in charge of jointly developing the initial concept for a space-based navigation system.

August 1973

The first system presented to the Defense System Acquisition and Review Council (DSARC) is denied approval. The system presented to DSARC was packaged as the Air Force's 621B system and therefore not representative of a joint program. Although there is support for the idea of a new satellite-based navigation system, the JPO is urged to broaden the concept to include the views and requirements of all the services.

December 17, 1973

A new concept is presented to DSARC and approval to proceed with what is now known as the NAVSTAR GPS is granted, marking the start of concept validation (Phase I of the GPS program). The new concept was really a compromise system negotiated by Col. Parkinson that incorporated the best of all available satellite navigation system concepts and technology. The approved system configuration consists of 24 satellites placed in 12-hour inclined orbits.

June 1974

Rockwell International is chosen as the satellite contractor for GPS.

July 14, 1974

The very first NAVSTAR satellite is launched. Designated as Navigation Technology Satellite (NTS) number 1, it is basically a refurbished Timation satellite built by the NRL. The second (and last) of the NTS series was launched in 1977. These satellites were used for concept validation purposes and carried the first atomic clocks ever launched into space.

1977	Testing of user equipment is carried out at Yuma, Arizona.
February 22, 1978	The first Block I satellite is launched. A total of 11 Block I satellites were launched between 1978 and 1985 on the Atlas-Centaur. Built by Rockwell International as developmental prototypes, the Block Is were used for system testing purposes. One satellite was lost as a result of a launch failure.
April 26, 1980	The first GPS satellite to carry Integrated Operational Nuclear Detonation Detection System (IONDS) sensors is launched.
1982	A decision to reduce the GPS satellite constellation from 24 to 18 satellites is approved by DoD following a major program restructure brought on by a 1979 decision by the Office of the Secretary of Defense to cut $500 million (approximately 30 percent) from the budget over the period FY81–FY86.
July 14, 1983	The first GPS satellite to carry the newer Nuclear Detonation Detection System (NDS) is launched.
September 16, 1983	Following the Soviet downing of Korean Air flight 007, President Reagan offers to make GPS available for use by civilian aircraft, free of charge, when the system becomes operational. This marks the beginning of the spread of GPS technology from military to civilian aircraft.
April 1985	The first major user equipment contract is awarded by the JPO. The contract includes research and development as well as production options for 1-, 2-, and 5-channel GPS airborne, shipboard, and manpack (portable) receivers.
1987	DoD formally requests that the Department of Transportation (DoT) assume responsibility for establishing and providing an office that will respond to civil user needs for GPS information, data, and assistance. In February 1989, the Coast Guard assumes responsibility as the lead agency for the Civil GPS Service.

1984	Surveying becomes the first commercial GPS market to take off. To compensate for the limited number of satellites available to them early in the constellation's development, surveyors turned to a number of GPS accuracy enhancement techniques including differential GPS and carrier phase tracking.
March 1988	The Secretary of the Air Force announces the expansion of the GPS constellation to 21 satellites plus 3 operational spares.
February 14, 1989	The first of 28 Block II satellites is launched from Cape Canaveral AFS, Florida, on a Delta II booster. The Space Shuttle had been the planned launch vehicle for the Block II satellites built by Rockwell. Following the 1986 Challenger disaster, the JPO reconsidered and has since used the Delta II as the GPS launch vehicle. Selective availability (SA) and anti-spoofing (AS) become possible for the first time with the Block II design.
June 21, 1989	Martin Marietta (after buying out the General Electric Astro Space division in 1992) is awarded a contract to build 20 additional "replenishment" satellites (Block IIR). The first Block IIR satellite will be ready for launch as needed at the end of 1996.
1990	Trimble Navigation, the world leader in commercial sales of GPS receivers, founded in 1978, completes its initial public stock offering.
March 25, 1990	DoD, in accordance with the Federal Radionavigation Plan, activates SA—the purposeful degradation in GPS navigation accuracy—for the first time.
August 1990	SA is deactivated during the Persian Gulf War. Factors that contributed to the decision to turn SA off include the limited three-dimensional coverage provided by the NAVSTAR constellation in orbit at that time and the small number of Precision (P)-code receivers in the DoD inventory at the time. DoD purchased thousands of civilian GPS receivers shortly thereafter to be used by the Allied forces during the war.

| 1990–1991 | GPS is used for the first time under combat conditions during the Persian Gulf War by Allied forces. The use of GPS for Operation Desert Storm proves to be the first successful tactical use of a space-based technology within an operational setting. |

| August 29, 1991 | The U.S. government revises export regulations, making a clear delineation between military and civil GPS receivers. Under the revised regulations, military receivers continue to be treated as "munitions" with strict export restrictions, while civilian receivers are designated "general destination items" available for export without restrictions. |

| July 1, 1991 | SA is reactivated after the Persian Gulf War. |

| September 5, 1991 | The United States offers to make GPS standard positioning service (SPS) available beginning in 1993 to the international community on a continuous, worldwide basis with no direct user charges for a minimum of ten years. The offer was announced at the Tenth Air Navigation Conference of the International Civil Aviation Organization (ICAO). |

| September 1992 | The United States extends the 1991 offer at the 29th ICAO Assembly by offering SPS to the world for the foreseeable future and, subject to the availability of funds, to provide a minimum of six years advance notice of termination of GPS operations or elimination of the SPS. |

| December 8, 1993 | The Secretary of Defense formally declares Initial Operational Capability of GPS, signifying that with 24 satellites in orbit, GPS is no longer a developmental system and is capable of sustaining the 100-meter accuracy and continuous worldwide availability promised SPS users. |

| February 17, 1994 | FAA Administrator David Hinson announces GPS as the first navigation system approved for use as a stand-alone navigation aid for all phases of flight through nonprecision approach. |

June 2, 1994

FAA Administrator David Hinson announces termination of the development of the Microwave Landing Systems (MLS) for Category II and III landings.

November 1994

Orbital Sciences Corp., a leading maker of rockets and satellites, agrees to purchase Magellan Corp., a California-based manufacturer of hand-held GPS receivers, in a stock swap worth as much as $60 million, bringing Orbital closer to its goal of becoming a satellite-based two-way communications company.

June 8, 1994

FAA Administrator David Hinson announces implementation of the Wide-Area Augmentation System (WAAS) for the improvement of GPS integrity and availability for civil users in all phases of flight. Projected cost of program is $400–500 million; it is scheduled to be implemented by 1997.

October 11, 1994

The Department of Transportation Positioning/ Navigation Executive Committee is created to provide a cross-agency forum for making GPS policy.

October 14, 1994

FAA Administrator David Hinson reiterates the United States' offer to make GPS-SPS available for the foreseeable future, on a continuous, worldwide basis and free of direct user fees in a letter to ICAO.

March 16, 1995

President Bill Clinton reaffirms the United States' commitment to provide GPS signals to the international civilian community of users in a letter to ICAO.

GPS COSTS

The various estimates for the cost of GPS that have appeared in GPS-related literature often fail to specify clearly what is included in the cost figure. A recent estimate by DoD puts the total GPS program cost at $14 billion (in 1995 dollars). This figure is based on data from the *Selected Acquisition Report* (SAR), the primary means by which DoD reports the status of major DoD acquisition programs to Congress.[69] This estimate includes costs associated with the development and deployment of all planned GPS satellites through Block IIF and with the development and acquisition of military user equipment, from program inception in FY 1974 through FY 2016. The GPS satellite and user equipment costs are shown in Table B.1. For a detailed breakdown of these costs over time, see Figures B.1 and B.2.

Additional GPS-Related Costs

The DoD definition of GPS system cost does not include the cost of launching the satellites. However, the ability to replace a GPS satellite once it fails in orbit is crucial to sustaining minimum GPS services and therefore warrants including booster and launch costs in the total cost of GPS. In this appendix we attempt to identify these costs, but industry proprietary concerns resulted in some gaps in the data. Also included here in the definition of system cost are costs

Table B.1

Basic GPS System Costs (1974–2016)
(constant 1995 dollars in millions[a])

Cost Category	FY74–95	FY96[b]	FY97[b]	Balance to Complete	Total
Satellite	$3,897	$179	$225	$4,264	$8,565[c]
User Equipment	$3,277	$315	$378	$1,554	$5,524[d]
Total	$7,714	$494	$603	$5,818	$14,089

SOURCE: December 1994 *Selected Acquisition Report* (SAR).

[a]The SAR reports these figures in then-year dollars. They are adjusted to 1995 dollars here using DoD deflators.

[b]Estimated.

[c]For 118 satellites.

[d]For 161,298 user equipment sets.

---

[69]*Selected Acquisition Report* (RCS:DD-COMP(Q&A)823) for the NAVSTAR GPS Program, as of December 31, 1994.

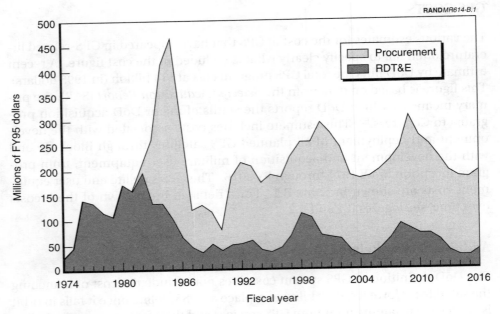

SOURCE: December 1994 *Selected Acquisition Report* (SAR).

Figure B.1—GPS Satellite Costs over Time

associated with nuclear detonation detection system sensors (often referred to as NDS or NUDET), which are carried on board GPS satellites as a secondary payload. Both costs were not included in the data presented in Table B.1. By including launcher and NDS costs, the total cost of the GPS program rises to almost $22 billion through 2016. As shown in Table B.2, more than $8 billion of this total has already been spent.

Launch Costs

Data on the cost of launching GPS satellites are not maintained separately. Nevertheless, the GPS Joint Program Office (JPO) provided approximated cost figures for launching GPS satellites, which are included in Table B.2 and are broken down by the type of launch vehicle that have been used for GPS.[70] The first GPS satellites (Block Is) were launched on Atlas boosters between 1977 and

---

[70]Cost figures for the Delta II launches are approximations provided by the JPO. Precise data on Delta II costs are not available at this time. A court injunction against the Air Force by the contractor (McDonnell-Douglas) prohibits public disclosure of this information.

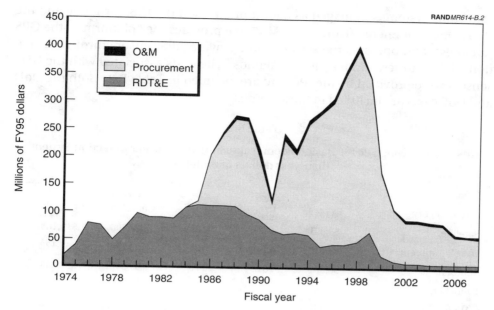

SOURCE: December 1994 *Selected Acquisition Report* (SAR).

Figure B.2—GPS User Equipment Costs over Time

1985.[71] Since 1989, the Delta II booster has been the launch vehicle for GPS satellites and is planned for use through the completion of the Block IIR satellites. The follow-on set of GPS satellites, the Block IIFs, will be launched on a new space vehicle known as the Evolved Expendable Launch Vehicle (EELV), which the Air Force hopes to develop by 2000. At the time of publication of this report, estimates for the cost of launching the Block IIF satellites on the EELV were not available.[72]

The Nuclear Detection System (NDS or NUDET)

Since 1980, GPS satellites have carried a secondary payload consisting of nuclear detonation sensors that provide worldwide, near-real-time, three-dimensional location of nuclear detonations. The GPS Nuclear Detonation

---

[71]Our cost data for the Atlas launches are based on figures published in the National Academy of Public Administration and the National Research Council, *The Global Positioning System: Charting the Future—Full Report*, National Academy of Public Administration, Washington, D.C., May 1995. However, the original source of these data was the GPS Joint Program Office.

[72]The budget for development of the EELV is $2 billion. For further information, see "U.S. Eyes Launchers With No Mil Specs," *Aviation Week & Space Technology*, p. 30.

Detection System is managed as a joint program of the U.S. Air Force and the Department of Energy (DoE). The Air Force provides the "platform"—the GPS satellites—and operates the system; DoE provides the sensors through its national laboratories, Sandia and Los Alamos. The costs associated with the NDS sensors were provided by the JPO and are included in Table B.2. Both the DoD and DoE costs are included in these figures.

Table B.2

**GPS Costs Through 2016: Basic System, Launcher, and Nuclear Detection System[a]
(then-year dollars in millions)**

Cost Category	FY74–95	FY96[b]	FY97[b]	Balance to Complete	Total
Satellite	$3,351	$221	$285	$7,306	$11,163
User Equipment	$3,010	$391	$485	$2,236	$6,122
Subtotal	$6,361	$612	$770	$9,542	$17,285
Launcher:					
Atlas	$238				$238
Delta[c]	$1,289	$177	$177	$1,882	$3,465
EELV	NA	NA	NA	TBD	TBD
Subtotal	$1,527	$177	$177	$1,882	$3,703
NDS[d]	$429	$82	$63	$199	$773
Total	$8,317	$871	$1,010	$11,623	$21,761

SOURCE: December 1994 *Selected Acquisition Report*, supplemented with additional data from the Joint Program Office (JPO).

[a]Figures not adjusted to 1995 dollars due to data constraints.

[b]Estimated.

[c]Data include costs for research, development, testing, and evaluation (RDT&E) as well as procurement.

[d]Data from 1989 through 2001 only.

GPS POLICY REFERENCES

1. Statement by the White House Principal Deputy Press Secretary, September 16, 1983.

2. Remarks by FAA Administrator James Busey to ICAO Air Navigation Conference, September 5, 1991.

3. Memorandum of Agreement between the Department of Defense (DoD) and the Federal Aviation Administration (FAA), Use of the Global Positioning System in the National Airspace System (NAS), May 15, 1992.

4. Letter from FAA Administrator David Hinson to Dr. Assad Kotaite, President of the Council, ICAO, October 14, 1994.

5. Letter from President Clinton to ICAO, March 16, 1995.

THE WHITE HOUSE

Office of the Press Secretary

For Immediate Release   September 16, 1983

STATEMENT BY THE PRINCIPAL DEPUTY PRESS SECRETARY
TO THE PRESIDENT

In their recent statements on the Korean Airlines tragedy, senior
Soviet officials have shocked the world by their assertion of the
right to shoot down innocent civilian airliners which accidently
intrude into Soviet airspace. Despite the murder of 269 innocent
victims, the Soviet Union is not prepared to recognize its
obligations under international law to refrain from the use of
force against civilian airliners. World opinion is united in its
determination that this awful tragedy must not be repeated. As a
contribution to the achievement of this objective, the President
has determined that the United States is prepared to make
available to civilian aircraft the facilities of its Global
Positioning System when it becomes operational in 1988. This
system will provide civilian airliners three-dimensional
positional information.

The United States delegation to the ICAO Council meeting in
Montreal, under the leadership of FAA Administrator J. Lynn
Helms, is urgently examining all measures which the international
community can adopt to enhance the security of international
civil aviation. The United States is prepared to do all it can
for this noble aim. We hope that the Soviet Union will at last
recognize its responsibilities, and join the rest of the world in
this effort.

# # #

REMARKS BY ADMIRAL JAMES B. BUSEY
ADMINISTRATOR
UNITED STATES FEDERAL AVIATION ADMINISTRATION
ICAO AIR NAVIGATION CONFERENCE
MONTREAL, CANADA
SEPTEMBER 5, 1991

Good Afternoon, Mr. President, Mr. Secretary-General, Members of the Secretariat, Fellow Delegates, Observers and Distinguished Guests:

It is a privilege to represent the United States at ICAO's tenth Air Navigation Conference.

As you know, it's been 15 years since our last air navigation conference. There have been many changes during those years, two of which demand our attention today.

First, aviation technology has become more complex, sophisticated -- and useful. And secondly, there has been an enormous increase in air traffic throughout the world.

The continuing increase in air traffic is straining system capacity to the limits in many places. Congestion and delays are increasing, efficiency is declining, and costs are going up. Most importantly, the current high level of aviation safety is threatened.

We must act to meet these challenges.

We must recognize, today, the urgent need to move forward, together, to build a system that will give us greater capacity, increased efficiency, and higher safety.

I think we all realize that the system of the future must be global.

Fortunately, now, for the first time in history, we have the technology to create a global air transport system.

- 2 -

But we will need a truly _international_ effort to build that system. And _that_ is what this conference is all about. Here we have the opportunity to agree on the cooperative steps we must take to solve our common problems and reach our common goals in aviation.

In developing the concept for the future system, the Future Aviation Navigation Systems (FANS) committee started with a clean sheet. It considered the shortcomings of the present system and every practical way to improve it.

Ultimately, the committee concluded that satellite technology offers the best way to achieve worldwide improvements in communications, navigation, and surveillance.

We are living in the age of satellites, and we are already reaping enormous benefits -- in science, in weather forecasting, in agriculture, and in many other areas.

Now it is time to apply this new technology to civil aviation -- so that nations and peoples in every part of the world can realize the _full_ benefits of modern air transportation.

There can be no question that a global satellite system will usher in a new aviation age -- in communications, in surveillance (tracking), and in navigation.

For communications and surveillance, satellites will provide links to aircraft anywhere in the airspace. For navigation, satellites will give us _one basic system_ that can safely handle all facets of flight -- en route, terminal area, and on the ground -- anywhere in the world.

The global navigation satellite system will give us more accurate navigation in high density regions as well as over the oceanic routes that are not covered by radar. And this will give us the ability to make substantial increases in traffic capacity.

And, with some associated ground equipment, satellites can provide near Category I (precision) approach and landing capability. This could make every runway in the world an instrument runway and open the way for increased air service in many regions.

The U.S., of course, strongly agrees with the FANS committee, and we intend to do everything we can to help fulfill its vision.

That is why I am announcing today that the United States government is offering its global satellite navigation system to civil aviation around the world for a minimum of ten years, starting in 1993.

- 3 -

We believe that the U.S. GPS system can help provide a basis for the transition to the new world air system we need so much.

Coverage will be worldwide. And there will be no charge of any kind affixed by the U. S. Government to the users of this service during the initial ten-year period.

In addition, the world's developing nations will no longer be faced with the need to make substantial investments in the ground-based navigation equipment that is required by today's technology. That will be a terrific boon for these nations. They could save millions of dollars.

Surely, the whole world will reap enormous benefits from satellite technology. When fully in place, the future system envisioned by the FANS Committee will mean not only increased capacity, but higher safety and efficiency everywhere in the world.

Satellites occupy a central place in the U.S. view of the future. We're investing more than $10 billion dollars in our Global Positioning System, and we plan to have it fully operational in 1993.

GPS will be a constellation of 21 satellites, plus three spares, 20,200 kilometers high, orbiting the earth every 12 hours. They will be spaced so that four will always be in view, 24 hours a day, everywhere in the world.

And it can be used in conjunction with other navigation systems, including the INS, Loran-C, MLS, and the Soviet Union's GLONASS satellite system.

In making GPS services available to civil aviation around the world, we will offer what we call a standard positioning service with an accuracy of 100 meters.

Now I want you to know that we recognize the obvious sensitivity involved in beginning the global navigation satellite system with the U.S. GPS.

We realize that there will be some concern about becoming dependent on the U.S. system. Some people may worry that we might suddenly withdraw or start charging high fees or take some other undesirable action.

Well, let me speak frankly. That is clearly not what we're planning. If we had anything like that in mind, I wouldn't be here today making this announcement.

- 4 -

Moreover, you may be interested in taking a look at one of the technical demonstrations we have brought to the conference. It shows how you can use off-the-shelf equipment to monitor the accuracy of the GPS signals, thus providing an independent assurance that the signals are usable.

And, of course, our satellites aren't up there alone. The Soviet Union is putting its navigation satellites into orbit too. And there may be other nations planning to do the same thing. We would welcome that.

In fact, we're working closely with the Soviet Union to develop civil avionics specifications and minimum operational standards -- and to develop an integrated receiver that can use signals from both systems. In addition, we're running cooperative satellite navigation flight tests, using both systems, over the North Pacific airspace right now.

If you're interested in how these two systems can work together, you'll want to take a look at our conference exhibit that demonstrates that technology.

The purpose of this conference is to endorse the FANS concept for worldwide implementation. The global community needs that endorsement so we need to begin the process.

We now have the opportunity, at this Conference, to choose a practical starting point for creating a global navigation satellite system. And we are offering our GPS system in the hope that it can serve as a practical starting point. It should be clear to everyone that other systems will certainly replace GPS in the future.

We view our offer of GPS as just the first step -- a first step that will provide the opportunity for all of us to work together to decide how we can cooperatively create the global navigation satellite system that will be so important to the future of aviation. Let me stress this point. The satellite systems that are being offered are essentially available platforms which the international community can use as starting points. But it is the international community which must decide in the coming years how to construct and operate a global system based on satellite technology. I pledge the full cooperation of the United States Government to that effort.

As I see it, we must now get started on the transition to the advanced, global system envisioned by the FANS committee. GPS will help us do that. It will give us the means to gather the operational data we need to test and refine the new technology.

While we're doing that, we must also prepare the agreements and mechanisms that will be needed to continue a satellite system after this initial commitment.

- 5 -

At some point down the road, the international community will have to deal with the question of replacement costs. We must recognize that the day when each nation could develop aviation systems and technology on its own is gone forever.

Now we have no choice but to create the institutional arrangements and economic structures that will be essential for maintaining the new global air control system on a continuing basis.

We have no illusions about the difficulty of coming up with a global approach to this question. It will require an unprecedented level of international cooperation, at all levels, in our governments and in the aviation world itself.

Our goal is to help build an _international_ system that will work well for _everyone_.

While we are addressing the institutional issues, we hope the world will join us in using the GPS system -- along with other systems other nations may offer -- for experimentation and development during this 10-year commitment.

I want to emphasize, however, that we fully support the eventual replacement of our system by other systems -- and we are certain that will happen.

Let's take this time to come up with a global system that makes sense -- and that works well.

There's a great deal of research and development that still must be done. We need to gain experience in using satellites for navigation. And we need the time to profit from that experience.

So this will be a testing period that will show us how well the U.S. and other systems work and that will give us the time to make them work even better.

And that is our main task in this decade.

The aviation world is challenged today as never before in history. The time has come to build a truly international air transport system. And we must do it in this decade.

The blueprint for the future aviation system has been developed by the world. The technology and expertise are available.

Now the entire international community must demonstrate the desire and the determination to get the job done. We need to make a common commitment to work together, in a spirit of creative cooperation, to achieve our common goals.

Nothing less will do. It's time to get started.

Thank you.

Memorandum of Agreement

between the

Department of Defense (DoD)

and the

Federal Aviation Administration (FAA)

USE OF THE GLOBAL POSITIONING SYSTEM
IN THE NATIONAL AIRSPACE SYSTEM (NAS)

1. PURPOSE

The purpose of this Memorandum is to establish an Agreement between the Department of Defense (DoD) and the Federal Aviation Administration (FAA) regarding use of the Global Positioning System (GPS) in the National Airspace System (NAS). GPS was developed as a military system. The viability and utility of GPS for military purposes must be maintained. In order to ensure continued military utility and achieve maximum benefits to the civil aviation community, appropriate working relationships need to be defined and implemented between the DoD, which developed and operates the GPS, and the FAA, the primary interface for civil aviation. This Interagency Agreement provides the basis for the necessary working relationships.

2. SCOPE

This Agreement defines cooperative efforts to provide GPS signals, coverage, and accuracy suitable for a worldwide civil aviation service and to promote and facilitate civil and military aviation uses of GPS within the NAS.

3. AUTHORITY

The FAA is authorized by statute to provide navigation services under sections 306, 307, 312, and 313 of the Federal Aviation Act of 1958, 49 U.S.C. App. 1347, 1348, 1353, and 1354. The Department of Defense is authorized to assist the FAA under the Economy Act, 31 U.S.C. 1553, in making available GPS service for civil aviation applications.

4.   **APPLICABLE DOCUMENTS**

The cooperative efforts outlined in this Agreement shall be conducted in accordance with the documents listed below:

o   DoD/DOT Memorandum of Agreement, *Coordination of Federal Radionavigation Planning*. September 1990

o   DoD/DOT Interagency Agreement, *Use of the Global Positioning System*. in coordination

o   *Federal Radionavigation Plan*. DOT-TSC-RSPA-XX-X, Current Edition

o   Deputy Secretary of Defense Memorandum, *GPS Positioning Services Availability and Accuracies*, May 26, 1983

o   Deputy Secretary of Defense Document, *Comprehensive Global Positioning System (GPS) User Policy (Revised)*, May 22, 1985

o   *DoD GPS Security Classification Guide*, 23 July 1984 with letter changes dated December 24, 1984 and May 26, 1989

o   ICD-GPS-200, *Navstar GPS Space Segment/Navigation User Interfaces*. 30 November 1987

o   DoD/FAA Interagency Agreement, *International Civil Aviation Use of GPS*. 9 May 1990

5.   **BACKGROUND**

GPS has the potential to provide numerous benefits to both DoD and civil users. National policy prescribes that the Standard Positioning Service (SPS) of the GPS be made available worldwide for international civil use. DoD/FAA working agreements regarding international civil aviation use of GPS are specified in an Interagency Agreement concluded on 9 May 1990 (Section 4 above).

6.   JOINT RESPONSIBILITIES

To accomplish the purpose of this Agreement, the DoD and FAA agree to:

a.   Designate points of contact within their respective organizations for GPS related matters.   The designated DoD point of contact for GPS and for oversight of DOD interface with FAA, including all NAS matters, is the Assistant Secretary of Defense for Command, Control, Communications and Intelligence (ASD (C^3I)).   The designated FAA point of contact is the Associate Administrator for System Engineering and Development (ASD-1).   When the DoD declares GPS fully operational the FAA point of contact will be the Associate Administrator for Regulation and Certification (AVR-1).

b.   Publish and continually review minimum system performance requirements for civil and DoD uses of GPS that are unique to aviation, and develop and refine information requirements for GPS notices to airmen (NOTAMs).

c.   Participate jointly in all long-range planning affecting aviation use of GPS. The FAA will consult with the DoD to develop a long-range plan for uses of the SPS applicable to civil aviation.

d.   Assist one another in conducting individual projects or portions of projects relating to aviation use of GPS. Specific activities of this nature will be conducted on a reimbursable basis and will be defined on a case by case basis in individual Annexes to this Agreement. These Annexes will be separately concluded but become part of this Agreement upon signature.

e.   Acknowledge the cooperation of the other agency in any public notice of any activity in which both agencies participate.   Press releases, descriptive literature, educational posters, etc. issued by either agency and affecting or referring to the activities of the other agency will be coordinated with the respective public information offices before release. Coordinate replies to correspondence which concern the operations of the other agency.

7.   DEPARTMENT OF DEFENSE RESPONSIBILITIES

In order to fulfill its responsibilities under this Agreement, the DoD will:

a.   Authorize the DoD GPS point of contact to:

1)   Act for the DoD on all matters related to aviation use of GPS in the NAS,

2)   Provide DoD GPS representation to other departments of the Federal Government, the aviation industry, and international organizations on aviation use of GPS,

3)   Advise the FAA GPS point of contact of the functions and capabilities of GPS organizations and facilities providing services to aviation,

4)   Act as liaison between FAA and DoD concerning GPS matters to ensure that the system remains responsive to civil aviation needs.

b.   Fund, establish, operate, and maintain a constellation of GPS satellites and associated ground control network to provide worldwide navigation signals suitable for military use with Precise Positioning Service (PPS) performance and for civil aviation use with SPS performance in accordance with the documents listed in Section 4.0 and the SPS Minimum System Requirements (Attachment 1). As described in the Federal Radionavigation Plan, radionavigation systems (including GPS) operated by the U.S. Government will be available unless otherwise directed by the National Command Authority (NCA) because of a real or potential threat of war or impairment to national security. Radionavigation systems (including GPS) will be operated as long as the United States and its allies accrue greater military benefit than do adversaries. Operating agencies may cease operations or change characteristics and signal formats of radionavigation systems (including GPS) during a dire national emergency.

c.   Coordinate with the FAA to achieve a capability to operate, on a worldwide basis, using GPS as the only external radionavigation system in aircraft avionics suites which provide the required level of navigation performance capability for all phases of flight except precision approach to landing.

d.   After GPS has been approved for civil use, coordinate and obtain agreement with FAA prior to making changes in GPS system technical parameters that may affect aviation safety. This provision does not limit in any way the authority of the DoD to act as described in Paragraph 7. b.

8.   **FEDERAL AVIATION ADMINISTRATION RESPONSIBILITIES**

In order to fulfill its responsibilities under this Agreement, the FAA will:

a.   Authorize the designated point of contact to:

1)   Act for the Administrator on all matters related to civil aviation use of GPS,

2)   Represent the Administrator on interdepartmental boards, panels, and committees related to the use of GPS by the civil aviation community,

3)   Act as the senior advisor to the Administrator on civil aviation uses of GPS,

4)   Provide appropriate FAA representation to other Federal Government agencies, the aviation industry, and international bodies on civil aviation uses of GPS,

5)   Serve in a collateral duty as staff advisor to the DoD point of contact on civil aviation use of GPS.

b.   Provide short-term and long-term plans for civil aviation use of GPS-SPS. Coordinate the development of minimum operational performance standards (MOPS) and the requisite GPS-SPS documents necessary to operationally achieve the civil use of GPS-SPS.

c.   Define and develop future civil requirements for use of GPS that may result from new air traffic control systems or aircraft. The FAA will be responsible for providing any resources necessary to modify or enhance the capabilities of GPS in order to meet such civil requirements.

d.   Provide a means of integrity notification for GPS-SPS users in the NAS.

e.   Authorize and control the civil aviation use of GPS-SPS in the NAS.

9.   DELEGATION AUTHORITY

The Director, Theater and Tactical C^3, is delegated to sign Annexes to this Agreement on behalf of the DoD. Authority to sign Annexes on behalf of the FAA is delegated to the Associate Administrators for Regulation and Certification and System Engineering and Development or their designated representatives.

10.   AMENDMENT AND TERMINATION

This Agreement will be reviewed annually by DoD and FAA to determine the need for amendment, modification, or termination. This Agreement may be amended by mutual agreement of DoD and FAA or may be terminated by either party. A minimum of one year advance notice of proposed termination will be provided.

This Agreement will terminate on 31 December 2005 unless extended by mutual agreement of the signatories.

11.   EFFECTIVE DATE

This Agreement is effective when signed by the DoD and FAA.

Assistant Secretary of Defense
Honorable Duane P. Andrews
March 13, 1992

Date

Administrator

MAY 1 5 1992

Date

ATTACHMENT 1

SPS MINIMUM SYSTEM REQUIREMENTS

1. Each GPS satellite will transmit navigation data and time signals on 1575.42 MHz in accordance with ICD GPS-200, 30 November 1987.

2. The SPS fix dimension will include 3 dimensional position, velocity, and time.

3. Daily predictable horizontal accuracy for any position will be 100m or better 95% of the time and 300m or better 99.99% of the time.

4. Daily, predictable vertical accuracy for any position will be 156m or better 95% of the time and 500m or better 99.99% of the time.

5. Time will be accurate within 300ns of Universal Coordinated Time (UTC) 95% of the time and 900ns or better 99.99% of the time.

6. There will be no ambiguity in position information.

7. User capacity will be unlimited.

ATTACHMENT

(e) MINIMUM SYSTEM REQUIREMENTS

U.S. Department
of Transportation
**Federal Aviation
Administration**

Office of the Administrator

800 Independence Ave., S.W.
Washington, D.C 20591

OCT 1 4 1994

Dr. Assad Kotaite
President of the Council
International Civil Aviation Organization
1000 Sherbrooke Street West
Montreal, Quebec, Canada H3A 2R2

Dear Dr. Kotaite:

This letter supersedes my letter of April 14, 1994.

I would like to commend, on behalf of the United States, the Committees on Future Air Navigation Systems (FANS) of the International Civil Aviation Organization (ICA0) for pioneering progress in the development of global satellite navigation for civil aviation. I note in this regard that the ICAO Council, on December 11, 1991, requested the Secretary General of ICAO to initiate an agreement between ICAO and Global Navigation Satellite System (GNSS) provider states concerning the duration and quality of the future GNSS.

I would like to take this opportunity to reiterate my Government's offer of the Standard Positioning Service (SPS) of the United States Global Positioning System (GPS) for use by the international community. As the United States made clear at the ICAO Tenth Air Navigation Conference and the 29th ICAO Assembly, the United States intends, subject to the availability of funds as required by United States law, to make GPS-SPS available for the foreseeable future, on a continuous, worldwide basis and free of direct user fees. This offer satisfies ICAO requirements for minimum duration of service (10 years) and freedom from direct charges. This service, which will be available as provided in the United States Government's technical sections of the Federal Radio Navigation Plan on a nondiscriminatory basis to all users of civil aviation, will provide horizontal accuracies of 100 meters (95 percent probability) and 300 meters (99.99 percent probability). The United States shall take all necessary measures to maintain the integrity and reliability of the service and expects that it will be able to provide at least 6 years notice prior to termination of GPS operations or elimination of the GPS-SPS.

The GPS/SPS is a candidate component of the future GNSS as envisioned by FANS. The United States believes that making the GPS available to the international community will enable states to develop a more complete understanding of this valuable technology as a component of the GNSS. The availability of GPS-SPS, of course, is not intended in any way to limit the rights of any state to control the operations of aircraft and enforce safety regulations within its sovereign airspace.

In the coming years, the international community must decide how to implement an international civil global navigation system based on satellite technology. The United States pledges its full cooperation in that endeavor and in working with ICAO to establish appropriate standards and recommended practices (SARP) in accordance with Article 37 of the Convention on International Civil Aviation (Chicago Convention). Consistent with this goal, the United States expects that SARP's developed by ICAO will be compatible with GPS operations and vice versa and that states will be free to augment GPS-SPS in accordance with appropriate SARP's. The United States will also undertake a continuing exchange of information with ICAO regarding the operation of the GPS to assist the ICAO Council in carrying out its responsibilities under the Chicago Convention.

I would be grateful if you could confirm that International Civil Aviation Organization is satisfied with the foregoing, which I submit in lieu of an agreement In that event this letter and your reply will comprise mutual understandings regarding the Global Positioning System between the Government of the United States of America and the International Civil Aviation Organization.

Sincerely,

David R. Hinson
Administrator

THE WHITE HOUSE

WASHINGTON

March 16, 1995

Greetings to all those gathered in the
beautiful city of Montreal for this important
meeting of the International Civil Aviation
Organization (ICAO).

As we approach the twenty-first century,
civil aviation is becoming increasingly dependent
on technological innovation. Satellite-based
positioning and navigation technologies will play
pivotal roles in the global aviation system of the
future. This technology, available today through
the U.S. Global Positioning System (GPS), can
serve to improve safety and reduce costs for
operators of all types of aircraft.

GPS, which was originally developed for
military use, has rapidly gained wide acceptance
in commercial applications. The United States
looks forward to the growing use of GPS and to its
incorporation in an integrated global navigation
satellite system.

The United States remains committed to
provide GPS signals to the international civil
aviation community and to other peaceful users
of radio navigation and positioning systems.

Best wishes for a successful and productive
meeting.

Bill Clinton

INTERNATIONAL LEGAL REFERENCES FOR GPS

INTERNATIONAL AGREEMENTS RELATED TO NAVIGATION AND GPS

The United States currently[1] has already made at least fifteen international agreements (other than treaties) that refer to global positioning, GPS, or NAVSTAR. None of these agreements seem to involve DGPS. The agreements cover diverse topics and fall into five categories:

1. *Basic exchange and cooperative agreements with Defense Mapping Agency* involving topographic mapping; nautical and aeronautical charting and information; geodesy and geophysics; digital data; and related mapping, charting, and geodesy materials in cooperation with the U.S. DoD's Defense Mapping Agency.

   Nicaragua (entered into force December 1, 1994. State Dept. No. 95–13)

   Albania (entered into force March 25, 1994. State Dept. No. 94–120, KAV No. 3834)

   Lithuania (entered into force February 15, 1994. State Dept. No. 94–78, KAV No. 3792)

   Estonia (entered into force December 7, 1993. State Dept. No. 94–13, KAV No. 3729)

   Latvia (Entered into force August 24, 1993. State Dept. No. 93–172, KAV No. 3662)

   Hellenic Republic (entered into force May 25, 1993. State Dept. No. 93–114, KAV No. 3573)

   Spain (entered into force June 29, 1992. State Dept. No. 92–176, KAV No. 3354)

---

[1] As of March 1, 1995.

Czech and Slovak Federal Republic (entered into force December 10, 1991. State Dept. No. 92-14, KAV No. 3122)

Norway (entered into force November 22, 1985. T.I.A.S. No. 11216)

2. *Basic exchange and cooperative agreements with DoD* involving military topographic mapping, nautical and aeronautical charting, geodesy and geophysics, digital data, and related MC&G materials in cooperation with the U.S. Department of Defense.

Hungary (entered into force December 9, 1991. State Dept. No. 92-13, KAV No. 3121)

Poland (entered into force November 10, 1991. State Dept. No. 92-254, KAV No. 3430)

3. *Agreement regarding installation, operation and maintenance of Global Sea Level Data Collection (GSL) Stations.*

New Zealand (entered into force November 18, 1992. State Dept. No. 93-2, T.I.A.S. No. 11973, KAV No. 3450)

4. *Memorandum of understanding* covering a cooperative program for harmonization, development, production, and support of a maritime patrol aircraft and the MPA-90 Program.

Federal Republic of Germany (entered into force April 5, 1989. State Dept. No. 89-129, KAV No. 689)

5. *Memoranda of agreement* specifically concerning the NAVSTAR Global Positioning System.

New Zealand (entered into force September 2, 1994. State Dept. No. 94-223, KAV No. 4015)

Australia (entered into force February 7, 1991. State Dept. No. 91-77, KAV No. 2856)

EUROPEAN POLICY ACTIVITIES RELATED TO SATELLITE NAVIGATION

In addition to public safety, the European Commission (EC) seeks ways to make its airline manufacturing and services industries competitive. Thus most EC documents related to satellite navigation are couched in terms of their potential benefits to the domestic aircraft manufacturers and service industries (see selected quotes below).

Recent EC Documents

Commission of the European Communities

Publication Date: December 31, 1994, 1994 OJ L 361

Document Date: December 15, 1994, 94/914/EC

Council Decision of 15 December 1994 adopting a specific program for research and technological development, including demonstration in the field of transport (1994 to 1998).

Selected quotes:

> Whereas, by Decision No 1110/94/EC (4), the European Parliament and the Council adopted a fourth framework program for Community activities in the field of research, technological development and demonstration (RTD) for the period 1994 to 1998 specifying inter alia the activities to be carried out in the area of transport; whereas this Decision takes account of the grounds set out in the preamble to that Decision; . . .

> A specific program for research and technological development, including demonstration, in the field of transport, as set out in Annex I, is hereby adopted for the period from the date of adoption of this Decision to 31 December 1998....

> Article 2
> 1. The amount deemed necessary for carrying out the program is ECU 240 million, including a maximum of 8,3% for the Commission's staff and administrative expenditure.
>
> 2. An indicative breakdown of this amount is given in Annex II.

Commission of the European Communities

Publication Date: November 5, 1994, 1994 OJ C 309

Document Date: October 24, 1994

Council Resolution of 24 October 1994 on the situation in European civil aviation

Commission of the European Communities,

Publication Date: July 29, 1993, 1993 OJ L 187

Document Date: July 19, 1993, 93/65/EEC

Council Directive 93/65/EEC of 19 July 1993 on the definition and use of compatible technical specifications for the procurement of air-traffic-management equipment and systems.

Older EC Documents on Air Traffic Control

Commission of the European Communities

Publication Date: November 12, 1984, 1984 OJ C 300

Document Date: October 11, 1984

Resolution on Eurocontrol

Commission of the European Communities

Publication Date: May 14, 1984, 1984 OJ C 127

Document Date: April 13, 1984

Resolution on the safety of air transport in Europe

Commission of the European Communities

Publication Date: May 16, 1983, 1983 OJ C 128

Document Date: April 14, 1983

Resolution on the Eurocontrol air traffic control center in Maastricht

Commission of the European Communities

Publication Date: July 19, 1982, 1982 OJ C 182

Document Date: June 16, 1982

Resolution on improvement of the European system of air traffic control

Commission of the European Communities

Publication Date: December 15, 1980, 1980 OJ C 327

Document Date: November 19, 1980

Resolution on the future of Eurocontrol

Commission of the European Communities

Publication Date: August 4, 1980, 1980 OJ C 197

Document Date: July 10, 1980

Resolution on the development of a coordinated European air traffic control system

INTERNATIONAL AIR NAVIGATION AGREEMENTS

The United States may want to make individual agreements with its major trading partners and allies that address GPS-related issues such as system availability, reliability, emergency procedures, liability, and mutual benefits. In reaching agreements regarding air navigation, the Secretary of Transportation and the Administrator of the FAA "shall act consistently with obligations of the United States Government under an international agreement" and "shall consider applicable laws and requirements of a foreign country."[2] We suggest here an approach to the aircraft/airways/airport navigation problem, rather than the merchant marine/sea lanes/harbor navigation problem, and introduce some of the pertinent domestic law of the United Kingdom as an example for preparing to negotiate with a specific country.

International Civil Aviation Organization (ICAO)

Members of the ICAO are free to bargain with other members for the provision of aids to navigation (i.e., the Chicago Convention 1944 is neutral on the question). Provision of air navigation facilities and services is the duty of the Contracting States within the limited range set forth in Article 28(a) of the Chicago Convention. Each signatory undertakes, so far "as it may find practicable," to provide in its territory radio services, meteorological services, and other air navigation facilities for international air navigation.[3] In 1987 a commentator on the work of the Future Air Navigation Systems (FANS) com-

---

[2] 49 U.S.C. § 40105(b)(1)(A)–(B). For the steps in making an executive agreement, see Congressional Research Service, *Treaties and Other International Agreements: The Role of the United States Senate*, S.Prt. 103-53, 1993, at xxi.

[3] Michael Milde, "Legal Aspects of Future Air Navigation Systems," 12 *Annals of Air and Space Law* 1987, 87–98, at 92.

mittee of the ICAO asserted that "nothing legally prevents several States from entering into arrangements or agreements under which one of the States or an entity created by the States or designated by them would provide certain aeronautical facilities and services to the collectivity of States concerned."[4]

Some national governments have crafted agreements regarding navigation aids that are not entirely under their sovereign control but rely to some extent on the cooperation of other countries. Examples of cooperative provision of navigation aids include: Denmark/Iceland joint financing agreements (DEN/ICE); Africa/Madagascar Agency for Air Navigation Safety (ASECNA); Central American Air Navigation Services Corporation (COCESNA); and Societe internationale de telecommunications aeronautiques (SITA).[5]

United States

Several kinds of U.S. agreements and treaties with major trading partner nations relating to commerce and navigation[6] may serve as models for understanding GPS and DGPS. Their titles suggest that civil aviation has been an arena of cooperation and exchange for many years.

Individual agreements related to navigation, often one of the first formal agreements entered into by the United States and other nations, have been largely supplanted by larger multilateral agreements in trade and commerce since WW II. This trend lessens duplication of effort and promotes uniform global practices. Global multilateral agreements have not been the rule in national security, however, where attention has focused on bilateral relations (e.g., U.S.-Soviet arms control) and regional security (e.g., NATO).

Some U.S. agreements are listed below:

Canada

Treaty of amity, commerce, and navigation (Jay Treaty) (1795). 8 Stat. 16.

Agreement concerning air traffic control (1963). 14 UST 1737, TIAS 5480.

Several agreements re Loran and Omega stations.

---

[4]Id. at 95.

[5]Id. at 96. Other organizations are ARINC, COSPAS/SARSAT, INMARSAT, and EUROCONTROL.

[6]U.S. Department of State, *Treaties in Force*, January 1, 1994.

United Kingdom

Treaty of amity, commerce, and navigation (Jay Treaty) (1795).

Memorandum of agreement concerning the provision of equipment and services for the development of civil aeronautics (1982). TIAS 10874.

France

Convention of navigation and commerce (1822). 8 Stat. 278, TS 87.

Agreement concerning air services facilities (1946). TIAS 1852.

Agreement concerning research and development of civil aviation (1980). 32 UST 2873, TIAS 9881, 1274 UNTS 201.

Memorandum of understanding concerning operation and maintenance of Omega station La Reunion (1981). 33 UST 2109, TIAS 10176.

Germany

Treaty of friendship, commerce, and navigation with protocol and exchanges of notes (1956). 7 UST 1839, TIAS 3593, 273 UNTS 3.

Memorandum of understanding relating to cooperation in the development of national air-space systems, with annex (1984). TIAS 11025.

Memorandum of understanding concerning air navigation services in Berlin, with related exchange of letters (1990). TIAS 11746.

Italy

Treaty of friendship, commerce, and navigation (1949). 63 Stat. 2255, TIAS 1965.

Six aviation agreements.

Memorandum of understanding concerning the installation and management of U.S. navigation aids (1985). TIAS 11191.

Japan

Treaty of friendship, commerce, and navigation (1953). 4 UST 2063, TIAS 2863, 206 UNTS 143.

Agreement relating to the establishment, operation, and maintenance of an Omega navigation aid station in Japan (1972).   23 UST 1480, TIAS 7428, 898 UNTS 55.

Implementing arrangement on cooperation in the field of national air traffic control service system, with annex (1985). TIAS 11141.

The Secretaries of State, Transportation, and Commerce, and the Administrator of the FAA have statutory authority to conduct "negotiations for an agreement with a government of a foreign country to establish or develop air navigation, including air routes and services."[7]

The Secretary of Transportation, subject to the concurrence of the Secretary of State and the consideration of objectives of the International Civil Aviation Organization, has the statutory authority to acquire, establish, and construct airport property and airway property (except meteorological facilities) in foreign territory.[8] A DGPS facility might qualify as "airport property."[9] And, although international agreements usually do not entail an exchange of funds, the Secretary of Transportation may accept payment from a government of a foreign country or international organization for facilities or services sold or provided the government or organization under this chapter.[10] An example of this kind of agreement is the Memorandum between the FAA and the UK Civil Aviation Authority, in which provision is made for the FAA and the CAA to furnish to the other equipment and services which the other has funds available for and has determined should be obtained from that source (see below).[11]

United Kingdom

The legal situation in the United Kingdom may be considered illustrative of the situation for other European states. The Civil Aviation Act of 1982 assigns the CAA the statutory duty to provide air navigation services in the United

---

[7] 49 U.S.C. § 40105(a). The FAA is further authorized to furnish equipment and services to particular countries by the Agency for International Development. Foreign Assistance Act 1961, 82 Stat. 963; 22 U.S.C . § 2357(a).

[8] 49 U.S.C. § 47302 ("Providing airport and airway property in foreign territories") para. (a)(1). (The Secretary of Commerce may acquire, establish, and construct meteorological facilities in foreign territory, para (a)(2).)

[9] 49 § 47301.

[10] Chapter 473—International Airport Facilities. The amount received may be credited to the appropriation current when the expenditures are or were paid, the appropriation current when the amount is received, or both. 49 U.S.C. § 47302(c).

[11] Equipment includes hardware (i.e., computer, radar, communications), software, material, and parts; services include information and personnel. Specific programs are to be described in Annexes to the general Agreement. NAT-I-1223, TIAS 10874; amended and extended Sept 12 and Oct 22, 1984 (TIAS 11405), and Mar 25 and Apr 15, 1986 (TIAS 11405).

Kingdom. This duty is proscribed by the extent to which it appears that such services are necessary and are not being provided by the CAA (either alone or jointly with another person) or by some other person.[12] Radionavigation aids in other European countries are likewise operated by a national agency.[13]

By these terms, GPS is a service that is being provided by some other person (which can be a foreign government), and thus the CAA may choose to allow GPS to be used in the United Kingdom and to not provide a redundant system. The Secretary of State of the United Kingdom may make regulations requiring the payment to any government outside the United Kingdom of charges for air navigation services provided by that government in pursuance of an agreement to which the United Kingdom is a party.[14] The CAA may undertake to provide air navigation services outside the United Kingdom, in pursuance of an international arrangement.[15] Thus it seems possible for the United Kingdom to establish DGPS sites for another country in the other country's territory.

Liability concerns are sometimes cited as reasons to assign navigation services to governments due to their supposed immunity to potential lawsuits. In the case of the United Kingdom, however, absolute domestic sovereign immunity ended with the Crown Proceedings Act of 1947.[16] The government is liable under ordinary rules of tort law, but public authorities may be authorized by legislation to perform acts that would otherwise give rise to liability.[17] Other G-7 countries have similar situations.[18]

If the United Kingdom were to seek an agreement with the United States on the use of GPS for air navigation, the CAA would have the statutory authority to: (1) accept GPS as an aid to air navigation; (2) make regulations requiring payment for GPS as an air navigation service; and (3) provide DGPS facilities outside the United Kingdom, pursuant to an international arrangement.[19]

---

[12]Civil Aviation Act 1982 § 72(1)(a). Reprinted in 4 Halsbury's Stat. at 190 (1991).

[13]Deutsche Aerospace, *Report on Assessment of Satnav Systems*, January 31, 1994, p. 9.

[14]Civil Aviation Act 1982 § 73(1)(b). Reprinted in 4 Halsbury's Stat. at 190 (1991).

[15]Civil Aviation Act 1982 § 72(1)(b). Reprinted in 4 Halsbury's Stat. at 190 (1991).

[16]10 & 11 Geo. 6, ch. 44 (1947); 13 Halsbury's Stat. 9 (4th ed. 1991). The State Immunity Act 1978 is the U.K. statute for foreign sovereign (limited) immunity, and it is similar to the U.S. Foreign Sovereign Immunity Act (FSIA) (28 U.S.C. §§ 1330, 1332(a), 1391(f), 1441(d), 1602–1611 (1988)), according to Joseph W. Dellapenna, "Foreign State Immunity in Europe," 5 *N.Y. Int'l L. Rev.* 51, 1992.

[17] Dellapenna, 1992; John Bell, "The Government Liability Law of England and Wales," in John Bell, and Anthony W. Bradley, *Government Liability: A Comparative Study*, United Kingdom National Committee of Comparative Law, 1991, pp. 17–44.

[18]Götz Eike zur Hausen, "Non-contractual Liability Under European Community Law," in Bell, and Bradley, 1991, pp. 275–290.

[19]Based on the 1991 edition (4th) of Halsbury's Statutes.

Existing agreements between the United Kingdom and the United States could provide additional assurances to the United Kingdom if it should choose to rely on GPS. These agreements include the use of overseas sites and exchanges of personnel that could be useful to GPS operations, such as:

Ascension Island

Agreement providing for the establishment of a lunar and planetary spacecraft tracking facility on Ascension Island (1965). 16 UST 1183, TIAS 5864, 551 UNTS 221.

Agreement relating to the expanded use of Ascension Island (1973). 24 UST 918, TIAS 7602.

Agreement relating to sharing facility construction costs on Ascension Island, with memoranda of agreement (1985). Consolidated Treaties and International Agreement (CTIA) No. 6209.000, London.

Diego Garcia

Agreement concerning a United States naval support facility on Diego Garcia, British Indian Ocean Territory, with plan, related notes, and supplementary arrangement (1976). 27 UST 315, TIAS 8230, 1018 UNTS 372.

U.S. Coast Guard

Memorandum of agreement on the exchange of personnel between the United States Coast Guard and the Royal Navy (1980). 32 UST 2403, TIAS 9849, 1267 UNTS 187.

Memorandum of agreement on the exchange of personnel between the United States Coast Guard and the Royal Air Force (1983). TIAS 10908.

SOVEREIGN LIABILITY RULES IN G-7 COUNTRIES

The subject of domestic sovereign immunity is not discussed or written about as frequently as foreign sovereign immunity is, but a particular state's approaches to foreign state immunity reflect its attitudes toward its own immunity to litigation.[20]   Ironically, the immunity of sovereigns in common-law countries today is determined by a statute that purportedly codifies the whole law on the topic. In civil-law countries (e.g., France and Germany), sovereign immunity largely remains (as it nearly always has been in the civil-law tradition) a judicial construct discoverable only from a study of the jurisprudence of the

---

[20]Dellapenna, 1992.

relevant courts.[21] Immunity and liability in several countries are summarized here.

France

The scope of immunity from noncontractual liability is very restricted. Apparently only in the conduct of foreign affairs does the State have any real immunity from suit in national courts. But when an international agreement has been incorporated into domestic law, it may be possible for a statute to exclude noncontractual liability.[22]

Germany

"The idea that there could be any state activity which may not be challenged in court is alien to German law."[23] Thus, the question of liability is not a barrier to negotiating or not negotiating an international agreement regarding GPS or DGPS.

Italy

The basis of the liability of public authorities is the same as the liability of private individuals. However, the discretionary power of a public authority is given (and limited) by statute or regulation.[24]

Japan

The situation in Japan is similar to that in Germany, where there is no immunity. According to a recent analysis of product liability law in Japan, much of Japan's civil and criminal codes are patterned after German legal codes:

> [T]he Japanese system does not recognize the notion of sovereign immunity and allows an injured party to sue the appropriate government ministry for breaching its duty to protect the public from a defective product. The Japanese government has been sued for negligence in defective design, manufacture, and warning cases for their failure to properly supervise the offending product or

---

[21]Id. note 84 and accompanying text.

[22]Dellapenna, 1992; Marie-Aimée de Latournerie, "The Government Liability Law of France," in Bell and Bradley, 1991, pp. 200–227.

[23]Wolfgang Rüffner, "Basic Elements of German Law on State Liability," in Bell and Bradley, 1991, pp. 249–274.

[24]Marcello Clarich, "The Liability of Public Authorities in Italian Law," in Bell and Bradley, 1991, pp. 228–248.

industry. Japanese law adds the government as another potential defendant who injured plaintiffs may sue for compensation in product defect cases to address cause-in-fact issues.[25]

Obviously, a look at existing international agreements may reveal clues to the risks the government is willing to take.

---

[25]Lucille M. Ponte, "Guilt by Association in United States Products Liability Cases: Are the European Community and Japan Likely to Develop Similar Cause-in-Fact Approaches to Defendant Identification?" 15 *Loyola Int'l & Comp.L.J.* 1993, 629, text at fn 213, 214, 215. Her sources: Kohji Tanabe, "The Process of Litigation: An Experiment with the Adversary System," in A. von Mehren, ed., *Law in Japan: The Legal Order in a Changing Society* 73–74; Younghee Jin Ottley and Bruce L. Ottley, "Product Liability Law in Japan: An Introduction to a Developing Area of Law," 14 *Ga.J.Int'l Comp.L.* 29, 32 (1984); Richard B. Parker, "Law, Language, and the Individual in Japan and the United States," 7 *Wisc.Int'l L.J.* 179, 202 (1988); David Cohen and Karen Martin, "Western Ideology, Japanese Product Safety Regulation and International Trade," 19 *U.B.C.L.Rev.* 315, 324–25 (1985); John O. Haley, "Law and Society in Contemporary Japan: American Perspectives"; "Introduction: Legal v. Social Controls," 17 *Law in Japan* 1, 1–2 (1984); Kijuro Arita, "Products Liability Law of Japan," in L. Frumer & M. Friedman eds., 3A *Products Liability* §§ 59.01–59.04, 1991.

Books and Reports

Aein, Joseph M., *Miniature Guidance Technology Based on the Global Positioning System*, RAND, R-4087-DARPA, 1992.

The Aerospace Corporation, *The Aerospace Corporation, Its Work: 1960–1980*, Los Angeles, CA, 1980.

———, *The Global Positioning System: A Record of Achievement*, Los Angeles, CA, 1994.

Aeronavigatsia State Research and Development Institute, *Assessment of Satellite Navigation System Study*, Department of Air Transport of Russia, Moscow, 1993.

Alsip, D. H., J. M. Butler, and J. T. Radice, *The Coast Guard's Differential GPS Program*, USCG Headquarters, Office of Navigation Safety and Waterway Services, Radionavigation Division, June 29, 1992.

Ananda, M., P. Munjai, R. Sung, and K. T. Woo, *A Simple Data Protection Scheme for Extended WAAS*, unpublished paper, The Aerospace Corporation, Los Angeles, CA, June 1995.

Applied Research Laboratories, *A GPS Information and Data System for the Civil Community: Vol. III, Interface Control Document for the Civil GPS Service Interface for the OPSCAP Reporting and Management System*, ARL-TR-88-11, Austin, TX, March 8, 1988.

ARINC, *User's Overview*, YEE-82-009D, Los Angeles, CA, March 1991.

Arnett, Eric H., "The Most Serious Challenge in the 1990s? Cruise Missiles in the Developing World," in Eric H. Arnett and Thomas W. Wander, eds., *The Proliferation of Advanced Weaponry: Technology, Motivations, and Responses,* American Academy for the Advancement of Science, Washington, D.C., 1992.

Barbour, Neil, John Elwell, and Roy Sutterlund, *Initial Instruments— Where To Now?* Draper Laboratory, CSDL-P-3182, Cambridge, MA, June 1992.

Bartenev, V. A., et al., *Russia's Global Navigation Satellite System,* National Air Intelligence Center, Wright-Patterson AFB, OH, May 1994.

Bell, John, and Anthony W. Bradley, *Government Liability: A Comparative Study,* United Kingdom National Committee of Comparative Law, 1991.

Black, Henry Campbell, *Black's Law Dictionary, Fifth Ed.,* West Publishing, St. Paul, MN, 1979.

Bowie, Christopher, et al., *Trends in the Global Balance of Airpower,* RAND, MR-478/1-AF, 1995.

Carus, W. Seth, *Cruise Missile Proliferation in the 1990s,* The Washington Papers #159, Praeger, Westport, CT, 1992.

Center for International Security and Arms Control, *Assessing Ballistic Missile Proliferation and Its Control,* Center for International Security and Arms Control, Stanford, CA, 1991.

Chairman of the Joint Chiefs of Staff, *CJCS Master Navigation Plan,* CJCSI 6130.01, May 20, 1994.

Clarke, Bill, *Aviator's Guide to GPS,* McGraw-Hill, Inc., NY, 1994.

Commission of the European Communities, *Satellite Navigation R&D Activities Under Way and Envisaged By the European Commission,* Draft, 1995.

————, *Satellite Navigation Services: A European Approach*, Commission of the European Communities, COM(94) 248 final, Brussels, 1994.

Currie, David P., *The Constitution in Congress: Substantive Issues in the First Congress*, 1789–1790, 1994.

Daggett, Stephen, *A Comparison of Clinton Administration and Bush Administration Long-Term Defense Budget Plans for FY1994-99*, Congressional Research Service, CRS Report for Congress, December 20, Washington, D.C., 1994.

DeBolt, Robert O., et al., *A Technical Report to the Secretary of Transportation on a National Approach to Augmented GPS Services*, U.S. Department of Commerce, National Telecommunications and Information Administration and U.S. Department of Transportation, NTIA Special Publication 94-30, December 1994.

Deutsche Aerospace AG, *Assessment of the Potential of Satellite Navigation Systems and the European Dimension of Their Utilisation*, Commission of the European Communities, Ulm, Germany, January 31, 1994.

Donohue, John D., *The Privatization Decision: Public Ends, Private Means*, Basic Books, NY, 1989, pp. 37–56.

Drezner, Jeffrey A., and Giles K. Smith, *An Analysis of Weapon System Acquisition Schedules*, RAND, R-3937-ACQ, December 1990.

Dyment, Michael J., *Differential GPS Markets in the 1990s: A North American Cross Industry Study*, KV Research, Inc., McLean, VA, 1992.

————, *North American GPS Markets: Analysis of SA and Other Policy Alternatives*, Final Report to the National Academy of Sciences, Committee on the Future of the Global Positioning System, May 1, 1995.

Electronic Manufacturing and Packaging in Japan, Japanese Technology Evaluation Center, National Technical Information Service, ISBN 1-883712-37-8, Washington, D.C., 1995.

Electronics Industry Association of Japan, *Report on the Japan GPS Market* (in Japanese), Tokyo, Japan, June 3, 1994.

Enge, Per, *Impact on Avionics of Moving the WAAS Signal to 1565.42 MHz*, unpublished manuscript, February 13, 1995.

Ergas, Henry, and Walter S. Baer, *Future Structural Options for INTELSAT: An Issues Paper*, RAND, DRU-925-CIRA, November 1994.

European Commission Space Advisory Group, *European Space Policy 2000*, Commission of the European Communities, Brussels, Belgium, July 1994.

Federal Communications Commission, *Final Report of the Majority of the Active Participants of Informal Working Group 1 to Above 1GHz*, MSSAC-41.6, April 1993.

Feld, Werner J., Robert S. Jordan, and Leon Hurwitz, *International Organizations: A Comparative Approach*, Praeger Press, Westport, CT, 1994.

Feldman, N. E., L. N. Rowell, and P. A. CoNine, *A Physically Survivable Backup for the NAVSTAR Global Positioning System*, RAND, R-1780-ARPA, December 1975.

Frost, Gerald, *Operational Issues for GPS-Aided Precision Guided Weapons*, RAND, MR-242-AF, 1994.

Frost, Gerald, and Calvin Shipbaugh, *GPS Targeting Methods for Non-Lethal Systems*, RAND, RP-262, February 1, 1994.

Garfinkel, Simon, *PGP: Pretty Good Privacy*, O'Reilly and Associates Inc., Sebastopol, CA, 1995.

General Accounting Office, *Global Positioning Technology: Opportunities for Greater Federal Agency Joint Development and Use*, RCED 94-280, Washington, D.C., September 1994.

Getting, Ivan A., *All in a Lifetime: Science in the Defense of Democracy*, Vantage Press, NY, 1989.

Haley, Ron, *Response to NTIA Special Publication 94-30*, Differential Corrections, Inc., Cupertino, CA, January 1995.

Harper, Lawrence A., *The English Navigation Laws*, Columbia University Press, NY, 1939, p. 276.

Harshberger, Edward R., *Long-Range Conventional Missiles: Issues for Near-Term Development*, RAND Graduate School, N-3328-RGSD, 1991.

Hemesath, N. B., "Performance Enhancements of GPS User Equipment," *Global Positioning System, Vol. I*, Institute of Navigation, Washington, D.C., 1980, pp. 106–107.

Hoshinoo, Kazuaki, *Integrity of GNSS for Civil Air Navigation in Japan*, Ministry of Transport of Japan, Tokyo, 1993.

Hurt, Gerald F., et al., *Preliminary Spectrum Reallocation Report*, Department of Commerce, NTIA Special Publication 94-27, Washington, D.C., February 1994.

Inmarsat General Counsel, *Inmarsat Basic Documents*, 4th ed., Inmarsat, London, 1989.

Isakowitz, Steven J., *International Reference Guide to Space Launch Systems*, American Institute of Aeronautics and Astronautics, Washington, D.C., 1991.

ITT Aerospace/Communications Division, *Future Civil Space Navigation System: Executive Summary*, ITT Defense & Electronics, Fort Wayne, IN, March 29, 1994.

Japan Ministry of Transport, Civil Aviation Bureau, *Multi-functional Transport Satellite (MTSAT) Aeromission*, Tokyo, 1994.

Japan Ministry of Transport, Civil Aviation Bureau and Meteorological Agency, *Description of Multifunctional Transport Satellite*, revision E, Tokyo, August 15, 1994.

Joint Department of Defense/Department of Transportation Task Force, *The Global Positioning System: Management and Operation of a Dual Use System, A Report to the Secretaries of Defense and Transportation*, Washington, D.C., December 1993.

Jones, Anita K., *Defense Technology Plan*, Department of Defense, Washington, D.C., September 1994.

Judycki, Dennis, and Gary Euler, *The Intelligent Vehicle-Highway Systems Program in the United States*, U.S. Department of Transportation, Washington, D.C., April 1993.

Kennedy, Charles H., *An Introduction to U.S. Telecommunications Law*, Artech House, Norwood, MA, 1994, p. xiv.

Koorey, Fred, *Navstar Global Positioning System Policy & Waivers (Updated Version)*, Science Applications International Corporation, A004-334, San Diego, CA, 1994.

Kramer, H. J., *Observation of the Earth and Its Environment: Survey of Missions and Sensors*, 2nd ed., Springer-Verlag, Berlin, 1994.

Lachow, Irving, *The Global Positioning System and Cruise Missile Proliferation: Assessing the Threat*, CSIA Discussion Paper 94-04, Kennedy School of Government, Harvard University, June 1994.

————, "GPS-Guided Cruise Missiles and Weapons of Mass Destruction," in Kathleen C. Bailey, ed., *The Director's Series on Proliferation #8*, Lawrence Livermore National Laboratory, Livermore, CA, June 1, 1995, pp. 1–22.

Logsdon, Tom, *The Navstar Global Positioning System*, Van Nostrand Reinhold, New York, 1992.

Lundberg, Olof, *Civil GNSS: The Inmarsat Vision for the 21st Century*, Royal Institute of Navigation, London, November 8, 1994.

McDonnell Douglas Aerospace, *TSPR GPS Block II-F White Paper*, Los Angeles, CA, May 27, 1994.

McMahon, K. Scott, and Dennis M. Gormley, *Controlling the Spread of Land-Attack Cruise Missiles*, American Institute for Strategic Cooperation, Marina del Rey, CA, January 1995.

Margo, Rod D., *Aviation Insurance*, Butterworths, London, 1989.

Mogee Research & Analysis Associates, *Global Positioning Systems Technology: An International Patent Trend Analysis*, Great Falls, VA, April 6, 1995.

National Academy of Public Administration and the National Research Council, *The Global Positioning System: Charting the*

Future—Full Report, National Academy of Public Administration, Washington, D.C., May 1995.

———, *The Global Positioning System: Charting the Future—Summary Report*, National Academy of Public Administration: Washington, D.C., May 1995.

National Research Council, *Forum on NOAA's National Spatial Reference System*, National Academy Press, Washington, D.C., 1994.

———, *The Global Positioning System: A Shared National Asset*, National Academy Press, Washington, D.C., May 1995.

National Research Council, Commission on Engineering and Technical Systems, Committee on the Future of the Global Positioning System, *Statement of Task*, n.d., 1994.

Navsat International, Inc., *Policy Options for GPS NAVSTAR*, Draft, McLean, VA, February 1994.

———, *Summary Business Plan*, second draft (unpublished), McLean, VA, February 1994.

Nolan, Janne E., *Trappings of Power: Ballistic Missiles in the Third World*, The Brookings Institution, Washington, D.C., 1991.

Overlook Systems Technologies, Inc., *Assessment of Recent SPS Performance Transients*, Vienna, VA., October 15, 1994.

———, *The Feasibility of a GNSS Exploitation Threat*, National Air Intelligence Center, Foreign Space Systems Analysis TAG 07-02, Wright-Patterson AFB, OH, April 25, 1995.

Peebles, Curtis, *Guardians: Strategic Reconnaissance Satellites*, Ian Allan Ltd, London, 1987.

Phillips, Charles F., *The Regulation of Public Utilities: Theory and Practice*, Public Utilities Reports, 1993, p. 9.

Poole, Robert W., *Building a Safer and More Effective Air Traffic Control System: Executive Summary*, Reason Foundation, Policy Insight No. 126, Santa Monica, CA, February 1991.

Potter, William C., and H. W. Jencks, eds., *The International Missile Bazaar: The New Suppliers' Network*, Westview Press, Boulder, CO, 1994.

Prabhakar, Anand S., *U.S. Coast Guard Radionavigation System User Survey*, U.S. Department of Transportation, DOT-CG-N-01-90, Springfield, VA, February 1990.

Preiss, George, et al., *Organising the Consultative Process for European GNSS User Requirements*, Commission of the European Communities, Brussels, December 19, 1994.

Royal Institute of Navigation, *Institutional Requirements for a Global Navigation Satellite System*, Draft, Royal Institute of Navigation, London, December 12, 1994.

RTCA, Inc., *Institutional Issues Discussion Draft*, RTCA Paper No. 210-92/TF1-23, Washington, D.C., March 1992.

———, *RTCA Task Force Report on the Global Navigation Satellite System (GNSS) Transition and Implementation Strategy*, Washington, D.C., September 18, 1992.

Scales, Jr., Brig. Gen. Robert H., Director, Desert Storm Study Project, *Certain Victory: United States Army in The Gulf War*, U.S. Army, 1993.

Schnier, Bruce, *Applied Cryptography: Protocols, Algorithms, and Source code in C*, John Wiley and Sons, NY, 1994.

Shetty, Sundar A., *Industry & Trade Summary: Navigational and Surveying Instruments*, U.S. International Trade Commission, USITC Publication 2730, Washington, D.C., February 1994.

Silva, R., and G. Murray, "Low Cost Quartz Rate Sensors Applied to Tactical Guidance IMUs," *IEEE PLANS-94*, Las Vegas, NV, April 1994.

Simpson, David, memo for the United Kingdom Home Office, *The Prospect of Referring British Admiralty Home Waters Charts Directly to WGS 84 Datum*, London, January 13, 1995.

Spilker, J. J., *Digital Communications by Satellite*, Prentice-Hall, Englewood Cliffs, NJ, 1977, pp. 528–608.

Tucker, Arnold J., ed., *A GPS Information and Data System for the Civil Community:* Vol. IV, *Synopsis of Civil GPS User Workshop (22 September 1987)*, Applied Research Laboratories, ARL-TR-88-11, Austin, TX, March 8, 1988.

Turner, David A., and Marcia S. Smith, *GPS: Satellite Navigation and Positioning and the DoD's Navstar Global Positioning System*, CRS Report for Congress, 94-171 SPR, 1994.

U.S. Congress, Office of Technology Assessment, *Assessing the Potential for Civil-Military Integration: Technologies, Processes, and Practices*, OTA-ISS-611, U.S. Government Printing Office, Washington, D.C., September 1994.

U.S. Department of Commerce, *Commercial Space Ventures—A Financial Prespective*, April 1990, pp. 25–31.

U.S. Department of Commerce, Institute for Telecommunications Sciences, *A National Approach to Augmented GPS Services*, NTIA Special Publication 94-30, December 1994.

U.S. Department of Defense, *Conduct of the Persian Gulf War: Final Report to Congress*, Pursuant to Title V of the Persian Gulf Supplemental Authorization and Personnel Benefits Act of 1991 (P.L. 102-25), April 1992.

———, *GPS Block IIF Initial Technical Package*, August 1994.

———, *NAVSTAR Global Positioning System User Charges: A Preliminary Report to The Senate and House Committees on Armed Services*, Washington, D.C., March 1, 1982.

———, *NAVSTAR Global Positioning System User Charges: A Report to The Senate and House of Representatives Committees on Appropriations and Armed Services*, Washington, D.C., May 31, 1984.

———, *Selected Acquisition Report* (RCS: DD-COMP [Q & A] 823) for the NAVSTAR GPS Program, December 31, 1994.

————, Office of the Secretary of Defense, *Defense Technology Plan*, Washington, D. C., September 1994.

————, U.S. Air Force, *Selected Acquisition Report for Navstar GPS*, RCS:DD-COMP(Q&A)823, December 31, 1993.

————, U.S. Air Force, *Selected Acquisition Report for Navstar GPS*, RCS:DD-COMP(Q&A)823, December 31, 1994.

U.S. Department of Defense and U.S. Department of Transportation, *Federal Radionavigation Plan, 1992*, John A. Volpe National Transportation Systems Center, DOT-VNTSC-RSPA-92-2, January 1993.

————, *1994 Federal Radionavigation Plan*, National Technical Information Service, DOT-VNTSC-RSPA-95-1/DOD-4650.5, Springfield, VA, May 1995.

U.S. Department of Transportation, Federal Aviation Administration, Satellite Program Office, *FAA Satellite Navigation Program Master Plan FY 94-99*, June 15, 1994.

————, *FAA Strategic Plan, Volume 2: Strategic Implementation*, 1994.

————, *Zero Accidents....A Shared Responsibility*, Washington, D.C., February 9, 1995.

U.S. Department of Transportation, Research & Special Programs Administration, *The RSPA Approach to Establishing the Civil GPS Service*, Washington, D.C., October 30, 1987.

U.S. GPS Industry Council, *GPS: A Dual-Use Technology Success*, Washington, D.C., 1994.

Watt, A., and J. Storey, *The Technical Implementation of a Common European Programme for Satellite Navigation*, EUROCONTROL, France, January 1995.

Wiedemer, Michael, *Proposed Guidelines for Compatible Operation of Radionavigation Satellites (Working Draft)*, Revision 3.6, NAVSTAR GPS Joint Program Office, January 10, 1995.

Periodicals

Adamson, Lee, "A Star to Steer By," *Ocean Voice*, January 1995, pp. 10–11.

"AF Says GPS Fully Operational," *GPS World Newsletter*, May 22, 1995, pp. 1, 5.

"Agency Initiatives Push Civil GPS Requirements, Agenda," *GPS World Newsletter*, October 27, 1994, pp. 1–2.

"Air Force Chops GPS Contract Plan," *Space News*, July 24–30, 1995, p. 1.

"Air Force Plans GPS Conference," *Aerospace Daily*, March 28, 1994, p. 484.

"Air Force Set To Release RFP on $2 Billion GPS Block IIF Contract," C^4I via NewsPage, May 11, 1995.

"Air Force Solicits Industry Comments on Plan to Change GPS Satellite Navigation Message," *GPS World*, November 1994, p. 16.

Andrews, Julie, "New Navigation Tool Works With Satellite," *Gazette Telegraph*, August 20, 1993, p. E1.

Anselmo, Joseph C., "'Smart Highway' Business Attracts Aerospace Firms," *Aviation Week & Space Technology*, January 31, 1994, pp. 56–57.

Arkusinski, Andy, and Ken Jongsma, *GPS Digest* (via electronic mail), Vol. 1, No. 2, March 9, 1993.

"Ashtech Wins USCG Differential Station Bid," *GPS World*, November 1994, p. 16.

"Aviation Markets Forge GPS Allies," *GPS World Newsletter*, December 29, 1994, p. 3.

Avionics, Vol. 18, No. 8, August 1994.

Baig, Edward, "On the Road Again—With a Digital Map," *Business Week*, June 20, 1994, p. 187.

Beukers, John M., "Global Radio Navigation—A Challenge for Management and International Cooperation," *NAVIGATION: Journal of The Institute of Navigation*, Vol. 23, No. 4, Winter 1976–77, pp. 325-333.

———, "Institutional and Financial Alternatives for Global Satellite Navigation," *GPS World*, October 1992, pp. 50–55.

Blackburn, Albert W., "GPS—A Technological Tidal Wave," *Professional Pilot*, November 1990, pp. 12–13.

———, "Internationalizing the Global Positioning System," *GPS World*, April 1991, pp. 44–46.

Blair Smith, Elliot, "Soviet Defense Technology Under Siege," *Houston Chronicle*, August 1, 1994, p. 8.

Boyer, William, "Company Introduces Nationwide GPS Correction Service," *Space News*, March 8–14, 1993.

———, "Randy Hoffman—President and Chief Executive Officer, Magellan Systems Corp.," *Space News*, January 10–16, 1994, p. 22.

———, "Trimble to Offer New Stock Shares," *Space News*, March 9–15, 1992, pp. 3, 21.

———, "U.S., Japan Foresee GPS Market Growth," *Space News*, November 16–22, 1992, pp. 10, 12.

Brown, Alison, "Expanding Horizons Through GPS Integrity," *GPS World*, 1992.

Burgess, Lisa, "GLONASS Expected To Be Operational in 1995," *Space News*, October 4–10, 1993, p. 6.

———, and Dennis Pidge, "Japan Plans GPS Adjunct," *Space News*, September 13–19, 1993, pp. 1, 20.

Bussert, Jim, "Russian Airport Control Systems," *Avionics*, Vol. 18, No. 8, 1994, pp. 32–34.

"Busy Summer for Satellite Launches," *GPS World*, September 1992, p. 20.

Butterline, Edgar W., "Reach Out and Time Someone," *GPS World*, January 1993, pp. 32–40.

Butterworth-Hayes, Philip, "Russian Keeps Faith with GLONASS," *Aerospace America*, August 1994, pp. 4–6.

"Car Navigation Expected to Spark GPS Growth," *Space News*, March 13–19, 1995.

"Cat 3 GPS Is 12 to 14 years Away, Study Says," *Aerospace Daily*, September 14, 1994, p. 416.

"Chinese 'GPS' Project Set," *Aviation Week & Space Technology*, October 17, 1994, p. 25.

"Civilian GPS Issues at DoD Elevated to Kaminsky's Office," *Aerospace Daily*, January 30, 1995, p. 145.

Collier, W. Clay, and Richard J. Weiland, "Smart Cars, Smart Highways," *IEEE Spectrum*, April 1994, pp. 27–33.

Communications, Navigation & Surveillance Outlook, Vol. 2, No. 2, February 15, 1994.

Cooper, Pat, "Navy Satellite System Aims to Deter ID Mishaps," *Defense News*, August 8–14, 1994, p. 26.

Cope, Lewis, "Satellites Help Mayo Medicine," *Star Tribune*, March 22, 1994, p. 1B.

Covault, Craig, "Space-Based ATC Liability at Issue," *Aviation Week & Space Technology*, October 18, 1993, p. 44.

Dana, Peter H., and Bruce M. Penrod, "The Role of GPS in Precise Time and Frequency Dissemination," *GPS World*, July/August 1990.

Day, Kathleen, "The Highway of the Future," *Washington Business*, March 14, 1994, pp. 1, 14–15.

———, "Orbital to Buy Positioning Firm," *The Washington Post*, November 29, 1994, p. C3.

Defense Electronics, Vol. 26, No. 9, September 1994.

DeMeis, Richard, "GPS Positions Itself for a Starring Role," *Aerospace America*, May 1993, pp. 32–35.

Dennehy, Kevin, "Where Military and Commercial Technologies Unite," *Via Satellite*, October 1993, pp. 61–64.

de Selding, Peter B., "Europeans To Pledge GPS Funds," *Space News*, May 1-7, 1995, pp. 1, 20.

———, "Eurospace Urges ESA Overhaul," *Space News*, June 12–18, 1995, pp. 3, 37.

"Dividends in Space," *GPS World*, June 1995, p. 16.

"DGPS Nets: China and Finland," *GPS World Newsletter*, December 29, 1994, p. 4.

"DoD/DoT Talks Get WAAS Back on Track," *GPS World*, April 1995, p. 18.

"DoT Restructures Civil GPS Policy Roles," *GPS World*, July 1994, p. 19.

"Drive Into the Future With TravTek," *AAA World*, March/April 1992, p. 29.

Drummer, Randyl, "Area firm signs accord for satellite dashboard devices," *Daily Bulletin*, August 27, 1993, pp. A1, A7.

"EC Satnav Report Focuses on GLONASS Industrial Policy," *GPS World*, November 1993, p. 12.

"EC Satnav Study Proposes Building on GPS GLONASS," *GPS World*, February 1994, p. 18.

"EC Set To Approve $202 Million in GPS Funding," *Global Positioning and Navigation News* via NewsPage, May 16, 1995.

Edwards, Steve, "GPS Tells You Where and When," *Defense Electronics*, September 1994, pp. 37–42.

"European Agencies Set Budget for GNSS Program," *GPS World Newsletter*, May 22, 1995, pp. 1, 5.

"European Consensus Emerges on GNSS," *GPS World*, Vol. 5, No. 11, November 1994, p. 16.

"European Representatives Air Concerns About GPS Availability," *GPS Report*, January 28, 1993, pp. 1–2.

Eustace, Harry F., "C3I Defense Conversion Markets Part 1: $15 Billion Spending on Russian Airways Modernization Will Use Many Western C3I Technologies Already Developed," *Defense Electronics*, June 1993, pp. 28–31.

"Executive Order 12906 Coordinating Geographic Data Acquisition and Access: The National Spatial Data Infrastructure," *Federal Register*, Vol. 59, No. 71, April 13, 1994, pp. 17671–17674.

"FAA Cancels MLS Work, Releases WAAS RFP," *GPS World*, July 1994, p. 19.

"FAA Chief Renews GPS Pledge to ICAO," *GPS World Newsletter*, October 27, 1994, p. 5.

"FAA, DoD Confer on Changes in Wide Area Augmentation System," *Aerospace Daily*, January 31, 1995, p. 153.

"FAA, DoD Confer on Wide Area Augmentation System Changes," *Aviation Daily*, January 30, 1995, p. 1.

"FAA Officially Accepts GPS," *GPS World*, April 1994, p. 16.

"FAA Should Have Its Own Navigation Satellites, Congress is Told," *Aerospace Daily*, March 28, 1994, pp. 483–484.

"FCC Allocates 33 MHz of Spectrum to MSS Opens Opportunities," *Mobile Satellite News*, December 22, 1993, p. 1.

Ferster, Warren, "Rockwell Sets Sights on GPS With Team Bid," *Space News*, January 30–February 5, 1995, pp. 1, 21.

———, "Russian Rocket Engines Vie for Role in EELV Effort," *Space News*, May 8–14, 1995, p. 12.

Fialka, John J., "Poor Man's Cruise: Airliners Can Exploit U.S. Guidance System, But So Can Enemies," *The Wall Street Journal*, August 26, 1993, pp. A1, A4.

Field, David, "U.S. to let airliners navigate by its satellites," *The Washington Times*, March 28, 1995, p. B7.

"Firm Enters DGPS-Correction Service Market," *GPS World*, July 1993, p. 60.

Fisch, Al, "GPS timing signals support simulcast synchronization," *Mobile Radio Technology*, May 1995.

Foley, Theresa, "On the Rise," *Ad Astra*, July/August 1994, p. 34.

Forum: Key Issues in International Aviation & Aerospace, December 1994.

Foster, Anthony P., "GPS Strategic Alliances, Part I: Setting Them Up," *GPS World*, May 1994, pp. 34–42.

———, "GPS Strategic Alliances, Part II: Dealing With the Legal Issues," *GPS World*, June 1994, pp. 28–32.

Fromson, Brett D., "The Agency Without Security," *Washington Post*, August 27, 1994, pp. F1, F7.

Fulghum, David A., "Competitors Protest UAV Design Selection," *Aviation Week & Space Technology*, October 17, 1994, pp. 21–22.

"GAO Questions FAA Progress on GPS; June 8 Hearing Planned," *Aerospace Daily*, May 22, 1995, p. 287.

Georgiadou, Yale, and Kenneth D. Doucet, "The Issue of Selective Availability," *GPS World*, September/October 1990, p. 53.

"GAO Questions Schedule for GPS Augmentation," *Aviation Week and Space Technology*, June 19, 1995, p. 42.

Gerold, Adrian, "Searching for the Holy Grail of Avionics," *Avionics*, August 1994, pp. 26–28.

Getting, Ivan A., "The Global Positioning System," *IEEE Spectrum*, Vol. 30, No. 12, December 1993, pp. 36–47.

Gibbons, Glen, "AF Says GPS Fully Operational," *GPS World Newsletter*, May 22, 1995, p. 5.

———, "Ashtech Scores Big with Coast Guard DGPS Win," *GPS World Newsletter*, September 29, 1994, pp. 1, 5.

———, "Being Civil," *GPS World*, July 1994, p. 10.

———, "DoD Dumps Selective Availability for Haiti Action," *GPS World Newsletter*, September 29, 1994, pp. 1, 5.

———, "EC Moves Ahead on GNSS," *GPS World Newletter*, September 29, 1994, pp. 1,5.

———, "Face to Face: Col. Mike Wiedemer, Director, GPS Joint Program Office," *GPS World*, April 1995, pp. 32–42.

———, "Falling Walls," *GPS World*, February 1992.

———, "Global Challenge," *GPS World*, March 1992.

———, "One Shoe Dropping," *GPS World*, January 1993.

———, "Panel Backs GPS Spatial Data," *GPS World Newsletter*, August 11, 1994, pp. 1, 5.

———, "Pioneers of GPS: Surveyors and Geographers," *GPS World Showcase*, August 1993, p. 36.

———, "Play Ball," *GPS World*, March 1995, p. 10.

Gilberson, Mark, "Magellan navigates $100 million deal with Japanese," *San Jose Mercury News*, August 27, 1993, pp. B1, B7.

Global Positioning & Navigation News, Vol. 4, No. 19, September 22, 1994.

"GLONASS: New Launch, Info Center, Web Home," *GPS World*, April 1995, p. 18.

"GLONASS Constellation Said Finished in 1995," *JPRS Report*, JPRS-UST-95-003, February 1, 1995, p. 6.

"GLONASS May Interfere with Big Leo Networks," *Mobile Satellite News*, November 24, 1993, pp. 3–4.

"GM Oldsmobile Will Be First in U.S. With GPS," *GPS World*, February 1994, p. 18.

Gouzhva, Yuri G., et al., "Getting in Sync: GLONASS Clock Synchronization," *GPS World*, April 1995, pp. 48–56.

———, "GLONASS Receivers: An Outline," *GPS World*, January 1994, pp. 30–36.

"GPS Aides Open Skies Treaty Monitoring," *GPS World*, November 1993, p. 12.

"GPS Changes Recommended To Ensure U.S. Control of Global Navigation," *Satellite Week* via NewsPage, June 6, 1995.

"GPS Firm Making a Difference in GIS Market," *GPS Report*, June 4, 1992, p. 6.

"GPS in the Federal Budget," *GPS World*, April 1994, p. 16.

"GPS in War," *GPS World*, March 1994, p. 20.

"GPS in Year 2000: $8 Billion," *GPS World Newsletter*, April 11, 1995, p. 1.

"GPS Marketplace: On the Road to Profits," *GPS Report*, April 9, 1992, pp. 1–2.

"GPS Measures Earthquake Motion," *GPS World*, September 1992, p. 20.

"GPS on Capitol Hill: Policy and Progress," *Professional Surveyor*, July/August 1994, p. 18.

"GPS on the Mississippi," *GPS World*, April 1994, p. 16.

"GPS Replacing MLS," *GPS World*, April 1994, p. 17.

"GPS Satellite Constellation Nears Initial Operational Status," *GPS World*, November 1993, p. 12.

"GPS System May Produce the Next Trade Flap With Japan," *Satellite News*, September 28, 1992, p. 5.

"GPS 2F Hinges on Procurement Strategy," *Space News*, May 1–7, 1995, p. 3.

"GPS Timing Applications Grow," *GPS World Newsletter*, December 29, 1994, p. 3.

"GPS to be Incorporated in Microlab-I Experiment," *GPS Report*, August 26, 1993, pp. 1–2.

"GPS to Test Nuclear Detonation Sensor," *Aviation Week & Space Technology*, August 27, 1979, p. 51.

"Greatest GPS Hits of 1994," *GPS World Newsletter*, December 29, 1994, pp. 1–2, 6.

Hamilton, David P., "Navigation Systems Set Course for U.S.," *Wall Street Journal*, February 13, 1995, pp. B1, B10.

Hanley, Timothy, and Harry Waldron, "1954-1994: A Look Back in Time," *Astro News*, July 1, 1994, pp. 2–14.

Harvey, David S., "Naval Aviators Play Catch-Up on GPS," *Avionics*, August 1994, pp. 30–31.

Healey, Jon, "Melding a Multitude of Maps," *Congressional Quarterly*, September 18, 1993, p. 2447.

Hewish, Mark, "Sensor Integration For Navigation and Survey," *International Defense Review*, No. 4, 1994, pp. 49–55.

Hirschman, Dave, "Need Futuristic Information? Beam it Down, Scotty," *The Commercial Appeal*, March 13, 1994, p. C3.

Hough, Harold, "A GPS Precise Timing Sampler," *GPS World*, October 1991, pp. 33–36.

"House Appropriators Cut GPS Block IIF, Add $100 Million For SBIRS," *Aerospace Daily*, Vol. 175, No. 17, July 27, 1995, pp. 129–130.

Hughes, David, "Aerospace Electronics May Guide Smart Cars," *Aviation Week & Space Technology*, November 8, 1993, pp. 63–64.

———, "Air Navigation Due for Dramatic Change," *Aviation Week & Space Technology*, October 31, 1994, pp. 51–59.

"ICAO Group Sees No Role for GPS in Global Navigation System," *Aerospace Daily*, July 28, 1993, p. 154.

"Implement GPS-Based Navigation for Aeronautics Now, Hill Panel Is Urged," *Mobile Satellite Reports*, Vol. 7, No. 14, 1993.

"In Japan They May Never Ask for Directions Again," *Wall Street Journal*, January 7, 1994.

"Inmarsat Invites Bids for GNSS Augmentation," *GPS World*, October 1994, p. 18.

"Inmarsat-3s Offered for Navigation," *Space Business News*, September 13, 1994, p. 4.

"International Community Seen Insisting on Bilateral Process for GPS," *Aerospace Daily*, June 25, 1993, pp. 522–523.

"IOA Reforms Under New Charter, Renamed as INA," *GPS World*, July 1993, p. 60.

"ITS Architecture Teams Boast GPS Expertise," *GPS World*, March 1995, p. 18.

"Jamming Danger Raises Doubts About GPS," *Aviation Week & Space Technology*, October 19, 1992, p. 61.

"Japan GPS Council," *GPS World*, January 1993.

"Japanese GPS Receiver Market: $240 Million and Climbing Fast," *GPS World Newsletter*, December 29, 1994, pp. 1, 4.

Jenks, Andrew, "Bursting into Bloom after Desert Storm," *Washington Technology*, October 8, 1992, pp. 17–18.

Johnson, Nicholas L., "GLONASS Spacecraft," *GPS World*, November 1994, pp. 51–58.

Kahn, Jeffery, *Building the Information Highway*, Summer 1993. (World Wide Web at http://www.lbl.gov/Science-Articles/Archive/information-superhighway.html).

Kane, Francis X., "Navstar GPS & Satellite Communications," *Satellite Communications*, 1994, pp. 44–46.

Kerr, Richard A., "A Military Navigation System Might Probe Lofty 'Weather'," *Science*, Vol. 256, 1992, pp. 318–319.

Kiernan, Vincent, "Civil GPS Advocates Lobby to Use Maximum Accuracy," *Space News*, April 29–May 5, 1991, pp. 3, 29.

Klass, Philip J., "FAA Cancels MLS in Favor of GPS," *Aviation Week & Space Technology*, June 13, 1994, p. 33.

———, "FAA Delays Awarding D-GPS Network Contract," *Aviation Week & Space Technology*, Vol. 142, No. 5, January 30, 1995, p. 35.

———, "GLONASS-M Readied," *Aviation Week & Space Technology*, December 12–19, 1994, p. 59.

———, "GPS To Be Tested For Cat.-3 Landings," *Aviation Week & Space Technology*, Vol. 142, No. 7, February 13, 1995, pp. 62–63.

———, "Inmarsat Plan Spurs GPS Debate," *Aviation Week & Space Technology*, July 26, 1993, p. 23.

———, "Missile Technique Aids Transport Landing," *Aviation Week & Space Technology*, August 15, 1994, p. 57.

Krakiwsky, Edward J., and James F. McLellan, "Making GPS Even Better with Auxiliary Devices," *GPS World*, March 1995, pp. 46–53.

Krawczyk, Thomas, "Outsmarting Traffic Jams," *Technology in Review*, February/March 1994, p. 14.

Kuritsky, Morris M., and Murray S. Goldstein, eds., "Inertial Navigation," *Proceedings of the IEEE*, Vol. 71, No. 10 (October 1983), pp. 1156–1176.

Kursinski, Rob, "Monitoring the Earth's Atmosphere with GPS," *GPS World*, March 1994, pp. 50–54.

Kuznik, Frank, "You Are Here: GPS Satellites Can Tell You Where You Are—Within Inches," *Air & Space*, June/July 1992, pp. 34–40.

Lachow, Irving, "The GPS Dilemma: Balancing Military Risks and Economic Benefits," *International Security*, Vol. 20, No. 1 (Summer 1995), pp. 126–148.

Langley, Richard B., "The Federal Radionavigation Plan," *GPS World*, March 1992, pp. 50–53.

———, "The GPS Receiver: An Introduction," *GPS World*, January 1991, p. 51.

Lardner, Richard, and Daniel G. Dupont, "Homemade Terror: Clear and Future Danger?" *The Washington Post*, November 6, 1994, p. C2.

Latham, Donald, "The GPS War," *Space News*, pp. 15, 19.

"Launch, Talks Bolster GLONASS Prospects," *GPS World*, October 1994, p. 18.

Lavitt, Michael O., "GPS Attitude Determination," *Aviation Week & Space Technology*, February 7, 1994, p. 13.

———, "Japanese Nav-Sats," *Aviation Week & Space Technology*, August 30, 1993, p. 13.

Leary, Warren E., "Civilian Uses Are Proposed For Satellites," *The New York Times*, June 1, 1995, p. A23

Lechner, Wolfgang, "ILS Into GNSS: Aviation's Difficult Transition," *GPS World*, July 1994, pp. 40–45.

Lehman, H. Jane, "Coming Soon: House Hunting by Computer," *The Washington Post*, November 26, 1994, pp. E1, E6.

Lenorovitz, Jeffrey M., "ESA Offers Updated Navsat Concept As New Civilian Navigation System," *Aviation Week & Space Technology*, January 25, 1988, p. 54.

———, "Russia Expands GLONASS Network," *Aviation Week & Space Technology*, August 29, 1994, p. 76.

———, "U.S.-Russian Teams Get Pentagon Funds," *Aviation Week & Space Technology*, August 8, 1994, p. 27.

"Lessons of the First Space War," *Space Markets*, April 1991, p. 12.

Liesman, Steve, "Russian-Rockwell Traffic Project to Speed Flights," *New York Times*, August 11, 1994, p. D3.

Loh, Robert, "Seamless Aviation: FAA's Wide Area Augmentation System," *GPS World*, April 1995, pp. 20–30.

"Loran Awarded Contract for Japanese Satellite," *Space News*, March 6–12, 1995.

"Manufacturers Hail Revise Export Rules, GPS Industry Council," *GPS World*, July/August 1991, p. 22.

"The Many Sides of Selective Availability," *GPS Report*, March 12, 1992, p. 1.

Marino, Karre, "Quake Aftershocks Under Study By Lab Scientists," *Jet Propulsion Laboratory UNIVERSE*, Vol. 24, No. 2, January 28, 1994.

Marks, Peter, "For a Few Lucky Motorists Guidance by Satellite," *New York Times*, April 2, 1994, pp. A1, A24.

Marsh, George, "Conference Explores Differential GNSS Policy and Technology," *Avionics*, August 1994, pp. 22–25.

McDonald, Keith, "Econosats: Toward an Affordable Global Navigation Satellite System?" *GPS World*, September 1993, pp. 44–54.

McKenna, Edward L., "Railroads Applying Infotech For Safety, Savings," *New Technology Week*, September 6, 1994, p. 7.

McLucas, John, "Smart Policy: Make Best GPS Data Available to All," *Space News*, April 1–7, 1991, p. 16.

———, "Use GPS for Cheap Weather Data," *Space News*, January 27–February 2, 1992, p. 21.

———, "Who Will Manage the Market for GPS Services?" *Space News*, April 8–14, 1991, p. 15.

McNevin, Ed, "GPS TurboRogue Provide More Precise Earth Measurements," electronic news clipping, March 29, 1994.

"Mexico Land Reform Program Adopts GPS," *GPS World*, September 1992, p. 20.

Miller, Brian, "Cellular Revolution Threatening E-911," *Government Technology*, October 1994, pp. 16–17.

Millett, Allan R., W. Murray, and K. H. Watman, "The Effectiveness of Military Organizations," *International Security*, Vol. 11, No. 1 (Summer 1986), pp. 37–71.

"Milspace Cuts Could Spell Commercial Opportunity," *Space Business News*, August 17, 1992, pp. 4–6.

"Minutes from a CGSIC Meeting," *GPS World*, July 1994, pp. 16–18.

Misra, Pratap N., et al., "GLONASS Performance in 1992: A Review," *GPS World*, May 1993, pp. 28–38.

"Mission a Success, Discovery Crew Prepares for Landing in the Dark," *The Washington Times*, September 21, 1993, p. 5.

"MLS Falters—Long Live GPS," *GPS World*, July 1994, p. 16.

"Mobile Satellite Officials Worried About GLONASS Signals," *GPS Report*, March 11, 1993, pp. 3–4.

Mogee, Mary Ellen, "Using Patent Data for Technology Analysis and Planning," *Research Technology Management*, July-August 1991, pp. 43–49.

Montgomery, Hale, "Academies Study GPS; Federal Budget; GPS Collars Fish Poachers," *GPS World*, April 1995, pp. 12–16.

———, "Congressional Changes; GLONASS Update," *GPS World*, February, 1995, pp. 16, 18.

———, "GPS for Ships and Planes a Bonus for Earth Science," *GPS World*, June 1994, pp. 12, 14.

———, "GPS in Transit," *GPS World*, March 1992, p. 16.

———, "GPS—Talk of the Town," *GPS World*, October 1993, pp. 14–16.

———, "Heading South—and East," *GPS World*, February 1992, pp. 12–15.

———, "High-Level U.S. Policy; Canadian Commitment," *GPS World*, October 1994, pp. 12–14.

———, "INMARSAT Goals," *GPS World*, September 1995, p. 16.

——, "National Academies' GPS Study; MLS Fades; CGSIC Notes," *GPS World*, July 1994, pp. 12–13.

——, "National Security Concerns, Rand Study, Space Ventures," *GPS World*, March 1995, pp. 12, 16.

——, "New U.S. Leadership Takes Up GPS GLONASS Issues," *GPS World*, June 1993, pp. 14–19.

——, "The Next Step: Global Differential," *GPS World*, November 1992, pp. 12–16.

——, "Reference Stations and EMS," *GPS World*, May 1994, pp. 12–16.

——, "Spectrum Fight Over GLONASS; Europe Looks at GPS Options," *GPS World*, April 1993, pp. 12–19.

——, "Task Force Differential In-Flight Differential and Video Van Mapping," *GPS World*, February 1994, pp. 12–16.

——, "The Winds of Change in Washington," *GPS World*, January 1994, pp. 12–18.

Mueller, Tysen, "Wide Area Differential GPS," *GPS World*, June 1994, pp. 36–44.

"Multiple Nations Should Manage GPS," *Aviation Week & Space Technology*, January 31, 1994, p. 66.

Nagle, J. R., A. J. Van Dierendonck, and Q. D. Hua, "Inmarsat-3 Navigation Signal C/A Code Selection and Interference Analysis," *NAVIGATION: Journal of The Institute of Navigation*, Vol. 39, No. 4, Winter 1992-93, pp. 445–461.

"NASA and Wilcox Complete Successful DGPS Autoland," *GPS World*, November 1993, p. 12.

Nash, Jim, "Lotus Deal Puts Strategic Company on the Map," *San Jose Business Journal*, June 20, 1994, pp. 3, 31.

"Navstar Global Positioning System Block IIF Acquisition—Intent to Release Draft Request for Proposal," *Commerce Business Daily*, May 18, 1995.

Nordwall, Bruce D., "Affordable Data Link to Benefit Small Aircraft," *Aviation Week & Space Technology*, July 18, 1994, p. 29.

————, "Aircraft Radar Used for Precision Approaches," *Aviation Week & Space Technology*, October 17, 1994, p. 51.

————, "Alenia Pushes Radar, Satellites for ATC," *Aviation Week & Space Technology*, July 4, 1994, pp. 64–65.

————, "Enhanced GPS Spawns Innovative Applications," *Aviation Week & Space Technology*, November 21, 1994, pp. 94–95.

————, "NAVSAT Users Want Civil Control Aviation Week & Space Technology," *Aviation Week & Space Technology*, October 18, 1993, pp. 57–59.

————, "Quartz Fork Technology May Replace INS Gyros," *Aviation Week & Space Technology*, April 25, 1994, pp. 50–51.

————, "Small GPS Receivers Open New Possibilities," *Aviation Week & Space Technology*, December 5, 1994, pp. 57–58.

"Old Navigation Systems May Go," electronic news clipping, May 30, 1994.

Pace, Scott, "GPS: Challenged by Success," *Space News*, August 30–September 5, 1993, p. 15.

Parkinson, Bradford W., "GPS Eyewitness: The Early Years," *GPS World*, September 1994, pp. 32–45.

Pearl, Daniel, "FAA May Spend Up to $500 Million to Track Aircraft," *The Wall Street Journal*, June 9, 1994, p. A5.

Phillips, Don, "Reorganization May Lead To New Air Traffic Agency," *The Washington Post*, December 1, 1994, p. A21.

Phillips, Edward H., "FAA Opens Bidding for Wide-Area GPS," *Aviation Week & Space Technology*, June 13, 1994, p. 34.

Polsky Werner, Debra, "Aviators to Use GPS," *Space News*, June 13–19, 1994, pp. 4, 29.

————, "Calif.-Based Firms Offer Highly Accurate GPS Services," *Space News*, November 29–December 5, 1993, p. 7.

———, "Clinton Lobbies for Global Satellite Navigation System," *Space News*, April 3–9, 1995, p. 35.

———, "Compromise Expected on Access to Precise Navigation," *Space News*, March 6–12, 1995, p. 8.

———, "Space-Based Navigation Undergoes Another Road Test," *Space News*, May 2–8, 1994, p. 22.

"Positive Steps," *Aviation Week & Space Technology*, August 29, 1994, p. 21.

Pound Dawson, Kate, "Japan Forms GPS Council to Avoid Tension with U.S. Firms," *Space News*, November 30–December 6, 1992.

———, "Japan Prepares To Meet Heavy GPS Demand," *Space News*, May 11–17, 1992, pp. 6,10.

Privor, Cheri, "GPS 2F Effort Hinges on Procurement Strategy," *Space News*, May 1–7, 1995, pp. 3, 21.

Proctor, Paul, "Making the World Smaller," *Aviation Week & Space Technology*, June 13, 1994, p. 15.

"Provision of Navigation Services through Inmarsat-3 Satellite Payloads," *GPS World*, September 1993, p. 18.

Raffi, Gregorian, "Global Positioning Systems: A Military Revolution for the Third World," *SAIS Review, A Journal of International Affairs* (Winter-Spring), Volume 13, Number 1, pp. 133–148.

Raymos, Dion C., "Liability of the Government for Improper Placement of Aids to Navigation," *Journal of Maritime Law and Commerce*, 1986, pp. 517–530.

Reason, Tim, "GPS on Capitol Hill: Policy and Progress, an interview with Senator Jim Exon," *Professional Surveyor*, July/August 1994, pp. 18, 21.

Reid, Rosalind, "Found: One Silver Lining (Global Positioning System Meteorology)," *American Scientist*, March/April 1993, pp. 126–127.

Rip, Michael Russel, and David Lusch, "The Precision Revolution: The Navstar Global Positioning System in the Second Gulf War," *Intelligence and National Security*, Vol. 9, No. 2, 1994, pp. 167–241.

Roos, John G., "A Pair of Achilles' Heels," *Armed Forces Journal International*, November 1994, pp. 21–23.

"Russia Sets Up GLONASS Information Center," *GPS World*, September 1992, p. 20.

"Russia to Proceed with GLONASS," *Aviation and Space Technology*, September 7, 1992, p. 38.

"Russian GLONASS Presentation at the RTCA GNSS Task Force Meeting, August 12–13, Herndon, VA, " *RTCA Digest*, No. 93, 1992, p. 13.

"The Russians are Here," *GPS World*, October 1992, p. 16.

"Russian Space Program Focuses on Communication and Navigation," *European Space Report*, March 1993, p. 2.

Scully, Michael, "Forest Service & Trimble Navigation: Pinpointing Animals in the World," *Technology Transfer Business*, Fall 1993, p. 46.

Seitz, Patrick, "Sony Sells Dashboard Navigator Tying GPS to Travel Data," *Space News*, January 9–15, 1995, p. 16.

Shank, Chris, and John W. Lavrakas, "Inside GPS: The Master Control Station," *GPS World*, September 1994, pp. 46–54.

Sharret, Patrick, Letter, *Space News*, April 29–May 5, 1991, pp. 18–19.

"SIC Effort Could Make GPS an Official Industry," *GPS World Newsletter*, October 13, 1994, pp. 1–2, 6.

"Skeptics Question DoD's GPS Jamming Policy, WAAS Approval," *Aerospace Daily*, March 23, 1995, p. 443.

Skinner, Liz, "Another Clash Over Territory In Outer Space," *Washington Technology*, August 11, 1994, p. 1.

———, "Global Positioning Systems' Place on Infobahn," *Washington Technology*, December 1994, p. 18.

———, "GPS Future Lies in Navigation Markets," *Washington Technology*, March 23, 1995, p. 16.

Sokolski, Henry D., "Nonapocalyptic Proliferation: A New Strategic Threat?" *The Washington Quarterly*, Spring 1994, Vol. 17, No. 2, pp. 115–127.

"Study Fault U.S. Daring in High-Volume Products," *New Technology Week*, May 30, 1995, p. 1.

"Study Puts Cruise Threat On Par With Ballistic Missiles," *Defense Daily*, January 12, 1995, p. 51.

Sugarman, Carole, "Sensors Software and Satellites May Hold Seeds of Better Yields," *The Washington Post*, September 7, 1992, p. A3.

Sugawara, Sandra, "Deep-Sixing the Sextant," *Washington Business*, November 29, 1993, p. 19.

"Survey Continues to be a Strong GPS Market," *Global Positioning and Navigation News*, May 2, 1995 via NewsPage on the World Wide Web at http://www.newspage.com/NEWSPAGE/newspage-home.html

Thomson, Allen, "Civil Satellite Vulnerability," *Space News*, February 20–26, 1995, p. 15.

"Time for Action on Global NAVSAT," *Aviation Week & Space Technology*, August 2, 1993, p. 70.

Toolin, Maurice J., "GPS in a Russian Telecommunications Network," *GPS World*, June 1992, p. 28.

"Trimble and Honeywell Sign Agreement for Strategic Alliance on GPS," *PR Newswire* via NewsPage, June 12, 1995.

"Trimble Discusses GPS Markets, Applications at the FCC," *Global Positioning and Navigation News*, May 30, 1995 via NewsPage on the World Wide Web at http://www.newspage.com/NEWSPAGE/newspagehome.html

"Trimble, Socket Develop PCMCIA GPS Sensor," *GPS World*, July 1993, p. 60.

"UNAVCO Offers Archived GPS Data to Researchers," *GPS World*, July 1993, p. 60.

Unwin, Martin, and Yoshikazu Hashida, "Found in Space: Tracking Microsatellites with GPS," *GPS World*, June 1993, pp. 32–38.

"U.S. Commerce Department Predicts Rapid GPS Growth," *Global Positioning & Navigation News*, January 27, 1994, p. 5.

"U.S. DoT Endorses 'Accelerated' GPS Schedule for Aviation," *GPS World*, February 1994, p. 18.

"U.S. DoT Fills Critical Policy, Staff Bodies," *GPS World Newsletter*, December 29, 1994, p. 5.

"U.S. Eyes Launchers With No Mil Specs," *Aviation Week & Space Technology*, May 15, 1995, p. 30.

"U.S. formally pledges free use of GPS," *Aerospace Daily*, October 19, 1994, p. 92.

"U.S./Japanese Governments Embark On Theater Missile Defense Study," *Inside the Air Force*, September 30, 1994, pp. 1, 6.

"U.S. Radionavigation Policy Sparks Overseas Concern," *Aerospace Daily*, August 25, 1994, p. 312.

"U.S. To Rule on GPS Management in '93," *Space News*, June 14, 1993.

"USDoT Looks to Survey Group for GPS Advisors," *GPS World*, October 1994, p. 18.

"USGIC Adds Membership Category and New Members," *GPS World*, July 1993, p. 60.

Van Zandt, David E., "The Lessons of the Lighthouse: 'Government' or 'Private' Provision of Goods," *Journal of Legal Studies*, Vol. 22, 1993, pp. 47–72.

Vartabedian, Ralph, "Eye in the Sky," *Los Angeles Times*, May 2, 1994, p. B5.

Verchere, Ian, "EC to Look at Russian Satellites," *Space News*, August 9–15, 1993, p. 17.

Victor, Kirk, "Air Waves," *National Journal*, February 19, 1994, pp. 418–421.

"Visit to GLONASS Center Is First for Outsiders," *GPS World*, September 1993, pp. 16–18.

"WADGPS Plans Continue to Generate Controversy," *GPS World*, March 1995, p. 18.

Ware, Randolph, "GPS Sounding of Earth's Atmosphere," *GPS World*, September 1992, pp. 56–57.

"Washington Outlook—Warning Signs," *Aviation Week and Space Technology*, July 24, 1995, p. 19.

Weber, Steve, "Army to Test GPS Technology for More Accurate Artillery," *Space News*, January 9–15, 1995, p. 19.

———, "GPS Studies To Probe Technical, Control Issues," *Space News*, August 1–7, 1994, p. 6.

Wechsler, Jill, "The Timing Subcommittee of the Civil GPS Service Steering Committee," *GPS World*, July/August 1990, p. 18.

Weintraub, Richard, "FAA Plans Satellite System to Reshape Aircraft Navigation," *Washington Post*, June 9, 1994, pp. D9, D11.

Werner, Udo H., "Improving Mobile Communications with GPS," *GPS World*, May 1993, pp. 40–43.

Williams, Trish, "Wall St. Sees Pentagon Control of GPS as Detrimental," *Space News*, March 21–27, 1994, p. 17.

"Worm Holes in GPS Coverage Raise Interference Concerns," *Aviation Week and Space Technology*, June 5, 1995, p. 32.

Yunck, Thomas P., "Earth Science Takes Off with Spaceborne GPS," *GIS World*, January 1993, pp. 60–62.

Conference Proceedings, Briefings, Speeches

Aerospace Corporation, "Status of GPS/GLONASS Compatibility Testing," briefing presented at the GPS Joint Program Office, Los Angeles AFB, June 16, 1994.

Air Force Space Command, "Satellite Roadmap," briefing charts, Boulder, CO, December 29, 1994.

Ananda, M., P. Munjal, and K. T. Woo, "Augmented Global Positioning System," paper presented at the 1995 National Technical Meeting of the Institute of Navigation, Anaheim, CA, January 18, 1995.

Anderson, Lynn, "Differential GPS Overview," briefing presented to the Defense Science Board Task Force on GPS, Los Angeles, CA, July 12–14, 1994.

———, "Direct Y-Code Acquisition for Precision Guided Munitions," briefing presented to the Defense Science Board Task Force on GPS, Los Angeles, CA, July 12–14, 1994.

———, "Enhanced GPS for Combat Systems," briefing presented to the Defense Science Board Task Force on GPS, Los Angeles, CA, July 12–14, 1994.

Arnold, James A., "FHWA Positioning," briefing presented to the National Research Council Committee on the Future of GPS, Washington, D.C., July 28–30, 1994.

Ashtech Inc., Motorola Inc., and Trimble Navigation Ltd., "Responses from the Civilian GPS Receiver Manufacturers to the National Research Council Committee on the Future of GPS," paper presented to the National Research Council Committee on the Future of the Global Positioning System, Irvine, CA, August 16–18, 1994.

Ballew, Robert, and Louis Decker, "NAVSTAR GPS: Future Requirements and Recommended Actions," briefing presented to the National Research Council Committee on the Future of the Global Positioning System, Washington, D.C., July 28–30, 1994.

Barbier, Jacques, and Thierry Trémas, "European Complement to GPS: Presentation of the Concept and Experimental System," paper presented at the 7th European Frequency and Time Forum, Neuchâtel, Switzerland, March 16–18, 1993.

Beukers, John M., "Administrative Procedures and Agreements Governing Global Radionavigation," paper presented at the *49th*

Annual Meeting Proceedings, Institute of Navigation, Cambridge, MA, August 1993.

———, "Civil versus Military Use of Satellites for Positioning and Navigation," *Planning for Global Radionavigation,* First International Radionavigation Conference, Moscow, Russia, June 26–30, 1995.

———, "The Compelling Case for a NavSat (GNSS) Council and Secretariat," paper presented at the Special Meeting of the International Association of the Institutes of Navigation, Paris, France, October 15, 1993.

———, "Institutional Inertia," paper presented at the Wild Goose Association (International Loran Association) 23rd Annual Convention and Technical Symposium, Newport, RI, November 3, 1994.

Blackburn, Al, "Presentation on Financing Alternatives," briefing presented to Scott Pace, Washington, D.C., October 1993.

Bobinsky, Eric A., "GPS and Global Telecommunications," briefing presented to the National Research Council Committee on the Future of the Global Positioning System, Washington, D.C., July 28–30, 1994.

Bogle, Andy, "An Overview of Commercial Marine GPS Applications," briefing presented to the National Research Council Committee on the Future of GPS, Washington, D.C., July 28–30, 1994.

Bottari, Maj. Elio, "User Equipment Overview," *The NAVSTAR GPS System,* Advisory Group for Aerospace Research and Development, Lecture Series No. 161, NATO, Neuilly-Sur Seine, 1988, p. 6–6.

Brown, Stephen, "Future of GPS," briefing presented to the National Research Council Committee on the Future of GPS, Washington, D.C., July 28–30, 1994.

Busey, James B., Administrator, United States Federal Aviation Administration, remarks made at the ICAO Air Navigation Conference, Montreal, Canada, September 5, 1991.

Calbi, Vito, "GPS Receiver Design for High Jamming Environments," briefing presented to the National Research Council Committee on the Future of the Global Positioning System, Irvine, CA, August 16–18, 1994.

Clark, John, "GPS Constellations Design: History, Options, Constraints," briefing presented to the Defense Science Board Task Force on GPS, Los Angeles, CA, July 12–14, 1994.

——, "GPS in a Challenged Tactical Environment: Security, Vulnerabilities, and Countermeasures," briefing presented to the National Research Council Committee on the Future of GPS, Washington, D.C., June 23, 1994.

——, "GPS Operational Principles," briefing presented to the National Research Council Committee on the Future of GPS, Washington, D.C., June 23, 1994.

——, "Status of GPS/GLONASS Compatibility Testing," presentation made to the RAND GPS study team, Los Angeles, CA, August 25, 1994.

Clynch, J., "Comparisons of DGPS Systems in a Dynamic Environment," *Proceeding of ION GPS-94*, Salt Lake City, UT, September 20–23, 1994.

Clynch, J., G. Thurmond, L. Rosenfeld, and R. Schramm, "Error Characteristics of GPS Differential Positions and Velocities," *Proceeding of the ION-GPS-92*, Albuquerque, NM, September 16–18, 1992.

Comsat Mobile, briefing charts on Inmarsat concepts, March 1994.

Danaher, James, "Integrated GPS/GLONASS: A Commercial Perspective," briefing presented to the National Research Council Committee on the Future of the Global Positioning System, Irvine, CA, August 16–18, 1994.

Day, Dwayne A., "A Comprehensive Rationale for Astronautics: Transformation of National Security Space Programs in the Post-Cold War Era," paper presented at the 45th Congress of the International Astronautical Federation, Jerusalem, Israel, October 1994.

Denaro, Robert, "GPS at Motorola," briefing presented to the National Research Council Committee on the Future of the Global Positioning System, Irvine, CA, August 17, 1994.

Dorfler, Joseph, "Project Introduction and Overview," briefing presented to the National Research Council Committee on the Future of GPS, Washington, D.C., July 28–30, 1994.

Dussell, William O., "Mobility, Location and the NII," briefing presented to RAND, Sunnyvale, CA, July 14, 1994.

Dyment, Mike, "Differential GPS in the 1990's: A North American Cross Industry Study," presentation made to the National Research Council Committee on the Future of the Global Positioning System, Washington, D.C., Sept. 29–Oct.1, 1994.

Ernst, Thomas J., "GPS Augmentation: An ITT Perspective," briefing presented to the RAND GPS Study Team, Washington, D.C., November 2, 1994.

Eschenbach, Ralph, "Overview of GPS in the National Airspace (NAS)," briefing presented to RAND, Sunnyvale, CA, July 14, 1994.

EUROCONTROL, presentation to RAND and NAPA on the European Satellite Navigation Programme, Paris, January 31, 1995.

Fleenor, Mike, "Jamming and Spoofing Test Results and Current Testing," briefing presented to the Defense Science Board Task Force on GPS, Los Angeles, CA, July 12–14, 1994.

Frost, Gerald, and Irving Lachow, "GPS-Aided Guidance for Ballistic Missile Applications: An Assessment," paper presented at the 51st Annual Meeting of the Institute of Navigation, Colorado Springs, CO, June 5–7, 1995.

Frost, Gerald, and Bernard Schweitzer, "Operational Issues for GPS-Aided Precision Missiles," paper presented at the 1993 National Technical Meeting of the Institute of Navigation, Washington, D.C., January 1993.

Galigan, R., and J. Gilkey, "Providing Highly Accurate Velocity Data for an Airborne Platform Using Differential GPS Velocity Corrections from a Non-Surveyed Reference Receiver," *Proceeding of* ION *National Technical Meeting,* San Francisco, CA, January 20–22, 1993.

Gecan, Anton, "GPS Technology Null Steering Antenna," briefing presented to the National Research Council Committee on the Future of the Global Positioning System, Irvine, CA, August 16–18, 1994.

Golden, Charles, "Anti-Jam Requirements and Specifications," briefing presented to the Defense Science Board Task Force on GPS, Los Angeles, CA, July 12–14, 1994.

———, "Anti-Jam Requirements and Specifications," briefing presented to the National Research Council Committee on the Future of the Global Positioning System, Irvine, CA, August 16–18, 1994.

———, "VECP for Antenna Electronics," briefing presented to the Defense Science Board Task Force on GPS, Los Angeles, CA, July 12–14, 1994.

Grace, Jim, "GPS Vulnerability," briefing presented to the Defense Science Board Task Force on GPS, Los Angeles, CA, July 12–14, 1994.

Gruber, Bernard, "Current and Potential Cryptographic Systems Used With GPS," presentation made to the RAND GPS study team, Los Angeles, CA, August 25, 1994.

Gunther, Tom, "The Potential of Loran-C Stations as GNSS Monitoring Sites," paper prepared for *ION GPS 1992,* Institute of Navigation, 1992.

Haley, Ron, "DCI Presentation to CGSIC," briefing presented at the 25th Meeting of the Civil GPS Service Interface Committee, Tysons Corner, VA, March 3, 1995.

Hart, Galen, "United States Department of Agriculture," briefing presented to the National Research Council Committee on the Future of the Global Positioning System, Washington, D.C., July 28–30, 1994.

Heckathorn, William, Col., "GPS Sustainment," briefing presented at the Air Force Industry Days Conference, Peterson AFB, CO, April 1994.

Inmarsat Comments in Response to an ICAO Secretariat Request for Information Concerning the Provision of Global Navigation Satellite System (GNSS) Services to International Aviation, London, 1991.

Inmarsat, "NAPA–Rand Update," briefing, London, February 3, 1995.

——, *The Possible Roles of Inmarsat in a Future Civil GNSS*, paper presented at a meeting of the Special Committee for the Monitoring and Coordination of Development and Transition Planning for the Future Air Navigation System, International Civil Aviation Organization, London, February 4–5, 1993.

International Association of Institutes of Navigation (IAIN), *IAIN Meeting on a Civil GNSS Office*, Paris, October 15, 1993.

Japan GPS Council, "Survey of Market Size by the Fields," presentation to the RAND GPS Study Team, Tokyo, Japan, October 19, 1994.

——, Potential Discussion Areas Posed to the JGPSC by the RAND GPS Study Team, presentation to the RAND GPS Study Team, Tokyo, Japan, October 19, 1994.

Japan Ministry of International Trade and Industry, "Feasibility Study on DGPS for Maritime Navigation," presentation to the RAND GPS Study Team, Tokyo, Japan, October 21, 1994.

Japan Ministry of Posts and Telecommunications, "State of the Studies in the MPT Concerning Positioning Satellite Systems," presentation to the RAND GPS Study Team, Tokyo, Japan, October 20, 1994.

Japan Ministry of Transport, Engineering Division of Ports and Harbours Bureau, "Real Time Kinematic Global Positioning System," presentation to the RAND GPS Study Team, Tokyo, Japan, October 21, 1994.

————, Maritime Safety Agency, "DGPS Program in Japan," presentation to the RAND GPS Study Team, Tokyo, Japan, October 21, 1994.

Johnson, Will, "Utilization of GPS by the NII," briefing presented at the Strategy Working Group meeting, Rockwell International, Crystal City, VA, August 17, 1994.

Jones, Ed, "Overview of GPS in Tracking Applications," briefing presented to RAND, Sunnyvale, CA, July 14, 1994.

Kevanney, Mike, "Transvision System," briefing presented to the National Research Council Committee on the Future of the Global Positioning System, Washington, D.C., July 28–30, 1994.

Kinal, George V., and A. J. Van Dierendonck, "Susceptibility of Inmarsat Navigation Payloads to Jamming and Spoofing: Fact or (Science) Fiction?" paper presented at the 1993 National Technical Meeting of the Institute of Navigation, San Francisco, CA, January 20–22, 1993.

Koerber, Berend, Vladimir Bacherikov, and Dennis Burnett, "Elekon," presentation to the White House Office of Science and Technology Policy, Washington, D.C., March 14, 1995.

Kursinski, E. R., G. A. Hajj, and K. R. Hardy, "Temperature or Moisture Profiles from Radio Occultation Measurements," paper presented at the 8th Symposium on Meteorological Observations and Instrumentation, American Meteorological Society, Anaheim, CA, January 17–22, 1993.

Latterman, Donald, "Global Positioning System Joint Program Office Top Ten Issues," briefing charts presented at the Strategy Working Group meeting, Rockwell International, Crystal City, VA, August 17, 1994.

Lundberg, Olof, keynote address delivered at the Royal Institute of Navigation Conference, Bristol, England, 1986.

————, "Waypoints for Radionavigation in the 21st Century," keynote speech delivered at ION GPS-94, Institute of Navigation, Salt Lake City, UT, September 20, 1994.

MacDonald, Mark, "NAVSTAR GPS Current Satellites Block II/IIA," presentation made to the National Research Council Committee on the Future of the Global Positioning System, Irvine, CA, August 16–18, 1994.

Marsh, Jerry, "IVHS America," briefing presented to the National Research Council Committee on the Future of the Global Positioning System, Washington, D.C., July 28–30, 1994.

Martel, John, Overlook Technologies, presentation to the 25th Meeting of the Civil GPS Service Interface Committee (CGSIC), Tysons Corner, VA, March 2, 1995.

McDonald, Keith, and Jim Nussbaum, "The Feasibility of Using Small, Low-Cost Satellites (Econsats) as an Augmentation to GNSS and as an Eventual Fully Capable GNSS," paper presented at the 1993 National Technical Meeting of the Institute of Navigation, San Francisco, CA, January 20–22, 1993.

McNeff, Jules, "GPS Signal Policy," briefing presented to the National Research Council Committee on the Future of GPS, Washington, D.C., June 23, 1994.

Meadow, Charles, "NAVSTAR GPS Current Satellites Block IIR," presentation made to the National Research Council Committee on the Future of the Global Positioning System, Irvine, CA, August 16–18, 1994.

Melbourne, William, "Spacecraft Uses of GPS," briefing presented to the National Research Council Committee on the Future of the Global Positioning System, Washington, D.C., July 28–30, 1994.

Melton, Walt, "Historical Overview of GPS," briefing presented to the National Research Council Committee on the Future of GPS, Washington, D.C., June 23, 1994.

Meyers, Tim, Joint Staff briefing to the National Research Council Committee on the Future of the Global Positioning System, Irvine, CA, August 16–18, 1994.

Minster, Jean-Bernard, "Some Applications of GPS in the Earth Sciences," briefing presented to the National Research Council

Committee on the Future of the Global Positioning System, Washington, D.C., July 28–30, 1994.

Mitchell, Mitch, "Air Force Modernization Planning," briefing presented at the Air Force Industry Days Conference, Peterson AFB, CO, April 1994.

Moody, Howard, "Presentation on the Uses of Global Positioning System in the Railroad Industry," briefing presented to the National Research Council Committee on the Future of the Global Positioning System, Washington, D.C., July 28–30, 1994.

Nagle, J. R., et al., "Global Navigation Satellite System (GNSS): Alternatives for Future Civil Requirements," paper presented at the IEEE Positioning Location and Navigation Symposium, IEEE Aerospace and Electronics Systems Society, Las Vegas, NV, April 12, 1994.

Nagle, Jim, "Waypoints to Radionavigation in the 21st Century," briefing presented to the National Academy of Public Administration, INMARSAT, Washington, D.C., November 18, 1994.

National Academy of Public Administration (NAPA) Panel on the Future Management and Funding of the NAVSTAR Global Positioning System, "The NAVSTAR Global Positioning System Considerations for the Future," briefing, Washington, D.C., September 30, 1994.

National Academy of Public Administration, notes and briefing charts presented at a meeting of the NAPA Panel on the Future Management and Funding of the Global Positioning System, Washington, D.C., August 5, 1994.

National Research Council, "Responses to the Federal Users Questionnaire," presentation made at a meeting of the National Research Council Committee on the Future of GPS, Washington, D.C., July 28–30, 1994.

———, "Summary of Federal Requirements," presentation made at a meeting of the National Research Council Committee on the Future of GPS, Washington, D.C., July 28–30, 1994.

NAVSTAR GPS Joint Program Office, "Augmented Global Positioning System (AGPS)," briefing presented to the National Research Council Committee on the Future of GPS, Washington, D.C., June 23, 1994.

————, briefing charts on the status of GPS and the Joint Program Office, February 25, 1994.

————, "NAVSTAR Global Positioning System (GPS) Block IIF Draft Baseline Concept Description," narrative outline presented at the Air Force Industry Days Conference, Peterson AFB, CO, April 1994.

Neves, Carole, "GPS International Issues," briefing presented to the National Academy of Public Administration GPS Study Panel, Washington, D.C., August 5, 1994.

Nichols, Mark, "Overview of GPS in Surveying and Mapping Systems," briefing to RAND, Sunnyvale, CA, July 14, 1994.

Orcutt, John A., and John Spencer, "Scientific Requirements for the Use of the Global Positioning System," report of a workshop held at UNAVCO, Boulder, CO, June 16–17, 1993.

Oster, Allan, "Anti-Jam Technologies," briefing presented to the Defense Science Board Task Force on GPS, Los Angeles, CA, July 12–14, 1994.

Overlook Technologies, "Assessment of Recent SPS Performance Transients," briefing to the Office of the Assistant Secretary of Defense (C³I), October 15, 1994.

Pace, Scott, "GPS Policy Study for the National Science and Technology Council and the Office of Science and Technology Policy," briefing presented to the National Academy of Public Administration GPS Study Panel, Washington, D.C., August 5, 1994.

————, "Overview of the GPS Policy Study for the National Science and Technology Council and the Office of Science and Technology Policy," briefing charts, August 19, 1994.

Privon, George, "U.S. Coast Guard Radionavigation Program," briefing presented to the National Research Council Committee on the Future of GPS, Washington, D.C., July 28–30, 1994.

Remondi, Benjamin W., "GPS Positioning Techniques," paper presented at the 48th ION Annual Meeting, Denver, CO, April 13–14, 1992.

—————, "National Geodetic Survey," briefing presented to the National Research Council Committee on the Future of the Global Positioning System, Washington, D.C., July 28–30, 1994.

RMB Associates, "Free Flight—Reinventing Air Traffic Control: The "Minimalist" Solution," paper prepared for the Measuring Operational Effectiveness Workshop, National Research Council/Transportation Research Board, Washington, D.C., October 3, 1994.

Saunders, John, "Infrastructure Needs for Space Industry Lift-off," paper presented at the 3rd Australian Space Development Conference, Sydney, Australia, September 8, 1994.

Schnabel, J., "Payload Performance Characteristics for the GPS Block IIR Space Vehicles," briefing presented to the National Research Council Committee on the Future of the Global Positioning System, Irvine, CA, August 16–18, 1994.

Seariver Maritime Inc., "Comments to the Committee on the Future of the Global Positioning System," briefing presented to the National Research Council Committee on the Future of GPS, Washington, D.C., July 28–30, 1994.

Serini, Peter, "A National Approach to Augmented GPS Services," presentation made to the National Research Council Committee on the Future of the Global Positioning System, Washington, D.C., Sept. 29–Oct.1, 1994.

—————, "Global Positioning System: Analysis of a National Approach to Augmented GPS Service," briefing presented to the National Research Council Committee on the Future of GPS, Washington, D.C., July 28–30, 1994.

————, "Should DGPS/Radiobeacons Be Used For," briefing presented to the National Research Council, Washington, D.C., September 30, 1994.

Shipton, Donna, "Requirements and Options for Block IIF Satellites," presentation made to the RAND GPS study team, Los Angeles, CA, August 25, 1994.

————, "Specification Requirements for Global Positioning System Sustainment (Block IIF)," briefing presented to the Defense Science Board Task Force on GPS, Los Angeles, CA, July 12–14, 1994.

Smith, Wayne, "GPS in Agriculture," briefing presented to the National Research Council Committee on the Future of the Global Positioning System, Washington, D.C., July 28–30, 1994.

Smolin, Les, "GPS Governance and Management Issues," briefing presented to the National Academy of Public Administration GPS Study Panel, Washington, D.C., August 5, 1994.

Stadd, Courtney, "GPS Commercialization Issues," briefing presented to the National Academy of Public Administration GPS Study Panel, Washington, D.C., August 5, 1994.

Swanson, Pete, "Timing Technology & Control in GPS," presentation made to the RAND GPS study team, Los Angeles, CA, August 25, 1994.

Trickey, Tyler, and Mike Yakos, "GPS System Security," briefing presented to the National Research Council Committee on the Future of the Global Positioning System, Irvine, CA, August 16–18, 1994.

————, "Rockwell Military GPS," briefing presented to the National Research Council Committee on the Future of the Global Positioning System, Irvine, CA, August 16–18, 1994.

Trimble, Charles, briefing presented to the National Research Council Committee on the Future of the Global Positioning System, Irvine, CA, August 17, 1994.

True, Scott, "Defense Mapping Agency Use of the NAVSTAR GPS," presentation made to the National Research Council Committee on the Future of the Global Positioning System, Irvine, CA, August 16–18, 1994.

U.S. Coast Guard, *Summary Record of the 25th Meeting of the Civil GPS Service Interface Committee*, Tysons Corner, VA, March 2–3, 1995.

———, *Summary Record of the 23rd Meeting of the Civil GPS Service Interface Committee*, Falls Church, VA, June 2–3, 1994.

———, *Record of the Sixteenth Meeting of the International Information Sub-Committee of the CGSIC*, Washington, D.C., June 1994.

U.S. Department of Defense, "GPS Signal Policy from DoD Directive 4650.5," briefing presented to the National Research Council Committee on the Future of GPS, Washington, D.C., June 23, 1994.

———, U.S. Air Force/SMC, "NAVSTAR GPS/Delta II," annotated briefing from the Launch on Need Study (unpublished), 1993.

U.S. Department of Transportation, "GPS Continuously Operated Reference Station(s) (CORS)," paper presented to the National Research Council Panel, September 30, 1994.

Van Dierendonck, A. J., J. Nagle, and G. V. Kinal, "Evolution to Civil GNSS Taking Advantage of Geostationary Satellites," paper presented at the ION 49th Annual Meeting, Cambridge, MA, June 1993.

Wainwright, David, Captain, "Control Segment Overview," briefing presented at the Air Force Industry Days Conference, Peterson AFB, CO, April 1994.

Ware, Randolf, briefing presented to the National Research Council Committee on the Future of the Global Positioning System, Washington, D.C., July 28–30, 1994.

———, "GPS/MET Presentation," briefing presented to the White House Office of Science and Technology Policy, Washington, D.C., July 25, 1994.

————, *Sensing the Atmosphere with an Orbiting GPS Receiver*, paper presented at a meeting with the White House Office of Science and Technology Policy, Washington, D.C., July 25, 1994.

Watrous, David, "Future of the Global Positioning System," briefing presented to the National Research Council Committee on the Future of GPS, Washington, D.C., July 28–30, 1994.

Weber, Lynn, and Anil Tiwari, *Performance of an FM Sub-Carrier (RDS) Based DGPS System*, Differential Corrections Inc., Cupertino, CA, 1995.

Weiss, Marc, "GPS-Relevant Atomic Frequency Standards," summary of a briefing presented at the Air Force Industry Days Conference, Peterson AFB, CO, April 1994.

White, Joe, "Spacecraft and Moniter Station Clocks," summary of a briefing presented at the Air Force Industry Days Conference, Peterson AFB, CO, April 1994.

Wiedemer, Mike, "Augmented Global Positioning System," briefing presented to the GPS Joint Program Office, June 1994.

————, "Global Positioning System: Wide Area Augmentation System (WAAS) Issues & Options," briefing presented to Paul Kaminski, Under Secretary of Defense (Acquisition and Technology), Los Angeles, CA, January 25, 1995.

————, "GPS System Health & Issues," presentation made to the National Research Council Committee on the Future of the Global Positioning System, Irvine, CA, August 16–18, 1994.

————, "An Integrated System Solution to Ensure Efective Dual Use of GPS," briefing presented to the Defense Science Board Task Force on GPS, Los Angeles, CA, July 12–14, 1994.

————, "An Integrated System Solution to Ensure Effective Dual Use of GPS," presentation made to the RAND GPS study team, Los Angeles, CA, August 25, 1994.

————, "Augmented GPS," presentation made to the RAND GPS study team, Los Angeles, CA, August 25, 1994.

Wilson, Jim, and Roger Sperry, "Project Plan & Schedule," briefing presented to the National Academy of Public Administration GPS Study Panel, Washington, D.C., August 5, 1994.

Young, William H., "Surveying with the Global Positioning System," briefing presented to the National Research Council Committee on the Future of the Global Positioning System, Washington, D.C., July 28–30, 1994.

Zaloga, Steven, "Harpoonski," *Naval Institute Proceedings*, February 1994, pp. 37–40.

Zumberge, J., et al., "The International GPS Service for Geodynamics—Benefits to Users," *Proceedings of ION-GPS 94: 7th International Meeting of the Satellite Division of the Institute of Navigation*, Salt Lake City, UT, September 20–23, 1994.

Congressional Testimony, Legislation, Government Agreements and Statements[1]

Baiada, R. Michael, President, RMB Associates, "Free Flight—Reinventing Air Traffic Control: The Economic Impact," statement before the U.S. House of Representatives, Committee on Government Operation, Subcommittee on Housing, Employment, and Aviation, August 9, 1994.

Bell, John, "The Government Liability Law of England and Wales," in Bell and Bradley, pp. 17–44.

Bell, John, and Anthony W. Bradley, *Government Liability: A Comparative Study*, United Kingdom National Committee of Comparative Law, 1991.

Clinton, Bill, President of the United States, letter to the International Civil Aviation Organization, March 16, 1995.

Clarich, Marcello, "The Liability of Public Authorities in Italian Law," in Bell and Bradley, pp. 228–248.

---

[1]See also Appendix D.

Code of Federal Regulations (CFR), Office of the Federal Register National Archives and Records Administration, 1993, Volume 15, Chapter VII, Part 799, Section 799.1, Item 7A03A.

Congressional Research Service, *Treaties and Other International Agreements: The Role of the United States Senate*, S. Prt. 103–53, 1993, at xxi.

Council of the European Union, "Council Resolution of 19 December 1994 on the European contribution to the development of a Global Navigation Satellite System (GNSS)," *Official Journal of the European Communities*, C 379, December 31, 1994, p. 3.

de Latournie, Marie-Aimée, "The Government Liability Law of France," in Bell and Bradley, pp. 200–227.

Denning, Dorothy E., Computer Science Department, Georgetown University, testimony before the U.S. House of Representatives, Committee on Transportation and Infrastructure, Subcommittee on Aviation, June 8, 1995.

Dillingham, Gerald L., Associate Director for Transportation Issues, General Accounting Office, "Perspectives on FAA's Efforts to Develop New Technology," testimony before the U.S. House of Representatives, Committee on Science, Subcommittee on Technology, May 16, 1995.

Donahue, George, Associate Administrator for Research and Acquisition, Federal Aviation Administration, testimony before the U.S. House of Representatives, Committee on Science, Subcommittee on Technology, May 16, 1995.

Dopart, Kevin P., and Kelley A. Scott, Analysts for the Energy, Transportation and Infrastructure Program, Office of Technology Assessment, testimony before the U.S. House of Representatives, Committee on Science, Subcommittee on Technology, May 16, 1995.

Dorfler, Joseph, Progress Update: DoD-DoT Wide Area Augmentation System Discussions, Department of Transportation, February 15, 1995.

Dorfler, Joe, SatNav Program Manager, "WAAS Frequency Offset," briefing by the Federal Aviation Adminstration, February 15, 1995.

Duncan, John J., Jr., Chairman of the Subcommittee on Aviation, statement before the U.S. House of Representatives, Committee on Transportation and Infrastructure, Subcommittee on Aviation, June 8, 1995.

European Union, Delegation of the European Commission, Demarche on the need for cooperation in the implementation of a global navigation satellite system, April 6, 1995.

Exon, Senator James J., "GPS's Limitless Potential," speech on the floor of the U.S. Senate, April 30, 1993, *Congressional Record*, p. S5274–S5276; reprinted in *Space News*, May 31–June 6, 1993; p. 15.

Götz, Eike zur Hausen, "Non-contractual liability under European Community Law," in Bell and Bradley, pp. 275–290.

Hinson, David R., FAA Administrator, letter to Dr. Assad Kotaite, President of the Council, International Civil Aviation Organization (ICAO), October 14, 1994.

Mead, Kenneth M., Director, Transportation Issues, Resources, Community, and Economic Development Division, General Accounting Office, "Assessment of the FAA's Efforts to Augment the Global Positioning System," testimony before the U.S. House of Representatives, Committee on Transportation and Infrastructure, Subcommittee on Aviation, June 8, 1995.

Milde, Michael, "Legal Aspects of Future Air Navigation Systems," 12 *Annals of Air and Space Law 1987*, 87–98, at 92.

Mineta, Norman Y., Congressman, opening statement before the U.S. House of Representatives, Committee on Transportation and Infrastructure, Subcommittee on Aviation, June 8, 1995.

National Academy of Public Administration, Committee on the Future of the Global Positioning System, *Statement of Task*, undated, 1994.

National Research Council, Commission on Engineering and Technical Systems, Committee on the Future of the Global Positioning System, *Statement of Task*, undated, 1994.

Noel, Bruce A., Vice President, Differential Corrections Incorporated, "Preventing Delays and Cost Overruns in the FAA's New Global Positioning (Satellite Navigation) System," testimony before the U.S. House of Representatives, Committee on Transportation and Infrastructure, Subcommittee on Aviation, June 8, 1995.

Peña, Luis, memorandum on the assignment of oversight responsibility for DoT Radionavigation and Positioning Management Activities, May 18, 1994.

Ponte, Lucille M., "Guilt by Association in United States Products Liability Cases: Are the European Community and Japan Likely to Develop Similar Cause-in-Fact Approaches to Defendant Identification?" 15 *Loyola Int'l & Comp. L. J.* 1993, 629, text at fn 213, 214, 215.

Rüffner, Wolfgang, "Basic Elements of German Law on State Liability," in Bell and Bradley, pp. 249–274.

Sperry, Roger L., and Arnold E. Donohue, GPS Project Directors, National Academy of Public Administration, testimony before the U.S. House of Representatives, Committee on Transportation and Infrastructure, Subcommittee on Aviation, June 8, 1995.

U.S. Congress, *Computer Security Act of 1987*, P.L. 100–235 [H.R. 145], 1987.

———, *International Maritime Satellite Telecommunications Act*, P.L. 95-564 [H.R. 11209], 1978.

———, House, "Civil Aircraft Usage of GPS," hearings before the committee on Transportation and Infrastructure, Subcommittee on Aviation, June 8, 1995.

———, House, *Department of Transportation and Related Agencies Appropriations Bill 1995*, 1994.

————, House, "GPS: What Can't It Do?" Hearings before the Committee on Science, Space, and Technology, Subcommittee on Technology, Environment, and Aviation, March 24, 1994.

————, House, Ways and Means Committee report, *New Tonnage Fees at U.S. Ports, Passenger Excise Taxes for Voyages Departing the United States, and Excise Tax on Liquid Fuels Used by Vessels Engaged in Foreign Transportation,* for USCG Maritime Safety and Navigation Services (Maritime Administration and Promotional Reform Act of 1994), 25 CIS/Index (July 9, 1994) H783-8.

————, Office of Technology Assessment, *Assessing the Potential for Civil-Military Integration,* OTA-ISS-611, Washington, U.S. Government Printing Office, September 1994.

————, Senate, *National Defense Authorization Act for Fiscal Year 1994,* 1993; *1995,* 1994; *1996,* 1995.

————, Senate, Committee on Armed Services, *Report on the National Defense Authorization Act for 1994,* July 28, 1993.

————, Senate, *Report for Department of Defense Appropriation Bill, 1990,* Report 101–132, September 14, 1989, p. 332.

U.S. Department of Commerce/National Telecommunications and Information Administration, *A National Approach to Augmented GPS Services,* Institute for Telecommunication Sciences, NTIA Special Publication 94-30, November 1994, p. G-9.

U.S. Department of Defense, *Global Positioning System User Charges,* Report to the Senate and House of Representatives Committees on Appropriations and Armed Services, May 1984.

U.S. Department of Defense and U.S. Department of Transportation, Federal Aviation Administration, *Memorandum of Agreement between the Department of Defense (DoD) and the Federal Aviation Administration (FAA): Use of the Global Positioning System in the National Airspace System,* March 15, 1992.

————, Revised statement on the status of discussions between DoT and DoD on wide area accuracy, Washington, D.C., January 27, 1995.

———, Statement on the status of discussions between DoT and DoD on wide area accuracy, Washington, D.C., January 26, 1995.

U.S. Department of State, *Treaties in Force*, January 1, 1994.

U.S. Department of Transportation, Federal Aviation Administration, *Wide Area Augmentation System (WAAS) Request For Proposal*, DTFA01-94-R-21474, 1994.

U.S. Department of Transportation, Office of the Secretary, "Civil Uses of GPS," September 1994.

U.S. Department of Transportation/U.S. Coast Guard, *U.S. Coast Guard GPS Implementation Plan*, June 1994.

U.S. General Accounting Office, *Global Positioning Technology: Opportunities for Greater Federal Agency Joint Development and Use*, GAO/RCED-94-280, U.S. Government Printing Office, September 1994.

———, *National Airspace System: Assessment of FAA's Efforts to Augment the Global Positioning System*, Statement of Kenneth M. Mead before the Subcommittee on Aviation, Committee on Transportation and Infrastructure, U.S. House of Representatives, GAO/T-RCED-95-219, June 8, 1995, p. 4.

U.S. Government, Joint DoD/DoT Task Force on GPS, *The Global Positioning System: Management and Operation of a Dual-Use System*, December 1993.

The White House, Statement by the President on the National Security Strategy Report for 1994, July 21, 1994.

———, Statement by the Principal Deputy Press Secretary to the President, September 16, 1983.

———, Office of the Press Secretary, Executive Order of the President, *Coordinating Geographic Data Acquisition and Access: the National Spatial Data Infrastructe*, April 11, 1994.

———, Fact sheet on the National Security Strategy, July 21, 1994.

Wiggers, George, Statement on the Department of Transportation's issues and concerns regarding the future of the Global Positioning System, June 23, 1994.

Personal Communication (letters, memoranda)

Baiada, R. Michael, President, RMB Associates, letter to Scott Pace, RAND, November 3, 1994.

Burgess, F. F., Jr., Chief, Maritime & International Law Division, U.S. Coast Guard, memorandum to the Chief of Radionavigation Division, U.S. Coast Guard, on private electronic aids to navigation systems, January 19, 1984.

Cochetti, Roger J., Vice President, Business Development and Planning, Comsat, letter to Gordon Smith, Assistant Secretary of Defense, U.S. Department of Defense, March 23, 1989.

Currier, D. G., Chief, Radionavigation Division, U.S. Coast Guard, memorandum to the Chief of Regulations and Administrative Law Division, U.S. Coast Guard, providing a legal opinion on electronic aids to navigation, December 2, 1983.

Danieli, Martin H., Chief, Office of Navigation, U.S. Coast Guard, memorandum to Chairman, DoT Navigation Council, providing position paper for U.S. Coast Guard assumption of Navstar GPS civil interface role, November 2, 1987.

Frost, Gerald, ION Conference and Industry Week Notes, September 1994.

McNeff, Jules, Responses to Questions on GPS by Dr. John McLucas, Aerospace Consultant, February 3, 1994.

Neves, Carole, questions posed by Carole Neves of the National Academy of Public Administration to the Japan GPS Council, October 1994.

Nichols, Mark, "Need for Nationwide Frequencies for RTK GPS Applications," memorandum to Ann Ciganer, Trimble Navigation, May 12, 1995.

Nishiguchi, H., personal communication responding to questions posed by Carole Neves of NAPA to the Japan GPS Council, October 25, 1994.

Paige, Emmett, Jr., letter to Frank Kruesi, Chairman, DoT POS/NAV Executive Committee, January 19, 1995.

Perry, William, Secretary of Defense, U.S. Department of Defense, letter to John McLucas, Aerospace Consultant, March 9, 1994.

Stephenson, Edgar L., Overlook Technologies, letter to F. Michael Swiek, U.S. GPS Industry Council, May 19, 1995.

Swiek, Mike, *Trip Report (visit to Beijing Research Institute of Telemetry)*, October 10, 1994.

———, personal communication, May 5, 1995.

U.S. Coast Guard, Coast Guard Recommendation/Position on Civil Access to the Precise Positioning Service, *circa* 1987.

———, Coast Guard Recommendation/Position on Generation/Distribution of Precise Satellite Ephemerides, *circa* 1987.

———, Coast Guard Recommendation/Position on GPS Near Real-Time Operational Status Capability Reporting System (OPSCAP), *circa* 1987.

U.S. Department of Defense, Under Secretary of Defense, memorandum to the Chairman of the Defense Science Board on the Terms of Reference—Defense Science Board Task Force on Global Positioning System, June 2, 1994.

Press Releases and Company Literature

Aviation Systems Research Corporation, "ATC Solutions Require Immediate Attention of Airline CEOs," press release, August 15, 1994.

Bell Communications Research, *In the Digital World, It's Always Time to Be Synchronized*, GR-2861-CORE, March 1995.

Federal Communications Commission, "FCC Takes Actions To Ensure Accessibility to 911 Services," press release, September 19, 1994.

———, "Action in Docket Case—FCC Takes Actions to Ensure Accessibility to 911 Services," press release, September 19, 1994.

Haley, Ron, *Response to NTIA Special Publication 94-30*, Differential Corrections Inc., January 24, 1995.

Inmarsat, *An Inmarsat Geostationary Overlay to GPS and GLONASS*, August 1994.

———, *Inmarsat Mobile Satellite Communications*, October 1994.

———, *Inmarsat Opens the Door to Civil Use of the Global Positioning System*, nr94/18/cfa, August 17, 1994.

———, *Inmarsat-P* "Steals the March on the Global Handheld Satphone Race", nr95/2/invcom, January 23, 1995.

Japan GPS Council, "Launching of the JGPSC," news release, 3-24-11 Yushima, Bunkyo-ku, Tokyo, 113 Japan, May 5, 1993.

Magellan Systems Corporation, "U.S. Commerce Secretary Ron Brown Joins Magellan Systems To Announce Export Agreement," news release, August 26, 1993.

Martin Marietta Astro Space, Inmarsat-3 brochure, 1993.

NASA Jet Propulsion Laboratory, "NASA Tracks Land-Surface Movement in Jan. 17 Earthquake," news release 94-19, February 4, 1994.

National Geodetic Information Center, *NGS Distributes GPS Orbital Data*, Department of Commerce, information flyer 86-2, 1987.

North, Oliver, and Robert Lilac, "Press Guidance Regarding Global Positioning System," September 15, 1983.

Orbital Sciences Corporation, *1994 Annual Report*, Dulles, VA, 1995.

Overlook Systems Technologies Inc., Graph of the estimated current radionavigation system user population, March 7, 1995.

Rockwell International Corporation. "Rockwell Team Wins Nunn-Lugar Award for Russian Defense Conversion," press release, August 4, 1994.

————, "Rockwell to Vie for FAA Sat-Based Navigation System," press release, August 18, 1994.

Royal Institute of Navigation, information brochure on the organization, 1994.

Trimble Navigation Limited, *Differential GPS Explained*, Sunnyvale, CA, 1993.

————, *GPS: A Guide to the Next Utility*, Sunnyvale, CA , 1989.

————, *1993 Annual Report*, 1994; *1994 Annual Report*, Sunnyvale, CA, 1995.

————, *Response from Trimble Navigation Limited to the National Research Council Committee on the Future of GPS*, Sunnyvale, CA, September 13, 1994.

————, *The SITE SURVEYOR System^{TM}: Real-Time Kinematic Surveying*, video, Sunnyvale, CA, 1993.

————, *Trimble Differential GPS Landing System*, video, Sunnyvale, CA, 1993.

UK Offshore Operators Association, brochure, 1995.

U.S. Air Force Space Command Public Affairs Office, "Global Positioning System Fully Operational," News Release, July 17, 1995.

U.S. Coast Guard, *GPS Facts & Figures*, revised October 1994.

————, *Loran-C Facts & Figures*, 1993.

————, *Navigation Information Service*, revised October 1994.

————, *Omega Facts & Figures*, 1993.

————, *Radiobeacon Facts & Figures*, 1993.

————, *U.S. Coast Guard Differential GPS*, revised October 1994.

———, *U.S. Coast Guard GPS Navigation Information Service (NIS) and its Function Within the Civil GPS Service (CGS)*, U.S. Coast Guard, Alexandria, VA, October 15, 1994.

U.S. Department of Commerce, *NGS:The National Geodetic Survey*, pamphlet, October 1988.

———, "Remarks by U.S. Secretary of Commerce Ronald H. Brown before the Magellan Systems Corporation GPS Consortium Announcement, San Dimas, CA," press release, Office of the Secretary, Washington, D.C., August 26, 1993.

———, "Remarks by U.S. Secretary of Commerce Ronald H. Brown before the Global Air & Space Conference, Arlington, VA," Office of the Secretary, Washington, D.C. May 2, 1995.

U.S. Department of Transportation, *GPS Background*, October 1994.

———, *GPS Information*, October 1994.

U.S. Department of Transportation, Office of the Assistant Secretary for Public Affairs, *Drivers and Surveyors to Get More Accurate Satellite Navigation Data*, press release DoT 174-94, December 8, 1994.

U.S. House of Representatives, Committee on Transportation and Infrastructure, "Chairman Shuster Announces Release of GAO Report on Global Positioning System," press release, May 17, 1995.

In addition to the works cited above, the following periodicals provided regular coverage of GPS-related developments and applications. They have been used extensively in preparing this report. Not all relevant articles from these periodicals have been cited individually due to space considerations:

Aviation Week and Space Technology

GPS World

GPS World Newletter

Space News

Washington Technology

United States–Government

Arms Control and Disarmament Agency

William Searle

Central Intelligence Agency

Terry McGurn

Department of Commerce

Office of the Deputy Secretary
Keith Calhoun-Sengor, Director, Office of Air & Space Commercialization

Department of Defense

Defense Intelligence Agency
Capt Barry Joseph, Space Systems Intelligence

Joint Chiefs of Staff
CDR Timothy Meyers, J6J

Navstar Global Positioning System Joint Program Office
Capt Bernard Gruber
2nd Lt Brian Knitt
1st Lt Donna Shipton
Col Michael P. Wiedemer, System Program Director

Office of the Assistant Secretary of Defense (C3I)
Jules McNeff

U.S. Air Force Headquarters
Maj Matt Brennan, SAF/AQSS
Maj Lee Carrick, SAF/AQSS

U.S. Air Force - National Air Intelligence Center
Maj Scott Feairheller, Technical Advisor on Navigation Satellite Systems

U.S. Air Force Space Command
John Anton, DR
LTC Mike Cimafonte, DR
Brig Gen Roger Dekok, XP
Lt Col Mike Kaufold

Col Bruce Roang, DR
1Lt Chris Shank
Maj Strouther, DOR
Maj Earl Vaughn
LTC Dan Wakeman, Special Operations
LTC Mike Wolfert, XPX
Col Pete Worden, Commander, 50th Space Wing

U.S. Navy, Headquarters Naval Satellite Operations
Mike Crawford

U.S. Space Command
Col Robi Chadbourne, J5
CDR Rod Trice, J3

Department of State

Embassy of the United States of America in Japan
Michael A. G. Michaud, Minister-Counselor, Environment, Science and
Technology Affairs

Oceans and International Environmental and Scientific Affairs
Tom Oldenberg, Office of Science, Technology, and Health

Treaty Affairs
Mary Brandt

Department of Transportation

Assistant Secretary for Transportation Policy
Joe Canny, Deputy Assistant Secretary

Assistant Secretary for Transportation Radionavigation Policy & Planning
Peter Serini
Heywood Shirer
George Wiggers

Federal Aviation Administration
Richard Arnold
George Donohue, Associate Administrator for Research and Acquisitions
David R. Hinson, Administrator
Mike Shaw, Satellite Systems Manager
Norman Solat, International Technical Program Manager

U.S. Coast Guard
CDR Wayne Raabe, Maritime and International Law Division
CDR Clyde Watanabe, Chief, Operations Division

U.S. Coast Guard Navigation Center
CDR Thomas Gunther, Commanding Officer

Executive Office of the President

Office of Science and Technology Policy
William Clements
Richard Dalbello, Assistant Director for Aeronautics and Space

Office of the U.S. Trade Representative
David Gutschmit, Director of Policy Planning for Japan and China

Office of the Vice President
Leon S. Fuerth, National Security Advisor for the Vice President
George Reed

National Security Agency

Guy Duffy
Clara McCullough
1st Lt Michael D. Codington, GPS User Segment Manager

U.S. Congress

Congressional Research Service
Marcia Smith

Office of Technology Assessment
Ray Williamson

Senate Armed Services Committee
Kirk McConnell
Eric Thoemas

United States–Industry

The Aerospace Corporation
John E. Clark, Systems Director, System Development and Analysis
Dave Nelson
Peter Swanson

American Medical Response West
Denis Jackson, Vice President, Technical Operations

American Mobile Satellite Corporation
Lon Levin, Vice President and Regulatory Counsel

Ashtech
Dr. Javad Ashjaee, President/CEO

AT&T Consumer Products
David Atkinson, Vice President

Beukers Technologies
John M. Beukers

bd Systems, Inc.
Teresa M. Dorpinghaus, Technical Staff

John E. Chance & Associates
Andy Bogle, Manager, New Business Development

COMSAT
Don Arnstein, Manager, Satellite Systems, COMSAT Laboratories
Jack Oslund, Director, External Affairs, COMSAT Mobile

Differential Corrections Inc.
　　Ron Haley, President
　　Bruce Noel, Vice President, Marketing

ITT - Aerospace/Communications Division
　　Peter T. Domanico, Director, Project Engineering
　　Thomas J. Ernst, Manager, Advanced Civil Navigation Programs
　　Dr. John A. Rajan, Manager, System Engineering

Joint Venture - Silicon Valley
　　Doug Henton

Leica
　　Sharon August Jones, General Manager
　　Thomas A. Stansell, Jr., Director of Advanced Programs

Lockheed
　　Eric. J. Christensen, Manager, CRSS Market Research

Loral Corporation
　　Dawn McKay, Public Affairs

Magellan
　　Randy D. Hoffman, President/CEO
　　James P. White, Public Relations Manager

MIT Lincoln Labs
　　William Delaney

Motorola
　　Robert P. Denaro, Director, Position and Navigation Systems Business

Navward GPS Consulting
　　Phillip Ward

Overlook Systems Technologies
　　Rob Conley
　　John Martel
　　Mike Sorrentino
　　Ed Stephenson

Rockwell Defense Electronics
　　Jack Murphy
　　Tyler Trickey
　　Michael Yakos

Rockwell Telecommunications
　　Thomas R. Damiani, Manager, GPS Key Programs Marketing

Sat Tech Systems
　　Keith McDonald

Smart Valley Inc.
　　Michael McRay

Trimble Navigation
　　Ann Ciganer, Vice President, Government Affairs
　　Jim Janky

Gary Lennen
Charles Trimble, President/CEO

U.S. GPS Industry Council
Mike Swiek, Executive Director

United States–Other

Consultant
Eric Bobinsky

National Academy of Public Administration
Arnold Donohue, GPS Project Director
Carole M.P. Neves, Project Director
Roger Sperry
Courtney A. Stadd, Consultant
Jim Wilson

National Research Council
Larry Adams
Allison Sandlin

Navstar University Consortium
Mike Exner
Randolph Ware

Resources for the Future
Molly Macauley, Economist

Australia–Government

Australian Surveying & Land Information Group
Dr. Ramesh Govind, Project Manager, Geodesy Research and Development

Department of Defence
Graeme G. Wren, Squadron Leader, Force Development (Air) Branch - Space Systems

Institute of Natural Resources and Environment
Jeff Kingwell, Manager, Science, Applications & Public Affairs CSIRO Office of Space Science & Applications

Europe–Government

Belgian Airports & Airways Agency
Eric De Backer, Acting Director of Administration, Air Safety Department

British Department of Transport
Stephen G. Frankiss, Head, International Aviation Division

Embassy of France
Bernard Luciani, Attache for Space

Eurocontrol
John Storey, Head, Sub-Division B2.4, Navigation and Surveillance Systems Group

European Space Agency (ESA)
Alexandre Steciw, General NAV & COM Mission Studies Coordinator

French Space Agency - Centre National D'Etudes Spatiales (CNES)
Alain Dupas, Consultant
Pierre Lafuma, Head of Radiocommunications Division

Norwegian Mapping Authority
George Preiss

European Commission

Delegation of the European Communities (Washington, D.C.)
Yves Devellennes, Counselor
Christopher Ross, EU representative and transportation consultant

Directorate-General VII - Transports
Jacques de Dieu, Principal Administrator, Maritime Safety Unit
Jürgen Erdmenger, Director
Giorgio Gulienetti, Consultant, Civil Aviation R&D
Claude Probst, Division Chief, Air Transportation Safety
Dinos Stasinopoulos,Principal Administrator
Luc Tytgat, Administrator

Directorate-General XII - Science, Research and Development
Pieter Van Nes

Europe–Industry

Consultant
Ron Bridge

Rascal Survey Limited
Gordon T. Johnston

Shell U.K. Exploration and Production
H.P.J. Edge, Head of Topographic Services

SubSea Offshore Ltd.
Tony Leary, GPS Manager

Europe–Other

General Lighthouse Authority for England and Wales
Captain Mac D. Turner

North Atlantic Treaty Organization (NATO)
Nicolas de Chezelles, Head Engineer of Defense, Joint Defense Council

Inmarsat
    George V. Kinal, Manager, Navigation & Multipoint Services Department
    Olof Lundberg, Director General
    Jim Nagle, Navigation Service Group Leader
    Bob Phillips, Director of Spectrum, Standards & Special Projects

International Institute for Strategic Studies
    Rose Gottemoeller, Deputy Director

Royal Institute of Navigation
    Walter F. Blanchard, President
    David W. Broughton, Director
    David M. Page, Chairman, Technical Committee

Japan–Government

Japan Defense Agency

Communications Division
    Dr. Masaki Kurosawa, Assistant Director, Equipment Bureau

Ministry of Construction

Geographical Survey Institute
    Kazuo Inaba, Head of Survey Guidance Division
    Masao Ishihara, Assistant Director, Geodetic Department

Geology Division
    Tomio Inazaki, Geologist, Public Works Research Institute

International Affairs Division
    Toru Kurahashi, Deputy Director, Economic Affairs Bureau

Ministry of Foreign Affairs

International Science Cooperation Division
    Takuya Tasso

Ministry of International Trade and Industry

International Research and Development Cooperation Division
    Makoto Kawari, Agency of Industrial Science and Technology

Space Industry Division
    Michio Hashimoto, Deputy Director
    Masashi Ishii, Assistant Chief

Ministry of Posts and Telecommunications

Aeronautical and Maritime Division
    Masato Iwasaki, Deputy Director, Telecommunications Bureau
    Akio Motai, Director General, Telecommunications Bureau

Space Communications Policy Division
    Fusaki Matsui, Director, Communication Policy Bureau

Standards and Measurements Division
Takao Morikawa, Chief , Frequency and Time Standards Section

Maritime Safety Agency

Aids to Navigation Department
Kenji Moribe, International Affairs Section

Ministry of Transport

Technology and Safety Division
Koichi Narisawa, Section Chief, Transport Policy Bureau
Yasusuke Yoshinaga, Special Assistant to the Director, Transport Policy Bureau

Engineering Division
Koichi Sahara, Deputy Director, Ports and Harbours Bureau

Air Traffic Services System Planning Division
Yukio Kita, Special Assistant to the Director, Civil Aviation Bureau

Japan–Industry

Japan GPS Council
Dr. Moriyuki Mizumachi, Professor, University of Tokyo
Hiroshi Nishiguchi, Secretary General